On College Teaching

A Guide to
Contemporary Practices

❀ ❀ ❀ ❀ ❀ ❀ ❀ ❀ ❀ ❀

Ohmer Milton
and Associates

❀ ❀ ❀ ❀ ❀ ❀ ❀ ❀ ❀ ❀

✾ ✾ ✾ ✾ ✾ ✾ ✾ ✾ ✾ ✾

On College Teaching

✾ ✾ ✾ ✾ ✾ ✾ ✾ ✾ ✾

Jossey-Bass Publishers
San Francisco • Washington • London • 1978

ON COLLEGE TEACHING
A Guide to Contemporary Practices
by Ohmer Milton and Associates

Library of Congress Catalogue Card Number LC 78-50892

International Standard Book Number ISBN 0-87589-377-5

Manufactured in the United States of America

JACKET DESIGN BY WILLI BAUM

FIRST EDITION

Code 7816

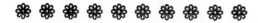

A joint publication in
The Jossey-Bass Series
in Social and Behavioral Science
& in Higher Education

A joint publication in
The Jossey-Bass Series
in Social and Behavioral Science
& in Higher Education

Preface

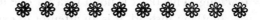

On College Teaching seeks to improve college teaching by encouraging everyone involved in undergraduate instruction to consider some new approaches as well as to improve old approaches to teaching. The book is beamed to all instructors in all disciplinary persuasions who are interested in teaching better—not simply the young and inexperienced, such as graduate teaching assistants and newly appointed faculty members but also the large numbers of experienced professors curious about approaches to instruction other than their own well-established ones.

A vast but scattered literature about college teaching already exists, as exemplified by the references at the back of this volume; new books and periodicals on the topic show little sign of abating. Some are substantively excellent, but few busy faculty members are going to ferret them out. Too many are written by specialists for specialists. Although they contain psychologically valid and impeccable information, much of it is not directly applicable to most professors' problems. For example, Finley Carpenter of the University of Michigan makes this lament about the psychological literature: "The assumption typically made by educational psychologists is that knowledge of the principles of psychology, plus a few illustrations, is sufficient to promote utilization of psychological knowledge to teaching. This assumption seems totally inadequate. . . . The link between theory and practice must be well comprehended by teachers before we can assume that they will make wise decisions in applying theory" (1975, pp. 569–570).

As a psychologist myself, I have dealt with this problem by asking expert teachers from a variety of disciplinary specialties beyond psychology to write the chapters included here. The result is a blend of explanation and critical commentary, along with portrayals of the approaches they find useful for contemporary college teaching. This book is not a plea for one instructional approach versus another; instead, it is an attempt to expound about all the major activities that fall under the rubric *instruction*. We cover traditional approaches, such as lecturing and discussion that are sound and that will continue to be used in hundreds of classrooms on thousands of campuses; and we explain newer ones, such as the Keller Plan and simulation that are being tried here and there in scattered classrooms. For the experienced faculty member, each chapter can stand alone. Such a professor may want to explore a single new approach or gain another perspective on a long-familiar one. For the inexperienced instructor, the chapters are meant to be complementary, pointing out the potential and problems of all approaches.

We do not devote separate chapters to every contemporary technique since a slight modification of one approach often results in a new name and more bewildering jargon rather than an actual difference in technique. Consider, for example, these acronyms for teaching methods: AI, CAI, CMI, IPI, ISP, PI, PLATO, PSI, RSVP, and TIPS. All together, they reflect only one or two basic notions; and we discuss these notions in two of our fourteen chapters—those on computers and on personalized systems of instruction (PSI).

In particular, we do not cover teaching by television for at

least three reasons: (1) In all too many instances, it is nothing more
than televised lecturing; (2) interest in it seems to be decidedly on
the wane; and (3) a comprehensive paperback (Crow, 1977) has
just been published that covers its advantages and disadvantages as
well as its legal issues, production costs, and other topics. Other than
this, we seek to describe all the major approaches to college teaching
currently in use in American higher education.

My major concern in compiling this book has been the disciplinary isolation so characteristic of higher education today—the
belief that members of one discipline cannot learn about teaching
from those in another. I disagree very strongly with that position.
My teaching experience over twenty-five years tells me that all students, whether they study elementary anthropology or advanced
zoology, have very much in common as they attempt to learn their
subject and that all teachers are people with some common instructional concerns across their disciplines. Each of my associates in this
book has sought to deal with this concern and minimize provincial-
ism by writing in standard English. All of us have struggled to avoid
words and phrases that, when used inappropriately or thoughtlessly,
not only obfuscate but bastardize our native tongue. These include
*classroom situation, dialogue, innovative, input, interface, linkage,
output, point in time, relate, relevant, thrust,* and *viable.* We may
have missed in a place or two, but we have aimed at clear English.

I am indebted to my colleagues for agreeing with me about
the importance of standard English and for their good will and good
humor as I prodded them to meet our deadlines. Of greater moment
for the cause of teaching and learning, however, I am grateful for
the mutual assistance in our scathing scrutinies of each others' draft
chapters. My chapters are clearer as a result, and several authors
have expressed similar sentiments about theirs. Surely these authors'
confessions about the value of criticism in clarifying their thinking
and writing has major implications for undergraduates in clarifying
their own thinking and writing—as well as for undergraduates helping teach one another by mutual criticism.

Knoxville, Tennessee   OHMER MILTON
February 1978

Contents

✿ ✿ ✿ ✿ ✿ ✿ ✿ ✿ ✿ ✿

The Authors

OHMER MILTON is professor of psychology and director of the Learning Research Center at the University of Tennessee, Knoxville.

Milton was awarded the Ph.D. degree in psychology from the University of Michigan (1950), the M.A. degree in psychology from the University of Kentucky (1941), and the B.A. degree in economics and psychology from Berea College in Kentucky (1940). In 1950 he joined the faculty at the University of Tennessee and helped to create the Learning Research Center in 1965.

Milton has published numerous articles and several books, including *Behavior Disorders: Perspectives and Trends* (with R. G. Wahler, 1973, 3rd ed.), *The Testing and Grading of Students* (with J. W. Edgerly, 1976), and *Alternatives to the Traditional: How Professors Teach and How Students Learn* (1972).

In 1974 Milton received the Distinguished Teaching Award from the American Psychological Foundation, and in 1975 he received a travel and study grant from the Ford Foundation.

PATRICIA W. BARNES-McCONNELL, associate professor, urban and metropolitan studies, Michigan State University

ROBERT M. BARRY, professor of philosophy, Loyola University, Chicago

ALFRED BORK, professor of physics and of information and computer science, University of California, Irvine

C. R. CARLSON, colonel, U.S. Air Force, and commandant, Academic Instructor and Allied Officer School, Air University, Maxwell Air Force Base

THOMAS CLARK, director, Center for Individualized Education, Empire State College

JOHN S. DULEY, assistant professor of education, instructional development consultant, Learning and Evaluation Services, Michigan State University

CHARLES F. FISHER, director, Institute for College and University Administrators, Office of Leadership Development in Higher Education, American Council on Education, Washington, D.C.

AUDREY D. LANDERS, assistant professor of psychology, University of Alabama

SUSAN M. MARKLE, professor of psychology and head, Instructional Design and Media Production Center, University of Illinois, Chicago Circle

MICHAEL J. ROCKLER, associate professor of education and chairperson, Department of Education, Rutgers University, Camden, New Jersey

JOHN SATTERFIELD, president, Wagner College, New York

WILLIAM J. SCHILLER, instructional psychologist, Adult Services Department, Illinois Institute for Developmental Disabilities, Chicago

Milton R. Stern, dean, University Extension, University of California, Berkeley

Gary A. Woditsch, consultant on Competency-Based Education (CBE), Flat Rock, Michigan, and former director of the Competency-Based Undergraduate Education (CUE) Project, Bowling Green State University, Ohio

On College Teaching

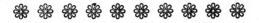

A Guide to Contemporary Practices

Ohmer Milton

Approaches
to Teaching

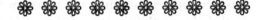

Although there has been clamoring over the years about the sad state of the art and craft of college teaching, it now appears that three trends are converging in the direction of its improvement.

First, experienced faculty members are questioning more than ever the effectiveness of their own teaching. Special teaching–learning centers have been inaugurated on campuses here and there to help faculty rethink their procedures; special local conferences about instruction are being offered; and regional and national meetings about teaching are increasingly well attended by faculty.

Second, increasing numbers of graduate teaching assistants are expressing a desire for help. The behemoth graduate schools are

1

beginning to concern themselves about the training for teaching that they provide; and occasional departments are introducing training programs for their graduate teaching assistants.

Third, philanthropists and legislators are becoming more and more impatient with excuses for inept instruction. Various public bodies are taking action, ranging from funding awards for good teaching to passing regulations about mandatory office hours and teaching loads. For example, in a positive move, the Tennessee Higher Education Commission (1977) has published the booklet *The Competent College Student* to promote faculty discussion about ways to facilitate student achievement, and it is assisting Tennessee colleges and universities to devise ways of demonstrating higher educational quality. And in lamenting that so few faculty members have concerned themselves with educational results, the Southern Regional Education Board warns that "it will be especially unfortunate if a sense of realism must be enforced from outside the academic community. There is still time for self-discipline and self-generated reform from within" (1976, p. 25).

So far, the instructional improvement conferences and faculty development activities reach too few faculty and are too limited in their focus; the concern of the graduate schools in far too many instances seems mainly to be public relations noise; and the actions of public bodies are too often merely barbed criticisms. Yet everyone is coming to agree that improvement is essential; the almost complete trial-and-error learning by faculty members about how to deal with undergraduate students—trials and errors that sometimes extend over a period of years for some instructors—is a luxury colleges and universities can no longer afford. The comforting rationalization that "we just don't know much about teaching and how students learn" is being recognized for what it is—professional excuse making.

Certainly there is more not known than known about college teaching, but for many elements or aspects of teaching, we need not wait for further scholarly research. All of us know a good lecture, for example, when we hear it. We can recognize dullness, indifference, and arrogance and know from personal experience as listeners that these flaws tend to interfere with our getting the message. As Kenneth Eble opined (1976, p. 11): "In my observations of teachers on many campuses over the past decade, I have seen fewer charlatans than mediocrities and have been less appalled by flashy deception than by undisguised dullness. And I have never encountered any evidence that a dull and stodgy presentation necessarily carries with it any extra measure of truth and virtue." Although the measurement of learning or testing as another example of teaching activity *is* inordinately difficult, there are sound principles and techniques for the process. Faculty members need not resist being deprived of their ignorance about such principles.

All of us know from our own experience, if not from psychology, that learning is facilitated when the student is active rather than passive. Despite the current public jargon to the effect that what the nation needs is better "educational delivery systems," we know better than to believe that teachers impart learning to students. Pray tell, since when was an education ever *delivered* to anyone? As a Chinese proverb puts it, "Teachers open the door. You enter by yourself." And as Galileo said, "You cannot teach a man anything. You can only help him to find it within himself."

If learning is thus correlated mostly with what the student does rather than with what the teacher does, if, in other words, teachers do not "learn" their students, what contribution can we as college teachers make to our students' learning? Each chapter in this book provides at least a partial answer to that question. Together, the chapters show how much we already know about helping students become self-motivated and self-directed learners, even if we often fail to put our knowledge into practice.

"Clarifying Objectives" opens the book as Chapter One by calculated design. Over the past twenty-five years it has become more and more apparent to me that the weakest area of collegiate instruction is course objectives; they are seldom made clear to students either at the onset of a class or during it, and they all too seldom mesh with students' learning objectives. As Robert M. Barry indicates in this chapter, faculty members, including himself, are often not too clear in their own thinking about course objectives. An associate professor once told me, for instance, that he would try to work them out *after* the course was completed. And even when they are clearly thought out, some instructors do not share them with students. The opening theme of this book, then, as well as one which occurs repeatedly in later chapters, is that of the desirability of making our objectives clear to students and of helping them clarify their own. I asked Barry, a philosopher, to develop this theme in Chapter One also by design because philosophers are embarrassingly masterful at forcing us to go beyond the pale and engage in serious and reflective thought about our own goals and about our means to these ends.

The lessons of the first chapter are indispensable for teaching effectively in either old or new approaches, but Chapters Two to Four turn to the lessons we can learn from the old approaches: lecturing, leading discussions, and conventional classroom testing. All three still hold prominent places as teaching practices and are likely to continue to do so.

In Chapter Two, John Satterfield, jazz musician and music professor turned college president, counsels in his inimitable style about the uses of the lecture, despite its disrepute, and about routes to better lecturing. No lecturer should minimize the amount of time and energy required, however, to follow his sagacious advice and achieve the standard that he sets for us—and that he exhibits in his own lectures.

If asked, significant numbers of faculty members will acclaim that one of their favorite teaching practices is discussion (Chapter Three) and that they frequently combine lectures with discussions. Yet most of us know how difficult it is to provoke lively and salient discussion; we know, too, as participants, how dull ones cause boredom, not learning. I have observed Patricia W. Barnes-McConnell in action among her students, and the verve with which she stimulates their participation is displayed equally in her chapter on the techniques she employs.

For Chapter Four on classroom testing, I was tempted to use the words of St. Augustine as its title: "For so it is O Lord, my God, I measure it. But what it is I measure I do not know." In that chapter, I offer some ideas about knowing better what it is we measure—and using these measurements for learning purposes as well as grading.

The next eight chapters turn to more recent techniques. In Chapter Five, C. R. Carlson extends my ideas about using testing for learning purposes into employing feedback for every teaching occasion. He illustrates the use of feedback at the Air University so thoroughly that there is little to be added, except an example from my own experience about the need for better feedback to instructors from students during the course. Not until the end of a course one year did one of my students offer the ambiguous observation, "I have enjoyed the course, and it required little study time. *However, I'm not doing exceptionally well."* By then it was too late.

Chapter Six is the most reasoned and balanced discussion of personalized systems of instruction (PSI), the so-called "Keller Plan," I have encountered. What a pleasure not to be proselytized by William J. Schiller and Susan M. Markle, even about a procedure that has more empirical evidence of its effectiveness than any other.

Chapter Seven, on computers in the classroom, illustrates explicitly the learning principle noted above: that learning is facilitated when students are active rather than passive. As Alfred Bork explains, computers force or require activity by the student whether the learning is simple or complex.

Contract learning (Chapter Eight) may be thought of as a formal procedure for clarifying course objectives, procedures, and testing from the very start: what students are to learn, how they can best learn, and how to determine what they have learned. Thomas Clark dispels the mystery and misconceptions about this approach with his samples of contracts and explanations of its use at Empire State College.

Gary Woditsch was reluctant to write Chapter Nine on competency-based teaching because much of what is labeled competency-based education (CBE) seems embarrassingly ludicrous, raising the prospect that CBE will suffer the fate of programmed instruction and teaching machines in the late 1950s after the Russian Sputnik: a sought-for panacea for educational woes, discarded because of overexpectations. CBE has caught the fancy of the nation, to be sure, as illustrated in part by the awesome number of legislative efforts to establish CBE requirements in teacher training and other programs (Pipho, 1977). Woditsch avoids seeing CBE as a panacea. With a philosopher's skill of analysis, he explains the implications of CBE for any teacher in any discipline, not simply those concerned with professional competence.

It is my guess that the case study method of instruction (Chapter Ten) is seldom considered as a teaching approach for undergraduate courses; instead, it is usually associated with business and graduate school offerings. From his vantage point at the American Council on Education, Charles F. Fisher emphasizes that the method can be an additional part of the undergraduate teaching armamentarium as well as a device for in-service faculty and administrative development.

In Chapter Eleven on simulation/gaming, Michael J. Rockler is so bold as to assert that even college learning should be fun. He cites research evidence indicating that favorable attitude changes take place with this approach, and his chapter is one of the few that addresses directly these issues of pleasure and attitude, or what has come to be called the affective domain.

Alfred North Whitehead wrote that "the tragedy of the world is that those who are imaginative have but slight experience, and those who are experienced have feeble imaginations. Fools act on imagination without knowledge; pedants act on knowledge without imagination. The task of a university is to weld together imagination and experience" (1949, p. 140). This welding has accelerated during the past dozen years not only through the use of vicarious experience by case studies and simulation or gaming but also through off-campus and "experiential" learning. I puzzled at length about the way to deal with such a broad topic and finally decided to focus on those aspects of it that are under the direct control of the faculty—consequently, Chapter Twelve on field experience learning. It was only natural to seek the services of John S. Duley because of his active involvement in the Society for Field Experience Education and the Council for the Advancement of Experiential Learning as well as his early leadership of field studies for Justin Morrill College of Michigan State University.

Chapters Thirteen and Fourteen do not deal directly with instructional approaches but with emerging issues that, like Chapter One on clarifying objectives, warrant attention by all instructors. Chapter Thirteen is included because of the marked changes now occurring among student bodies. Colleges and universities are no longer the province of only eighteen- to–twenty-one-year-olds. Middle-aged and even older students are returning to college both for career advancement and for personal development, and legislatures in several states are offering encouragement to retired persons by making it possible for them to attend tuition-free. From his perspective as dean of University Extension for the University of California at Berkeley, Milton R. Stern discusses these nontraditional students who are beyond the traditional college age and the implications of their attendance in our classrooms for our teaching.

Chapter Fourteen on evaluating teaching is included for two reasons: (1) Faculty evaluation is here to stay, and most faculty must be much more sophisticated and informed, particularly about many technical details, then they now are; and (2) research results in this area have important things to say about improving instruction, and Audrey Landers is a superb translator of these research findings. If Chapter One can be considered required reading for the cause of student learning, I recommend her chapter as required reading for the cause of faculty welfare.

"Required" reading smacks too much of imposed assignments, compulsory reading lists, and gloomy reserve book shelves. The following chapters and my summary comments at the end of the volume are not texts to be endured by the unwilling reader and the threatened instructor; instead they are a combination of research findings and informal ideas from experienced teachers to their colleagues about their mutual craft. For these colleagues who need no external compulsion to continue their efforts at improvement, who seek to learn more about teaching because of their own desire to excel, these chapters should offer pleasure and reassurance, and my concluding remarks after them can point to further reading for further learning.

1

Robert M. Barry

Clarifying Objectives

As college teachers, very few of us have ever been taught our craft. Our teaching habits have been formed somewhat casually—for good or bad—over the years, during which we progressed through the primary, secondary, and finally the higher levels of education. This is not to suggest that most of us are not effective and interesting but rather that many of us show little concern for ensuring the effectiveness of our own teaching procedures.

If the teaching careers of others are similar to mine, and comments from colleagues suggest they are, then few of us have the opportunity or the desire to retreat from the daily routines in order to be knowingly concerned with our approaches. We just teach! Seldom, if ever, do we reflect about teaching before or during a course. Moments that could be spent in self-reflection about what is happening in our classes are devoted either to reading the most recent book in our field or to thinking about our discipline. Prepara- tion time is spent essentially with subject matter: How can course content be related to the interests of students while, at the same time, expanding those interests? Are there new books to be mentioned? Are there new articles to be added to the reading list, and what new topics for term papers must be added to the regular list?

These concerns, and similar ones, are valid and appropriate; to ignore them is to fail to prepare adequately. Vital though they are, however, they will not receive attention here. By themselves, they are not enough. Deeper and different issues are raised by such reflective questions as "What am I trying to accomplish with stu- dents?" and "What do I wish them to be able to do at the end of this course?" If these questions remain unanswered, then instructors will have no reasonable norm for selecting methods of instruction and will never truly know what has been accomplished, nor will most students have the opportunity to do anything more than rou- tinely listen to our material and try to understand their assignments. As paradoxical as it may seem, the perceptive, and at times even brilliant, analyses that we demonstrate in class are frequently lost on our students or confuse them unduly because we fail to anchor them within the reasonableness of clear aims or objectives.

Recently, in one of my courses, a series of events gave me a good deal of insight into the importance of being reflective about course procedures and clarifying aims or objectives for students. This chapter uses this experience as its focus. I admit that it is uncom- fortable to discuss publicly what went on in the privacy of my class. I am sufficiently part of the culture of the academic world—twenty- five years' worth—that I realize teaching is ordinarily considered a private affair. It is done mostly behind closed doors, and its private character is affirmed by the gentleman's agreement among instruc- tors to avoid commenting on each other's approaches to instruction. I have had some fine moments in class over the years—I still savor them, and they will remain forever in my substance. Now and then, I have reported a few words about them to my wife, and maybe, just maybe, an occasional mention to some trusted colleague. But such reporting is rare, for when the door is closed, our culture tells us that the *sanctum sanctorum* begins.

It is thus doubly uncomfortable to report a mistake. It seems a violation of trust—what trust I am not certain! Yet there is only one way to overcome the restriction of such privacy: We must learn to share what we have experienced in our classes if the stupidity of repeating mistakes is not to be continued under the guise of the privilege of privacy. The fact that it took me twenty-five years to recognize some very ordinary truths about teaching and learning seems so patently wrong that I feel obligated to call attention to what I learned from that class. What I learned, I am sure, has been known by some other teachers, but no one told me. This practice ought not be continued.

The Setting

The course was "Philosophy of Man": a required introductory course that the entire faculty of my university firmly believes is essential for students to take if they are to consider themselves educated. Its objective, according to the catalogue, is "to develop the capacity for a growing reflectiveness on such fundamental issues as the meaning of man." During an early session, I informed the students of my own major objective for the course: to help them explore and understand their own experiences, since philosophy is basically an attempt to understand all human experience. The inadequacy of these statements, I am embarrassed to admit, only became evident to me during its seventh week.

The first five weeks of the course were used to explain that philosophy focuses on human experience and to show that philosophers have tools and concepts which can be used to illuminate and understand aspects of ordinary experience. Class presentations examined the roles of time and space in experience, the influence of culture on experience, the cognitive and aesthetic dimensions of experience, the contrast between thought and action, and the notion of freedom within the context of culture. Technical terms had to be introduced, and particular classical philosophers were mentioned as their general theories related to an understanding of humankind. But since the course was designed for nonmajors, exclusive emphasis on the technical aspects of philosophy was unnecessary. Forty-five students were enrolled. Most were sophomores, but a few were juniors and seniors. Their open discussion, even focused conversation, was encouraged; but they knew that I did not grade them for class participation, since I hoped to eliminate the aggressive sort of participation that often results when students are encouraged to speak in class because they know their grades will be affected.

In the sixth week there was a brainstorming session to determine the six topics to be explored philosophically during the remainder of the course. The students suggested about fifty, reduced these to fifteen by a voting procedure, and then attained a rank order of the top six by a second vote, with each student having six choices. (Death topped the list—a primary selection for six straight years; "Is College Worth It?" came in second; and interpersonal relations—a topic not chosen previously—was third.) I explained that I would serve as a resource person in the exploration of these topics. I would draw on my philosophical training to make certain that the insights of the classical philosophers were brought into class discussion. My task, accordingly, was threefold: (1) to monitor the discussion by way of giving and maintaining direction, (2) to make certain that the philosophical rigor of the discussion was adequate, and (3) to help the students recognize how the use of philosophical perspectives and terminology would provide both insight and clarity in understanding ordinary experience.

There would be no textbook for these discussions; instead, both articles and books would be used for supplemental readings. Since the class discussion would provide students with ongoing feedback about their progress, frequent examinations were not needed, but for those students who wanted greater feedback than this, they could hand in several pages detailing what had been said in class after each topic had been discussed. These pages would receive detailed commentary by me, and I would return them with a grade. The final examination would be standard: Students would write an evaluation of a selected number of the discussion topics by using the norms of experience that had been discussed in the first portion of the course.

I had taught the course in this manner for several years, and student response had been good. Better students enjoyed the participation and opportunity for sharing responsibility for the topics, whereas average students liked it well enough, even though it meant that they had to do some thinking—and that was work! As a result,

I thought I was on top of a well-taught course—until I was confronted with the events of the seventh week.

The Events

During class one day that week, a student who had earlier remarked casually that he was taking the course just to get it out of the way to get on with his major asked, "What do you expect us to do on the exam?"

I confess I was a bit nonplussed. The group came alive; even the students who had suffered previously from terminal lethargy and were not massive note takers whipped out their pencils and ballpoint pens and poised them expectantly. It was as if I were about to make a special revelation!

The implication of their reaction was only too obvious: they were not interested in the topic under discussion but with what was coming on the final. Over my years of teaching, it had always annoyed me that students seemed merely to want to know what the questions would be. It was as if the only significant parts of the course had to do with what was going to be on the exam. And since their interest in this question today was so divergent from what seemed to me to be appropriate, I had to discourage the build-up of a wrong attitude. "Before we copy any notes about the final evaluation," I suggested, "perhaps we should talk a bit about what is happening here."

They were cautious, but curious. I asked if anyone remembered the discussion in an early class session about the objectives of the course. One student, Jim, commented that there had been no *discussion:* I had merely *told* the class what to do. Another, Debbie, disagreed: "You tried to get a discussion going, but we wouldn't respond, probably because we didn't believe you wanted a discussion."

Tom started speaking as soon as his hand went up. He had said little in the course but appeared now to be quite annoyed, even angry. "You know, I really don't know why we are trying to talk about objectives or exams or final evaluations. What really bothers me is why I have to take this course! I know what my major is, and I know what I want to do when I graduate. There's a job waiting for me, and I didn't come to college to take philosophy. I'm going to be an accountant. So why do I have to take this course?"

It was clear that Tom's position was shared by many, although philosophy was hardly the only course that the college required for graduation—and so I decided I might as well begin at the beginning.

"Today, parents and their college-bound teen-agers seem to know more clearly the vocational possibilities that exist after college than did prior generations," I said. "Certainly more students have a sense of what they want to do after college." The students seemed to be listening, so I continued. "Parents in my day did not always have a sense of the relationship between a college degree and a vocational field. That is, few saw college as a preparation for a specific vocation. Most parents knew, though, that if their son or daughter graduated from college, he or she would get ahead in the world. I would imagine it was a combination of some sort of faith in the American system, combined with some awareness of the broad goals of higher education. Today it is quite different. Both students and parents recognize that college is a major step toward a *specific* career."

Most students were following every word, but then they always did when I spoke about vocations or jobs. The body language of most of the class indicated an intensity of concern.

I pursued. "But college is not a vocational school; the primary goal of college is to help you become an educated person. Since our society needs specific, technically trained persons, colleges function, in many cases, to provide that training. But vocational training or skill training is not the primary task; the primary task is to educate persons. To train persons in specific occupations is not necessarily to educate them."

Tom may have felt slightly guilty for raising the topic and identifying his own concern as primarily job oriented, for he spoke out with vigor, "Do you mean that I won't be educated because I want to be an accountant?"

"Of course you will be educated," I replied. "I mean you will at least have the opportunity to be educated. But that opportunity will not come exclusively from the accounting program. When you take an accounting sequence in college, you are really studying something broader; only about a fourth of your courses are in that field. The other courses make certain that your program is broadly based and takes cultural issues into account."

"If you had learned your accounting via on-the-job training, then you would have been involved in merely learning the skills of accounting. But such learning is generally dull and extremely demanding by way of learning routines. Although the discipline involved may be helpful to the formation of proper habits, the dull routines that never stimulate the imagination will, over a period of time, squeeze out the connections that must be made between the facts you learn in accounting and their broad-ranging implications. And, the paradox in this is that the reward for good performance in skill tasks is usually promotion into a position that will require the ability to draw imaginative connections between the specific skills and the broader issues of society or civilization."

Not many of the students were in the business field, and I did not want to convey the impression that I was insensitive to business students. "Chemists, as well as scholars of the Greek and Latin languages, could possess the same limitations as the person who had merely good accounting skills. Chemists could be good technicians, with fine laboratory skills, and yet be insensitive to the broader issues of, for example, chemistry and the environment. A specialist in Greek and Latin, with fine skills of translation, could be unable to relate the languages to the cultures of Greece and Rome. The issue is not that of training in skills but of relating the skills to the broader issues of civilization and even to history, of having one's learning enlightened with imagination."

I had to relate my comments back to Tom's question, for the session was coming to an end. "Even in accounting, or chemistry, or whatever, college offers the opportunity for receiving an education—for not merely learning facts or skills but for becoming aware of the relationship between these facts or skills and general principles. Education is imaginatively conceiving facts so as to have a sense of their broader implications."

I announced that the topic would be continued on Friday and mentioned that many of my ideas about education came from

Alfred North Whitehead's (1949) article "Universities and Their Function," which was available for students to read.

Class on Friday began with a brief summary of what had happened during the last session. I asked, "Are there any questions about the last class?"

Suzanna, who had mentioned previously she was majoring in communication arts, responded: "Now I'm pretty sure I understand what you said, but let me say what I heard and then you react to me. You are telling us that college teaches us some things that are . . . like on-the-job training from a theoretical perspective. But that the really important thing is that it teaches us to have an imaginative dimension linked to our learning the facts about things."

I agreed that she had said what was being taught, but I wanted to emphasize—probably in an upstaging manner—that the imaginative dimensions of facts allowed for a full range of human concern. "The possibilities in facts involve the dimension of values, the sorts of things for which people in the past have chosen to die." I explained that very few Americans would commit their lives over the fact of having a Bill of Rights but that the imaginative possibilities of the Bill of Rights were quite far-reaching and embraced significant dimensions of human values. It was these that would get taught at college, along with the factual basis of the subject matter.

Carolyn, whose eyes had indicated she had been following the discussion closely, said, "But you have explained why we should come to college, rather than merely have on-the-job training. I thought you were going to talk about why we all have to take this course, even though it is not part of our major requirement."

I acknowledged she was right in her appraisal but that it was necessary to understand the significance of college before we spoke about the role of a specific course. I explained that it was the broadening of perspective, the development of a sense of openness and sensitivity, the understanding of the development of civilization that really takes place in college. Thus, an entire series of courses outside one's major explores questions about the development of humankind through history, about the operation of government, and about the values that function within human civilization. The courses raise the questions that have to do with the meaning of life as well as with personal decisions about one's own life. I pointed out that the teaching which takes place in college is directed to those who, within two generations, will be future leaders. For some students, of course, this was pure rhetoric; for others it was right on target because they knew they would some day be managing corporations or presiding over boards of directors.

Carolyn was not to be contained; she inquired again, "Why do we have to take this course, since it isn't part of our major program?" There were other hands raised. Bill suggested, "This is not the only required course outside of our major. Why do we have to take any of them outside of our major?"

I explained that education is not a precise process and that a single course, or series of courses, no matter how valuable, is generally not sufficient to educate a person. Parents may send their children to college so they can learn or develop a vocation, and young people may come to college to secure a better job, but as good a personal reason as this may be, it is not the reason colleges and universities continue to exist. The purpose of college is to educate citizens. Colleges have to do with subtle things, with long-term, rather than direct and immediate, values.

"There are many reasons for required courses outside of one's major program," I explained. "Different courses do different things. Students frequently approach college in a piecemeal fashion; having to register for each course, they are inclined to look at college as if it were merely a series of specific courses. But college also must be seen from an overall perspective; the whole program of courses when taken together must be seen to possess some reasonableness, some purpose, that may not be recognized from the piecemeal vision."

Almost all students were listening carefully; a few were even selecting some ideas to be written in their notes, and the usual three or four were copying down every word. I sensed that few had ever considered the meaning of college from a single overall perspective. I was providing a new way to look at college and giving them some overall meaning to their habitual routines: coming to class each day, time in lab, time in the library, conferences with teachers, even registration itself. As I spoke, I could almost see them piece together many of their different activities into a single whole. It was interest-

ing to recognize—though I dared not tell them—that their seriousness in listening was having an impact on me.

I continued, "All the courses together have a significance.
Though it is difficult to be precise about the import of a college
program, since students vary so much in interests and goals, there
are overall goals that faculty and administration have in mind for
those who come through the undergraduate program. First, all the
courses together help students to acquire information and knowledge, the very basis of all intellectual activity. Since there has been
a knowledge explosion—an almost unimaginable expansion during
the past ten years—students should have the opportunity to develop
quickly a firm base. Second, all the courses help students develop
intellectual skills and habits of thinking that are of basic importance
in being educated. Students should develop the ability to communicate in both oral and written form with precision and style. Students
have the opportunity to learn how to learn. Thus, learning can be a
continual affair throughout life. Also, students should learn to read
and write a foreign language to give them access to an alternate
culture and the literature appropriate to the culture.

"Third, there can be a development of what is vaguely referred to as qualities of the mind. Students are offered the opportunity to learn to be open-minded, to respect other points of view.
Students can learn a capacity for commitment and a comfortable-
ness with facts. Also, students will have the opportunity to develop
an appreciation of, and even love for learning and understanding.
This appreciation should continue even after the college years.
Fourth, college students have the opportunity to nourish literary,
artistic, and musical sensitivities. And last, many courses will be of
assistance in the development of the ability to make reasoned judgments and to discern significant values."

I summarized, "It is important to affirm that the college
program, although at times it may seem to have little reasonableness
about it, has been put together with the assumption that the final
product—the student—will have had the opportunity to become
educated. Unlike bicycle riding, which, when performed, can be
recognized easily even by nonriders, education—that is, genuine education—is not so obvious; nor is it generally discernible to the
noneducated."

Since I had taken many of these ideas from Bok (1974), I noted that his article was available for all to read. Then, to provide an overall perspective, I explained that if students were to take courses only in their major, they would be well trained, but hardly educated. "What it means to be educated can be spoken about only in bold lines. Only by taking courses in literature can a student develop a critical taste in reading. Only by reading in broad, general areas can a student develop a writing style. Only by having courses in logic or dealing with various logical forms can a student consciously learn to use valid arguments. Only by dealing with past human actions, periods of both greatness and weakness, can a student develop a sense of discrimination in human affairs. These are some of the things a person must be able to do to be considered educated. One of the real problems is that education is so complicated and subtle that colleges can never really tell in a precise manner how it is to be done. Thus many courses must be taken."

I asked if there were any questions. Carolyn was quite patient, but she was also persistent. "You have told us quite a bit about what colleges want to do, and you have even suggested why students have to take courses outside of their major. But you know you have not yet said why we have to take this course."

She was right, and as the bell rang I attempted to point out that before students could understand the purpose behind any particular course, they had to have some clear sense of the operation of the whole university. It was a strange feeling, but every time Carolyn asked her question something in me triggered a flight pattern. I really was not sure what she was asking, and, at the same time, I felt uncomfortable with her question. I was thankful for being rescued by the bell, and I vowed to myself that I would complete some work before the next class meeting.

Two questions were still hanging: What is going to be on the exam and why does a student have to take this course? As I reflected, I realized that I was disturbed about both of them. It became apparent that I had avoided them by suggesting that they meant something else; in both instances I transformed them into larger and more complex issues. I was controlling the questions— for what reasons I was not precisely sure—and forcing the students to look at the questions they had raised by moving over to a larger area of concern, an area of concern that was, at best, complex and shadowy. I realized that teachers had done this to me when I was a student. There were times when it was an appropriate move, but there were other times when I had a sense that the teacher felt uncomfortable with the question which had been raised and had used the maneuver for either rescue or to get away from the precise topic.

One thing was plain. I was dragging my feet on the issue of student questioning about course objectives. I seemed to have a problem at the point where the content of the exam intersected the question of specific objectives.

I used the weekend preparing for Monday's class. Half was spent searching in the library; the other half involved reading those books I brought home. It became certain that too many books had been written about "objectives," but there were some good ones: Alexander and Davis (1977); Mager (1975); and Cohen (1970).

Some things began to surface as a result of my readings. First, I had not made egregious mistakes during the discussion of objectives. Some points had to be clarified, some had to be changed, but generally the discussion had not run counter to what the best informed sources had to suggest. Yet, second, all was not so simple. Although I was relieved that my concerns were right-headed, I realized that my procedures or skills were clearly naive and counterproductive. I had been teaching for almost a quarter of a century, and I had spoken of objectives quite frequently but in a vague manner. I had always wondered what students were really learning in my classes; now I was beginning to wonder if they had been learning anything! Perhaps I was being too hard on myself, but at least I was beginning to develop a sense of the basis for my own uneasiness: There was much that I had to learn about teaching. My ignorance was embarrassing, but then it always has been. I had never before reflected so much about my teaching, and it all made embarrassingly good sense.

Monday seemed to come earlier than usual; the class was in its typical posture for the day. I have long suspected that motivation and energy could be doubled if Monday were eliminated from the college schedule. I began with a brief summary of the last day of class, and I repeated the two outstanding questions. I then said the usual things that professors are obligated to say about examinations:

prepare ahead, don't cram, get a good night's sleep, and the like.

Jim, the one who first asked about the final exam, said he thought I did not understand what he was asking. He said he wasn't interested in knowing exactly what the questions would be, but he wanted to know the general area of the questions.

Other students spoke up. Mary said, "Knowing what is going to be on the final exam helps give us a perspective on the entire course. The only way to get any overview of a course, to really see where it's going, is to get a sense of what's going to be on the final."

A chorus of supportive faces agreed with her. I countered, "It seems to me that what students have typically done is to reduce their studying to the questions that will appear on the final."

"What's wrong with that?" inquired Mark. I was not quite sure of the implications of Mark's objection, so I just hesitated slightly.

My hesitance was interrupted by Bonnie raising her hand. Bonnie was a large woman who seldom spoke. She seemed always to have some authoritative command over student opinion; when she spoke, others were quiet. "I work more than twenty hours a week," she began, "and the only way I can get my hand on what is taking place in a course is to know where we are supposed to be when the course is over."

Carolyn interjected, "That's why we have to know why a student should take this course." She hesitated, but there was no stopping her. As if answering an unposed question, she continued, "I don't have any real objection to taking this philosophy course even though it's required. What I want to know is what do you want me to learn in this course? It really annoys me that the faculty make requirements for students and then don't explain what the required courses are supposed to do for us. I mean, like, I can live with taking a required course, but it's like you don't think I—I mean the students—can understand what you have in mind. That's really putting us down, you know!" Her face was flushed, but there was not a single embarrassed face in the class. She was speaking for everyone. Even the most lethargic student had his head set in an expectant posture. It was not quite a revolt; it was clear the issue was one of honesty and openness.

I knew the students had to know I was receiving a clear message and perceiving the class accurately. "What you are telling me," I began, "is that you are annoyed, not because you have to take a required course, but because the faculty, in this case me in particular, seem to refuse to explain the purpose of the course. You want the teacher to be clear about the outcomes, what we will achieve by the time the course is completed." Many heads nodded affirmatively, and I continued, "You feel that the faculty is putting you down by not seeming to let you in on what should be the final objectives. Are you asking to be that involved in the course?" Susan suggested, "I like to know what is supposed to happen to me in the course, and I would like to be in on what's happening, you know, just so I can tell if the right things are really taking place." Bill added, "I like to be involved in what I am learning, and I think I learn best when I can have a positive sense of being involved. I like to know what's happening and to be able to have a sense of direction." I inquired whether the feedback I gave on their written reports was sufficient. Most approved, but Bill said: "The feedback is good, but I like to know, I like to have a sense of where I am. Grades or evaluations are good, but I want to know more. I want to be able to locate what I am learning in the total plan for the course. It gives me a sense of direction."

At that moment, I recalled at least the words of some of my colleagues about what happens in a classroom, and I suggested that when it comes to teaching a subject, the reason that students are in the classroom is to learn; it is the teacher who has the information. Since I did not want them to think I had changed my position, I said, "A professor–friend of mine believes that teachers are obligated to teach because they know something, and students are there to learn because they don't know anything."

Tim, a Vietnam veteran, took exception: "Not quite true, prof." Tim always spoke as if he knew exactly where he was going, though his tests indicated he was merely clever. "You are part right and part wrong. Teachers are trained and have the responsibility of teaching, but students—whatever or whoever they are—have the responsibility of learning. And we have to pick up on that responsibility. Sometimes we can't learn because we have a poor teacher or, if you don't mind my saying so, because we have a dumb teacher."

Bill interrupted, "He doesn't mean you!" Tim agreed. He continued, "We have the obligation to learn. Teachers can help us or even sometimes get in our way by confusing us; but learning is something that students do—we do it by ourselves."

I was about to make the distinction between negative confusion and creative confusion, right out of Plato's "allegory of the cave," when Susan spoke up, "You know, teachers sometimes think they are all that happen in class. But I have to take what a teacher is trying to teach me and translate it into something I learn, and that has little to do with the teacher. The learning is what I do."

It was so clear to me that Susan was using the rhetoric of a woman's lib group that I was about to dismiss her comments mentally. That is, until I glanced about the room and saw that some of my best students were nodding their heads in support of Susan's position. There were even more men than women in agreement with her. I realized that I had always thought teaching was active but that learning was somewhat passive and that students were merely recipients of my teaching. It really had never occurred to me before that teaching and learning are both active, positive processes.

I thought I should probe a bit. "Susan, don't you think that what you said is probably more true if you have a poor teacher? With a good teacher isn't it easier to learn?" "I'm not sure," she replied, "but, for me, it sometimes doesn't make any difference who the teacher is; I still have to learn by myself—and *for* myself!" It was clear to me that she used her hesitation to give emphasis to that last phrase. It was both a statement and a challenge. There was no shift in posture among the students. They were not putting me down personally, but I was being told that two things happen in a classroom: teaching *and learning*. They were honestly announcing that they were in charge of learning and it was something they did by themselves and, lest I forget, *for themselves*.

This was insight I had tended to ignore. Probably many teachers tended to overlook it. Teachers seemed to take full credit for any learning that took place in *their* class and with *their* students. It occurred to me that a teacher's language, when referring to students in the class, was "*my* students," but that students spoke mostly of "*the* teacher." What Susan said ran counter to teachers' language. She said the teacher owned the "teaching" but students owned themselves as well as their "learning." If she was correct, then the subtle structure of the classroom was not perceived correctly by teachers such as myself, who took credit for the learning that was happening under their supervision.

The issue was significant, so I decided to probe further. Not wanting to close off the discussion, I raised an objection. "Many of my colleagues believe that only the brightest students want to assume responsibility for their own learning. Those students who are not so bright do not assume responsibility for their own learning."

Tim said, "That tells us a good deal about what teachers think of most of us, for they automatically assume that most of us will not accept responsibility for our own learning. I don't think that's right." After a pause, he corrected himself, "I mean, I don't think it is correct that the not-too-bright students refuse to assume responsibility for their own learning."

John had never before spoken in class; he now indicated that he had something to say, "I don't have fantastic grades; I mean, with my job, I don't have too much time to study. I'll graduate, but when I have a sense of where the class is going and what it is going to do, I can study better. So if you want to consider me to be one of those 'not-so-bright students,' then I want to say it isn't so. I mean, even students like myself want to know where the class is going and what we are supposed to be doing."

Charles was shaking his head in a manner that was clear, but he obviously did not want to confront the rest of the class. I called on him. "I don't think it's right for students to worry about objectives or why they have to take the course. To be a doctor, all I want out of this class is something that will help me with my MCATs. If I don't get an A and some information that will give me some advantage in the MCATs, then the course is a mistake for me; but I don't care about anybody coming up with objectives."

Some students in the rear commented, in a stage whisper: "He's just a scientist!"

Jerry quickly said, "I'm a scientist too, but not all science students are alike. My major is physics, with a minor in astronomy, and I agree with the rest of the class. I want to know the objectives so I can structure the course for my own learning."

The class had achieved a critical position: They wanted to have some sense of the objectives of the course, for they saw that the objectives would permit them to play a more significant role in learning. But with the awareness that objectives played a role in the learning of students, would we be able to by-pass the common belief that objectives are usually thought to be exclusively for the help of the teacher?

"Perhaps this is the best point at which we can begin to speak about the reasons for taking this course," I suggested. "Then, we can discuss the final evaluation, or the final exam, as most of you call it." The soft nodding of many heads indicated we were setting off together.

First, I explained, it was necessary to distinguish the general sorts of things that the community and the Board of Trustees expect to happen to students during the time they are at the college; these may be called goals. Objectives are the particular intellectual aims toward which students strive. Their attainment means changes that take place in students (or are supposed to) as a result of taking a course. "Then why don't the professors tell us what is supposed to happen within us?" asked someone in a stage whisper from the back of the class. There was a chorus of titters. "I really do not know, though I suspect that most professors believe that their enthusiasm for the subject matter is all that is needed for a successful course." I tried to explain that in general my colleagues were most interested in communicating their enthusiasm for their subject matter along with some understanding of it. Most professors have a love affair with their field and want their students to develop the same sort of affection.

Some students were moved by my words—although they were not said with that intent—whereas others took serious exception. Paul suggested that it was dumb. Tom, the accountant, suggested he did not want a love affair with philosophy; he just wanted to understand why he had to take the course. And Susan inquired, "What are the things that are supposed to happen within students in this class?"

There were other things I wanted to explain about objectives before responding because otherwise my explanation would be sloppy. But I decided to respond to the students' interest, hoping that even a sloppy explanation in response to student questions could lead to fruitful learning experiences.

Based on Bloom's taxonomy of educational objectives (1956), I suggested six things should happen to students in the class. They should learn (1) some technical terms, facts, theories, methods, and principles (which may be called knowledge or information); (2) to comprehend, translate, or interpret the knowledge; (3) to apply it to concrete and particular situations; (4) to analyze the knowledge by recognizing relationships, discriminating elements, or picking out forms and patterns; (5) to synthesize portions of experience by bringing together elements of the above in new relationships or combinations; and (6) to evaluate some portion of experience from the perspective of, for example, its goals and its internal and external criteria. I finished by explaining that in describing these six objectives, I had merely applied levels of cognitive learning to the basic format of the course.

The reaction of the class was quite mixed. Some looked astonished. Others nodded by way of confirmation. Some just smiled with that sense of "I knew it all the while." There was a whole series of underbreath musings as others turned to their neighbors to comment, creating a general noise that really did not communicate anything specific.

I sensed it was not fair to dump that formidable list on them and then ask for instantaneous responses, so I simply asked for general reactions. This gave them a few minutes to get collected. Then Jim volunteered, "This course is a heavy trip!" Susan said: "I'm almost sorry I pushed for an answer!" And Tom asked, "Just out of curiosity, do those things that we should learn apply to other courses? I mean, you sort of suggested it, but do you really mean that?" Bill interrupted and said, "Before you answer Tom, would you tell me the relationship of the six things to each other. I mean, is there any priority? You seemed to be hinting at priorities."

"There are priorities," I suggested, "and each successive level is a sort of prerequisite for the next one. The six levels can be called knowledge, comprehension, application, analysis, synthesis, and evaluation. They are related in a ladderlike fashion; one level must be learned before you can go on to the next. Unless a teacher either teaches particular knowledge or assumes it has been acquired in a prior course, then anything that would presume to take place on the levels of comprehension or application would be unreasonable."

To answer Tom, I then said that the classification of levels would, in general, be appropriate to all courses in the college. The only exceptions would be courses that focus upon one or more of the lower levels of the classification. For example, in a first foreign language course, the major focus would be on learning the facts of the language, the words, the vocabulary, and perhaps some of the rules of word order, or the peculiarity of verb tenses. Certainly for any course beyond an introductory stage, most of the levels would be involved.

Bill asked, "Can you run through them again and explain each one so we can understand how they apply to this course?" I agreed and proceeded. I explained that the definitions of experience, knowledge, time, space, and so on were the items that comprised the first level. At the second level the students should learn to understand these items and their implications by themselves. Then, the students should be able to apply these items to their own or other persons' situations. Additionally, on the fourth level, students should be able to discern similarities of the structure of experience among persons involved in different events. I continued on through the six levels.

No sooner had I finished when the bell rang and the class was over. Two students immediately raised their hands. I called on Jim, who asked, "Will you give us a copy of these levels?" I replied, "Yes, but we have to discuss the issue a bit more." Most of the students were ready to leave, but I recognized Tom, who also had his hand raised. "It will keep to next class," was his reply as the class emptied with a rush.

I duplicated the list of levels for the next meeting. On Wednesday I passed it out and reiterated that although these categories could be used for many courses, in this course they were to be applied to its content of human experience. I then asked for questions. "I have a problem with them," suggested Paul. "You seem to have included all possibilities of learning; I mean, you seem to have excluded nothing. Suppose somebody comes up with something they have learned that doesn't fit into the categories but that the student believes would be important to mention—what does the student do?"

I explained that there were other kinds of things learned, such as the entire range of affective or feeling or value processes which constitute another type of learning, and a third type dealing with psychomotor skills, such as athletics, ceramics, voice control, and so on. To my knowledge little significant work had been done in the latter, and, in addition, the range of psychomotor skills had almost nothing to do with our course and could be ignored safely. I suggested that students who were majoring in physiology or psychology might keep the psychomotor range in mind as a possible subject of exploration for an advanced degree.

Tim asked, "Aren't we really talking about what is usually called behavioral objectives? I'm in the middle of a management course, and it seems to me you are really talking about what management people call behavioral objectives." I affirmed that although I knew little about corporate operation, I sensed that behavioral objectives were those specific goals identified and adopted by sections of a corporation so that they could be achieved more readily. Some educators had used this idea of activities or behavior as goals of corporations and applied it to the classroom and the school. Thus, behavioral objectives in the area of education state clearly and specifically what a student can do at the end of a particular course of instruction. For example, arithmetic is designed to teach students to add, subtract, multiply, and divide. Thus the objectives of a given arithmetic course would be the kinds of problems students should solve, ways in which they would do so, and so on.

Apparently I had communicated a negative attitude that I did not intend, for Tim asked, "What's wrong with that?"

"Nothing, really, but let me give an example from my grammar school days, when students had to prepare for state regents exams. Rather than studying history of a given period or of studying literature, we studied old regents exams in those areas in the hope of passing forthcoming ones. In all of these we used each regents exam as a sort of behavioral objective. Certainly we learned some history and some literature, but our goal was to pass the exams, not to learn."

"The difficulty with behavioral objectives is that they can become endpoints in the use of time and energy. In many ways they can corrupt the process of education by promoting the belief that a specific activity or range of activities is equivalent to the objectives of the course. At the same time, the whole notion of behavioral objectives is quite important for it stresses that each course should have a series of specific objectives and it forces awareness or recognition of exactly what a student must do to demonstrate achievement—for example, the appreciation of music." (I did not inform the class, but the notion of behavioral objectives was helping me clarify much of my own thinking.)

Carolyn, obviously deep in thought, suggested, "That is why you want us to play a role in the setting of objectives in this course. I mean it's why you want us to recognize that learning is a process and the objectives should play a role in that process, rather than objectives merely being things that we aim at." I agreed.

Evelyn chuckled and then blurted out, "You know, you have been really telling us what is going to be on the exam!"

I asked her to explain. She was happy with her discovery and just poured out, "When you started telling us what things we should be learning, I just made a mental note that seemed to tell me what I would be writing when I took the exam. I don't know how to explain it, though!"

She was right, and I agreed. "When a student knows what the course is attempting to teach, the mind seems to create categories and then it records those portions of the course that fit into particular categories. It's as if the mind, while in the process of learning, prepared itself to write the final evaluation. What makes it even more interesting is that as we go through the course, the mind continually rearranges and reassembles information. The information truly becomes *ours*; the mind seems to put its personal stamp on our acquisition. What we learn when we play an active role in the learning process seems to become something we own, that we identify as ours. Thus the exam, or final evaluation, is merely an opportunity to display our personal learning. Yes, Evelyn, you are correct; to know what should be happening to you, by way of what you should be learning, is to categorize the information in a manner that seems almost to develop into an evaluation experience, namely the final exam."

Bill was shaking his head, as if conversing with himself. I

asked him if he had a question. "Not really," he responded, "but there is a problem I can't seem to get straight. How are these things that should happen to students in this course going to be evaluated? You haven't indicated the amount of accuracy, the time, or even how long these things are supposed to be. I'm really lost!"

He was, of course, correct. The things that should happen to students are objectives, and they cannot really be spoken of without some specific reference to *performance*. Students should know what they are supposed to be able to do, the conditions under which they are to perform, and the standard or performance criteria by which they will be judged.

I suggested we use the lowest level of objectives—the technical philosophical terms—as an example. In the first portion of the course, students were supposed to have learned these terms, and they would be expected to be able to identify the terms by matching two columns: one containing the terms and the other column containing thirty items, some of which were accurate, some of which were partially true, and others which could only be applied erroneously. One-half hour would be allowed for getting at least sixteen items correct.

Bill said he understood, but he inquired how we could test the next level—comprehension. I suggested an exam on which all terms were listed; a student would have to paraphrase each term within thirty minutes. Apparently most students grasped this, but almost in unison they inquired about the final category—evaluation. I admitted this would be very difficult because of the complexity of that category. "You will have to understand this requires more attention than I have given it to this point, but I do have some ideas. Evaluation would be about almost any significant experience you have had. It could include the class itself (for this is an experience), some other personal experience, perhaps an experience had by a friend or even by parents, or another course. Possibilities include a movie, a drama, a television program or production, or a novel. The evaluation would be done in a written form. It would have to include, in a conscious fashion, use of technical philosophical terms and an application of these terms by way of both analysis and syntheses, and finally, a judgment of the experience by both an internal and external standard. It would also have to be completed within a designated time and be of a particular length. Use of a specific number of philosophical terms would be required."

Tom asked what I meant by internal and external standards. Since we had not gotten that far in the course, I said that those terms would be difficult to explain now. If, for example, the student selected the process of this class as the experience, then the standard could be the extent to which what was learned helped the student understand portions of past experience, confirmed past beliefs, or brought new insights, or, on the other hand, the extent to which the class did not do these things. In this latter case, it would probably be necessary to have some sense of why the experience was not as fruitful a learning experience as it could have been.

Many of their faces broke into smiles, and Paul said, laughingly, "How many teachers would pass you for the course if you said their class was a 'bummer'?" I had to admit that was a problem; yet, at the same time it seemed to me that a positive critique of why things did not go well could be the basis for a good grade.

Bonnie said she felt as though she now knew what the course was trying to do, and she felt satisfied. She now wanted to get on with other topics. Other students agreed. The event had come full cycle; they now wanted to return to the process of the class.

Three class sessions had been used, but it seemed worth the time. It was one of the most significant experiences I have had in teaching, and those students still tell me it was one of the most valuable portions of any course they ever had. Although I recognize their tendency to exaggerate, my portion of their experience has been confirmed. Once they raised the question "What do you want us to learn?", class discussion explored many corners of teaching and probed issues that required my personal reflection. They were issues that were not rooted in the discipline of philosophy but had to do with the process of teaching itself. Not only did the students learn from the events, I learned from them in reacting to their concerns.

Finale

The significance of this experience for my teaching colleagues is, of course, an additional and very crucial question. To what extent can the fruitfulness of this exchange in one course be translated to another course? I readily concede that college professors are rewarded on the basis of developing a narrow area of expertness, and in light of this, it is quite easy to understand the response of some of my colleagues that their area of specialization is so unique that little is to be gained by attempting to apply what may work in some other area to their area of specialization. For many of them this is an honest response, although I suspect more automatic than the result of reflection and offered by way of a protective defense mechanism. But surely there is little exquisite uniqueness in the vast majority of introductory courses, and from my experience in teaching in two departments other than philosophy —sociology and American religious thought—there is little doubt in my mind that at least some of my learning from the event is applicable in other disciplines.

All things considered, these three precepts now make sense to me in the writing and use of objectives and can be considered, I believe, fairly universal:

1. Instructors should write their own course objectives. None should be imposed from without. There is little doubt that specific courses fulfill requirements of a whole series of persons and groups: professional agencies; boards of trustees, in the case of college or university requirements; deans and their advisers, in the case of sector requirements; department members, in the case of department requirements; and others. These requirements are important, and the advice of one's disciplinary colleagues is most useful and should be sought and used in the writing and rewriting of one's objectives. But no matter what requirements the course fulfills, the objectives must be developed to the satisfaction of the instructor.

2. The development of course objectives must be done in conjunction with the students. This is not intended to suggest that students dominate the class but that objectives be seen as part of the learning process and not as some goals removed from the concern of the class. The development of objectives permits and then encourages what might be called student ownership of the course. Students should be helped to recognize that although the instructor has the responsibility for the teaching of the course, the learning which occurs depends on their feeling of ownership. The objectives

must become an integral part of the students' thinking. It is this transformation of objectives, seen as ends, to objectives viewed as part of the entire learning process that is crucial. If students are not able to bring the objectives into play, then the objectives serve dominantly as a limiting force, even militating against the very development of the imagination. Each course, each classful of students, by its unique individuality, in essence creates a course different from any other. Classes of students differ in such things as ranges of ability, mix of personalities and variant experiences; and one way this diversity can be accommodated is through student participation in the development of course objectives. Basically this can be accomplished in two ways: by encouraging students to react to instructor-presented objectives and by having them select alternate methods for implementing and attaining them.

3. At no time is it possible to have completed the development of objectives; it is an ongoing process. Clarifying objectives, however, is not external to the teaching-learning process but is an intimate part of it. Just as students are expected to take a significant role in the development of their lives, both teachers and students are expected to take significant roles in the living process they share. Insight, understanding, awareness, reflection, and appreciation play important roles, not only in the living of life, but also in the teaching-learning process. Without backing off from the hard-nosed position that the teacher is the trained person, the professional, frequently with years of experience, it must be acknowledged that the process of teaching is not a private process; it is done in front of, and in conjunction with, students. The medium through which teaching becomes learning is the process of communication. This is not a sometime thing but an ongoing sharing, and both faculty and student must be involved continually.

Three final comments are in order. First, in retrospect, did I not waste an entire week of classwork discussing objectives with my students? The answer is both yes and no. Certainly the students missed a week of course content—and knowing well the continual pressure in most disciplines to cover the material, I am not suggesting that any colleague use a week doing what I did. All I hope is that colleagues make use of the knowledge I gained from my slow, plodding method of handling the question of objectives during that week. The sadness in my self-reflection is that it took me a quarter of a century of teaching and that week of class meetings to become suddenly and acutely aware of the importance of clarifying objectives *with* and *for students*! To the extent that others avoid my personal traumatic learning process, the experience can benefit more than my students and me.

Second, do I really believe that the notion of objectives approached from the perspective of the level of cognitive learning can be used in all courses, from anthropology to zoology? Yes, I do. Since all courses presume to be dealing with cognitive skills, then the statement of objectives as herein outlined would be clearly applicable.

And third, am I opposed to the love affair that teachers have with their field of study? Certainly not! Yet, by itself, it can be destructive, for it seems to set norms for students that are unrealistic; students can easily perceive that only those who have a love affair with the subject matter will succeed in particular classes, whereas what teachers usually want to communicate is that their feeling for their discipline comes after they develop knowledge and skills in the discipline. This is not always communicated clearly, and students have been known to feign love for the sake of a grade. Like most love situations, the love that has depth can only come after much knowledge.

Thus, to the extent that a course has some sort of objectives, that students are involved in the course, and the teaching-learning process is an ongoing one, it seems appropriate to suggest that the process of clarifying objectives is one that can be fruitfully used by all who teach.

2

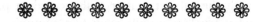

John Satterfield

Lecturing

In the Preface, our editor describes this as a "how-to" book. My contribution to it can hardly be so massive as an exhaustive "how-to lecture."

All good teaching opens doors. To open doors by yourself is only one way to learn; otherwise stories would be "The Lady or the Tiger." We can learn much from the conclusions—their watched entrances through doors they have opened—of surpassers with unusual insights, persons like J. S. Bach, Cézanne, Michelangelo, Flannery O'Connor, Dylan Thomas, and an equally tight catalogue of natural scientists, social scientists, jazz musicians, theologians, politicians, comedians, and some other teachers. Here I point to some doors that others have opened and invite you to enter, to consider some categories of practice which both you and your students can enjoy.

34

The unlively aura of the college classroom has long called up savage remarks about lectures and lecturers: "That professor would be dull on free love." "Stay out of that course; each lecture in it is better than the next one." "I wish the dean would take those two hacks out of the classroom and put them at something harmless like campus landscaping, but they'd probably sod the roofs." "Class dismissed *physically* now, maybe, but *psychologically* fifty minutes ago." "If it's sociology, it's either obvious or not true." "The most forgettable character I ever met."

These old laments received fresh pungency and poignancy from the recent complaint of Professor Walter Kaufmann (1977, pp. 187–188):

> Lectures are . . . highly problematical, and most of them are certainly a waste of time. If the lecturer does not write them out, chances are that they will be greatly inferior to something available in print that could be assigned instead. And if he does write them out, there seems to be no need for him to read them off because they could easily be made available to the students to read for themselves in half the time. . . . Does it make any sense for people who are bad at lecturing to go right on doing it for decades and alienating students? It seems obvious that at the very least something should be done to decrease the percentage of poor lecturers. But in fact there are thousands of colleges and universities in North America alone, the number of professors at many of them is several hundred, and hardly any of them have ever received any advice, not to speak of instruction, about the art with which they earn their living. I doubt that the great majority have ever given very much thought to the point and aims of lecturing. What, if anything, can be achieved in this way that could not be done far better by adding another assignment?

Regardless of such abhorrence of it, however, lecturing is likely to remain the most prevalent practice of college teaching; and in spite of its disrepute as a teaching method, the orally delivered essay can be magnificent. (I have heard a few terrific ones myself.)

The modest goal of the suggestions to follow is to improve at least some lectures. Perfecting all to magnificence would be an immodest hope. The demand put upon the college lecturer is enormous, so great that it cannot begin satisfaction if the standards approach perfection. At one hundred and fifty words per minute (maybe an average rate of speaking), the lecturer must produce seventy-five hundred words for a fifty-minute lecture. Twelve different lectures a week require ninety thousand words. Hardly any writer could be so prolific and at the same time exercise all the careful revisions the craft necessitates to produce excellent prose. The lecturer has to fill a verbal space that nobody could fill truly well in a like period—nobody, not Herman Melville, not St. John. Aside from the system's not wanting the teacher's best, aside from the lecturer's lack of specific preparation—a lack including the practical neglect of language itself (neglect that both undergraduate and graduate curricula cannot justify for prospective professors)—the very working conditions of nine to fifteen lectures each week during the academic year militate against good performance. The most gifted writer would be unwilling to submit ninety thousand or more words per week to an editor.

Still, we lecturers should not say with despair that we are doing our best under adverse circumstances. Our lectures could be—should be—better. Most of us might shrug off the comment that our lectures are unesthetic, it not having occurred to us that communication—presentation—has rigors of its own which are not identical to disciplinary rigor. "Unesthetic? Of course! I'm a scholar, not an artist," says the rationalizer. But no professor can justify lectures that are anesthetic. The lackluster talk finds a match but no reflection in the glazed eyes of bored students.

Note the word "talk." My first piece of advice to the lecturer, whether beginning or continuing, is to separate ordinary talk from lecturing. Useful as words may be for spleen venting, preening, and reducing anxiety, talk is frequently not a transmitter of substance. (What does the phrase, "I don't like chocolate," for example, tell a hearer about chocolate?) Most wordage may be self-therapy to keep the human organism functional as other than a direct communicator.

People mostly talk *at,* only sometimes *to,* and very rarely *for* one another. On a city bus in Atlanta, a passenger cannot miss overhearing an exchange between two women on the seat just ahead, the one woman on the aisle balancing several packages as she joins the other.

"Hot, ain't it, honey?"

Does the one by the window confuse temperature and time? "I doneven know what day it is. My husban's been in the hospital more'n a week, and I been there mostly night and day."

"Did you git by Rodgers' for the sale? I declare I lef early this morning to miss em picky bargain hunters, and the bus was loaded with em. I been promisin myself some open-toe pumps, so today was the time, but that crowd packed downtown like high heels jam toes in pointy shoes. I had to stand in line even to git in Rodgers'es basement. Tha's where the sale is."

"He had this here growth on his groin. I never seen nothin lak it. He finely had to have it cut off, and I ain't sure he got it done in time."

"You should seen them biddies pickin away at everthang. When I finely got a seat in the shoe department, I had to just sit for three girls who came after me to try on shoes standin up. I ast the clerk how come he waited on *them* first, and he couldn't do nothin but blush."

"He thought it was a bruise—just kinda dark— when he first seen it, and it won't very sore, but he dint show it to me until it begun to swell, look lak a egg, all blue with red streaks in it. I tol him to go right away to a clinic, but he said it'd go away."

"A buncha women huntin bargins sure do make me sick, standin' aroun lookin over my shoulder with gripey faces—after all, I dint try on but sevun styles. I went back to number six. They blue with this white on the instep and a little white band where the toe opens. 'Stoo cumberful with all these bags, or I'd show you. Rang that bell, will you, honey? My stop's nex."

"He dint go 'til it swoll out on a kinda neck and look lak a droopy light bulb turnin all green and festerin. Tha's when it commence to smell, and I guess that odor finely run him to the doctor. He never come home

from the office, went slapdab into the hospital, and was
in the operatin room in a hour. He's still delirious, and
he ain't passin no water."

"I git off here. Nice talkin to you. Try to git
down to Rodgers' while the sale's still going."

"Good to talk to you. Keep well, you hear?"

That we mostly talk *at* one another is a primary premise
overworked by the theater of the absurd. Only the craft of melding
material and style into form—Samuel Beckett has the craft—can
successfully prolong a basic absurdity by giving it apparent development, rich implication, and ultimate consequence in a circumstantial
symmetry. But dwelling on that premise through two and a half
hours of little development, implication, and consequence is as dull
as a lecture redacting encyclopedias on pre-Darwinian conjectures
about evolution. Yet most college lectures are absurd in every sense,
including the recent technical and philosophical ones cultivated by
existentialists. The ordinary academic use of talk is poor both
stylistically and formally. Every reader of these pages already knows
how little of this talk has substance of any greater import than a
typical line from a soap opera.

But I am not conspiring to change conversational habits:
I am pointing out that a college lecture has a different purpose from
ordinary talk. The lecture should be better. It has no purpose but to
communicate memorably and well.

Consider the importance of the development of content, rich
implication, and ultimate consequence in achieving this goal.

Content and Context

All communicative techniques and utter skill in delivery
cannot overcome empty content. In the practice of democracy,
process is probably more important than product; but in education,
product—substance—is the measure. We are not educating when
we deserve the criticism often given to John Updike: "He hasn't
got anything to say, but he says it awfully well."

The content of the good lecture may be old, but it cannot
be obvious—except occasionally as a joke. No professor should

seriously tell a class, "There are three kinds of time: past, present, and future." Star that he could be, even Aristotle underestimated his audiences and readers with similar sentences: "Let us begin, as is natural, with primary matters first" (1942, p. 1), and "A beginning is that which of necessity does not follow anything, while something by nature follows or results from it. On the other hand, an end is that which naturally, of necessity, or most generally follows something else but nothing follows it. A middle is that which follows and is followed by something" (1942, pp. 15–16). Pedantry is where you find it—sometimes interspersed among the startling insights of a mastermind.

Many—I hope all—college students do not need an explanation of this sentence: "Glimpsing an ominous sky through a window, Pushinsky picked up his umbrella as he left his house." But Heaven help students! Many professors practice the equivalent of telling how a confluence of signs—clouds, their shape, their swiftness, their color, the color behind them, and others—make the sky a warning that rain may shortly fall; an umbrella has a design and a material which protect its carrier from rain, and that is why Pushinsky picked his up as he left his house. Does such material express condescension toward or contempt of an audience, or is it an illustration of the human mind at *work?* Maybe *a* human mind, but scarcely that of the typical student admitted to college. Lectures, like most textbooks, carry the freight of uselessly explaining the already understood: dead weight.

Good content—especially in fine contexts—should be challenging, not so familiar that it never sends a student to a reference or a new experience. Is not one purpose of education to enhance curiosity while showing how to satisfy it partially? However, the material cannot be totally unfamiliar and remain so throughout the lecture successfully. That extreme induces the same classroom comas as the obvious. The lecturer needs to know how much the class already knows and to take its members across some new thresholds. Judgment is necessary. Suppose church architecture is the subject. Confessing that the statement is ridiculously anthropomorphic, the lecturer might say, "Although I'd really be everywhere if I were God, I'd mostly be at Chartres, Coventry, Köln, and Ronchamp instead of at the Riverside Church in Manhattan or at the First

Baptist Church in Orangeburg, South Carolina." Who knows
whether a student may someday find a good reason for going to the
Riverside Church or even to Orangeburg, South Carolina?

Good content usually is not exclusively personal opinions of
the lecturer, but just as surely it usually is not only opinions of
others. Separating content from style and form is tricky on this
point, but a good lecturer who is also a good scholar and thinker
ought to arrive at some personal conclusions and expose them to
students. Otherwise, why study and think? Besides—here the separa-
tion of content from model behavior may be impossible—the professor who wants students to reach conclusions should show them
how to do it.

Should the professor write his lectures to ensure quality content? In view of what I have already said and what I will say later
about form, my answer is yes. No professor with whom I have
studied did so; among them were some good teachers (in modes
other than lecturing), and occasionally I heard one present an excellent, prepared address, a paper not for the classroom. Although
the professors varied in ability to improvise lectures, the height
reached by the most skillful few was only tolerability. I have heard
and known only one professor who could appear before an audience
and improvise a superbly argued, informative, attention-keeping
speech for fifty minutes. A very few others—Ernest Bloch among
them—were themselves, as personalities, as much their individual
subjects as those advertised; learning such as they dispensed had
many values, including some inspirational ones, but characters
strong enough to teach through mildly disguised display of self-hood
are typically too strong to remain on an institutional payroll; we
have to learn from their creations rather than directly from them.

Many members of audiences and faculties resent well-prepared, rehearsed speakers. Consideration in getting ready for hearers
gets different interpretations: insecurity, inability to think on the
feet, overformality, lack of spontaneity—all clearly related to manner and not at all to content. Although I understand the torpor
induced by the poor, slow, monotonous reading of bad writing, I
can think of no greater inconsideration of audiences than that shown
by the typical, improvised college lecture, full of faults from a compendium that these pages hardly begin. Polish and precision do not

eliminate spontaneity, as a sonnet by Shakespeare and a theorem by Pythagoras demonstrate. Some results of spontaneity are worth the effort to polish and make them precise. The "down-to-earth" speaker may be "one of us" and keep us comfortable, but our relaxation may not be the reason for our attending lectures. A professor recently told me, "I never prepare a lecture. Students today don't want to hear anybody lecture. They just want somebody to talk." Their almost universal condemnation of lecturers *in the classroom* says that they want something better than talk.

I recommend a prepared lecture—as many written as possible. For each one a clear outline done in complete sentences and with logical subordination could go to students. The students could then listen, taking few notes. Part of the distributed material might be sentences (sometimes definitions) especially fancied by the lecturer. Under such conditions the following all-too-familiar episode need never occur again on a college campus.

Lecturer: Ontogeny—don't worry; I'll spell it for you in a minute— recapitulates phylogeny—and I'll spell that, too, but it is a sentence that should be remembered because it is an important concept in your understanding of the biological concepts that will be taken up as we consider the influence of genetics. You'll probably be examined on this, so I repeat it is important for you to get this, and I'll repeat it slowly so you can take notes and get it. Now,—Ontogeny—that's O-N-T-O-G-E-N-Y—recapitulates—uh, maybe I'd better spell that—R-E-C-A-P-I-T-U-L-A-T-E-S—and the last word is "phylogeny", and it is spelled P-H-Y-L-O-G-E-N-Y —that's something you'll want to remember because it will help you in the rest of the course and may show up on an examination.

Student: What does "recapitulate" mean?

Lecturer: Well, it means "to repeat" maybe or "to do over again"— uh, the same patterns that show up in phylogeny will show up in ontogeny and that's why we say ontogeny recapitulates phylogeny—but you'll see what I mean when I give you definitions of "ontogeny" and "phylogeny"—and I guess I'd better get to those right now—now ontogeny— O-N-T-O-G-.

During analogous episodes, how many ticks of college's clocks have moved them toward the sun's final exhaustion? How many hearts have beat toward the last beat as if every pulse were not a time for recognizing, enjoying, and acting upon the gift of life? The written lecture and the distributed outline (and glossary when necessary) can reduce the boredom of the classroom, increase the effectiveness of the lecturer and the students, and save more time than anybody has measured.

The distributed outline is one kind of audiovisual aid. My topic—lecturing—prevents my dwelling on such aids. Still, maps, charts, tables, photographs, recordings, moving pictures, printouts can make some points with greater speed, clarity, and context than spoken words. Lecturers might appeal to the audiovisual aids to make such points, but often professors must make their own software. The aids should be only supports for the lecture. When they dominate, the mode of teaching is different from lecturing.*

More important to the content of the lecture than these aids is significant context. Since I will argue that significant context is a vital but mostly absent element of college lectures, I need to establish a contextual perspective for my own remarks.

In a paper rejected by periodicals but widely circulated "underground" before publication in a book of his essays, Carl Rogers charged graduate departments of psychology with rejecting the most creative candidates for advanced degrees and thus be-

---

*The insistence on the importance of such aids comes mostly not from lecturers but from people who want lectures replaced by other means of instruction. Audiovisual equipment (the machinery itself) is impressive in demonstrations. (For this chapter let us ignore the failures of staff to deliver the machinery at the right place on time, loss of power at the electric company, and the short circuits, blown bulbs, defective resistors, and million other untoward eventualities for which we have heard a billion rationalizations.) The machinery—from the slide projector to the computer—*is* impressive, the messages provided for the machinery to convey not very. When the "software" becomes products of creators like Herman Melville, we may say that the load is better than the truck carrying it. Not so now. Almost all material for audiovisual presentation that I have seen came from commercial hacks or the equivalent of high-fidelity fanatics—people who listen with delight to the tweeter and the woofer whatever they are reproducing, even the singing of Carmen Lombardo. "Multimedia" events typically compound the already insuperable difficulties of opera. In audiovisual software "the state of the art" is sad, unworthy of the technology ready to transmit it.

coming routine mills (1969, pp. 169–197). "Respectable" academicians may not be incompetent to work on the meanings of the
facts they seek and sometimes find, but they mostly choose the security of narrow—and usually dull—contexts. The same content—
especially in but not restricted to the humanities and the social
sciences—can often be stark and without explored implications and
arresting form, or it can be lush with allusion to many contexts and
made indelible by grace of style and compelling shape.

Content becomes significant by context achieved through
reference to other contents. I do not urge name dropping, padded
inventories, or any other excess, but the presentation of isolated,
mechanically sorted facts—what academic respectability likes most—
is an excess that needs moderation. If facts out of context have little
meaning, using them in isolation can lead the academic astray. "The
scholarly enterprise" altogether wrongly exploits material out of appropriate context. The vivisection of Raquel Welch a loss entails.

The purpose of higher education as carried out in the classroom—the purpose of the classroom lecture as communicating
information memorably and well—needs a more distinguished judgment than mine. I appeal to Justice Oliver Wendell Holmes
(quoted in Black, 1946, p. 345): "The recording of facts is one of
the tasks of science, one of the steps toward truth; but it is not the
whole of science. There are one-story intellects, two-story intellects,
and three-story intellects with sky lights. All fact collectors, who
have no aims beyond their facts, are one-story men. Two-story men
compare, reason, and generalize, using the labors of the fact collectors as well as their own. Three-story men idealize, imagine, and
predict. Their best illumination comes from above, through the sky
light."

Higher education overcautiously directs its laborers to stay
on the ground floor collecting facts. Its overspecialization, particularly in graduate schools, tells the laborer that risk lies in comparison
outside the speciality and inhibits generalization, and the program
keeps formal study so tightly within the discipline that comparison
outside it is impractical. Holmes's third story, where imagination
lives, is even more inaccessible. In my graduate schooling (for
music—of all subjects) "imaginative" was more often a pejorative
adjective than a compliment, whether applied to a composer, a pub-

lished scholar, or a student. For Holmes to attribute illumination to a skylight is wrong in every academic sense. He may be saying that we cannot yet "explain" the arrival of insight or the accident of genius, but he may metaphorically be talking about providential intervention, Plato's sun as the source of all good, Promethean fire, or many other conjectural or superstitious items. What respectable scholar resorts to metaphor? Only a poet would do anything so irrational.

So the graduate student of music should know on that first story the exact year in which Chopin migrated from Poland to France and became, as the historians have it, very much a product of his time and his environment. The student should not ask why Chopin, among the products of his time and environment, should be so far superior to all others. What graduate student has the—the what?—the temerity? the knowledge? the *right*? to ask a question that the history of music—as a discipline—refuses to acknowledge as conceivable? The normal requirement that a doctoral dissertation contribute to knowledge finds satisfaction in the addition of a fact to the collection on Holmes' ground floor.

The collector of facts looks no higher. Once I suggested to an historian that a collation of all examinations given in colleges and universities on, say, European history from World War I to date would probably present a professorial consensus on about one thousand indispensable facts. Why not mimeograph the thousand statements for students entering the course and then lecture on what certain ones or groups of the facts might mean? "Because," the historian said, "students should be busy learning a second thousand." Such a mind can say approvingly that learning is drudgery, but it does not know that insight is joy—maybe because it never had a synthesizing insight.

My second piece of advice to the lecturer, therefore, is to defy the higher educational system by getting off Justice Holmes' ground floor. Consider and explore contexts. For the majority of professors that means a new, major, and endless reading (and seeing and hearing) assignment, the required reading of each, perhaps through several degrees, having mostly been shelved in one place in the library. It also means a new, major, and endless self-education, but I have never known a professor who persisted in it and did not find it infinitely more illuminating than the education he received formally. Not having practiced their literacy outside their respective disciplines, most professors may be correctly cautious to refer to only what they have read, yet the persuasions that narrowed their reading were incorrect. One frequently heard remark on campuses is that professors' spouses outread professors, possibly not true in volume but likely true in catholicity.

Some evidence comes from two informal and small but convincing surveys I have conducted. At separate institutions I have asked representative upperclass members to check the names of authors and artists whose work professors had assigned for study. (Because nonverbal accomplishment is significant, I included names of architects, painters, and composers whose works students had met in assignments.) The names were sometimes glorious, sometimes those of discipline founders; they included Freud, Comte, Adam Smith, Marx, Plato, Darwin, Einstein, Augustine, Tillich, Homer, authors of biblical books, Sophocles, Thucydides, Gibbon, Goethe, Shakespeare, Hawthorne, and peers ancient and modern—even the drafters of the Constitution of the United States. The paucity of names that the students checked (in these surveys architects, painters, and composers almost never received checks, and the Constitution received them by no more than 1 percent of the students) would shock anyone who still believes (What do college and university catalogues say? What is the definition of an intellectual? an academic? an educated person?) that erudition is a goal of American higher education. A tour of any college bookstore will convince the tourist; the average quality of the texts there simply cannot bear comparison with that of a longer list which continues the short one I wrote above as token.

But worse news came; when I took the survey results to a large group of representative faculty members on each campus, I at first met a defensive phalanx protesting, "You want everybody to be a Renaissance man." After my mild statements that it seemed likely that the exposure to several dozen unique creations by luminous individuals could make professors' lectures more interesting and more significant and that nobody hoped to put a Leonardo da Vinci behind every lectern, some defensiveness subsided. Admissions arrived that most had never done any such study—even reading—as I had suggested, and too many admitted never having read works by the founders of their respective disciplines. Fortunately, on both campuses some faculty members recognized the seriousness of the most widespread curricular oversight in the United States: Except on a very few campuses, faculties do not have any convention about what students should study to receive diplomas (save exposure to some disciplines), and only rarely do professors know what their students study other than their own assignments. With some professors participating, both campuses introduced modest programs to ensure that students would to some extent practice literacy in other than books written to be college texts. Small progress maybe, but any move toward a more erudite populace is worth making.

Delivery and Style

Specific illustrations about how to improve content and context are difficult in a general chapter about lecturing on almost all subjects. Illustrations are easier to make when discussing manner of delivery and style. I recommend that all lecturers hear some recordings of their respective classroom performances. Each lecturer should then jump on the recordings with both ears. A report that Flaubert cried when he discovered that he had allowed to go to press a succession of two prepositional phrases beginning with the same preposition may be apocryphal, but it illustrates well the persistent, ruthless self-criticism the lecturer should exercise. The evaluative hearing of their own lectures may spur professors to begin improving elements of them.

A moment ago I pleaded for avoiding the obvious in the classroom. But bad habits in lecturing may, like body odors, escape the notice of offenders grown accustomed to them; under stress at work a sweating race driver may feel no need for a pit stop. Nonsense syllables have no place in college lectures, but they teem, and not only in college lectures. President Carter recently pronounced seventeen "uhs" within three improvised sentences for television. Walk along the hall of a campus classroom building, or arrange another way to hear professors perform. "Er," "ah," "um," "uh," "eh," and even the literary (especially British) "harrumph" are modes of breaking wind to relieve the lecturer's tension or results of careless indecision. They are ugly wastes of time by professors insensitive to their audiences. Hearing recordings of themselves as they indulge in such cacophony, lecturers can understand that a silence is superior to a meaningless vocable. They can act on the understanding. Having found that from 5 to 20 percent of lecture time went to nonsense syllables (or after improvement to silences anything but pregnant), professors could close verbal gaps and temper their chronic complaints that semesters are too short for their subjects.

To assume that most professors would prefer correct to incorrect grammar is dangerous, "like it is" and "where the students are at" often appearing in lectures but no longer just for humor or social criticism. Since precision helps in attempts to tell a truth and since correct grammar is an aid in being precise, proper usage is important to lecturers. Those who say as a beginning, "In Greece they . . ." and who hear themselves say it on a recording are not likely to know what is wrong with the sequence. The many professors—and newscasters—who treat "phenomena," "data," "criteria," and "agenda" as singular nouns will not learn that each is plural only by hearing themselves say it (presumably newscasters do hear themselves sometimes after their programs are on magnetic tape, but their grammar is not improving—if "different than" is a measure). I recommend that lecturers make a conscious, intense, everlasting effort to use language well. One delightful bolster for the person trying to reduce errors is the short, sharp book by Strunk and White, *The Elements of Style* (1962). Reading it and listening to themselves, many lecturers will improve not only their grammar but also their taste. Books on grammar vary from the tedious to the stimulating, from the stuffy to the happily practical, and all emphasize the individual demons their respective authors want to exorcise. Strunk particularly hated the construction "the fact that," apparently necessary in the minds of most lecturers but an ostentatious waste of words since everyone supposes professors deal with facts (Strunk and White, 1962, p. ix). *The Elements of Style,* far from exhaustive, implicitly urges acquaintance with Fowler (1965) and with a dictionary large enough to give examples of entries in historical and idiomatic usage.

This chapter cannot linger on the specifics of grammar, but

it must insist on their importance. That Abraham Lincoln split logs may have had no bearing on the quality of his presidency (never mind his "image"). Lyndon Johnson split infinitives.

Having eliminated various grunts and other nonsensical ejaculations from their talks and having—through listening to themselves and studying the conventions—arrived at correct grammar, lecturers should concentrate on style, a large part of it governed by diction. In this chapter "diction" means "choice of words," not "enunciation."

Academic language is notoriously bad. Gibes at its being needlessly polysyllabic, turgidly involuted, and simply overabundant do not really account for its dullness. The scholarly vocabulary picks words of Greek and Latin origins, derivatives that tend toward the general, over words from the Anglo-Saxon, the rejects usually being short and more specific. It prefers the abstract to the concrete. Therefore, long words ending in "–tion," "–ness," and "–ment," for instances, greatly outnumber words like "dank" and "brown." (The examples for the comparison come from my memories of James Joyce, who knew the difference as well as anybody.) The resultant fault in academic diction—this sentence illustrates it—is that it does not offer images to the senses; it has the opposite effect of alerting: it is soporific. "The ability to think abstractly" is a virtue in professors' recommendations of students and peers, but every good writer from Homer to Bellow has used concrete language without impairing demonstrations of thought on all levels.

The difference between the learned abstract and the careful concrete affects the quality of the message itself. Compare Keats' "To Hope," studded with abstract nouns, with his "Ode on a Grecian Urn," vividly concrete; he probably would have earned oblivion with the former, but he did earn eternal reference with the latter. Poetry aside, see the brilliant simplicity (the simplicity becoming overwhelmingly complex through evocative images for the senses) of Carlos Castaneda's narrative in *The Teachings of Don Juan: A Yaqui Way of Knowledge* (1974). Then read his appendices, where he tried to reorganize the compellingly narrated experiences in language suitable for a dissertation at the University of California, Los Angeles. A typical sentence from the former: "I moved through the water of the black lake perched on a piece of soil that looked like an earthen log" (Castaneda, 1974, p. 112). From the latter: "Don Juan may have produced this second special state in order to strengthen the link between ordinary and nonordinary reality by developing the possibility that most, if not all, of the component elements of ordinary reality could lose their capacity to have ordinary consensus" (Castaneda, 1974, p. 283). Although to improve their work, college lecturers will have to overcome many kinds of scholarly prejudices and preferences, they will make their talks more communicative and rewarding to their students if they will accept and act on this premise: Since the adjective they earned came from their attention to language, good writers are better models to follow than academicians, most of whom pay little attention to language. Clear, precise language must have a high correlation to clear, precise verbal thinking. The occasional exception is only that and extremely occasional. Kant deserved the wit that said, "Don't worry about his translator's ability; Kant loses something in the original."

Listening to themselves on recordings, lecturers can discover and remove some verbal tics. Those ending in "-wise" ("family-wise") and "-ize" ("finalize") are symptoms of an illness worth curing. A teacher who said "ostensible" eighty times in fifty minutes might look up a synonym, or better, recognize that if it were not "ostensible," "apparent," or "manifest" to somebody (the lecturer here), nobody would be saying it. Uses of such words should be rare, each with point. That understood, the unemployment rate for "ostensible," "apparent," "manifest," and "obvious" could easily rise 98 percent.

A former lecturing colleague could scarcely get through a sentence without "exceedingly" or "thoroughly." After hearing him several times, I concluded that he found "very" an overused intensifier—a true finding. But he must also have found "very" in itself a cliché. He therefore substituted "exceedingly" or "thoroughly" for every "very" without recognizing that neither of the longer words means—is a suitable substitute for—"very."

During the 1950s I heard a baccalaureate sermon largely about a Scottish tour given by a congregation to a Presbyterian minister and his wife. "On the deck of that great ocean liner, as I heard the deep-throated blahst of the whistle," set the scene. "The

deep-throated blahst of the whistle" got repetitions in seven succeeding scenes and another in the ending. Hearing himself could
not have helped that speaker; his bloated, self-stroking, aural love
for his broad "A" and his own atonal epithets deafened him to anything else. (Where was onomatopoeia? "Blahst" doesn't sound like
a blast; "blast" does.) Others, able to be self-critical, can profit by
hearing themselves. That sermon occurred some years before the
advents of Miss Lovelace's well-known movie and the Watergate
conspiracy. How about John Dean's "at this point in time" for
"now" and "at that point in time" for "then"? They are products
of people willing to say "plus and in addition to" rather than "and."
A government employee so inefficient with words is shamelessly
wasting taxpayers' money and may be plotting to run away with
their civil rights. We probably could end the fad of pornography in
the United States if somebody would produce the ultimate dirty
movie, *Linda Lovelace Meets the Roto-Rooter*. I have not con-
ceived even a probable way to end corruption in government.

Diction results from taste and is therefore—contrary to the
proverb—subject to disputing. Although we cannot agree exactly
where the line lies between good and bad taste and good and bad
diction, we have some descriptive words for excess. We can tolerate
an English professor's use of "patina"; not a household word, it
nevertheless has a specific and concrete meaning. For the same
reason we should not complain about the young Thomas Wolfe's
"phthisic," exactly right where he put it and probably not replace-
able by a single word as precise. We cannot easily forgive "ambi-
ance" (particularly with an attempted French pronunciation) because it appeals to current chic (hangs out a blatant sign reading
"I'm hipper than thou") and is very loose as often used. We might
hear "aubusson" as neatly fitting for a particular red, but it is not
right for any red. Some short-story writers for *The New Yorker*
like to call colors "mauve," "chartreuse," "ecru," "ocher," and the
like; they avoid "green," "red," "yellow"—and become precious.
One once named the stir of air from a fan in a city elevator "a
sirocco." Linguipotence is less the extent of vocabulary than the
expressive control of the right one (which need not include "linguipotence.") Sometimes we can forgive an English professor's use of
"conceit," "trope," and "metaphysical," because with the critic's

special definitions they are part of the trade's necessary (technical) jargon. Unnecessary jargon belongs nowhere. From further mention in these pages I dismiss it—*social scientists, now hear this!*—with the lethal sentence the poet Conrad Hilberry gave me: "The plural of 'interface' is 'interfeces'." So much, as Aristotle might say, for diction.

Clichés (tired language) usually occur as more than one word. Neither "vast" nor "majority" is a cliché, but since the latter hardly ever sounds without the former, "vast majority" is a fatigued and fatiguing sequence. Lecturers, listening to themselves, should cut such clusters from their material.

One group of phrases—used as catch-up moments by the brain that pauses while the larynx continues to churn—are objectionable on at least three counts: they waste time; they are pale; and they do not mean anything. They include "as a matter of fact," "for the simple reason that," and "in a very real sense." They show up in speeches by people who carelessly dangle "hopefully" anywhere, modifying nothing in its sheltering sentence.

Passive voice is a plague on academic language. Combined with expletive constructions, it is deadly: "It might be said that. . . ." Checking a dozen pages of academic prose in books and periodicals chosen at random, I found three sentences in the passive voice to every one in the active. In the committee work of faculties, the passive voice helps to secure anonymity: "It was recommended that . . ."; "The subject of credit was introduced and discussed, but no action was taken"; "It was moved and seconded that . . . ; the motion was carried." Compare those fragments with "Jack and Jill went up the hill" and with "Tom, Tom, the piper's son, stole a pig and away he run." In the latter examples we know who did what. Active language makes us alert; committee minutes put us to sleep. Unfortunately, professors must associate the passive voice with elegance, as—when writing—the older ones (anyhow) follow the received opinion that the first person is inelegant. Can you (second person) invent anything more pompous and a bigger fake (claim to objectivity) than my (first person) referring to myself (first person) as "the present writer" (third person)? Acknowledgement of help to authors normally and abnormally ends with a sentence like this: "It is to be hoped that errors have been avoided, but in any case those that have not been excluded are not to be attributed to any of the counselors to whom the writer is indebted, but are to be ascribed to the writer alone." Better: "Thanks to my advisers. Errors are mine." A past participle will often do the work of the passive voice. "The courses that are required should be taken first" is less simple and less efficient than "Take the required courses first." Elegance is not eloquence; the latter is better.

For oral delivery sentences should be fairly simple and clean. Too many qualifying phrases and clauses can lose the ear. In this chapter I have used visual signs (dashes and parentheses, for instance) as guides through long sentences. Those signs on the pages reach no ears hearing them read. Asked to make an oral presentation of the chapter, I should revise and shorten these sentences.

These suggestions on style—at the levels of word, phrase, sentence, and voice—are surely not exhaustive. They are a token list to which the improving lecturer will add many more items, negative and positive, through self-study and the study of work by others.

The subject of speaking is tender, but it will not go away. Manner is important in lecturing, and some difficulties with it respond to correction. On hearing themselves, lecturers must ask about the sounds of their individual voices. How loud is the voice? Loud enough to hear from any point in the room but not so loud that it is oppressive? Good. How about the tone? A paper-thin, high-pitched rasp is unpleasant, but so is a basso profundo rumble with indistinct consonants. One of my graduate schoolmates unwittingly invited (and got) as epithet "the human oboe," but he could have worked at lowering his average pitch (and closing some entrances to his squeakily resonant sinus cavities) when speaking. If recorded voice sounds to the lecturer like angry horse flies trapped in a Mason jar or like a swinette, it needs cultivation. (The swinette may resemble in tone quality a kazoo or humming through a tissue-wrapped comb; an instrument from the mythology of jazz, a swinette is three hairs stretched across a pig's behind.)

Correction does not imply affectation like pulpiteer's or mortician's unction. Walk down the line at a reception by the music faculty; hear "Hello," "Good to see you," "Glad you could come," and similar cordialities; then receive a heartlessly too-hearty (proof of vigor?) handshake from a party who overenunciates in a voice too mellifluent, too rich, "Howd *doo* you DOO?" You are in the presence of a smothering euphony and also of the choral director, the kind who has a choir sing, "Going ginto Jerusalem."

The land of John Knox is a Mecca for Southern Presbyterian ministers. One trip to St. Andrews is enough for each to acquire a flutter-tongued "R," meant as a Scotch burr but closer in sound to a Bronx cheer (in the pulpit the tongue stays in the mouth —at least down South). The noise of a ratchet is not among the vocables of English. Other affectations of speech are less rattly, but all are silly.

More annoying than basically bad vocal quality is monotony of quality. Henry Kissinger is the nonshining example of both. Couldn't he change the pitch and the pace with varying content? Are all sentences, all paragraphs, all subtopics of equal importance? They are not. Descriptions, narratives, explanations of process, conjectural probes call individually for suitable pitch, pace, diction, sentence structure, mode of emphasis—all dimensions of style. I advocate the merger of style and content, not artificial devices. Coached in the "selling" of the song, some popular singers bring the same body English, flapping of hands, bubbly grins, and perky, canned melismas to "Keep Your Sunny Side Up" and "Gloomy Sunday." The moribund professorial delivery does the opposite of "selling"; it does not bubble and perk for any subject.

Even more tender than vocal mannerisms are the topics of visual appearance and activity for the eye. Style of harness and currying is probably not important in the stables of thoroughbreds that we advertise our faculties to be, but having detected—in walks past many stalls—some suspiciously long ears, I offer basic suggestions. Clean people are easier to watch than dirty ones. Droopy hose are distracting to audiences of women in skirts, and men in pants should keep them zipped. If everybody on the campus wears jeans and sweatshirts, men and women should close zippers.

Lecturers might arrange to see themselves on videotape and learn to avoid habitual diverting actions: the placing of a forefinger on the upper lip to indicate pondering (which should have preceded the presentation); the quickly too-cute, repeated drawing of quote marks in the air with two fingers of each hand; gesturing

with no meaning; scratching with meaning. Since students' evaluations of faculty have become widespread, I have seen some professors begin to walk all about the podium, waving their arms, jerking
both index fingers into points on every accented syllable, and otherwise being lively. Everything they say (recordings verify it) and do
(videotapes verify it) has become wildly emphatic—a manner
finally as pallid as that of the catatonic monotone. Hyperactivity is
especially pathetic when the routine content deserves no fervor. I
recommend as much movement as necessary to keep numbness of
limbs away, but I also recommend that the lecturer be visually
unobtrusive.

Beyond the self-help that the lecturer can manage with recordings, videotapes, and study, assistance can come from supportive
critics among friends who have the advantage of some detachment.
Find some; submit to them. The Great Lakes Colleges Association
responds to requests for help in teaching by sending critics from
campuses other than the lecturer's own; that practice increases the
detachment of the critic and the security of the professor seeking aid.

Form

Content in expanding contexts got first place in this chapter
on lecturing. Among the several means of conveying content, the
total means being style, emphasis fell on verbal diction and vocal
and visual manner. The most integrative, however, and therefore
the most important of the means is form. Although delivered in
interesting contexts and with crisp diction and alert, appealing, but
unobtrusive manner, good substance still needs organization in convincing shape. At their respective and interacting bests, content and
form transcend symbiosis in which each remains identifiable. In a
transcendant synthesis they become practically identical, each so
largely dependent on the other that distinguishing between them
becomes difficult and inappropriate. Such a synthesis defies analysis
that could say anything which the synthesis has not already said
better. A synthesis so cogent is rare enough even in art, but pieces of
art and expository prose improve as they aspire toward integration
and resist explanatory paraphrase.

Some epigrams—very small forms that stand alone—and

some single lines of poetry—normally written as parts of larger forms but as quotable as epigrams—illustrate the resistance of successful synthesis to paraphrase. An outstanding example—a line of poetry—is from a Scottish song: "the brokenhearted ken no second spring." Nobody could say it better, and any English speaker who needs explanation of it is pathetic, probably beyond help from a college faculty or any other profession.

This chapter cannot quote entirely a large synthetic form, but it should contain an illustration longer than one line. A sonnet by John Keats serves exactly.

"On First Looking into Chapman's Homer"

Much have I travell'd in the realms of gold,
And many goodly states and kingdoms seen;
Round many western islands have I been
Which bards in fealty to Apollo hold.
Oft of one wide expanse had I been told
That deep-brow'd Homer ruled as his demesne;
Yet did I never breathe its pure serene
Till I heard Chapman speak out loud and bold:
Then felt I like some watcher of the skies
When a new planet swims into his ken;
Or like stout Cortez when with eagle eyes
He star'd at the Pacific—and all his men
Look'd at each other with a wild surmise—
Silent, upon a peak in Darien.

"Form" often means outer shape perceived through relatively gross measurements, thus macroform. The sonata, the arch, the syllogism, and the sonnet have largely external measurements and are macroforms, the much-used but fairly few constructions human beings make to organize material. They are containing patterns that exist independently of the values found in what they individually contain. Keats' poem above is a sonnet because it has fourteen lines and deploys both a rhyme scheme and a meter conventional in sonnets. Since many other poems with the same number of lines and the same rhyme scheme and meter are far from the quality of Keats', macroform, however necessary, is not an important determinant of quality. Thousands of other poems, also sonnets with the same macroform, are not worth the time required to read them.

"Form," as I use the word in this chapter, includes macroform, but its emphasis is on microform: the multiple cross relations among details of the work. The high tonal and other integrities of the many interrelationships among internal details of "On First Looking into Chapman's Homer"—its microformal organizations—make it a great expression. Understanding the meanings of Keats' words and references (a dictionary and an encyclopedia are sufficient tools) or following a careful and imaginative explication of them, a reader cannot doubt that the poem is a magnificent synthesis with unique and inseparable content and microform.

A college lecture is not a sonnet, not a poem. But a lecture needs the same compressed energy and the same forceful integrity of synthesis—close care about each detail and its relation to other details and a comprehensive grasp or an immaculate intuition about the complex interactions of all microformal elements contributing to the synthesis.

Regardless of the academic discipline, most of us usually organize our lecture material by categorical lists, by chronology, or by both, but all are weak and aesthetically not developmental. If disciplinary rigor impels us to put each statement under the correct rubric or in chronological order, it does not provide aesthetic form for our lectures. Without a specified discipline, algebraic unknowns can illustrate the dry form of the lecture that runs through annotated categories: Subject x has the remarkable elements a through m. Having given that information, the lecturer tells about a, then about b, and down the alphabet. Why are a through m in their order of appearance? Relative importance? If so, how significant is the content after it passes g? To what conclusion is it heading? The least important remark about the least important element, m? Professors who present material in the categorical pattern do not worry about whether they finish one lecture or begin the next one before a class period ends. Having all their lectures precisely timed for fifty minutes each would add minimum tidiness but no development. In the categorical-list schematic, where are active such considerations as comparisons, cross relations, evaluations, personal insights except at minute levels and with little contribution to a subsuming synthesis? Otherwise (many college lectures fit this "otherwise"), analysis is taking a clock apart with no intention of reassembly but too often with the pretense that the clock is the subject of study and with the sheer pretentiousness that time is the subject.

Countless other lectures move chronologically. A number of disciplines order their curricula, if not chronologically, in chunks of chronology. The resulting absurdities shoot down major claims of the university about its purpose. In their survey of literature, students likely meet Lord Tennyson because he was representative of his century, school, nation, or all of them and likely do not meet Rabelais, Virgil, or Dante at all. Since we cannot cover everything, all defensiveness removed from the typical plea, why don't we cover in our limited time what is best? The chunks-of-chronology plan implies that the chunks are more important than the values emanant from what they contain and that the chunks offer the best organizing principle. Made explicit, some deductions from those implications are ridiculous: "I specialize in the seventeenth century"; "One of the advantages of being a medievalist is that you don't have to know anything that has happened since the Middle Ages."

That events temporally succeed one another is an insufficient truth on which to build a lecture, but observation tells me that the insufficiency has no wide recognition among college professors. History—the occurrence of events, here not the knowledge or the narrative record of their occurrence—may be more aleatory than Westerners can allow themselves to believe, but chronology alone does not change that quality. We lecture and talk as if it did, attributing more philosophical power than it can generate to the ubiquitous connective that is a frail tie, "and then . . ." Our superstition about chronology produces a pathetic condition in higher education: A student asks, "How did this come to be?"—a question about justice (do all the faculty members who say they teach by the Socratic method know Socrates' chief concern?)—and a professor replies with an "explanation" rather than a justification and with a series of statements more or less relevant to the question but held together primarily by chronology ("You'll understand it better if I give you a little history."). Chronology is weak glue; a fine lecture depends on other organizations than chronological chance.

The formal principle of a presentation should be appropriate to the content. The usual "congregational prayer" in Protestant churches is a curiosity under that consideration. The minister asks a blessing on those in the sanctuary, those unavoidably away (particularly the sick), those avoidably away ("have mercy"), those in the state or in the denomination, those in regions of the United States where recent catastrophes have happened, the leadership of the country, those suffering in other nations, and the leadership of the world. Thus from the pulpit comes a lesson to the congregation (who may need it) and to the Almighty (Who may not) in political geography, a singularly mundane and unfitting organizer of supplication to the Divine. If there had not been a Forgiver, it would have been necessary to invent One.

Closer to home, on the campus, the lecturer comparing two objects, phenomena, works, or wholes of any kind gets advice from teachers of rhetoric and their textbooks. Lay out the comparison in one of three (the "three" is presumably exhaustive) patterns: all about whole A followed by all about B (vice versa must be a variant of the pattern), all the mutual likenesses of A and B followed by all the differences between them (or vice versa), a list of the categories present in A and B with remarks on the pair's likeness or difference in each category (with a possible appendage of categories belonging to only one of the pair—a kind of difference).

Not all lectures have to be informational and practical, but if integration of material, whether informational, practical, or otherwise, is important, the first pattern looks weakest; all about A and all about B might be separate lectures. The second pattern— "the likeness-difference method"—must refer throughout to A and B, has better integration than the first pattern, but still has a schism between its halves (if likeness and difference get equal time). The categorical comparison offers the best integration of the three patterns, but it has all the weaknesses mentioned earlier of lectures built on lists; especially it may integrate remarks on A and B but have no synthesis of its own. Teaching diagnosis, a medical lecturer might be most successful in presenting two syndromes by talking exclusively about one before talking exclusively about the other, but the lecturer's success, reflected by students' ability to diagnose the two diseases, is not a success of comparison. The pattern—all about A and all about B—takes comparison away from the lecturer and leaves it up to the students.

Thousands of comparative lectures or sections of lectures could follow plans superior to those offered by the rhetoricians. Having analytically compared as private preparation, the lecturer could compare synthetically in the classroom. What insights came from the comparative analysis? How do they relate to other insights in the subject and other fields? What subsuming argument, thesis, or revelation might issue from all this pondering? In what order do its premises belong? Can the lecture grow toward a conclusion and develop increasing interest among listeners as it approaches its disclosure? Ordered by answers to those questions, the lecture might use remarks appropriate individually to one of the rhetorical patterns, all three represented, each remark subordinated to a statement developing the thesis, none of the rhetorical patterns being the whole.

Comparison is only a token kind of lecture in these pages; undiscussed kinds are ample. All of them need the greatest creativity the lecturer can bring to them, but the academy has not encouraged the lecturer to work creatively. Creators have encouraged lecturers and everybody else, one implicit message of every creation being the parabolic "Go thou and do likewise." Aside from creations themselves, the improving lecturer may get help from essays, studies, and reports like those assembled by Brewster Ghiselin in *The Creative Process* (1952).

Chaos is not long tolerable to living beings, but rigid, dimvisioned organizations of its elements stimulate nobody's imagination and are simplistic distortions of the truth. Chaos, because it calls forth organizing activity, may be a better stimulus to creativity among students than the weak, dull structures of most lectures. The latter stimulate nothing more active than inattention.

Writing these pages, I have taken much from Aristotle. Although an analyst by temperament, he could not have called Homer divine without knowing that the whole may be greater than the sum of its parts. The whole is not always greater; when it is so in a

work of art, it probably is so not only because "De cerebrum connected to de cerebellum" but also because "De brain connected to
de thyroid gland" and to the parathyroid, the pineal, the pituitary,
the anterior pituitary, the adrenal, and the gonads—and to the
eyes, ears, nose, mouth, and skin—among other things. Ironically
Aristotle's *Poetics* is not greater than the sum of its parts; it is a
series of short arguments that call for unity but have no synthesis to
weld them together. I have said all along that analysis (the academic means to smaller means) is not enough. Lecturing well is not
just analysis, not just speech techniques, not even just communication science. Lecturing well is an art.

A lecture is fifty or more times longer than a sonnet. The
classroom speech need not be so tight and intense. It can vary its
intensity in several ways, and it can contain relevant diversions and
asides; these help with transitions between intensities and can both
relax and realert listeners; humorous or serious they should not be
altogether extraneous and are best when they reinforce major points
of the lecture; they should *belong* to the synthetic whole.

My selective description of the good lecture called for important substance in broadening contexts. The importance of the
substance at the level of the single fact may not be apparent without
context. Who cares that the body temperature of a normal chicken
is 107 degrees? Certainly nobody preparing for Graduate Record
Examinations. Does anybody want to earn a living taking the
temperatures of chickens? But suppose the task is to design a hen-
house so its occupants will flourish in all seasons. What does it need
for heating and cooling? The new context has improved the value
of the fact formerly isolated.

My description recommended diction that is appropriate,
lucid, free of jargon and cliché, and active. I urged close attention
to precise language and correct grammar, anything less than either
flawing the lecture and putting bad examples before students.

My description suggested an unobtrusive manner for lectures. Nobody appeals to everybody else (President Eisenhower
tried). Arriving on the planet as a male, Southern, whitish but of
mongrel ethnicity, genetically and environmentally subject to some
certain and some uncertain predilections, prejudices, and even a few
pleasant addictions, and recognizing that everybody else arrived
with analogous (many happily different) conditioners of appear-

ance and manner, I believe that all lecturers should cover the external idiosyncracies that they can control and intrude only through the creation of the lecture itself—not through overt mannerisms not germane to the presentation.

My description also emphasized the requisite of formal synthesis. The choice of Keats' sonnet as illustrative was a fortunate one for this chapter. "On First Looking into Chapman's Homer" made in fourteen lines of poetry all the important points that I have made clumsily in much longer expository prose. If nobody will admit to talking *at* students, the common idiom says that we lecture *to* them. At our best, however, we lecture *for* them.

Aristotle not filling all my needs for a model, I turn to Keats. Join me, please, in the special delight of considering a philosopher *himself* as necessary but insufficient (nobody could make that remark about Beethoven). We would be too demanding to expect every professor to create a stunning new insight for each lecture. We would be perfectionist and misanthropic, but the modest wish of this chapter is only to improve some lectures at some colleges. It does not express the attitude, "If you're not Benny Goodman, how come you're standing there with that clarinet in your hand?" To borrow fitting syntheses is a means of giving lectures stature, and professors, who borrow most of their material anyhow, should not hesitate to borrow a big insight as an enveloping clincher. The subsuming synthesis to integrate this chapter is on loan from John Keats.

What is the purpose of education? To enhance curiosity that leads to insight. In good lectures we bring to students our gifts of insight to serve as hones for theirs. Keats did just that for us, and his poem has the right substance for this chapter. It is about synthetic insight, the wondrous kind that satisfies some curiosity while introducing more. The sonnet reflects Keats' insight, Chapman's, Homer's, an unnamed astronomer's, some explorers' (one mistakenly named), and ultimately everybody's. The goal of education should be to bring every student to the top human joy of "a wild surmise" that sends each forever chasing other insights.

A good lecture, like good teaching in any mode, is *for* the students in the class; it guides them toward those moments that we most profoundly wish them to have, when each can stand "Silent, upon a peak in Darien."

3

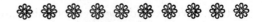

Patricia W. Barnes-McConnell

Leading Discussions

Whether a class is large or small, successfully handled student participation is an important means by which students assimilate course material and become involved in an atmosphere that supports both personal and academic growth. The discussion process can be the principal means by which course objectives are attained and by which individual students develop important new insights that precipitate fundamental attitude change. Class discussions, therefore, can be among the most rewarding of class activities for instructors and students alike.

 As is painfully apparent to well-meaning instructors who have tried to stimulate classroom discussions by simply showing up, successful and exciting discussion sessions do not just happen. Successful discussion leaders, like successful athletes, require a great deal of preparation preceding seemingly effortless performance. In an instructor's case, performance is the professional behavior that stimulates students to participate enthusiastically in the verbal exploration of a topic. Adequate instructor preparation involves not only a detailed knowledge of the topic but also the acquisition of specific discussion skills and the development of a basic sensitivity to student needs.

Opportunities for Discussion

Many educators agree that discussions are most successful when the material is controversial. My own feeling is that controversy is less important than emotion. As with any lively discussion with one's friends, there must be an atmosphere that raises adrenalin. Emotions must be incited somehow. The emotion may come from the poignance of a common experience that touches the participants in unique ways, with the discussion sharing these unique perspectives and leading to new understandings and a new reality for each of them. It can come from problem-oriented materials that readily lend themselves to emotionally involving discussion. It can even come from the sense of integration of complex and difficult material, if handled well.

In contrast, some materials do not lend themselves well to the discussion technique. For example, new instructors often mistakenly assume that because an assigned reading makes an important point, it will automatically engender class discussion. But in the context of student views, "important" is a very relative term, and the reading may be taken at face value, engendering little in the way of a response. There are few things deadlier in a classroom than attempts to discuss straightforward, unchallenging facts—particularly those that only the instructor perceives as important.

Besides the topic, three other factors are important in planning to use the discussion method: (1) session objectives, (2) group size and mix, and (3) space and time. All three factors are heavily interrelated, and each is strongly influenced by the other two.

Objectives. The most crucial factor is that of objectives. Objectives are required not only for deciding whether or not the discussion technique is appropriate but for assessing which discussion methods to use.

Appropriate objectives for discussion sessions include problem solving, the integration of course content, cross-peer learning (particularly appropriate in heterogeneous classes), increased sensitivity to complex issues, and the clarification of values, attitude change, and increased understanding of a phenomenon as it operates in an applied setting or of a theory in application. Thus Alexander and Abramson (1975, pp. 2–3) reported that such objectives as increasing skills in interpersonal relations, modifying opinions, and working out the applications of course concepts are appropriate for the discussion technique.

By defining the objectives in terms of the behavior that students are expected to exhibit at the end of the course, an instructor can determine whether discussion seems an appropriate means to these ends.

Group Size and Mix. Group size and mix must be considered in evaluating the appropriateness of the discussion method. Many instructors feel that they cannot hold a discussion session in a large class, but this is not at all the case. Although the ideal discussion group is about fifteen to twenty students, large groups of fifty, seventy-five, one hundred, or more can be broken up into small groups in different parts of the room, facilities permitting. In this case, the instructor can float from group to group to monitor activity. Although the noise level may be a bit high, this can contribute to the excitement up to a certain point rather than being a source of worry. Even if the group cannot be subdivided, several techniques are useful for pulling its members together. The instructor can either move around, so as to be in physical proximity to everyone at some time, or stay as close as possible to the middle of the room (without having his or her back to anyone) and having frequent eye contact with everyone, alternating from one side of the room to the other.

Indeed, a small homogeneous group may be more difficult to get going than a large heterogeneous one because it may lack the tension, anxiety, cross-peer curiosity, and values conflict of the larger group. The instructor may find a greater identification with a small group, making for easier personableness and intimacy; but this situation must be monitored with caution: An attitude of mutual dependence in a small group is not the same as mutual inquiry.

(Other approaches, including panels, symposia, debates, and fish-bowl discussion, may facilitate group interaction in those cases in which general discussion is inappropriate. These techniques for gen-erating student participation were reviewed by Bergquist and Phillips, 1975.)

Space and Time. Classroom size, moveable seats (or com-fortable carpeting), available equipment, and adequate time are additional factors to be considered. (I resist with a passion, for example, the fifty-minute class.) Some discussion techniques require the informality and freedom of movement prohibited by fastened-down seats; others require a blackboard or overhead projector for posting ideas. Although structural constraints do not determine ob-jectives, they obviously must be considered in planning the ways to achieve them.

Instructor Attitude and Behavior

Being successful as a discussion leader requires an attitude of openness and mutual inquiry on the part of the instructor to encour-age student participation and support the development of a basic level of trust within the group. Curwin and Fuhrmann (1975, p. xvii) emphasized the importance of self-awareness and self-knowl-edge in making the discussion leader's role effective. This openness to personal and professional growth supports an openness to ex-perimentation with alternative response patterns in teaching. Ap-proaching the class with this personal attitude of openness and mu-tual inquiry, the instructor sets the stage for a balanced relationship between the students and him- or herself. Whatever the topic under discussion, the instructor may know more information about it than any student, but the students bring varied perspectives within which this information must be applied. The application of this informa-tion may well require adjustment or modification or reorganization of the subject matter, an exercise that becomes a learning experience for the instructor as well.

The importance of this attitude of mutual inquiry is espe-cially apparent in student-faculty interactions with adult learners as a significant percentage of the student group. For them, as well as many of the increasingly sophisticated younger students, traditional hierarchical messages directed at keeping students "in their place" must give way to an atmosphere of "I'm OK, you're OK" (Harris, 1969). Today, some professors are not much older than the children of these older students, a situation making even more ridiculous the traditional student-teacher relationship, which as Margolis said, was "painfully hierarchical" and required "a degree of obsequiousness" on the part of students that is best forgotten (1974, p. 35).

Why is this emphasis on an atmosphere of mutual inquiry and basic trust so crucial for successful discussion? Clearly there is no better way to declare one's own stupidity to the world than to share a thought out loud to a group and have the teacher not only reject it but reject it in such a way as to make one look like a fool. Many of us have experienced that kind of pain during our twelve years' confinement in elementary and high schools. In all too many college classes it is reinforced. It dries up any chance of open discussion. For this reason, basic trust in the professional integrity of the instructor, the feeling of a supportive environment of mutual inquiry, and the assurance that all ideas are an important contribution to the group are essential.

A variety of cues suggest to students the orientation of a faculty member in this direction. Some, such as the syllabus, are explicit even before the class gets under way.

Course Description and Objectives. I have found the stage is best set through a course introduction written in conversational prose, emphasizing the importance of the integration of course material. Course objectives should include the oral communication of ideas.

Assignment Structure. A clearly written-out set of assignments (readings, research, and so on) should be organized under course subtopics that are consistent with the course outline. This helps the students organize their own thinking and have a better understanding of the instructor's frame of reference.

Statements of Course Expectations, the Grading System, and Criteria for Evaluation. In the syllabus, I frequently write a statement such as "thinking and integration of class experiences and materials are more important than rote memory." For that reason, if I do give an inclass examination, it allows open book and open notes. The grading system further reflects this emphasis with class discussions receiving a reasonable percentage of the grade. Criteria for evaluation include the integration of class experiences and materials, the development of pertinent ideas, insights, or points of view, the sharing of exemplary experiences, asking of crucial questions or building on provocative points made by others.

Some other cues that students use to assess the orientation of faculty are implicit.

Opening Session. Starting the class the first day with non-threatening, personal sharing is often an appropriate way to begin: name, family data and hobbies, academic major and career interests, why are you interested in the course, one important question you'd like this course to help you answer, and so on. I usually have each student tell these things to a partner (opposite sex, if possible), who reports it to the group. The particular method of personal sharing is much less important than the actual participation in this first exercise in trust building and in sensing that all ideas are important to the group.

This trust building is much more difficult than it sounds. Many student utterances do not sound like much at first, and their contributions may easily be taken lightly or passed over when, in fact, they are quite personal and important to the student. It is thus very appropriate to suggest to students in the first session that should you inadvertently do or say something insensitive, they should speak up in class or speak to you after class, but they should not just sit and simmer. Mutual learning requires mutual exchange without defensiveness. Affirming such an orientation requires positive action. In his recent book, Kenneth Eble (1976) further developed the importance of instructor behavior such as this, and I recommend the book for more information.

Verbal Cues. Success for faculty members in leading discussions frequently requires having a view of themselves less as judges or dispensers of wisdom and more as resource persons. Examples of comments I have used frequently to support an atmosphere of trust and mutual inquiry include:

1. Does my thought make any sense to you?
2. Can you think of a situation in which this notion might apply? Might not apply?

3. That's an interesting idea, tell me more.
4. I don't know either, but that's a very interesting question. Let's write it down, think about it a while, and come back to it after we've gotten more information.
5. Interesting, you might find some help with that idea in Birch's book.
6. You know, I hadn't thought of that.
7. Can anyone help us unravel ourselves here?
8. Both of you have a point. Maybe each of you should try to think of an instance in which your respective idea would fit best and one where it would not fit at all.
9. I'm not sure I understand. Were you saying that the survey questions were too personal? Can you give me an example?
10. Feels to me like we've kind of strayed from the point. Have we?
11. Let's not forget the basic problem we're trying to solve.
12. What's the first step?

Nonverbal Cues. These cues include the physical proximity of the instructor to students, the physical mobility of the instructor and students, and the instructor's facial expression and eye contact.

In terms of physical proximity of the instructor to students, by drawing an imaginary circle around the students, one can assess whether the instructor is characteristically within that circle or more remote, such as behind a desk or on a stage. For larger groups proximity is difficult to achieve, and one is often reduced to the tactics of talk-show personalities, such as walking among the students.

In terms of instructor and student physical mobility, freedom to move as appropriate is important to everyone, as in using the blackboard to make a point, changing seats, and so on. This is not to imply that pandemonium is conducive to learning. On the other hand, physical rigidity encourages mental rigidity and a more formal learning environment than that generally observed in active discussion groups. Recently I observed a teaching assistant come out from behind a desk, firmly plant his chair in front of it, and sit there at the head of the class for the duration of the session. With head frequently lowered and reading from notes, he occasionally asked unsuccessfully for questions or comments. The instructor gave the impression that he was just as withdrawn and inaccessible as if he had stayed behind the desk. Having the group move their seats in a more inclusive, circular manner with a more mobile instructor would have encouraged greater interaction.

Regarding eye contact and facial expression, enthusiastic behavior on the part of the instructor gives outward indications that the student is being heard. Furthermore, it suggests to students that "somebody's home" and interested in receiving their contributions. Student enthusiasm, either for the material or for each other's comments, usually does not exceed that expressed verbally or nonverbally by the instructor.

Personal Anecdotes. The creative use of an anecdote from the instructor's own personal life lends an air of intimacy difficult to achieve, especially in large groups. It is no accident that the most successful comedians or talk-show personalities often tell stories about themselves, their families, or their pets. They are aware that this is necessary for the stranger to identify with them by identifying with the human behavior common to us all.

In like manner, instructors become human, trustworthy, when they occasionally share a personal experience in the appropriate student learning context. Rather than sneaking in an anecdote with a guilty chuckle, a planned, well-thought-out anecdote can be very effective. For example, relevant experiences in a preprofessional class might include the following: an early incident of naïve professional behavior of which the instructor is now most sincerely ashamed, a difficult time or incident in the instructor's life that fits a particular theorist's concept, or anecdotes from the instructor's children facing some relevant problem. These are the things that make students feel they know the instructor better. Furthermore, as McKeachie (1969a, p. 50) suggested, they "convey the relevance of the course material to what is worthwhile and exciting in life . . . the intellectual matters under discussion are not irrelevant to the conduct of a life . . ."

One of my favorite stories on myself, which I use in a pre-community internship class, demonstrates the complexity of people's lives and the danger of the do-gooder approach. Early in my research work with low-income families, I encountered a mother living alone in an old dilapidated house with her children and a stopped-up toilet. I called my son to come with the plunger, and the toilet was soon taken care of. The next week I returned to find the same condition; it was obvious that something was wrong with the plumbing. I discussed the situation with a Ph.D. friend, who identified the problem and verified that a plumber was needed. He then called the landlord, identifying himself as Dr. _____ in his usual manner, stating that young children were in that home and that the situation had to be rectified. The landlord falsely claimed that he had known nothing of the problem but that he would certainly pay; all the tenant had to do was call the plumber and have the bill sent to him. Not only had he not told this to the tenant, but this particular tenant was illiterate and could not have read the yellow pages. After my friend's call, the landlord, in a rage, called the tenant, swore at her for having called the health department on him (his supposition), and told the woman to get out of his house (it was in the middle of the winter). The mother had to plead with the landlord before he eventually cooled down. He subsequently paid the plumber's bill, and the matter was laid to rest. But in my haste to "do good" I nearly had a family evicted in the middle of winter and did cause the mother a great deal of anguish, embarrassment, and loss of self-esteem. Although I still might have chosen to handle matters as I did, my lack of understanding of potential outcomes did not speak well of my level of professionalism. That incident was a very instructive one for me and for many of my naïve students. Others nod their heads with a knowing smile and share similar experiences.

For many reasons, it is important that these personal anecdotes not be self-aggrandizing but in fact cast the instructor in a very human light that all students can understand. Dr. Herman Blake (1977) emphasized the importance of failure, and often a great deal of failure, as a part of the success process. He pointed out that this understanding must be made clear to students, especially to those who do not see themselves as winners or as members of a group that is generally successful. Many students who do not identify with the dominant culture in the class are likely to need the reassurance that these kinds of anecdotes provide. The university world often looks so strange and omnipotent to them that they welcome this glimpse of a fellow human being. Even when their instructors provide them with highly successful female, minority, and other role models, they assimilate the societal stereotype that these instructors are "special" or "unusual" but that they themselves are ordinary and could never be that successful. These students gradually must be made to understand that the so-called special people are plain, although often stubborn, persons who are essentially no different from themselves. Dr. Blake sensitively addressed the understandable reticence of some teachers to relive their past hurts, frustrations, and pain for the edification of their students. Nonetheless, he was sure that such sharing would be required to maximize the potential of the role model in the academic lives of struggling, atypical students. The use of personal anecdotes is the appropriate vehicle to support such student motivation and growth.

One word of caution must be mentioned here. The overuse of personal anecdotes can become a form of instructor therapy. Purposeful attention to objectives and planned use will help instructors guard against this problem.

Discussion Techniques

There are many different techniques for leading discussions, from the most nondirective to the most programmed. Within the general process of leading discussions, I will describe a few techniques that seem to be the most appropriate for most classrooms. Keep in mind that, at least from my perspective, the greater the emotional involvement—that is, the greater the controversy or the "closer to home" the issue—the greater the chance for a successful discussion session. Obviously, the more emotional the student involvement, the more astute the instructor must be in managing student interactions.

Laying the Common Ground. To discuss anything productively, all students should have at least one, and preferably multiple, common experiences or frames of reference from which to begin. Examples include a written common experience such as a case history, a story, a report, a news article, a book, and so on, the reading of which is required of all students. It might be a class handout or homework assignment. A common verbal experience might be a lecture, a speech, a guest presentation, or a panel. Movies, slide shows, television programs, or media interviews are common audiovisual experiences. A common simulated experience might be a role-playing session or a simulation game, and a common real-life experience might be participation in a community research survey, individually assigned visits to community agencies, group field trips, or observation of some community activity.

Starting the Discussion. The group should reconvene as soon after the common experiences as is practical. The greater the time between the experiences and the discussion, the greater the likelihood of loss of personal involvement. If the experience and the discussion are separated by a great deal of time or if the experience was so poignant that students have trouble expressing their feelings out loud, written feedback on the common experience may be appropriate. When collected or verbally shared, these comments can become the basis for starting the discussion. Instructor silence after a particularly poignant experience will allow the discussion to generate spontaneously, particularly if an attitude of trust has already been established. Verbal, open-ended, nonspecific questions—What do you think? Where are you? What are you feeling now? Any thoughts on this problem?—are frequently ineffective unless emotions are quite high. Specific questions are usually more promising in a less electric atmosphere: If you were in that situation, what would you do? What is the real problem here? Were the community resources really sensitive to the needs of the people? How did each of you feel in your role? A single written task can be passed out. For example: "Using your procedural outline, design a plan to alleviate the problem." Students working in groups are then told they are on their own with so much time to get the job done. At the end of the allotted time, they would be expected to report orally or in written form. The procedure can be repeated in a stepwise fashion.

If, even after a common experience, you suspect the group will be reticent, you may bring in an assistant (a graduate student, a faculty colleague) to get into a heated debate with you. Students should be encouraged to break in at any time. This debate, of course, must be carefully prepared from beginning to end with "spaces" for "thinking" and controversial analogies that pull the students in. This technique has only worked for me in a small group. Large groups tend to slide easily into an audience role and just observe.

It is clear that regardless of whether questions are asked in verbal, or in written form, the phrasing by the instructor is very important. McKeachie (1969a, p. 54) suggested: "One of the common errors in question phrasing is to ask questions that obviously have only one right answer, which the instructor knows. . . . Rather, discussions need to be formulated so as to get at relationships, applications, or analyses of facts and materials. . . . A second common error in framing questions is to frame the question at a level of abstraction inappropriate for the class. . . . Discussion questions need to be phrased as problems which are meaningful to the students as well as the instructor. Such questions can be devised more easily if one knows something of the students' background."

Curwin and Fuhrmann (1975, p. 201) agreed that if the object is to promote active thought and discussion, instructors might either ask "questions that require students to look for relationships and underlying concepts" where there are many possible responses or "questions that ask for divergent thinking including personal opinions and responses and solutions to hypothetical situations for which . . . any response is acceptable."

Keeping the Discussion Going. Instructor prediscussion preparation and discussion monitoring are essential in keeping the discussion focused on the original objectives. The instructor must stay as objective as possible, assessing when the group is taking a nonproductive direction, is beginning to operate under some false assumptions, or is too broad or narrow in its perspective. If the students are on their own, working in small groups on a task handed out in the beginning, the instructor may listen in from time to time and perhaps post helpful hints on the board, such as "minutes left ————," "listing constraints is part of defining a problem," or "focusing an attack on personalities is to lose the issue." The instructor may function as a facilitator, perhaps clarifying specific questions raised, getting clarification of ideas from students and posting them, asking questions about their discussion process, reminding students to stick to ground rules (that is, focus conflicts on ideas not personalities, brainstorm hypotheses without being judgmental), and reinforcing the contributions of the less vocal students in the group.

Instructor behavior throughout the session is crucial to the success of a discussion group whether the role is a more or less active one. The following behaviors have been found helpful:

1. Make clear the ground rules (focus conflict on ideas not people, try not to interrupt, resist being judgmental, all ideas are legitimate although not necessarily agreed to).
2. Post an agenda of issues on the board to be worked through and share objectives with the group. Ask for additions. Pay attention to this agenda during the session so that the logical flow of discussion attains these objectives.
3. Be willing to hear out emotional outbursts of students, encouraging them to continue until they feel they've said it all. Clarify in your own words what you thought you heard, get verification from that student, and accept that point of view as legitimate for that student.
4. Watch for stumbling blocks to constructive discussion (personality conflicts, instructor domination, and so on). Point them out or have students discuss the problem.
5. Encourage a student making unclear contributions to give examples. Restate points for verification or rejection by that student.
6. For students making hesitant contributions, inquire further, ask for elaboration and examples as appropriate with nonverbal reinforcements (smiles, nods, and later references to that student's point).
7. Tolerate silence! If there is a task or issue on the table, it is okay for students to think without having the instructor put words in their mouths. An instructor who cannot tolerate silence may come across as tense, unstable, and untrustworthy.
8. Reinforce student freedom to talk by not cutting them off and by asking them to respond to one another. Either do not talk too much or change back to lecture format.
9. When the discussion is going well, summarizing ideas on the board is an excellent way of keeping control of the direction without verbally interrupting the students.
10. Keep adrenalin up by alternate use of humor and tragedy.
11. Encourage and make time for neighbor interaction. Twosomes may be requested to join to make foursomes for some task, or,

for a second task, students may be asked to relate to some person other than the original neighbor.

Student responses in a discussion are by definition verbal, but at various predetermined places in the process, a written response may be appropriate. The following points may be considered:

- Instructor may require that all responses indicate a reference to class experiences.
- The responses may give an analysis of some aspect of group activity at that time.
- The responses may give implications of decisions made by the group.
- The responses may reflect individual students' own personal-professional goals in relation to discussion topic, indicating if there has been any change or impact.

Ending the Discussion. The end of the discussion is a critical part of the process. Instructors doing a good job of monitoring the process are aware of the problems that need resolution as the discussion ends. Some students need instructor reinforcement; it should be given verbally, by a pat on the back, a smile, a nod, a handshake, an "I'll see you next time." If the student is upset, ask him or her to speak with you after class. At that time acknowledge your concern and give reinforcement. Other students are not forceful enough to get their ideas in. Ask if they would give a closing comment about the topic (without calling attention to their timidity). A summary statement should be made by the student spokesperson and the instructor.

Student Feedback

From the instructor's point of view, student feedback is the most important part of the discussion process. It directs instructor learning and provides data for course modification. It also acts as a tool for increasing student involvement, particularly in large classes. Providing feedback is no light responsibility, and students must be impressed with its importance in overall class functioning. Students usually take this responsibility seriously if feedback is requested regularly and anonymously and actual consequences of the feedback are made apparent. I have found it helpful to emphasize that I would like negative as well as positive feedback and, especially in the case of negative feedback, that I would like constructive suggestions for change. That is, I ask for suggestions for fixing the problem students have identified.

The request for feedback can come at the end of the common experience ("Should the experience be kept or deleted from the curriculum?"), or it can come at the end of the discussion session. It can be formal (a printed student evaluation sheet) or informal ("On a piece of paper, state how you feel about today's session.").

In subsequent class meetings refer to different points made in the feedback from time to time. ("By the way, I'd like the student who said I talk too fast to know I'm trying to talk slower; let me know how I'm doing." "Because many of you indicated a need for additional information, I'm handing out copies of this organization chart; let me know if you need anything further.") Occasionally the feedback will be a personal attack on the instructor. The response must be nondefensive and exploratory. Remember, it takes two to fight, but acceptance of students' frustrations reduces their hostility and often makes students feel they are getting the level of respect they think they deserve. ("Will the student who feels I am chauvinistic please write down each time such an incident happens and pass it up to me at the end of each class? I want to continue to learn, too, but I have a hard time seeing my own behavior and evaluating it without specifics to go on. I'd appreciate that.")

It is important to understand that student feedback is a crucial tool for instructors to use in keeping up with their students. Nothing can be taken for granted in classrooms today. Written, regular feedback is the only way to verify that you are not expending a lot of energy for naught.

Instructor Feedback. Instructor feedback to students is also quite important. Since students have a responsibility in mutual inquiry as well as instructors, it is most appropriate that the instructor regularly indicate whether or not the class is meeting academic expectations. Judgments of this sort are best done against course or task criteria for evaluation as outlined in the course syllabus. Frequent constructive feedback from students and faculty to each other can only help the development of a supportive academic environment and subsequent individual growth.

Evaluation. I have found it helpful to run an informal student evaluation at the beginning and end of the term. After the introductory lecture that sets the stage for the course, I ask students to write on a piece of paper—anonymously—"where they are" relative to the course material, the personal and professional (or preprofessional) resources they bring, their needs and expectations, and their overall thoughts. I emphasize my request for a very personal response, not general university jargon. These little pieces of paper, some of which have been quite personal, have been most helpful in course discussion design and in subsequent lecture development. At the end of the course, I repeat the process, comparing statements to assess whether students' needs were met and how. I match papers on the basis of both parents' initials, student social security number (not useful if foreign students are in the class), or some little drawing they put at the top of the paper to aid in the "pre-post" match. A charge could be made against the instructor, however, that this information was used in the assignment of grades. In small classes this can be a problem since instructors quickly learn individual students' handwriting and writing styles. This is yet another example of where a well-established atmosphere of trust and mutual inquiry operates for the benefit of faculty and students.

Interpersonal Perception and Student Mix

Successful instructors are aware that much depends on their specific responses to individual students, responses that are based on the accuracy of skills in interpersonal perception. In his excellent little book *The Art of Empathy*, Bullmer (1975, p. 1) pointed out that such perceptions are really "inferences concerning the emotions, intentions, attitudes, traits, and other internal properties of the perceived person. In this sense, since so many human properties are internal rather than external and cannot be observed visually, persons are not so much perceived as they are judged." He discusses the influence of the perceiver's past learning experiences and thinking process in making the judgment. This emphasizes the magnitude of potential error since the perceiver is basing his or her judgments in perception on his or her own beliefs, attitudes, values, and motives. "These beliefs, attitudes, and values may form a relatively fixed set of biases about what other people are like and how they operate and lead to serious errors in our attempts to perceive others" (Bullmer, 1975). Instructors seriously concerned about their professional competence work diligently to increase their skill in interpersonal perception.

Such is the orientation of faculty who have spent some time understanding themselves and their own motivations and are now ready to enter into an atmosphere of mutual inquiry with students whom they respect as human beings. Such is the basis of trust.

Student mix can be one of the most trying factors in maintaining the atmosphere of trust discussed above; it is also one of the most valuable factors in establishing mutual inquiry. After all, it is especially difficult to learn anything, to grow and expand in understanding, when one is surrounded by people who are carbon copies of oneself. Recent and continuing trends have fortunately opened up higher education to heterogeneous populations varied by age, career status, race, and socioeconomic background. This heterogeneity can make for rich and exciting classes. At the same time, it can be quite volatile by supporting the instructor's easily broadcast biases and playing into the weakness of the students. But this is no cause for alarm. When conflicts about values arise, the instructor's goal should be to help students identify and become more aware of the actual values involved in the conflict. The conflict itself then becomes an aid to learning. The instructor can list these values and their implications on the board in a nonjudgmental "if-then" format, rather than frantically trying to smother them. Rigdon (1977) suggested that coming to grips with diverse traditions and values is essential in the teaching-learning process if students are to (1) fully comprehend their own values and beliefs, (2) critically evaluate what is necessary for their further development, and (3) ultimately make a conscious commitment to their expression. His viewpoint is that the rich diversity within a heterogeneous student population is a resource far too valuable to waste. Trust, self-confidence and eagerness to participate evolve from an atmosphere of overt caring, respect, and fairness in student-faculty interactions. From the outset, the instructor must set the tone for the establishment of this atmosphere. Four categories of students deserve special note here: adults, minorities, women, and the poor.

Adult Students. Among the students who have started to appear in increasing numbers are adults interested in mid-life career changes. Undoubtedly, lifelong education is a concept whose time has come. Boyer (1975, p. 20) stated that "occupational and career changes and shifts in intellectual disciplines are occurring so rapidly that no college program—no matter how ingenious—can possibly prepare all college students completely for life, work, and leisure (in their first college years) . . . our formal learning schedule must consider, and be balanced by, people's needs to feel useful, loved, active, or engaged." He suggests that "increasing numbers of adults want to learn more," including college graduates who are ready to return to college for more professional training or intellectual development. Another group consists of returning adults who did not complete a degree program during their younger years but now wish to do so. The traditional instructor attitude, however, strains the helpfulness of the college experience for these students.

Furthermore, adult students often find loneliness a difficult and unanticipated aspect of returning to college. Margolis (1974, p. 36) wrote that "some of us dominate classroom discussions with the experience of our years—trying perhaps to catch the professor's notice, to share something with the only age-mate around." Margolis implied that this behavior should be a signal to the instructor that the student feels a lack of belonging and needs instructor reinforcement and support. I have found the acceptance of this behavior as the sharing of "a case in point," an appropriate context to establish. It enables the instructor to either encourage a clearer definition of the specific point or to reinforce the example by asking for further such examples from other members of the class as well. The idea that classroom dominating behavior is often an attempt to establish oneself as a worthwhile member of the group suggests that the instructor should be alert for and responsive to such apparent calls for help. Class activities, assignments, and so on can be handled in a way that encourages the inclusion of all students. The overt caring, respect, and fairness just mentioned are again quite crucial; see Chapter Thirteen of this text for a more thorough report of the needs of this group.

Minorities. Minority students must deal with deeply imbedded feelings that they cannot depend on others to treat them as

human beings. Withdrawn, noncommunicative behavior and ob-
streperous behavior are frequently designed to reaffirm that attitude.
Pifer (1973, p. 42) wrote about the new black students from urban
ghettos who "felt strange, lonely, unwanted, and fearful in what
they saw as an alien and even hostile white world. They withdrew
from social contacts with whites and sought only the company of
other blacks . . . in some cases a kind of paranoia set in, which
even caused black students to arm themselves."

For many minority students, the sudden change of environment, of expectations for behavior, and of ability to predict how
others will react result in a sort of culture shock similar to that experienced by many from the white American business community
who have been transferred to foreign countries. As one might guess,
many minority students do what their business community counterparts who huddled in American compounds in countries all over
the world did. Minority students often seek solace and safety in each
other. Furthermore, as their numbers grow, their behavior becomes
quite assertive, an interesting phenomenon also observed frequently
in many white Americans abroad. This behavior can be viewed as a
necessary step in minority students' own subsequent growth. Hood
(1973, p. 107) reported, "When black students indicate solidarity
in terms of personal tastes and experiences . . . [they] are often
reaffirming their beliefs in themselves as persons and their desire to
be recognized as a meaningful group." Hood's comments have important implications because, unlike members of the business community, minority students often begin the process with a powerful
negative self-image. Close ethnic identification provides these minority students with the safety of a social organization, a peer society
necessary to realistically assess their personal-social position and its
consequences.

If the classroom activities begin to get difficult, the sensitive
instructor continues to:

1. Address all students by using their surnames, being careful to
   refer to them as person, young man or young woman ("There is
   a person here who disagrees with you, I think!").
2. Push for point clarification ("Are you saying that the author
   missed an important point?") while being constantly ready to

post on the board specific statements that move the discussion along.

3. Insist on the maintenance of ground rules ("Well now, Ms. Smith is certainly entitled to her opinion. As a matter of fact, we might well look for additional situations where her idea would be appropriate. We may have overlooked something.").

The point here is that it is necessary to treat minority students with the same ease, fairness, and respect accorded all students, a situation which does not always come easy to the inexperienced teacher.

Undoubtedly a secure sense of humor is invaluable too ("Ah, come now, Mr. Brown, I think you're pulling my leg. Do you really mean . . . ?"). I have discovered that I can better control and offer support to a student demanding attention by briefly moving physically closer to him or her. This allows for such subtle behaviors as a quick knowing smile, direct eye contact, or touching that student's desk and using him or her with others in an analogous example of some point. I try to be careful not to close in like a school marm but to drift in and out of the immediate area like someone who is OK and thinks the student is OK too. Being acknowledged, respected, and appreciated by instructors is new for many students. It is without doubt an important step in individual growth and development and the initiation of personal and social change. Rather than resist the difficult behaviors of minority students, the instructor might well use them to increase motivation and to channel energies toward even greater personal growth.

Women. Many female students have similar problems, but traditionally they have taken a more passive role. Instructors must be alert to their first hesitant efforts to contribute to the class so that these students not find themselves shut out by those who are more vocal. Furthermore, female students still find themselves taken less seriously than their male counterparts as they struggle for academic achievement and recognition. The persistent myth of the nonworking wife indicates the subjective evaluation of both counselors and professors who unconsciously decide not to spend too much time with the woman student who will probably "just get married and have babies."

Using data from a survey conducted by the American

Council on Education, Tidball (1973, p. 386) explained: "The data are consistent with the ideas that . . . men faculty perceive women students as sexual beings and as less serious and capable students than men, thereby excluding women students from full partnership in collegial relationships." The lack of equal academic opportunity for women means not just benign chauvinism but a destructive lack of access to the supportive academic "good life" that renews the motivation of discouraged males to continue their struggle toward greater academic achievement. The opportunity for working in a supportive atmosphere of mutual inquiry has usually been available to male students who could frequently study quite closely with a same-sex, role-modeling mentor available more or less constantly to support their academic and sometimes even personal growth. This professional collegiality and support is what has been denied female students who have the added burden of trying to define their own identities through a personal reconciliation of their professional and feminine roles in society.

The Poor. For those students who come from low-income or poverty families, problems in the classroom are often based on an inability to respond with "privilege." Such families have not had the "privilege" of being free from the demanding, continuous pressure of egocentric decision making for survival, free from ill health, free from malnutrition and its stubborn effects of missed school days, free from listlessness and difficulty in memory, concentration, and abstract thinking (Montagu, 1974). Students from low-income families may not have had the "privilege" of healthy and secure parents, an environment that supports solid and pervasive learning, or immediately available resource people who could answer questions and provide that all-important role model. Yet a few make it to college! And it is important for the instructor to perceive such students as persons whose perspective, although different, is no less valid than that of the traditional student. In fact, it is just such a student who can validate the legitimacy of the instructor's perspective.

The problems of all these groups are brought into the classroom. It is from their respective vantage points that students must enter into academic relationships with faculty and each other, a difficult task for such a diverse group. Yet it can be this very diversity that makes for an exciting, alive, rich learning environment. Cross fertilization of ideas, cultures, and orientations becomes the stimulus for active involvement. As Hood (1973, p. 111) stated, "When cultural difference is stigmatized as 'inferior', the educational value is lost. When it is appreciated as a different way of thinking and doing, it becomes a unique human expression." McKeachie (1969a, p. 81) suggested that the larger and more heterogeneous the group, the more resources there are available within the group. Making use of the resources relies heavily upon the level of communication; instructors must be ready to assist this process.

Intrigued by the possibilities in heterogeneous classrooms, many faculty can explore new roles for themselves in interpersonal perception. For students, this change means greater responsibility in the fashioning of their own learning strategies and the building of their own dreams. The importance of faculty behavior to the heterogeneous group should be clear. "To meddle so smugly in someone else's daydream is to limit all dreamers to your fantasies. The worst danger of all is that you might succeed" (Noonan, 1977).

Sensitive Course Materials

Nowhere will the level of trust in a heterogeneous student body be more apparent than in the identification of sensitive course materials. Sophisticated faculty know that they can sometimes miss the often very subtly demeaning nature of some materials. Even being a member of the group demeaned does not make one immune to these oversights. Students are reassured if professors are sympathetic to finding such incidents and particularly so when specific action is taken as appropriate, such as writing a letter to the author and publisher, deleting the material from course requirements, or adding an appropriate rebuttal or interpretation to the original material.

Trust is undermined when demeaning material against groups not present, such as an ethnic joke, is intentionally used. Representatives of other groups can be seen glancing at each other in a knowing fashion when it becomes apparent that the professor's sincerity and genuineness evaporate behind closed doors.

On the other hand, where professors have really accepted

the notion of mutual inquiry and learning, the identification of demeaning material will be accepted as a positive occurrence and a chance to understand more of the underlying dynamics of our Western culture. Undoubtedly the urge to evaluate such an identification as "picky" is quite tempting at times. Yet it must be remembered that (1) if the student feels it, it is real (regardless of intention), and (2) it can be an excellent opportunity to explore the real life implications of such material. Frequently more traditional students must be reminded of the importance of such sensitivity and its own potential implications for their personal and professional development.

The following examples are illustrative of comments I have used in dealing with the identification of sensitive issues:

1. That article seemed biased to me. Did it strike anyone else that way?
2. I think I just put my foot in my mouth with that phrasing. What exactly did I say?
3. OK. That's a reasonable interpretation, although surely not intended. Let's omit or reword it.
4. We must all help one another to become sensitive to the subtle ways in which we attack different groups. If you felt it, although not intentionally, it was there. Thank you for helping us understand.
5. Your statement made me uncomfortable. It could be interpreted as saying . . .
6. I don't think I quite understand that point yet. Explain that again . . . yes, keep talking.
7. I have a funny feeling from your comments that there's something about this that rubbed you the wrong way.

Example: Guided Design

A good example of discussion methods is Guided Design, an educational strategy developed by Charles E. Wales and Robert A. Stager (1976).* Its premise is that a range of subject matter can

*Descriptive material taken from *Guided Design, Part I* by Charles E. Wales and Robert A. Stager. The author appreciates the cooperation Dr. Wales gave in the preparation of this section.

be successfully taught by the active participation of students in small groups, working their way through a hierarchically organized set of decision-making steps to the resolution of real-life problems.

This strategy is quite similar to earlier work by Maier (1952), who coined the term "developmental discussion" "to describe a problem-solving discussion technique in which the teacher breaks problems into parts so that all group members are working on the same part of the problem at the same time" (McKeachie, 1969b; Maier, 1963). The present work by Wales and Stager goes further in the structural development of the idea and its applicability to a range of disciplines.

The structure of Guided Design clearly defines the process. Essentially, a problem under study is divided into a series of steps that the students must resolve in a set order. The students devise a work plan for each step, including deciding on the information they will need to successfully address that step of the problem's solution. Anticipating these informational needs, the instructor is to have prepared reference material for them (books, films, tapes, and so on). Students are expected to consult these materials. After having arrived at a first step decision, the students are given written feedback sheets prepared in advance by the instructor. The feedback sheets present the range of decision options that were available to the students, elaborating on the strengths and weaknesses of each. Students are expected to compare their decision with that of the professional, an exercise that usually generates further motivation as well as learning. Students are then given the second step in the problem's solution, and the process repeats itself. The specific preparation of the problem steps and the feedback sheets by the instructor are based on student skills, the subject matter, and the objectives. The steps in decision making followed in Guided Design are:

- Gather information (a component of each of the steps).
- Identify the problem.
- State the basic objective or goal.
- State the constraints, assumptions, and facts.
- Generate possible solutions.
- Evaluate and make a decision.

- Analyze elements of chosen solution for implementation.
- Synthesize elements into detailed solution.
- Evaluate solution against objectives and whether solution is feasible, practical, economical, safe, legal, and moral.
- Report results and make recommendations.
- Implement decision.
- Check results.

These steps may be modified as appropriate.

The role of the instructor in Guided Design is not one of the traditional actor on the stage, but it is best described as one of a consultant, manager, or coach. Through the carefully presented options given in the feedback sheets, the teacher brings together the freedom in decision making with the subsequent responsibilities entailed in specific choices. The students gradually learn the consequences of misplaced constraints, poor analyses, and myopic vision. Guided Design has been reported to have a number of advantages: students' ability to develop creative ideas, individualized instructional material, greater retention of learned material, better student communication, shift in student attitudes. But these results are not guaranteed. Although the potential is there, successful adaptation in a given course by a given instructor requires that the instruction be very carefully thought out, well prepared, presented, measured, and evaluated with subsequent modification as appropriate.

Wales (1977) reported that at West Virginia University, where he and his colleagues developed the method, exciting data are emerging. For example, since the introduction six years ago of Guided Design in a six-credit freshman engineering program, "50% more students graduated, and these students earned grades that are 30% higher than those earned by transfer students who did not take these courses." Furthermore, he reported a significant decrease in the drop-out rate from the engineering program. Many factors are accounted for in these data presented, but it has yet to be determined whether the addition of better problem-solving skills alone or this addition plus the added attention and enthusiasm of the faculty are the basis of this phenomenal improvement in student performance.

Undoubtedly, this particular instructional method, which

uses discussion as a principal tool in decision making, has a great deal of merit. However, I think it is worthwhile to note that in a Ed.D. thesis ("Evaluation of Guided Design in a Technology Course") by Richard E. Landers done at West Virginia University, reported by Wales and Stager (1976), one class of students did not find Guided Design significantly more democratic, flexible, fair, or novel. In view of the importance of trust and the accompanying attitude of mutual inquiry stressed earlier in this chapter, one may suspect a problem associated with the feedback sheet is that by being done in advance, it sets up the student-instructor relationship as a master-disciple or expert-child one. For many purposes, such a relationship is far from optimal. In the technical sciences, this relationship may not be much of a problem, but in their application for use in the social sciences, one need not go far to discover that the experts are less expert, less sensitive to the real problems, and less creative in devising workable, acceptable solutions than many lay persons. Another possible problem is the tendency of sophisticated students to resist what appears to them to be the structure's "busy work," which often seems to be associated with many programmed approaches. Nonetheless, the structure is Guided Design's strong point when it is applied to interdisciplinary problems. Whatever the case, the instructor using Guided Design must guard against preoccupation with the form that would replace the give and take of mutual inquiry, the special and unique potential of discussion groups.

The following strategy, The Fishing Trip, written by Charles E. Wales and Gene D'Amour (used by permission of Charles E. Wales), is an example of Guided Design.

The Fishing Trip—An Introduction to the Decision-Making Process

Introduction

Many of you have probably gone on an automobile trip only to have the car break down on the highway. Although this can be inconvenient and annoying, help is usually within walking distance and there is little danger involved. In contrast, imagine the problem you might

have if you had a breakdown while out in a boat on a fishing trip in
the Gulf of Mexico. That's the situation we want you to deal with in
this one-hour project. You will be asked to participate in this situation
in two ways. First, there is an *individual exercise* in which you are
asked to rank a list of items. Second, you are asked to work as *part of a
team* to explore the best way to deal with the problem.

The Setting

It was the first week in August when four friends set out on an
overnight fishing trip in the Gulf of Mexico. Everything went well the
first day—the sea was calm, they caught fish, and later camped out on
a lovely little island. However, during the night a very strong wind
pulled the anchor free, drove their boat ashore, and the pounding
waves broke the propeller. Although there were oars in the boat, the
motor was useless.

A quick review of the previous day's journey showed that the
group was about 60 miles from the nearest habitated land. The small
deserted island they were on had a few scrub trees and bushes, but no
fresh water. They knew from their portable am-fm radio that the
weather would be hot and dry, with daytime temperatures expected to
be over 100°F the rest of the week. They were all dressed in light
clothing but each had a Windbreaker for the cool evenings. They
agreed that whatever happened they would stick together.

The families back on shore expected the group to return from
their trip that evening and would surely report them missing when they
didn't show up. However, they realized that it might take time for
someone to find them because they went out further than anyone might
have expected.

While some members of the group were quite concerned about
this predicament, there was no panic. To help keep the group calm, one
of the group, Jim, suggested that, just to be safe, they inventory the
food and equipment available to them. "It might be several days before
we are safe," Jim said, "and I think we should prepare for that." Kate,
Tom, and Ann agreed, and their effort produced the following list
of items.

First Exercise—Individual Work

*After the list was complete, Jim suggested that each person in-
dependently rank these items according to the importance of each item
to the survival of the group.* Each member of the group agreed to do

this. Without discussing the problem with anyone else, they would individually rank the items from number "1," for the item which was most important, to number "14," the item least important to survival.

(We would like you to assume that you are a member of this group and individually rank these items on the form provided. *Write your list of numbers in the space marked Column A.*)

Items Available	*Column*				
	A	Z	B	Y	X
Each person has					
a. one windbreaker					
b. one poncho					
c. one sleeping bag					
d. one pair of sunglasses					
The boat contains					
e. a cooler with two bottles of pop per person and some ice					
f. one large flashlight					
g. one first-aid kit					
h. fishing equipment					
i. matches, rope, and a few tools					
j. one compass mounted on the boat					
k. two rear-view mirrors that can be removed from the boat					
l. one "official" navigational map of the Gulf area where you are					
m. one salt shaker (full)					
n. one bottle of liquor					

Second Exercise—Group Decision Making

Form groups of four to seven people.

Introduction. The material you are about to use is concerned with decision making, a basic intellectual process which makes it possible for each of us to face and solve new problems. This material is organized in an "Instruction-Feedback" pattern so you can participate in the solution of the problem. Each instruction presents a question the group on the island raised about one step in the decision making process. We suggest that each member of your group read each Instruction, *discuss it with your team, decide on a group response,* and then compare the decision with the printed Feedback which your teacher will provide. This Feedback offers a summary of what your group has probably discussed and presents the decision made by the group on the island. You should realize that the purpose of the printed Feedback is to allow everyone to compare their reasoning with that of other people. No one should feel that they have to accept any of these decisions.

Each group should *appoint a secretary to record* the decisions made by his or her teammates. When the group feels they have completed their answer to the Instruction, ask the teacher to come to the group to check the work or have the secretary take the record to the teacher. If the teacher believes the work is acceptable, the secretary will receive copies of the Feedback and the next Instruction to give to the group. If the work is not yet acceptable, the teacher may ask questions to stimulate further thinking.

Instruction A—The Problem. When the group on the island finished their work on the list of items, Tom, who was visibly shaken, spoke up. "I'm not sure that what we have done so far makes any sense. I'm really worried!"

"Do you want to make a group list?" Jim asked.

"No," Tom said, "I think we should *talk about what we are going to do about our problem.*"

(Assume you are the group on the island and discuss what you would do about this problem.)

Feedback A. The four friends had quite an animated discussion about what to do. Some of their ideas were to:
• Row to shore.
• Stay on the island and gather wood.
• Build a fire.
• Ration food and water.
• Catch fish.
• Build a shelter.
• Take the mirrors off the boat.

Instruction B—Identify the Problem. Tom, who had now calmed down, spoke again. "I think we're making progress now, but I'm *not* sure we're on the right track. I get the feeling that all the ideas we listed should be called possible solutions—we talked about *what we should do to solve our problem, but not about the problem these solutions are supposed to solve.*"

"Tom's right," Kate said, "We can't generate intelligent possible solutions unless we know exactly what the problem is we face. Let's see if we can *agree on the problem we want to solve.*"

The others agreed and they proceeded with this task.

Feedback B. This time the group came up with a list of what they thought were potential problems. They said the problem is:

• We are stuck on this island.
• The propeller is broken.
• Survival.

Instruction C—Identify the Problem. "Wait," Jim said, "I think we've got problems mixed with causes. It's a subtle difference, but an important one. The broken propeller and the fact that we're stuck here got us into trouble—they caused our problem, but the immediate problem we face is survival."

"I agree," Ann said, "but survival is too broad a word. We can't generate good solutions unless we *pinpoint* the problem that threatens our lives. I think we've got to define the most basic problem we face. *What is the specific problem that is most likely to threaten our survival?*"

Feedback C. After a brief discussion the group agreed that the immediate threat to their lives was either starvation, sunburn, or dehydration. Then they decided that they could get out of the sun and avoid a "burn." They could also eat fish so they wouldn't starve. But they had no source of fresh water. Thus, dehydration seemed to be the most serious problem and the one on which they should focus.

"It seems clear to me," Ann said, "that we have not only identified the problem we face, but stated the goal of our work as well, our *goal* is to stay alive by avoiding dehydration." The others agreed.

Instruction D—Facts, Assumptions, Constraints/Choose a Solution. "OK," Tom said, "our goal is to prevent dehydration. I suggest we pool what we know and list the facts, assumptions, and constraints which affect this goal."

"The *facts* are easy," Ann said. "We're stuck sixty miles from the nearest habitation where we can get help, and it's going to be hot and dry during the day."

"Yes, and we can *assume* that our families will miss us and someone should be looking for us tomorrow," Kate added.

"And," Tom continued, "the *constraints* are that we have only the items on our list to work with plus the few trees, bushes, and the sand here on the island.

"Given this state of affairs," Jim added, "let's *make a list of the things we must avoid to forestall dehydration and then make our choice, either to stay on the island or to row to shore.*"

Feedback D. The group generated the following list. To avoid dehydration they would have to:
• Do as little exercise as possible.
• Keep out of the sun and wind.
• Eat nothing.
• Avoid alcohol and salt.

"I think we've got a good list," Tom said. "Now let's see if we can use it to *choose the best possible solution.* Since our goal is to avoid dehydration, the question we must answer is, How can we best avoid dehydration? We have two options, stay or row to shore. Which should we do?" After a short discussion, the group agreed that staying on the island was the best possible solution because it would be easier to avoid dehydration if they could avoid the open water and the exercise involved in rowing the boat.

Instruction E—Analysis/Synthesis. "We've done a good job," Ann said, "and now is the proper time to use the list Jim had us develop earlier. Now is the time to *rank the items we have available.* Why don't we see if we can make more sense out of the list now that we know our goal is to prevent dehydration and the best possible solution is to stay here on the island."

"When we're done with our work on the list," Kate added, "I suggest we *synthesize our thinking into a short statement that represents our final plan.*" The group agreed and together they proceeded with their new ranking of the items.

(Each person should write the numbers selected by the group in Column B—leave Column Y blank for now. Please do not change the work you did earlier in Column A.)

Feedback E. The result of this Instruction is your ranked list of items.

The group summarized their thinking in the following way. Given all this information, the group's final decision was to stay on the island and wait for rescue. They would protect themselves from dehydration, from the sun and the hot, dry air, by wearing the sunglasses and the windbreakers and developing a shady shelter with the ponchos and sleeping bags. The mirror, flashlight, and a fire would be used to signal rescuers. The pop and ice water would be used as needed, but no food or liquor would be consumed.

Information F—Evaluation. The group implemented their plan quite effectively and with excellent results. Everyone was in good shape when, three days later, a search plane came near enough to the island for them to signal with the mirror. A few hours more and a Coast Guard vessel came into view and the four friends were soon aboard enjoying a sweet sip of water. After they had rested, the captain dropped in to ask them how they had survived in such good shape. The group told him about their decision making and the lists they had prepared.

"I know a good deal about survival," the Captain said. "Why don't I rank the list of items and you can check your work against mine."

The group agreed and the Captain gave the following explanation.

(Write these numbers to the right, in Column X.)
1. (k) *Two rear-view mirrors*
   "The best way to avoid dehydration is to be rescued, so your first concern should be to develop a signal system. Because a search is most likely to take place in daylight, the mirrors are of prime importance—with a mirror you can generate a beam of light that can be seen a long way. You might get as much as 6 million candle power on a bright day. The chance of being rescued is very high if all you have is a mirror and sunshine."
2. (f) *One large flashlight*
   "To complete your signaling potential, you should count on the flashlight. With the light and the mirror you can signal at night as well as in the daytime."
3. (i) *Matches, rope, and tools*
   "Matches plus parts removed from the boat and/or gasoline provide another signaling device, a fire. The flame at night or smoke during the day should provide an excellent signal. In addition, the rope can help you create a daytime shelter."

4. (a) *Windbreaker*

"Your second concern should be to slow down dehydration by reducing both respiration and perspiration. To be effective at this task you should put yourself in the place of those who know how to survive in a hot, dry climate—the animals you have seen over and over again in Walt Disney movies and on Wild Kingdom TV shows. Animals, who live in a hot, dry climate, survive by staying out of the sun and limiting their activity. You can do the equivalent by staying quietly in the shade to reduce respiration and insulating yourself from the hot, dry air with the Windbreakers. This will increase your survival time significantly."

5. (b) *One poncho each*
6. (c) *One sleeping bag each*

"These two items are considered together because both, in combination with the rope, can be used to create enough shade to reduce the temperature by up to 20%. This is an important reduction which can prolong life. You might also be able to use the poncho to create a solar still and produce some fresh water."

7. (d) *One pair of sunglasses each*

"By the second day, the intense sunlight can produce serious eye problems, equivalent to snow blindness. The shade provided by the shelter will help, but sunglasses offer additional safety."

8. (e) *The cooler of ice and pop*

"This amount of liquid will not offset the inevitable effects of dehydration. Thus there is no point in rationing the pop and water. Instead, it should be consumed when you are thirsty, on the first day, so you can keep a clear head as you make the important decisions that will affect your survival."

9. (g) *First-aid kit*

"This kit would be of value if anyone were hurt, but the island is likely to be a very healthy place because it is so dry. Even if someone were cut, they would not be likely to bleed because their blood is dehydrating and thickening."

Items of Little Value

10. (l) Navigation map
11. (j) Compass

"These two items are of value only if the group tries to row to shore, which is likely to be a fatal mistake. If no one were looking for you, this might be a option, but it is not in this situation. You should use the map for a sun shade, to build a fire, or as toilet paper."

12. (h) Fishing equipment
13. (n) Liquor
14. (m) Salt shaker

"The fishing equipment could be used to catch food, but the activity would dehydrate you even faster. In addition, eating requires water for digestion so you would accelerate dehydration by eating.

"The liquor may be liquid, but in this case it's liquid death. Alcohol is a dehydrating agent so if you want to go fast, but happy, you should drink the liquor. It might better be used to cool the skin.

"Salt also acts as a dehydrating agent. You do not need to replace the salt in your blood, it is already too salty because you are dehydrating. Therefore, avoid the salt."

At this point Kate interrupted with a question. "I understand and agree with what you've said, but some of us felt that fixing a shelter was more important than worrying about rescue because we knew you wouldn't even begin to look for us until the next day."

"That's a good point," the Captain responded, "and I couldn't argue if you switched the list around with shelter first. The point is to avoid dehydration by either reducing it or getting off the island."

Instruction F—Evaluation. "The success of your plan was demonstrated when you were rescued in such good shape," the Captain said, "But let's see how well your choices stacked up against my evaluation. To determine how your group did compared to my advice, I suggest you score your work in the following way:

First Exercise—Individual Scores

1. "Subtract to obtain the *'absolute difference'* $A - X$, the difference between Column A (your individual ranking) and my ranking (X). Write the result in Column Z.
2. "Each person should add all the 'difference' numbers in their Column Z to get a total for their work.
3. "Calculate an average individual score for your group: the sum of the Z results divided by the number in your group."

Second Exercise—Group Decision Making Score

4. "Subtract to obtain the *'absolute difference'* $B - X$, the difference between Column B (the group ranking) and my ranking (X). Write the result in Column Y.
5. "Add the 'difference' numbers in Column Y to get a total score for the group ranking."

Feedback F. The Captain suggested that to see the evaluation of their scores, the group compare the average individual score (Z) with the group decision-making score (Y). The point was well made because the four friends could see that their group score (Y) was lower (or closer to the Captain's evaluation) than the individual score (Z).

The Captain summed up this work with the following points:

1. "The more you know about the key elements involved in a problem, the more successful you are likely to be at finding a workable solution. For instance, in this problem, the more you know about dehydration the more likely you are to survive. In other words, the things you study and learn, whether in school or out, can help you be a more effective problem solver.

2. "A group can usually arrive at a better decision than an individual, especially if the people in the group understand how to work together to share what they know and what they think.

3. "Your decision-making work is likely to be much more effective if you know which steps to take and how to use each step. If you are skilled at this process you are less likely to commit one of the classic errors, such as generating possible solutions before you identify the problem to be solved. After you properly define both the problem and the goal, you are also in a much better position to decide what information you need to proceed intelligently.

"Perhaps I should stress," the Captain continued, "that identifying the problem and stating the goal are extremely important steps in the solution of any problem. If you have not done these steps properly, you are not likely to produce the best solution; you may miss possible solutions which should not be missed or perform an excellent analysis of the wrong problem. An example of this occurred in the early development of the U.S. space program when a problem similar to the following was posed: Find a material which will withstand a temperature of 14,000°F for five minutes. Of course this problem was related to the re-entry of a space capsule and the enormous amount of heat generated during the process.

"A great deal of time and money was wasted trying to solve this problem because there was no known material which would withstand the required temperature. Finally, someone realized that they were trying to solve the wrong problem. The new problem was stated as follows: Find a way to protect a capsule and the person inside during re-entry. This problem was solved very quickly with the ablation system now in use."

"The problem you faced on the island was very similar to this re-entry problem," the Captain said. "If you focus on getting to shore and not the real problem of dehydration, then you are likely to miss the solution that results in survival."

Epilogue. Through this problem we have tried to indicate in a very brief way that many steps are required in the solution of an open-ended problem. In the more involved problems which follow you will be asked to perform these steps, learning as you go how to perform them with greater and greater skill. As you work on each problem, you will be expected to use what you already know and to learn new fundamental principles which are required to produce the desired result. In this sense, you will be operating exactly like a problem solver in the real world, who commands a broad background but must often search out new information and skills to produce the best solution.

Before we move on to the next problem, it would be well for you to review the steps we have performed here. Although the order in which these steps are used may vary from problem to problem, the steps themselves are an important key to successful work. Try to list the steps we have used, then check your list against our "Steps in Decision Making."

Debriefing. Congratulations!

You have just completed your first Guided Design class. If you decide you'd like to try this approach in a class you are presently teaching, you should reproduce enough copies of our Fishing Trip project so each student can have one set. *You have our permission to do this, as long as you give proper credit.* This material should not be collated because it will be passed out one page at a time. (Note: these "debriefing" paragraphs should be deleted from the students' copies.)

If you decide to adopt the Guided Design style for your class, this "Introduction to Decision Making" is extremely important because it helps the students understand the process which will be a prime focus of their work throughout the course. However, we should point out that this introduction has one unique feature which is not present in a typical Guided Design project, that is the scoring at the end of the project where the students compare their solution with that of the captain. As you will see in the other examples presented in this book, the usual pattern used in Guided Design does not include this type of comparison and scoring.

Even if you don't plan to convert your course to Guided Design you may find this project valuable because of what it can contribute to your students' abilities. For example, this material would be par-

ticularly appropriate in any course where the teacher already devotes
some time to discussion activities. In fact, if you choose to teach the
decision-making process in such a class with this material, we expect
you will find the quality of the students' discussion improved.

Guided Design has been supported by the Exxon Education
Foundation, which provides two opportunities for further learning
in this methodology:

1. A 25-minute, 16mm, color film (#31864), complementing the
   material presented in Guided Design, is available rent-free from
   Film Scheduling Center, Modern Talking Picture Service, Inc.,
   2323 New Hyde Park Rd., New Hyde Park, NY 11040; Telephone: (516) 488-3810.
2. Impact grants through 1978 made available two opportunities to
   attend Guided Design writing workshops at West Virginia University and to visit courses there where Guided Design has been
   implemented.

The interested reader may write to Dr. Wales, Director,
Freshman Engineering, West Virginia University, Morgantown,
WV 26506 for further information.

Summary

As is apparent from the range of possibilities presented, instructors who employ discussion techniques may define their role as
active and directing, or they may define it as more passive and
facilitative. Session objectives and other planning factors previously
discussed will help decide how to proceed. Instructors may wish to
vary their role from time to time to receive new data and explore
new possibilities. Session objectives also help the instructor decide
whether or not a discussion session is the most appropriate teaching
tool to use. An early, clear formulation of such objectives is very
important throughout, from planning to evaluation.

Furthermore, the success of discussion sessions depends not
only on thorough knowledge, adequate planning, and appropriate
techniques; it also depends most heavily on instructors' ability to
build a level of student-faculty trust and an atmosphere of mutual

inquiry. These latter conditions depend on the openness of instructors' attitudes, their ease and fairness in working with a heterogeneous student population, their willingness to understand sensitive issues, their judicious use of personal anecdotes, and their openness to student feedback. These points appear to draw pretty heavily on the ego strength of instructors, suggesting that instructors who anticipate conducting discussion groups should look very closely at their own behavior and motives before attempting to raise the level of class interaction.

Some faculty may find this whole presentation on discussion highly antithetical to their own way of viewing their professional responsibility. In fact, it would not be at all unusual for any instructor to feel a great deal of anxiety and personal ambivalence when moving from the lecture to the discussion method of teaching. To be told further that his or her personal life must somehow be touched could be too much! Indeed, if this were to be the case, such an instructor might well explore those feelings and use the resolution of them as an excellent avenue to professional growth. A healthy respect for one's own feelings supports a similar respect for those of students. Such respect is often mirrored in the students themselves. (There are many excellent publications on professional growth and personal development, examples of which are suggested here: Johnson, 1972; Fox, Lippitt, and Schindler-Rainman, 1973; and Pollak, 1976.)

Successful discussions require more than a knowledge of mechanics and the polished execution of technique. Indeed, I suspect that all the concerns and admonitions written about in previous sections, including the building of trust and the emphasis on mutual inquiry, dangle quite badly without addressing the creative perspective into which they all fit.

Creating exciting, alive, and mutually stimulating classroom interactions should become a challenge that, when successful, is tremendously rewarding. It is, in fact, art—full of frustrations and achievements, latent and realized potential, mystery and magic. Frustrations are overwhelming when, after hours of planning and preparation, the discussion is somehow flat and lacking in vigor. There are also achievements when everything seems to click and both the students and teacher leave the class feeling that something important had happened to them. Some instructors seem to have a talent for inspiring positive interaction. Others must doggedly pursue that elusive, creative potential within us through painful trial and error. I have no formulas for accomplishment, but I do know when art is being created. The mystery in each student becomes infectious! The thread in the common experiences involves us all in a personal way! The feeling of collegiality, even in dissent, fills the room! And there is magic in the air!

Richard Caemmerer (1977) suggested that art is the celebration of a moment in time. Perhaps it is that sense of celebration and its potential for spontaneity, freshness, and creativity which lift the complacent discussion to the level of art. But it is not the work of art. Caemmerer also stated that art is process, not the product of that process. In the celebration of a moment in time, art is the creative using of that moment's resources to communicate its meaning.

The result of the creative process, on the other hand, is its product—what is left when the art is done, when the moment is gone. We call that product the work of art, the artifact, the solution. The product's existence, its representation of that moment, can scarcely convey the full experience of its production. As with any reproduction of human experience, much is lost in its representation.

This position is no attempt to denigrate the frequently magnificent product. Indeed, the desire for the product, as in problem solving, is often the motive for initiating the process. But it is important not to lose the potential in the creativity of doing by concentrating on its possible result. In group discussion, a product may be rejected shortly after its formulation. Yet each act of expressing makes a contribution to the creative process, and we become aware of the art we are creating together. T. S. Eliot (1958) chided us not to be concerned about the harvesting but to concentrate on the sowing.

How does one find the mystery in one's students? How does one stimulate magic in one's classroom? How does one create art through human interaction? I cannot answer, for I have failed more times than I have succeeded. The best I can say is that it feels as though the process for each of us begins within ourselves, for each of us is also—art!

4

Ohmer Milton

Classroom Testing

This chapter focuses on perhaps the most neglected feature of good instruction: testing. Its primary proposition is that improved classroom testing will improve the quality of learning for many students (even if those who care not about learning will not be touched). Its secondary proposition is that classroom tests should be improved out of sheer fairness to students, since major decisions are made about their lives on the basis of test scores or their haloed derivative, the grade point average.

Testing and Grading

Unfortunately the terms *testing* and *grading* are often used interchangeably to refer to the entire process of assessing the course performance of students. Yet a distinction must be made between them. Each endeavor encompasses quite different concepts. The cause of learning will be enhanced and progress in evaluating students is more likely to occur if they are kept separate in our thinking. This will be difficult; testing and grading are very emotional topics, and reason frequently flees at their mention.

As used here, *testing* refers to those activities of instructors in *preparing to assign* a letter grade or symbol. It includes (1) writing single questions or items, (2) selecting several items or questions to comprise an exam, (3) setting conditions under which the test is administered, (4) scoring each individual item for each student, (5) assigning a score of number or quantity to the whole for each paper or exam, and (6) determining the frequency of administering tests in a given course. Some faculty refer to this process as *measurement*. Others are offended by that label, but what the process is called is not too important. What is important is that the process is thought of as being distinctly different from the act of assigning a grade or letter symbol.

For the most part, grading—the assigning of this symbol—is used for making comparisons among students and for record-keeping purposes—not for informing students of the details of their successes and failures. More specifically, as is well known, grades are used to rank students from high to low, whether by A's, B's, C's, D's, and F's, or by percentages, numbers, or pluses and minuses. Undoubtedly their use as a personnel screening and selection device will continue for many years, and since grading for selection purposes will more than likely continue to be an integral part of instruction, faculty members will have to perform better in this area. It is too bad, of course, that tests administered for these grading purposes are not used more extensively for providing substantive feedback to students and aiding their learning during the course.

Grading and grades receive more public and professional scrutiny than tests and testing. Millions of words continue to be printed, both praising and damning the grading system, with wailing about grade inflation being only the most recent expression of concern. It is my considered opinion, however, that grading is *not* the fundamental issue; it merely touches the surface of a bewilderingly complex problem. The basic problem is testing. If the process by which any product is produced is faulty, then the product will be faulty. In the case of grades, clever and sophisticated statistical manipulations often are employed to improve the interpretation of faulty symbols stemming from faulty measurement. This only compounds and obfuscates the original procedural errors.

Impact of Testing

Setting aside this issue of grading and of sheer fairness to students for the moment and concentrating on the proposition that improved classroom testing can improve the quality of learning for many students, this proposition is based on evidence that the testing to which students are subjected influences how they study and what they learn. This evidence can be summarized by a principle that has been known to experimental scientists for many years: The act of measurement has an effect on the object or phenomenon being measured. Just as in a blood-pressure reading, where at least two features of the act of measurement can distort the true reading or measure—(1) the pressure of the inflated cuff, and, for some people, (2) the very thought of the procedure itself—so in education: The act of testing affects the learning being tested.

As an example of anecdotal evidence about testing influences, a little over fifty years ago in a survey at the University of Minnesota (Douglass and Talmadge, 1934), a majority of students reported that when studying for multiple-choice and true-false tests, they learned minute details and tried to remember the words of the book; on the other hand, while preparing for essay examinations, they tried to form personal opinions, understand relationships, and draw tentative conclusions about the material. At about the same time, Meyer (1935) found indirect evidence of this principle by analyzing notes made in the booklets that contained new material to be learned by students at the University of Michigan: Of those students who were to receive an essay test, a smaller percentage used underlining and a greater percentage made summaries than did those who were to take multiple-choice and true-false tests.

During the early 1930s Wert (1937) found that students

performed better on nonfactual test questions than on factual ones
and that the better performance endured longer. During the course,
exams were developed very carefully to measure achievement of six
objectives in elementary zoology: (1) naming animal structures,
(2) stating functions of structures, (3) terminology, (4) other facts,
(5) interpreting new experiments, and (6) applying principles to
new situations. There was special emphasis upon the latter two.
Equivalent forms of the tests were administered to the same students
at the end of the course, one year later, and two years later. There
were significant losses over the two-year period in the first four objectives; performance continued to be high for the other two.

In 1964, following a review of the literature, Balch (p. 177)
concluded that although "our understanding of both *how* and *why*
testing influences learning is incomplete," the consensus was "that
the use of an evaluating instrument (as opposed to not using one)
and the nature of the instrument used influences students' learning."
But more recent direct evidence by Thomas and Augstein (1970)
offered further understanding of the how and why of testing influences, as well as further support for this consensus about influence.
They found that students who studied a paper on genetics, having
been informed that the test would be an essay one—but in fact took
essay and multiple-choice–true-false ones—performed better on all
tests than did students who studied the same material under the impression that their test would be multiple-choice–true-false—but
actually received both. Furthermore, the essay students performed
better than did the others on repeat tests one week later.

For most of us, the most compelling evidence supporting the
proposition that classroom testing influences learning is not experimental along these lines but is instead indirect and anecdotal. "Will
that be on the final?" is a question common to the ears of all experienced teachers; if the answer is "no," the fate of this particular subject matter is immediately sealed—and virtually doomed. Very important evidence may come also from our own psyches (if we are
honest!) regarding the extent to which potential tests influenced our
own learning when we were students. On the other hand, more professors than many of us realize may present the following sort of
paradox to their students, which occurred at a most prestigious in-

stitution. "I observed the professor in one class beginning the term by explaining that the students were expected to be creative and involved. . . . They would have the opportunity to take intellectual risks, to make mistakes. . . . Five weeks later the first quiz was given. The students found that they were asked to return a large amount of information that they could only have mastered by memorization. . . . The consequences for the students varied: Some became cynical and said, 'Okay, if that's the way you play the academic game, if that's what he really wants, I won't make the same mistake again. Next time I'll memorize the key points. . . .' But a large group approved the quiz. They . . . were relieved to find that rote memory would suffice to get a superior grade" (Snyder, 1970, p. 17).

This same principle of the power of testing is illustrated outside the academy by the effects of standardized testing on school teaching. In reporting that the College Entrance Examination Board was likely to start testing the writing ability of students, the *New York Times* (Maeroff, 1976, p. 1) quoted Albert G. Sims, a board vice-president, as saying, "What the teachers are saying to us is that if the College Board does not require writing as part of the basic testing program, then writing won't be valued in the schools, and teachers won't require it of their students."

Direct evidence about the *quality* of classroom tests and testing practices is scanty. There are literally thousands of studies about grading but very, very few about the tests from which they are derived. One study was found (McGuire, 1968) in which three judges independently categorized test questions in such fields as physiology and chemistry. There was unanimous agreement that over half of the items required predominantly either recall or recognition of isolated information. Fewer than one fourth of the questions were thought by any single judge to require even simple elements of interpretation of data or of problem solving. Inspection by a panel of faculty members of large numbers of test questions from several member schools in the Kansas City Regional Council for Higher Education (KCRCHE) revealed that most sought only factual information (McNames, 1977).

At least two surveys of students tend to corroborate these

findings. In one survey (Spencer and Stallings, 1970), 82 percent of almost 3,500 students at the University of Illinois (2,300 on the Urbana-Champaign campus and 1,100 at Chicago Circle) agreed with this statement: "Despite instructors' insistence that they do not teach 'facts,' most grades are based on tests which are primarily factual in content." In the other survey, conducted at the same school, 88 percent of an additional 500 students agreed with this statement: "Most objective examinations call for factual information."

As for testing practices, such as the types of tests used, two studies provide most interesting comparisons among several institutions; to my knowledge, these are the only studies of this kind. One was at the University of Illinois (Spencer and Stallings, 1970), and the other included two member schools of KCRCHE (McNames, 1977). Table 1 indicates the frequencies faculties reported they used these most common test types (percentages rounded):

Table 1. Faculty Use of Test Types, in Percentages.

	Ill	KCRCHE		Ill	KCRCHE
Essay	17%	13%	Multiple-		
Short-Answer			Choice	14%	17%
Essay	24	16	True-False	9	13
Completion	12	10	Matching	7	9

That there are similar frequencies of use of certain of these types—multiple-choice, true-false, and matching—at a large university and at the very small member schools of KCRCHE is an enigma. Giant schools are accused of relying too heavily on these types of items because of large classes, yet small schools in this sample utilize them to a comparable degree. There are several plausible explanations: (1) Both groups have fallen into the trap of what they consider to be the easy way out, when in reality the construction of reliable and valid recognition items is both difficult and time consuming; (2) the cult of pseudoobjectivity is the culprit—many faculty and students really believe that classroom multiple-choice and true-false items are objective; and (3) faculties have oversimplified a very complex issue because of ignorance. There is insufficient

recognition that the measurement of human achievement is inordinately difficult.

Improving Test Quality

What is meant by improved or quality classroom tests? Note
first that *improved* and *quality* are relative, not absolute, terms.
They refer, in the main, to increasing a test's reliability and validity
(also relative characteristics).

Reliability means the dependability or consistency of students' scores; that is, if the test were repeated, would the test scores
remain essentially the same? To put it another way, is a given student's performance on a particular test an accurate representation of
that student's achievement?

Increased reliability for classroom tests is crucial because we
are *comparing* students one against another, and our comparisons
should be fair. Student complaints suggest that most classroom tests
are not very reliable. In the only investigation of classroom test reliability that I have found (Spencer and Stallings, 1970), 182 classroom tests in several subject-matter areas were analyzed, and their
reliability coefficients ranged from .96 down to −.01—in other
words, from excellent all the way to abominable. (A .00 coefficient
indicates no dependability or consistency; 1.00 indicates perfection.)
To be acceptable, a reliability coefficient should be .70 or higher;
and Spencer and Stallings found that fully 40 percent of the tests
they analyzed failed to be this reliable.

There are several kinds of validity, but most important here
is *content validity:* the degree to which a test measures what it is
supposed to measure—for example, critical thinking in political
science, problem solving in thermodynamics, comprehension of the
principles of literary criticism, or knowledge of a foreign language
vocabulary. As for the validity of classroom tests, studies have suggested (as mentioned) that the great majority of tests seek primarily
factual knowledge or isolated bits of information. Yet most of us
claim and advertise that we wish students to think critically or reason, to comprehend, to apply what they have learned, and so on. If
there is a paramount discrepancy between what we say we teach

and wish our students to learn and what our tests measure, then classroom tests tend toward invalidity.

If by learning we mean far more than an ability to recognize or recall specific factual information and instead mean at the very least the ability to deal with and manipulate facts in a variety of ways—comprehending or understanding, being critical or reasoning, interpreting, and applying them—quite obviously, the learning or achievement we hope to see happen is far more complex than that called for on many tests. Moreover, if we wish students to learn more than factual information and want this learning to endure far beyond the termination of our course, then we will increase the chances of their doing so if we give them test questions that require the added performance.*

Objectivity

Before making detailed suggestions about increasing reliability and validity, clarification about another term—objectivity—is in order. Many people separate tests into two major types: "objective" (short answer) and "subjective," (essay) mainly on the basis of the scoring of the test. My feeling is that these two particular categorizations obscure more than they clarify. They cause undesirable blanketing and incorrect assertions about the merits and demerits of each type of test, when the central issue is grasp of factual information, comprehension, facility in providing evidence, and so on. What seems to be happening is that many faculty members confuse measurement and evaluation in equating testing and grading. Some comment, "If only evaluation could be objective!" Evaluation perforce is subjective in that it entails human judgment.

To be objective, a test score must reflect primarily the per-

---

*Incidentally, there are very, very few studies of the extent to which learning endures beyond the end of a course. One of the most interesting and comprehensive investigations (Bach and Saunders, 1965, 1966) involved about 5,000 persons who had been out of college for varying periods of time and who had taken varying numbers of economics courses. They had attended all types of schools—ranging from the most to the least prestigious. Performance on a specially devised Test of Economic Understanding was quite poor; performance was better on factual items than on those focusing on concepts and problems.

formance of the student being measured rather than the idiosyncracies of the instructor making the measurement. It is true that the scoring of multiple-choice and true-false tests is more objective—*after* a key is prepared—than is the scoring of an essay one, but the scoring or quantifying of any test is only one element of its composition. To say then that multiple-choice and true-false tests are objective is simply false; they may or may not be. As a matter of fact, I would argue that most multiple-choice and true-false classroom tests are not objective because they tend to be constructed hurriedly and carelessly. Even questions that are supplied with many introductory texts are suspect.

Unfortunately, the very act of quantifying tends to be equated with objectivity and sanctity. As Hofstadter (1966, p. 339) explained: "The American mind seems extremely vulnerable to the belief that any alleged notion which can be expressed in figures is in fact as final and exact as the figures in which it is expressed." Kenneth Boulding remarked that we exhibit a certain obsessiveness with arithmetic by believing that once a number has been arrived at by a recognized statistical ritual, something has been accomplished. This mindlessness about numbers helps account for the worship of the grade-point average, but in fact it is one of the most meaningless statistics ever devised.

Gronlund (1977) has proposed the terminology *selection* and *supply* rather than *objective* and *subjective*. In the former, as the name implies, the student selects an answer, such as in multiple-choice, true-false, and matching. In the latter, the student constructs or supplies the answer; essay, short-answer items (a phrase or phrases), and completion or fill-in-blanks are examples. Research has shown that selection items tend to be easier than supply ones; the cognitive activity required is recognition. We know also from personal experience that a sort of lesser level of learning is needed to be able to recognize than to recall. Of course, students must exhibit much more cognitive ability than recall on good essay type items and questions.

The fundamental but by no means sufficient route to increased reliability and validity is clear, unambiguous individual test items, whether of the "selection" or "supply" variety. My impression is that unclear and ambiguous questions constitute the major weaknesses in classroom tests. These major weaknesses exist even in mathematics tests, much to the surprise of many; these deficiencies were documented by Crouse and Jacobson (1975). There are at least three explanations for unclear and ambiguous questions: (1) There are many words in the English language that are used ambiguously; (2) item writers are often not too clear in their own thinking about the particular mental attribute they wish to tap; and (3) the writing is often hurried and careless. To compound these difficulties, students probably give words in test questions more critical attention than any other words they read and, as a consequence, misconstrue many of them.

Constructing Quality Tests

The most common advice offered about constructing valid and reliable classroom tests is to the effect that questions should be written at the language level of the students because to be valid a test should not resolve into one on English vocabulary or into a series of verbal puzzles. On the face of it, such advice appears fairly easy to follow. It must be remembered that all written tests (except foreign language ones, obviously) use the English language, and it is assumed that college students have attained a certain level of mastery.

Recent complaints in the press about student writing and my personal observations cause me to wonder about the true significance of the advice. For example, this statement (if it can be called that) appeared on a course evaluation questionnaire: "Very helpful course, and I gained much more enjoyful readings in this class as I had in another class, that pertained to different readings also." Another student was heard to say: "The relationship was a Plutonic one." How does one tap the vocabulary level of these two "scholars" so as to determine their attainments in a course?

As an illustration of vocabulary ignorance, the following item was used in a psychology research methods course at a major university (Wright, 1976, p. 187) and was designed to test for understanding of concepts about operationalism:

A. "Love is the indescribable joy I feel when my
lover is with me to share my triumphs and sorrows, the

anesthetic agony of my lover's absence and the sensual
ecstacy of our oneness."

B. "One male and one female subject was confined to the experimental room and deprived of food
for 48 hours. At the end of this deprivation period, the
female subject was given a 12 ounce chocolate bar and
was told she could eat all of the chocolate bar or share
it in any way she wished. The number of ounces of
chocolate she gave the male subject was used to define
how much love she felt for him."

1. Which of these two definitions of love is the
more explicit?

2. Which is the operational definition? (Explain
your choice.)

3. The definitions used here illustrate the principal advantage and disadvantage of operationalism.
Discuss them.

Many students who answered questions two and three correctly missed question one. Sleuthing by the instructor revealed students were missing question one because they did not know the definition of explicit. It is incomprehensible to me that college juniors
and seniors do not know the meaning of that word—just how far
should we go in using one syllable words in tests?

With this caveat, strive for item or question clarity. Thorough mastery of the subject matter, a rational and well-developed
set of aims for instruction (see Chapter One)', proficiency in written
communication, and knowledge of the special techniques of item
writing are mandatory for attaining the goal. Large investments of
time, thought, and editing are compulsory.

Although volumes have been written about the details of
test construction, limitations of space dictate that only a few basic
notions be introduced here. More thorough and extensive treatments
are in Ebel (1972) and Gronlund (1977)'. Since multiple-choice
items are seemingly the most widely used of the selection type, some
major special techniques for preparing them will be discussed briefly.
The sample items were chosen deliberately to illustrate and emphasize each technique, not because of their simplicity.* Although there

*These are from Robert L. Ebel, "Writing the Test Item," in *Educa-
tional Measurement,* E. F. Lindquist (Ed.) (Washington, D.C.: American

are marked differences of opinion among faculty, many believe that carefully constructed multiple-choice items can measure much more than grasp of factual information: understanding of relationships, ability to make predictions, ability to recommend appropriate action, and so on.

Include in the stem or body all necessary qualifications that are needed for answer selection. Consider:

If a ship is wrecked in very deep water, how far will it sink?
1. Just under the surface.
2. To the bottom.
3. Until the pressure is equal to its weight.
4. To a depth which depends in part on the amount of air it contains.
The instructor intended alternative 2 as correct, but several capable students chose 4 because they considered the possibility [which the instructor failed to exclude] that a wrecked ship might not sink completely.

Generally, omit nonfunctional words; they tend to interfere with comprehension:

Although many in the United States feared the inflationary effects of a general tax reduction, there was widespread support for a federal community-property tax law under which:
1. Husbands and wives could split their combined income and file separate returns.
2. Homesteads would be exempt from local real estate taxes.
3. State income taxes might be deducted from federal returns.
4. Farmland taxes would be lower.

Comprehension of this item may be facilitated by rewording it as follows:
Community-property tax laws permit:
1. Husbands and wives to split their combined income and file separate returns.

Council on Education, 1966), pp. 214ff. Used by permission. Portions of this material appeared also in Ohmer Milton and John W. Edgerly, *The Testing and Grading of Students* (New Rochelle, N.Y.: Change Publications, 1977). Used by permission.

2. Homesteads to be exempt from local real estate taxes.
3. State income taxes to be deducted on federal returns.
4. Farmland taxes to be lowered.

Sometimes, though, it is useful to include introductory statements that help to emphasize importance:

The pollution of streams in the more populous regions of the United States is causing considerable concern. What is the effect, if any, of sewage on the fish life of a stream?

1. It destroys fish by robbing them of oxygen.
2. It poisons fish by the germs it carries.
3. It fosters development of nonedible game fish that destroy edible fish.
4. Sewage itself has no harmful effect on fish life.

Beware of unessential specificity or trivia. Consider:

What percent of the milk supply in municipalities of over 1,000 was safeguarded by tuberculin testing, abortion testing, and pasteurization?
1. 20.3 percent
2. 31.5 percent
3. 51.9 percent
4. 83.5 percent

This item, encouraging rote memorizing, is an illustration of the trivia about which so many students complain. Furthermore, such figures are seldom as precise as they appear.

Be certain the stem is accurate. Consider:

Why did Germany want war in 1914?
1. She was following an imperialistic policy.
2. She had a long-standing grudge against Serbia.
3. She wanted to try out new weapons.
4. France and Russia hemmed her in.
Who is in any position to say that Germany wanted war? Such inexactitudes may strengthen student misinformation.

Adapt the level of difficulty of the item to the group and to the purpose for which the item is intended. Consider:

If a tree is growing in a climate where rainfall is heavy, are large leaves an advantage or a disadvantage?
1. An advantage, because the area for photosynthesis and transpiration is increased.
2. An advantage, because large leaves protect the tree during heavy rainfall.
3. A disadvantage, because large leaves give too much shade.
4. A disadvantage, because large leaves absorb too much moisture from the air.

The above item illustrates an increased level of difficulty because it requires knowledge of both the answer and an explanation for it.

Do not use a negatively stated item stem. Experience has shown that these tend to confuse students. Consider:

Which of these is *not* one of the purposes of Russia in consolidating the Communist party organization throughout Eastern Europe?
1. To balance the influence of the Western democracies.
2. To bolster her economic position.
3. To improve Russian-American relations.
4. To improve her political bargaining position.

Which of these is *not* true of a virus?
1. It is composed of very large living cells.
2. It can reproduce itself.
3. It can live only in plants and animal cells.
4. It can cause disease.

Some items contain two and three negatives and are intricate verbal puzzles.

Be certain that the correct answer is one on which competent critics agree. Consider:

What is the chief difference in research work between colleges and industrial firms?

1. Colleges do much research, industrial firms little.
2. Colleges are more concerned with basic research, industrial firms with applications.
3. Colleges lack the well-equipped laboratories that industrial firms maintain.
4. Colleges publish results, whereas industrial firms keep their findings secret.

Competent authorities could not agree upon the best response to the above. If this type of item is to be used, a qualification should be offered in the stem, such as, "According to ———, the chief difference. . . ."

Avoid answer alternatives that overlap or include each other. Consider:

What percent of the total [property] loss due to hail is the loss of growing crops?
1. Less than 20 percent
2. Less than 30 percent
3. More than 50 percent
4. More than 95 percent

If 1 is correct, then 2 is also correct; and if 4 is correct, then 3 is correct.

Avoid stereotyped phraseology in the stem and in the correct alternative; this will tend to defeat the rote memorizer. Consider:

What is the biological theory of recapitulation? Ontogeny repeats phylogeny (one of the alternatives).

Avoid irrelevant sources of difficulty. Consider:

This item was intended to measure students' understanding of the *principle* of price discounts:
• Mr. Walters was given a 12½ percent discount when he bought a desk whose list price was $118.75. How much did he have to pay for the desk?

If the item is missed, is it due to calculation errors or to not understanding the principle? To test the principle alone, consider:

• Mr. Walters was given a 10 percent discount when he bought a
desk whose list price was $100. How much did he have to pay for
the desk?

Omit clues to the correct response. Items that contain clues
or cues are not measuring what the instructor intended. They
measure test-taking ability, not achievement. Including clues is perhaps the most frequent error made in multiple-choice tests. In the
following item, it is necessary only to know that "exert" is commonly used with "pressure":

What does an enclosed fluid exert on the walls of its
container?
1. Energy
2. Friction
3. Pressure
4. Work

In the next item the stem calls for a plural answer, which occurs
only in 4.
Among the causes of the Civil War were:
1. Southern jealousy of Northern prosperity.
2. Southern anger at interference with the foreign slave trade.
3. Northern opposition to bringing in California as a slave state.
4. Differing views on the tariff and Constitution.

In the next item, the correct answer has been stated more precisely
and at greater length than the others. Students catch on quickly to
such a clue.
Why were the Republicans ready to go to war with England
in 1812?
1. They wished to honor our alliance with France.
2. They wanted additional territory for agricultural expansion and
   felt that such a war might afford a good opportunity to annex
   Canada.
3. They were opposed to Washington's policy on neutrality.
4. They represented commercial interests which favored war.

In the next item, there are common elements in the stem and in
the answer:

What led to the formation of the States Rights Party?
1. The level of federal taxation.
2. The demand of states for the right to make their own laws.
3. The industrialization of the South.
4. The corruption of many city governments.

Finally, such specific clues as "all," "always," "certainly," and "never" are to be avoided. Moreover, scholars are leery of absolutes and should encourage students to be.

Some psychometric authorities applaud or at the least approve the use of true-false tests. One of their major arguments is so many more questions can be asked in a given period of time that there is a more representative sample. This may be sacrificing validity for reliability. I am opposed to the use of true-false tests at the college level; the writing of good ones requires too much time. I have seen too many that were nothing more than sentences copied directly from the book, with "is" changed to "is not" or "does" to "does not," for example. This surely encourages rote memorization and nothing more. As I have already tried to make clear, my position is that most of us wish to promote a higher order of learning.

Another criticism of true-false testing is the predominant role that chance or guessing may play. If there are 50 items on a quiz, sheer guessing will yield a score of 25. In addition, if the student knows just a little bit, his or her test score reflects a false picture of achievement.

Essay questions, the most important of the supply type, can test how students approach a problem, what information they think is important to record, the soundness of their conclusions and so on. Most importantly, they must write. These are all important abilities in educated persons. Many faculty members are convinced that the proper development of these qualities has been hindered (and I agree with them) by the excessive use of selection tests. Recall in this connection that the use of selection tests is similar in frequency at large and small schools. Although the major problems in multiple-choice tests are encountered during the preparation of the items, the major problems in essay testing are encountered during the scoring. The use of certain techniques during the writing of essay questions will aid in scoring them later.

Limit the scope of the question. Such broad questions as

"Analyze cultural bias in standardized testing" cannot be scored fairly. The scope may be limited in several ways: Ask students to compare, contrast, note limitations, draw inferences, and so on. Call for brevity and conciseness and even specify the amount of space to be used, such as a half a page.

Do not use items or questions that ask for personal feelings. "How do you feel about . . . ?" "Do you relate to . . . ?" "Do you believe . . . ?" "What is your opinion of . . . ?" These questions encourage unfair and improper judgments by instructors, especially if the students' expressions do not agree with theirs. Remember that you are working toward assigning a symbol (ABCDF) that will become part of the student's permanent record. Discuss opinions, feelings, and attitudes freely and openly; grade them—no.

Be certain that adequate time is allowed for the test. Are you trying to get at speed of response or substance?

There is one major additional tactic for increasing content validity. Seek the advice and counsel of colleagues. Prior to consulting them, specify, preferably in writing, what cognitive activity each question is designed to measure—for example, understanding. Then ask at least one colleague to read each item for clarity and ambiguity and to specify what the question is measuring. If there are substantial differences in opinion about given items, rewrite them.

Two techniques for increasing reliability have been mentioned—unambiguous items and scoring objectivity. What are some additional ones? A given test composed of *x* number of questions is always a sample of those that could have been asked. The point is that questions asked should be representative of the major objectives of the course. There are no hard and fast rules for attaining representativeness; it is a matter of approximating it. Some faculty use charts such as the one shown in Table 2 as a guide.

The number or percentage of questions for each topic and for each learning outcome should reflect the relative importance attached to each one throughout the course. If you have insisted, for example, that knowledge of facts and principles is not too important, then it would not be representative for 60 percent of your questions to be of that type. In this regard note again the learning-testing paradox I referred to earlier in this chapter.

Table 2. Designing a Test About Test Construction.

Subject Matter Topics	Knowledge of Facts and Principles	Learning Outcomes Understanding of Facts and Principles	Application of Facts and Principles	Total
1. Planning the test	5[a]	5		10
2. Constructing multiple-choice items	5	10	10	25
3. Constructing essay questions	5	5	5	15
4. Assembling the test	10	5	15	30
5. Using and appraising the test	5	5	10	20
Total	30	30	40	100

[a] Either the number of items or the percentage of items may be recorded in each cell.

Source: Norman E. Gronlund, *Constructing Achievement Tests*, 2nd ed., 1977, p. 9. Reprinted by permission of Prentice-Hall, Inc., Englewood Cliffs, New Jersey.

Another tactic is to call on a colleague and ask for an opinion about representativeness. Also to be considered is the length of the test; the greater the number of questions, the greater the likelihood of representativeness. This is one reason selection type tests tend to be more reliable than supply ones. More questions can be asked in a given period of time, and the greater the number of questions, the greater the likelihood of a representative sample. Still another way to increase reliability is by the number of tests during a course. The performance of all of us varies from day to day. Several tests will tend to average out these variations and tend to yield a more accurate measure than would a single test.

For essay tests, there is the added problem of scoring reliability or consistency. These procedures will help ensure fairness in scoring. Minimize, as far as possible, cues that will identify the owners of the papers; at the very least remove the names. It is all too easy to allow extraneous knowledge about a student to influence

the marking of that paper. Such precautions, too, should help to
assure minority students that the marking process is free of discrimination. Write out an ideal answer ahead of time and ask a colleague to do likewise; combine the two into a standard with which
students' replies can be compared. Complete the reading and scoring
of a given question for all the papers before going to another question. Score each item on a point scale without reference to a letter
grade.

Testing Frequency

As for the frequency of administering tests and its influence
on learning, two recent studies provide some very helpful insights.
Gaynor and Millham (1976) found that students who received
weekly tests answered significantly more course examination questions than did those who received only mid-term and final examinations. This study was a bit unusual in that the goals of the course
were reported; they and the tests were aimed at much more than
recall or recognition of facts. The central focus of the course was on
process rather than content; as one example of emphasis, students
were required to question and evaluate critically the current methods by which psychologists go about confronting and investigating
major concerns. Very serious efforts were made to prepare test items
that measured something other than knowledge of facts:

> According to the "frustration-aggression" model, the
> more children are punished, the more strongly they will
> want to misbehave (i.e., the more frustration, the more
> they will be aggressive). Some parents of children are
> interviewed with a tape recorder, and each family is
> given a "punishing" score. The teachers of the children
> write short essays describing each child, and each child
> is given a "misbehavior" score. Suppose that there is a
> significant trend ($r = .54$, $p < .01$) for children with
> high "misbehavior" scores to have parents with high
> "punishing" scores. From this one study, we can con-
> clude that: (a) the model is proved, (b) the model is

disproved, (c) the model is supported and fits the available data, (d) none of the above [Gaynor and Millham, 1976, p. 313].

In the other investigation (Dorsel, 1977), two pertinent findings emerged. First, students who had taken equivalent forms of
quizzes until a predetermined criterion (score) was attained performed better on an end-of-course exam than did students who took
a given quiz only once (see Chapter Six). Second, students who
took several short tests performed better on an end-of-course exam
than did students who took the same questions and the same number
of them massed into fewer but longer tests. (These current findings
are quite consistent with those of similar studies over the years:
Frequent testing enhances learning.)

At least some small schools are more accommodating of these
testing practices than are the large ones. The pattern of (1) a final
examination only, (2) a final examination and a mid-term, or (3)
a final examination and at least two hour-long tests account for only
30 percent of testing at the two KCRCHE schools (McNames,
1977). On the other hand, 68 percent of the testing at the University of Illinois is accounted for by this pattern (Spencer and Stallings, 1970).

It should go without saying that comfortable seating and
adequate lighting and ventilation are necessary for optimum performance; testing conditions must be such that no student can get
help from another.

Epilogue

The assessment of student achievement is an inordinately
difficult and time-consuming task. Faculties should not be expected
to shoulder all the responsibility for improvement, although I believe we should press for reforms. The institution should provide
such support as materials, clerical assistance, and funds for workshops and consultation with testing specialists. At the department
level, there should be emphasis on peer review of tests and increas-

ing use of test banks. It is here that computers can be of incalculable benefit because departments of the same discipline but in different institutions can be tied together easily. Questions that go into the computer can, of course, receive extensive review and editing for both clarity and quality. Investments of time and effort by a single faculty member will be reduced markedly. I am inclined to think that some system of this sort is the way out—few faculty will ever have sufficient time to devote to test construction.

In the meantime, the burgeoning wave of serious public criticism now being directed toward standardized testing may forbode similar criticism of classroom tests. Ralph Nader is blasting the products of the Educational Testing Service, and at least one bill has been introduced in Congress—The Testing Reform Act of 1977—by Michael J. Harrington. H. R. 6776 states: "The Congress finds that . . . standardized tests play a major role in education despite the fact that the reliability of these tests is uncertain, and the results of such tests are often misleading and at best can give only an approximate evaluation of an individual's abilities. It is, therefore, the intent of Congress in enacting this Act to enable test subjects to more fully exercise their rights with respect to standardized testing, and to make test subjects and persons who use such tests more fully aware of the implications of using such tests in education."

The bill provides penalties unless the standard error of measurement is reported along with test scores; this statement must be included also: "These scores are approximations. The standard error of measurement reported with each score represents the statistical probability of the test subject achieving a score within the indicated range on repeated administrations of this examination." Penalties are provided, too, for failing to inform the test subjects prior to the examination "the manner in which the test is scored, the statistical accuracy of such score, and the significance of such score in terms of the skills and knowledge it represents."

This bill asserts that standardized tests tend toward unreliability and invalidity. The facts of the matter are that scores from them are misused often. Although difficult to document and although some documentation has been offered in this chapter, most classroom tests are much more unreliable and invalid than are standardized ones. Moreover, scores from classroom tests are more abused than are standardized test scores, as when a grade point average is used as a screening device. A student with a 3.50 grade-point average receives further consideration, whereas one with a 3.49 does not.

Finally, if we as faculty, both individually and collectively, do not improve assessment practices, it seems quite likely that there will be direct intrusions from without. Already the courts are beginning to intervene, and although the intervention has been mostly in graduate and professional programs, undergraduates who see textbooks on educational measurement that are allotting increasing space to many of these issues, especially the Civil Rights aspects of them, may seek redress.

The case of Laurence Levine (1976) is an excellent example of court intervention in academic matters and the substitution of the judgment of the court for that of the faculty. This young man failed a major course during his second year of medical school, and although he could have been dismissed at that time, he was allowed to remain by repeating all second-year courses. He was admonished that a repeated performance of marginal quality would result in harsh measures.

Levine passed all the courses on the second try, but in each one he ranked at or near the bottom of the class. Such performance was judged marginal and out he went. It developed that the concept of marginality had been debated by the faculty over many years, and yet it remained undefined. A Superior Court of the District of Columbia ruled that the student should be allowed to continue his medical studies on the grounds that "what the Medical School may not do—any more than any other institution, public or private—is enter into a contractual arrangement with an individual upon which that individual reasonably relies, and then provide, to the individual's own detriment, its own subjective interpretation of the agreement after the fact and without prior notice." (p. 10) In other words, an institution must be clear and specific about what is meant by marginal performance and communicate that fact to students before courses rather than after. If we simply abbreviate the term *marginal,* then the parallel with grades is obvious.

In commenting on this case and related ones, McInnis (1977) observed that courts do not want to substitute their judgment for that of the faculty in academic evaluation but that courts need reassurance that faculties are clear about assessment criteria. Perhaps if faculties become more knowledgeable about testing practices than now seems to be the case and also attempt to follow the suggestions made in this chapter, the courts may be reassured.

5

❀ ❀ ❀ ❀ ❀ ❀ ❀ ❀ ❀ ❀

C. R. Carlson

Feedback for Learning

❀ ❀ ❀ ❀ ❀ ❀ ❀ ❀ ❀ ❀

We are all familiar with college-level courses that consist of readings, lectures, an assigned paper or project, and tests. Aside from the lectures, most information from instructors to students is limited to grades or scores on papers, quizzes, hour exams, and the final course grade. Information of this sort all comes well *after* students have been evaluated on their work; if there is any impact on learning, it will come in the next phase of the course, during the next term, or in some follow-up activity on the job. But such grade-oriented post-mortems contribute little to student learning. On the other hand, providing information that students can use to improve themselves *during* the course may be one of the most important teaching functions. Such information guides students while they can still take corrective action and also gives the teacher clues when a change in approach may be needed.

125

In order to differentiate between grading and this other information the teacher may provide during a course, some educators borrow the term *feedback*. I define it as *authoritative information students receive that will reinforce or modify responses to instruction and guide them more efficiently in attaining the goals of the course*. Some schools also use feedback *from* students for evaluation and improvement of the educational system (curriculum and faculty), but this chapter will concentrate on feedback that aids student learning.

McKeachie (1976, p. 824), one of the best-known writers on college teaching, recently asserted "that the more feedback given, the more learning results." Bloom (1976, p. 212) has stressed the need for a system of feedback to the teacher and the students that "can reveal errors in learning shortly after they occur . . . a self-correcting system so that errors made at one time can be corrected before they are compounded with later errors." For some time, Gagné (1970, p. 315) has included feedback as a major component of teaching, stressing that "some means or other must be provided during instruction for [the student] to perceive the results of his activity . . . some feedback that enables him to realize that his performance is 'correct'."

Unfortunately, except for grades, most college teachers do not consider feedback important and rarely provide it. Yet many different forms of feedback can contribute to learning, and generally, the more feedback, the more effective the teaching. Feedback is especially effective when used to prevent errors and to provide a student with direction and a sense of achievement.

Included in this chapter are suggestions for establishing the proper conditions for feedback and descriptions of a number of types of feedback that can be used in both large and small classes. Some of the types of feedback discussed, such as ungraded practice sessions, instructor and student critiques, videotaping and graphic rating scales, apply best to skill oriented courses. Emphasis is given to types of feedback such as diagnostic tests, comments on outlines and drafts of written assignments, class discussions, group problem assignments, and suggestions for how to study a particular discipline for courses in which the objectives are less precise. For large classes, suggestions are made for preparing students to make their own assessment of their work by careful specification of the objectives and expectations of the course, providing examples and standards for student work and giving students access to the instructor's check list or grading guide.

Feedback in this chapter differs from Chapter Four on classroom testing principally in that the feedback is part of the teaching rather than the assessment process. The feedback emphasizes progress toward the course objectives and the expectations of the instructor rather than assessment and comparisons among students. Other forms of feedback are discussed in Chapter Six on using PSI.

Academic Instructor School

Planned feedback to students is an important part of the curriculum at the Academic Instructor School (AIS), a part of the Air University located at Maxwell Air Force Base in Montgomery, Alabama. Because there are several differences between AIS and most civilian instructor training schools, I would like to describe it briefly before discussing our experience with feedback, which can be applied in the college classroom.

AIS came into being in the late 1940s, primarily to train instructors for Air Force Reserve Officers Training Corps (ROTC) who were not nearly as well qualified academically as they are today. The school still trains instructors for ROTC in its two summer classes, but the other five classes a year service a wide range of instructors from all major commands of the Air Force, including men and women from the Air Force Institute of Technology and the Air Force Academy (both degree-granting institutions). Graduates instruct in a wide range of schools, including leadership academies and the Air War College, with instruction often at the graduate level. The word *academic* in the school's name differentiates it from other Air Force instructor training schools responsible for technical and flying training—entirely separate operations that are conducted elsewhere.

The typical AIS student is a college graduate (usually an officer, a noncommissioned officer, or an Air Force civilian), whose primary training has been in another discipline. The five-week, intensive course (212 hours of instruction with suggested accreditation of 9 semester hours) is a survey of teaching–learning theory and practice at the level of an upper-division college course. The school is frequently called on to give workshops in faculty development for other universities and professional organizations, and a limited number of civilian faculty members are invited to attend the school as observers. The editor of this book was perhaps the first to attend. The school's faculty all hold graduate degrees, with a number at the doctoral level.

Apart from the quality and homogeneity of its students, a principal feature of the AIS is the emphasis on practice with different teaching methods. Each student presents four practice teaching exercises (PTs) to different groups of students and is evaluated by different instructors. Typical methods are the lecture, the guided discussion, the case, and the teaching interview. For each of the PTs, the student is scheduled for workshop sessions in lesson planning and delivery skills with his or her "homeroom" instructor. Although students take pre- and posttests and unit surveys (like hour exams), these examinations are designed purely as learning experiences to allow students to see their progress, and no examination grades are awarded.

Despite the lack of a formal grading system, honor graduates, or an "order of merit" (all features of other service schools), student dedication and morale are high, with astonishingly few motivation problems. And despite the pressure of a five-day, forty-hour-a-week class schedule, all students spend appreciable amounts of their free time on school work, so intense is the peer pressure to succeed.

Compared to the problems of motivation at the typical university, AIS may seem utopian in its approach and atmosphere; on the contrary, the school is highly structured and intensely practical, with feedback given freely and systematically at every turn. Instruction in AIS and the schools where AIS graduates teach must be effective and efficient. The time students spend away from operational or staff duties must be used to the best advantage, and military students soon become impatient with instruction that does not make a tangible and direct contribution to their professional development. When these considerations are combined with the insistence of the members of Congress that military education and training costs be kept as low as possible, Air Force educators are forced to adopt feedback techniques that prevent errors, improve student performance, and increase the rate of learning. The AIS students receive so much feedback that they, in turn, become very critical of all faculty performance, a reciprocal arrangement that keeps the faculty on its toes.

Feedback at AIS

Students start to receive feedback almost from the first day at the school when they spend an hour meeting the "homeroom" seminar, a group of seven to nine plus an instructor. This time spent in "breaking the ice," discovering the commonality and diversity of the student group, is repeated each time the student is assigned to a different group to give his or her PTs, what the school calls "scatter" seminars. This opportunity for feedback among students is unusual in the typical college classroom, even in graduate seminars, where students may attend the same class for an entire semester and not really know one another. Getting to know others in the group sets the stage for communication within the group, rather than having all the communications one-way, from instructor to student.

Another instance of feedback occurs early in the first week of the course when students give impromptu speeches of three to five minutes; these are video recorded and played back and are also critiqued by the instructor and the homeroom members. The speeches are not graded, because the emphasis is on reinforcing good communication techniques and identifying areas for improvement. As the students are all involved in the speeches and critiques, they profit from all the feedback, whether it be directed to them or not. Later there is a similar process with short, prepared speeches, also delivered to the homeroom and also video recorded; these acquaint the students with the AIS lesson format and reinforce their self-confidence in speaking in a low-threat environment. For all student presentations, the instructor uses fairly detailed graphic rating scales augmented with his own written and verbal comments, which make the feedback as precise as possible. The critique is also video recorded for subsequent review by the student, either on the classroom monitor or in a carrel.

Between these formal opportunities for feedback, the students receive continual informal feedback from their instructor in workshop sessions designed to help all students write their lesson plans. One feedback tactic used in these workshops is to have each student write his or her version of the assignment (a lesson objective, a series of main teaching points, sample questions) on heavy acetate with a grease pencil. (Recycled, exposed x-ray film works well.) The instructor then reviews each student's work by projecting it via an overhead projector; the entire class suggests revisions; and the student reworks the proposal until it meets with general agreement. How different from the average college student chewing on a pencil at a dormitory desk waiting for inspiration to strike!

Once the general teaching outline is set, students work up lesson plans and test items independently, with further feedback from the instructor at inclass conferences or, if necessary, after normal class sessions. Office conferences are infrequent up to this stage because time for feedback is scheduled as a formal part of the curriculum.

When the lesson plan is complete, students practice ten- to twelve-minute portions of the lesson before the homeroom seminar or try out a line of questioning and again receive feedback from both class and instructor. When students finally teach their lesson "for record" in a higher-threat environment of different students and a different instructor in the scatter seminar, they have a better-than-average chance for success because of the constructive feedback already received. The PTs taught to the scatter group are thirty-five minutes long, leaving time for a ten-minute critique. Again there is self-confrontation with the video recording, which includes a recording of the critique, and the completed set of graphic rating scales, which aid the scatter instructor in the critique. This written critique is sent back to the homeroom instructor to become part of a cumulative record that provides a base for future feedback when more information on student performance has been made available.

This process of feedback from the low-threat homeroom instructor in practice sessions followed by critical but still constructive feedback from the higher-threat scatter instructor repeats itself for each of the four PTs in a cycle that takes about a week.

Interspersed with this activity, students encounter other feedback in the form of three unit surveys and a posttest. Again, formal classroom time is scheduled for a thorough review of each test item both for content and for the form of the item (as writing test questions is one of the important subjects in the curriculum). Posttest and pretest scores are compared. These test discussions provide both reinforcement and feedback, as students compare their performance with those of their peers. No sterile testing followed by an impersonal letter grade on a bulletin board!

A further feedback technique is the final PT in which students stay in the home seminar to present a forty-five minute PT that has been developed with little or no help and with practice on the students' own time. Rather than neglecting this final assignment because of the low-threat environment, students often work even harder to impress their fellows. Although they often teach a subject from the curriculum of the school where they will be assigned, students go out of their way to choose topics that are interesting or challenging, often combining methods freely. The final PT thus becomes a true culminating experience. Feedback is provided by the homeroom instructor in a private conference, which includes a review of progress from the first day of school and possible suggestions for future development.

Final feedback at AIS is a quiz show, modeled on the "College Bowl," which is telecast by means of closed-circuit cable during the noon hour of the last days of the course from the school's television studio. The questions are all taken from required lectures and readings and thus reinforce the curriculum to the entire school. (Viewing the program is optional, but most students cut their lunch short so they can watch in the studio or in a classroom.) Each home seminar elects two quiz show participants who compete with other seminars in an elimination contest. The winners are duly recognized, and in this one instance in the school, feedback deliberately pits one student's achievement against another's. The quiz show becomes an opportunity for the exceptional student who thrives on competition, while at the same time not destroying the self-confidence of the less competitive students, who may still, in their own way, have profited greatly from the course. Mature adults become as excited as youngsters during the quiz show, and when a recent class president (the senior officer student, in this case a full colonel) was also the quiz show winner, he gloated like a proud papa, showing those youngsters there was life in the old boy yet!

Still another kind of feedback—among instructors and their supervisors—occurs in weekly faculty conferences where a very open atmosphere of participatory management encourages frank discussion of common problems. Teaching by the instructors is frequently observed by colleagues, both live and on videotape, and new instructors are scheduled to observe experienced ones. The faculty board, the director, and the commandant are continually bombarded with fresh data on which to base academic decisions and are in no danger of suffering from an ivory-tower syndrome. The continual quality and variety of feedback—both to students and among faculty—is one factor that makes the AIS an exciting place in which to teach and to be taught, and everyone appreciates the openness of a classroom environment that plans for feedback.

The Feedback Process

Feedback is important to students. Students seek individualized guidance and correction because it is efficient. Whether students are in a technical school, a military staff course, or a graduate school, feedback aids learning and provides a sense of accomplishment that can carry the recipient through to higher academic achievement or to greater confidence on the job. Feedback requires observation and evaluation of a student response or performance, which, in turn, is based upon earlier instruction. The instructor and frequently the student sense the response, and the student response can be modified or corrected as needed. The student can be "corrected" or advised in time to shape or modify the final outcome. Feedback may be given in an oral or written critique, coaching, supervision of performance, review of responses to tests, or in reaction to progress in either individual or group problem solving.

Clearly, the number of students enrolled determines the extent to which the instructor can look at individual responses and make corrections. Although there is no doubt that Mark Hopkins was a stimulating teacher, most college teachers feel they, too, could do much better with one student on the end of a log. This ideal student-to-teacher ratio does not exist in today's colleges. Some teachers, faced with large classes and less-than-satisfactory class-room arrangements, have given up on any notion of giving indi-vidualized feedback to student work. On the other hand, there are teachers who have experienced the results of feedback while teach-ing small groups, and they are looking for ways—and the time—to provide similar guidance to students in larger classes.

Some college instructors have grown comfortable with large classes and the standard lecture method because of the large number of research results in which there was no demonstrated advantage for small classes. McKeachie (1972, p. 3), who has conducted several studies of his own and has followed this question closely over the years, came to a new conclusion after his last major review of the literature: "If one considers the basic outcomes of retention, problem solving, and attitude differentiation, the weight of the evidence clearly favors small classes." McKeachie further asserts that "in large groups more time is devoted to lecturing than in smaller classes." With large classes the easiest thing to do is to lecture. Although teachers in small classes may, and often do, lecture, they seem less apt to do so. McKeachie (1972, p. 4), finds that "small classes are more important for some students than others." But of more significance, "the importance of class size depends upon educational goals." Although large classes are as efficient as small classes in communicating knowledge, they are not as effective for retention, attitude change, and critical thinking.

There are usually two stages in the feedback process: The instructor gathers evidence of student attainment and then relays corrective information back to the student. There is no way to cut short what can be relatively long and time-consuming. However, with imagination and the use of educational hardware where ap-propriate, it is possible to devise feedback situations in which the information comes back directly to the student. This shortcut can save instructor time and still be very useful if the student is prepared to handle the information and make his or her own corrections. Several suggestions in this chapter take this form.

The idea of telling students their "correctness" is not new. In courses in which correct answers serve as check points and there

are agreed-on steps for arriving at those answers, the technique is
routine. Mathematics and physics students find the correct answers
in the backs of texts. For years it has been common practice in
these subjects for students to work at the chalkboard, with the instructor checking their work and correcting it. In typing classes, the
number of words typed per minute gives clear feedback, and the
instructor watches student technique to detect and correct flaws
before they can interfere with correct habits. When skills are taught,
coaching—a basic form of feedback—is readily accepted as appropriate. It has not been as widely recognized that students need
similar monitoring and guidance when they are dealing with controversial social problems, reading complex materials, or analyzing
economic trends. In courses in which such requirements exist—
most courses in colleges and universities—imagination and effort are
needed to accomplish this feedback step.

College teachers have tended not to concern themselves with
teaching students how to study or to provide students with feedback
on progress with the content of the course. Individual differences in
achievement are often considered merely a reflection of differences
in inherent traits or abilities students bring with them, which cannot
be modified in college. In Air Force schools we have found that
students will profit from suggestions on how to study that are based
on samples of their work. The college teacher needs diagnostic information on possible student difficulty with the study process as
well as with the content of the course. Smaller classes would help,
but they are not likely to be arranged. With deliberate planning for
feedback, however, the instructor can improve learning not only in
smaller classes, which are skill oriented, but with relatively large
classes and in courses in which the outcomes are not as directly
observed.

Grading or Feedback?

To illustrate some of the issues involved in planning for
feedback, let us consider for a moment a class in the Academic Instructor School. A student has just finished teaching a thirty-five
minute lesson to seven student peers. Ten minutes is available for a

critique by the instructor. The instructor is known for his excellent lectures and special training in speech.

In most schools the instructor would be expected to grade student performance and then provide as many constructive suggestions as possible that would apply to other students in the class as well. In this situation which function would have priority, grading or student learning? How should the instructor proceed? What should the course planner do to provide the best results for both grading and learning? Can good results be expected for both purposes?

It is the rare student whose foremost concern is not the grade. With few exceptions, the reaction is the same for both enlisted and officer students, for high school graduates and students with graduate degrees. The sensitive and skillful instructor will recognize this preoccupation and try to minimize it. At the outset, the instructor may tell students whether they passed. However, merely indicating satisfactory performance will not be sufficient for students who want to excel. Such students will look for grade-related indicators: either adjectives such as *excellent, good, outstanding* or points toward final class standing or a grade, and this information has limited, if any, value in helping shape or improve the next performance because it does not tell the student specifically what to do to improve. A common penalty students pay is that they do not listen to the feedback for learning.

A second penalty results from the pressure on the instructor to provide the kind of feedback the students seek rather than prescriptive information that will improve future performance. Many instructors feel that their primary task is to make value judgments in such situations, to reduce these observations and judgments to grades and report the grades to students. The student need is satisfied, but the potential for learning is seriously reduced.

One consequence of this pressure is an influence on the type of observation form that might be devised for a student performance or product. If grades are the primary objective, the scales will contain numbers or single adjectives such as *average* and *superior,* arranged in order of merit to assist in differentiating among the students. On the other hand, if the instructor wishes to emphasize development and improvement, the scales will be descriptive and phrases will be used that are typical of performance at different skill levels, phrases that also indicate what is expected as a student advances. For example, in a course that emphasizes development and improvement, three of the levels on a five-point scale for rating the "motivation" step in a speech might be described as follows:

- Level 1: "Lacking or inappropriate; little or no attempt to show relationship of subject to listener needs."
- Level 3: "Appealed to personal and social needs and showed benefits of subject."
- Level 5: "Realistic; relationship of material to audience is challenging."

These descriptions show both the student and the instructor what is expected at each level of competence or development. In most applications, numbers are assigned to descriptions to form a "graphic rating scale," which can then be useful for both feedback and grading.

Proper Conditions for Feedback

Student preoccupation with grades is well known to all experienced teachers. Competition and the selection process make this preoccupation even more pronounced as students advance. What can instructors do to recapture the attention of students for feedback for learning?

One suggestion is to separate grading from feedback for learning. Busy teachers who already feel they are devoting too much time to testing and evaluation will probably wonder if such a notion is practical and if the effort will help students. Obviously, only instructors and their students can answer this question. However, the positive student response to well-planned feedback experiences can be very convincing, particularly when the suggestions from the instructor are based on student work that is not graded.

Fortunately, in many courses a self-contained grading system already exists in the form of tests made up of questions from an item bank. The questions are kept secure and any attempt to teach by reviewing the test items would compromise the grading system. Feedback plans need not interfere with such an arrangement, and the very independence or separateness of the testing process can improve the feedback for learning.

The notion of separating the grading and teaching functions is not new. Visiting examiners have been used successfully at Swarthmore (Milton and Edgerly, 1976, p. 53) and at Colorado College. At the University of Chicago, a Board of Examiners functioned for two decades (Bloom, 1954). Under that plan there was an opportunity for the teacher and the student to work together to excel in the eyes of a third-person examiner. More recently, the authors of a policy paper written for *Change* magazine recommended a system of "detached" evaluation, "judged by others in the university or perhaps by outsiders" (Group for Human Development in Higher Education, 1974, p. 59). The authors perceived a conflict in roles when the teacher is both the helper and the certifier and described a plan whereby the amount of grading done by members of an academic department would be approximately the same, but they would be grading students taught by someone else.

It may not be practical to arrange for a colleague to be the evaluator. In the following example, the grading and feedback functions were not assigned to different individuals, but the feedback step was kept quite separate, and increased acceptance by the students was achieved. In one school of the Air University, each student completes as many as twenty-nine written assignments and fourteen assigned speeches during a ten-month course. The evaluation policy has been to provide direct feedback for improvement with as little threat as possible. Grades are not assigned on these individual assignments, but students receive oral feedback, completed rating forms on their effort, and comments on the text of the papers. As a separate step, the instructor who does critiques for these individual efforts in the first of four phases of the course assigns a phase grade for writing and another for speaking before the student moves on to work with the instructor in the next phase.

Another promising means of arriving at grades with a

minimum of disruption for feedback plans is the trend toward
grading "contracts." When the student and teacher agree early in
the course on the evidence of accomplishment that the student will
produce, the teacher usually is relieved of giving interim or "part-
score" grades until the final product has been submitted. The contract may provide for grading by another instructor. While the
course is in progress, the teacher can devote full attention to feedback for the improvement of the final submission. The discussion
in Chapter Eight should be considered when planning for feedback.

In some classes it is possible to establish a simple "pass–
fail" grading policy. Under such a policy much less attention is
given to the grade, and the instructor can devote more time to
teaching and feedback. Since some provisions are still retained for
determining a failing grade, the remaining grading procedures
should be kept separate from the principal feedback process to the
maximum extent. There are many instructors who view "pass–fail"
and experiments with eliminating the failing grade as an erosion of
academic standards. Some feel the incentive of grades and the
possibility of failure are needed, and they hesitate to depend on the
intrinsic interest and value of their courses for motivation. Once
these instructors have seen students respond positively and show
evidence of learning more, they will be more willing to devote class
or other teaching time to feedback.

Any steps the college teacher can take to isolate the grading
process will improve feedback for learning. Instructors in a variety
of disciplines in several colleges and universities are already separating the two functions to a significant degree, to the benefit of their
students.

Feedback When Objectives Are Less Precise

The techniques discussed to this point apply most directly
in those aspects of college courses in which the objectives can be
precisely stated or observable student skills are developed. For example, feedback is often an integral part of teaching mathematics,
speech, music, or laboratory skills. It is much less likely that feedback is provided in courses, or for those objectives within a course,

in which the outcomes are not so specific. In a school of business the precise objectives in accounting are quite different from those in management or business law. Philosophy, literature, and the social sciences are other examples where providing feedback is less common. Four techniques that have proven successful with such objectives include tests, written assignments, class discussion, and group problem-solving techniques. Additional suggestions are to be found in the section on Feedback in Large Classes.

Perhaps the most common means of providing feedback is some version of a written test. Even though the technique is fairly common, the tests are often not designed for feedback, and there is an understandable reluctance to review and discuss test items that will be used with succeeding classes.

One of the most useful descriptions of how to design tests for feedback can be found in the *Handbook on Formative and Summative Evaluation of Student Learning* (Bloom, Hastings, and Madaus, 1971). In this book, testing for grades is designated as *summative* (see Chapter Four of this text), whereas the term *formative* describes testing for instruction and student learning. Systematic procedures are described for building both kinds of tests. Most college teachers probably do not have the resources available for building an additional set of "formative" tests with diagnostic scoring keys. However, the instructor can write informal quizzes with relatively simple true-false or short-answer questions—*these are not to be graded*. Wrong answers will reveal student misconceptions. By correcting the quizzes in class and by bringing out the "why" or the "because," the instructor can bring the class to a fairly common level before proceeding with new work. An occasional open-book test may give some insight into study habits and ability to generalize when the facts are readily available. If possible, the quizzes should represent the sampling pattern and content emphasis of the examinations for grades, thus making the student more aware of the instructor's priorities.

College students can benefit from a pretest—even a simple true-false form—to obtain an indication of their entry level. Often such tests are built around the myths or fallacies that exist about the course content. The following example of five true-false questions was designed by a member of the staff of Educational Testing Service (Dobbin, 1976) to introduce a unit in intelligence testing.

T   F   1. The IQ is a relatively stable index of native brightness or intelligence.

T   F   2. Children grow in intellect until they are about sixteen years old; then their intellect declines gradually from that point to senility.

T   F   3. Children with IQ's below 100 are to be regarded as subnormal.

T   F   4. A child with an IQ higher than 140 probably is a genius.

T   F   5. I can't change my child's IQ much, because if the test is any good it measures innate ability acquired through the genes.

As Dobbin says, all five are "dead wrong." It is now commonplace in colleges for adult students to appear who are returning to school after an interruption of several years (see Chapter Thirteen of this text). Often new information and earlier generalizations have changed, or the students may simply have forgotten earlier lessons. It can be useful to administer appropriate pretests such as vocabulary, geography, computational skills, grammar and punctuation, or sample items from prerequisite courses. Students are motivated and guided in their study from their results of such pretests. The same questions can also provide the instructor with an excellent discussion vehicle.

A second feedback vehicle—and one of the best—for classes in which the objectives are less easily measured is the written assignment. Unfortunately, often the only feedback the student receives is a grade. Making comments on written papers takes time and special training. Some instructors frankly recognize that teaching writing per se, particularly to advanced students, is a specialized field. Their feedback comments are based solely on the content once students have demonstrated a basic writing ability. Suggesting style books and making model papers available can be helpful in reaching an acceptable format so students can concentrate on the course objectives.

Some instructors allocate more time to student outlines and drafts than to the final product. Effort expended at the outline stage may well have more impact on learning. When the instructor is grading the final paper, little can be done to help students develop. An outline, including key references, can provide a feedback opportunity in time to help them make adjustments and profit from the instructor's experience. This procedure also makes it more difficult to employ a "ghost writer." Sharing the instructor's checklist or critique form with students can be as effective with written as with oral assignments. Students can do a great deal of "self-correcting," and the final grade will be easier to understand and accept.

Class discussion is another technique that is widely used when objectives are less precise. Discussion in class does provide feedback, but some cautions are in order about the validity of the information. Most experienced instructors can recall how impressions of students gained from class discussions can change when their written papers come in and the examinations are graded.

To make the most of this method, the discussion should be planned, in many respects as carefully as a lecture. Although spontaneous questions from students are useful, such questions can lead the instructor away from his or her objectives as a result of student premeditation. The instructor should plan the main questions and provide direction and feedback by periodically summarizing both student responses and instructor reactions. With small groups— twelve or less—discussions can provide feedback both to the instructor and to students. Even with a small number of students, however, obtaining a sufficient sample to correct or modify student reactions and progress requires skill. Better information for feedback can be expected from a series of class meetings with the same group.

Although classroom discussions have many advantages (see Chapter Three), a modification involving small group problem solving may be more effective for feedback. This approach may also be more practical with larger classes. Several small groups can be formed, and the feedback takes a different form. Some super-

ficial feedback may be obtained by listening to each group. The
primary information, however, would come from an assigned group
product, prepared under the direction of a group leader and
recorder.

Some examples of group projects in the AIS include developing rating scales, refining statements of several types of learning
objectives, writing test items, and describing the attributes of a
competent instructor. All students contribute to the final product,
and occasionally each student in the group is asked to submit his or
her own version of the conclusions of the group. A variation of this
approach is to ask the seminar group to collectively comment and
make suggestions on individual student work, such as draft test
items or samples of writing or speaking.

In this section, we have discussed four techniques that can
be effective in courses in which the objectives are less precise. Before
going on to additional feedback techniques for use with large
classes, a few general comments about written feedback, managing
the instructor's time, protecting student privacy, and accessibility of
the instructor are offered. Although it is not always possible, the
instructor should try to give feedback that "leaves a trace," such as
written comments on student papers. Comments written immediately adjacent to the phrase in question are ideal, although admittedly time consuming. Check marks on a completed rating scale
can be a helpful substitute. Another practical measure is to develop
a list of the most common corrective or prescriptive statements and
merely write the number on the student paper where appropriate.

There is no question that providing feedback, like so many
other improvements in teaching, takes time. To find time may require managing time more efficiently and changing to different
methods of initially presenting the course content. Obviously, if
virtually all the class time is devoted to lecturing, no feedback time
in class will be available. Oral presentations to either large or small
classes are not very efficient if the same material is available in
written form; such presentations can take two or three times as long
as reading in some disciplines. Although some lecture time will
probably always be appropriate, using assigned readings, learning
centers, and other techniques for initial exposure to the information

can free class time. Techniques such as those described in Chapter Six should be considered as an alternative to the lecture for presenting course material.

The conscientious instructor who is trying to save time may forget the importance of protecting the privacy and self-esteem of students. Written comments on papers, completed observation forms, and similar feedback should be returned directly to the student without an intermediary. Avoid discussing one student's private comments with another, even when it may look like a teaching opportunity. When serious academic counseling is in order, use the office, not the classroom or the halls. When good conditions for feedback have been established, students will feel free and secure enough to respond openly—even to make mistakes— but their personal privacy should be considered in planning.

A word or two about the general accessibility of the instructor, including office hours, may be in order. To be equally accessible to all students, some instructors poll their students before setting the time for office hours for the term. Also, feedback techniques may require additional office time. Instructors often unintentionally let some students monopolize their time to the exclusion of others equally deserving. It has been helpful to ask an observer to come to class occasionally to check the instructor's distribution of questions and the responses to student questions. Some students want to ask all the questions and other students who need feedback may be ignored. Managing an instructor's time includes distributing both class time and office time to give all students equal opportunity to interact while retaining a "cushion" for those students who may need extra attention.

Feedback in Large Classes

Large classes pose special problems in providing feedback and may be the most important reason why college instruction so often fits the pattern of readings, lectures, written papers, and examinations—with grades as the only feedback. When working with a large class, even the most skillful instructor has difficulty because often the sampling of student responses on which to base feedback is fragmentary and unreliable. Also, time to work with individual students is scarce if available at all. Two of the techniques from the previous section, using tests and group projects, can be used with some measure of success. Written assignments require an inordinate amount of instructor time if feedback comments are provided, and a great deal of imagination and the help of teaching assistants are required if discussion is to be used for feedback. Although the suggestions that follow are far from perfect for classes of, say, twenty or more, they have been used to good advantage and show particular promise for preparing students to make their own corrections.

The first suggestion is to inform the students completely and specifically about the objectives and expectations of the course. For college courses in which the objectives are not quantitative or are less easily observed, this step is analogous to the modeling provided to students learning a skill. Prepare students well so they can compare their progress with your published goals. For example, if you tell students at the outset that they will be expected to "define the five characteristics of evaluation" and "state the relationship between validity and reliability of a test," they can be expected to proceed with little further "correction" or modification from you. To be sure, a detailed listing of the course objectives may be so voluminous as to discourage students, and it may be desirable to give them out in smaller increments. The statements of objectives are not intended to duplicate the readings but to guide students by clearly indicating priorities and emphases. When objectives are presented properly, many more students should be able to match the "best" students in the ability to see what is needed to reach the instructor's expectations.

Along with the stated objectives, students need examples of the type of problems to be solved. The instructor should aim for the efficiency of the answers in the back of mathematics texts. When it is not possible to see each student's work, provide examples of the "method" or "process" used to arrive at the answer. Then students should be asked to "show their work" when solving problems. In the social sciences, there is no single best answer to most problems. In such a case, it is helpful to provide the criteria used to evaluate and compare solutions. The fact that a discipline deals with "shades of gray" or "best" solutions does not decrease the need for guidance.

Students should be prepared to note "the principal disadvantages" of a particular course of action or to rank alternatives in the same way they might be asked to choose the "best" alternative in a multiple-choice test.

There are college courses such as art, creative writing, and musical composition in which this much structure might be considered inhibiting. Even in such courses, students will benefit from a clear explanation of the instructor's expectations and standards for acceptability to help keep their study and creative effort in focus. Portions of the earlier reference on summative and formative evaluation (Bloom, Hastings, and Madaus, 1971) can be useful, particularly Chap. 15, "Language Arts"; Chap. 17, "Art Education"; Chap. 20, "Literature"; and Chap. 21, "Writing."

In addition to the statements of objectives and samples of problems, guidance to students in large classes should include the instructor's checklists or observation scales. They will be particularly helpful for feedback if the observation scales contain descriptions of the levels or stages in development such as those presented earlier. In many courses, the ultimate level of achievement sought—particularly for gifted students—is to produce perceptive critics of performance or products in the subject area. The observation scales need not, and for feedback purposes probably should not, be related to grades, even though students will press the instructor for that kind of information. The example of a rating or observation scale that follows indicates how the descriptions in the scale can give students information for judging their own product, whether or not the instructor is available.

In the Instructional Aids Laboratory of the AIS, students are taught how to prepare a color "transparency" for an overhead projector by the "color-lift" process, working from color photographs in a magazine. The objective is to set the standard and permit student self-evaluation. The product is evaluated as "satisfactory" or "unsatisfactory" on the following factors: (1) free from distracting* fingerprints, (2) free from distracting scratches, (3) color transfer complete, free from blank spots or bubbles, (4) distracting clay residue removed, and (5) completed within six minutes. Student use

*Distracting is defined on the scale as "anything that interferes with, or draws attention away from, the visual content of the slide."

of a product-rating scale for self-evaluation not only relieves the busy teacher, but is more convincing and probably better retained.

Students welcome an opportunity to compare their work with an authoritative standard. All of us who had the experience can remember using a piece of litmus paper to test the acidity of an unknown chemical solution. Test-answer sheets have been developed that can be peeled back to reveal the key, and the better programmed texts and computer-based learning programs make use of this principle of timely reinforcement.

Another suggestion related to the use of observation or rating scales is to ask the students to devise portions of the scale themselves. Although a faculty-developed scale is useful for the students, the opportunity to construct a scale—usually in a small group of students—can be a significant step toward better performance. To save time, some teachers start the students with poorly constructed scales to modify, or partial scales that can both be improved and completed. Samples prepared by previous classes can be useful. As the students formulate descriptions of the various levels of competence for the rating scale, they review and better understand the standards. Advanced students can start with the objectives for a class period and prepare an observation or rating scale. Both performance scales and product scales make useful exercises, the choice depending upon the objectives of the course.

In similar fashion, students can be asked to write test items from the course outline, from written objectives, or from the lecture and readings. It is probably best to start with simple true-false questions or easy multiple-choice questions where the alternatives are essentially true-false items grouped around a general topic. When students attempt to write multiple-choice questions, they are virtually forced to read with greater understanding. Student-prepared items, with an occasional "straw vote" on the keyed answer and the alternatives, can provide useful feedback. Selected items can be projected on a screen, and the large class can be divided into smaller groups for discussion and comment. Student incentive can be increased by including a certain number of items prepared by students in the course examinations.

A final suggestion, which is applicable for any size class, is to provide instruction and feedback on how to study. Each academic discipline has its own particular requirements, such as library research, computational skills, variable reading rates, laboratory technique, and note taking. Even among the most successful students, there are differences in approach to a discipline, and instructors often are not aware that students may not know how to study efficiently. One of the most common weaknesses is poor or inflexible reading habits. Often students who are oriented to science or mathematics will apply their slow, methodical reading habits to a survey course and not know that a faster rate is not only possible but more appropriate. After a check on the time students need to complete a reading assignment, referral to a reading clinic may be in order. The student may not need a complete course to develop a more appropriate reading rate. Often students are able to work on assigned readings in the clinic.

Success in college courses often requires memorizing a considerable amount of information such as classification categories in the sciences, chronologies of events, and formulas. If so, tell the students and give examples of mnemonic devices and proven ways to aid recall.

Taking notes, both in class and from assigned readings, can also be a source of difficulty for students, and feedback is easily provided. Some students laboriously take detailed notes on the examples and support materials, when broader generalizations are the objective. It will help to point out the kinds of questions that will be asked on the tests and to relate note taking to the course objectives. There also may be a need to indicate the relative priority among the suggested readings. It is helpful to provide examples of how the instructor took notes on a sample from the assigned readings. Some lecturers furnish a "note-taking device," which consists of an incomplete outline that the student can fill in while listening. This device eases the pressure on the student to reconstruct the lecturer's outline. Students are able to concentrate on the major generalizations and are more likely to interrupt their note taking to answer questions and participate in the feedback process with the instructor.

Students often go to a teaching assistant for suggestions on how to study. It can be very helpful to schedule a voluntary or optional period in which successful graduates (preferably more than one) can discuss study methods used in a particular course. Feedback on study habits can be important. Not only the marginal student but those expecting a "C" can be helped to achieve more.

Instructor Feedback Skills

Whether teaching large classes or small, there are certain skills that are useful to the instructor, skills that are easily developed once the purpose is recognized. One of the most important is to reduce—or remove, if possible—the inherent threat and negative student reaction to evaluation and feedback. It is not sufficient to praise first in a critique, for example. Students detect this pattern very early, and it has been said that the only one fooled is the instructor.

We suggested previously that the grading process should be separate, if possible, with provision for planned evaluation sessions included solely for feedback. When grades must be given as part of a critique, get the grade out of the way early, at least in general terms. "You passed, that's for sure," or "It will be better than a C, but I'm not sure how much better" are useful opening statements. Keeping comments as impersonal as possible reduces the threat. Small differences in approach can help a student on the defensive. Rather than placing all the responsibility on the student with a statement such as, "You did not make it clear," the instructor can be more helpful by saying, "I did not understand." Instead of "What you did wrong," or "What you should have done," the performance can be separated from the student by saying what might have been done to make the speech better. Some corrections and suggestions can be presented as deficiencies that are common to a larger group of students. Feedback comments made to the class as a whole should only be those that provide a needed reteaching opportunity. Other comments can be saved for an individual critique session.

Contributions to the critique by fellow students can be a useful feedback opportunity but can be threatening unless the instructor is prepared to moderate and put comments in perspective. A variety of situations should be planned in which it is possible for the instructor to observe and listen. Instructors have to listen to students, and listening skill is essential for the instructor who wants to give useful feedback.

Another skill that can easily be developed is the ability to collect descriptive data while observing student performance and to avoid or postpone making value judgments as long as possible. Collect descriptors first, without ranking or rating the observations. The data will usually take the form of brief notes on what the performance or product was, not how good or bad it was. Later, the value judgments or grades can be assigned. The descriptors will be much more helpful for future student development than adjectives such as *excellent* or *fair*. It might be useful to make an analogy between the observations of a skilled instructor and the feedback from a video recording. The recording is a collection of data, an objective report without any qualitative indicators except in the opinion of the viewer. The recording provides an excellent basis for feedback. Although no instructor can achieve this degree of "objectivity," it can be a useful goal. The instructor's descriptive observations, coupled with informed and authoritative suggestions for improvement, provide a sound basis for learning.

Although the admonition to be "constructive" may seem trite, such an approach to students is essential if instructor feedback is to be accepted. Too often college instructors are described as "negative," "patronizing," "sarcastic," or "condescending." A useful feedback comment is one that includes support for the suggestions with a liberal dose of the "why" or "because." Also, no matter how perceptive and accurate the observations and suggestions, the instructor's manner must offer hope or optimism that the student can profit and make progress.

In addition to skill in reducing the threat, listening to students, collecting descriptive data, and being constructive, the instructor must be able to handle student reactions to correction or other feedback. Teachers soon become aware of the wide variations in student reaction and may become concerned about their ability to interpret the reaction and respond appropriately. Occasionally academic encounters become quite emotional, resembling those encountered by psychologists or other clinicians. College teachers cannot be expected to have the skills of such specialists.

First, the instructor should be very wary of judging from the outward or visible reaction. Most students have developed great skill in hiding their true feelings, particularly from their teachers. It is very easy to come to wrong conclusions about a student's motivation and acceptance of suggestions. Second, it is probably safest to assume that all students, no matter what the academic or experience level, would rather not be evaluated, even for pure development or learning. A corollary of these two points is that the instructor should expect any corrective comment, no matter how constructive, to be uncomfortable, and even hurtful. How much will depend both on the students and the atmosphere instructors can establish, but they should not expect to be able to tell how students are affected just by watching or listening.

Instructors usually feel they should be able to determine the true feelings of their students and then tailor the feedback to the individuals involved. The instructors are aware, however, that some of the most able students have only rarely been corrected and even a minor suggestion can be severe. Other top students virtually demand suggestions, no matter how uncomfortable, to help themselves become even more competitive. There are also students who will say they want to be evaluated but later admit that they were not prepared for even skillful and forthright suggestions.

Knowledge of individual students will help, of course, but instructors should be very cautious about their ability to tailor their feedback to students' idiosyncracies. The objective is to improve the chances that instructor feedback will be accepted by making the evaluation as nonthreatening as possible. If questionable assumptions are made about the technique that is best for a particular student, about whether to be gentle or firm, or about the "thickness of the student's skin," the actions of the instructor are probably going to be more threatening than they need to be and less effective. Tailoring feedback to individual students is a specialized skill. Although some instructors have special training and experience, most instructors are better advised to minimize their "analysis" of students and try to be as consistent and impartial as possible in responding to all students. Instructors can do this best by striving to relate their feedback and comments as impersonally as possible to the model, to the objectives, to the expectations that were set out for that particular aspect of the course. When students understand and accept the course objectives, they welcome feedback as an important, though often neglected, step in teaching.

Summary

Much of the discussion of feedback in this chapter is based on experience in the Academic Instructor School of the United States Air Force. Feedback is defined as authoritative information students receive that will reinforce or modify responses to instruction and guide them more efficiently to attaining the goals of the course. Feedback for curriculum improvement has not been included.

Although feedback is very common in coaching and similar teaching activities, the only feedback in many college courses is grades. To be effective, feedback for learning must be separated from the grading process as much as possible. Most students resist being evaluated, and they are cautious of feedback because it appears to be related to grading. Specific feedback opportunities should be planned as an integral part of college teaching.

The most common source of feedback information is written tests. Written assignments also provide feedback opportunities, particularly during the outline or early planning stages. Group discussion and both individual and group problem-solving assignments can be useful. Although small classes make it easier to provide feedback, more can be done with large classes. Students must be prepared to benefit from feedback. An important part of that preparation is to provide a thorough understanding of the model, the instructor's expectations, and the course objectives. Suggestions such as providing students with copies of the observation or rating scales in advance of completing the assignment prepare students so more "self-correcting" can take place.

Students profit from feedback about study methods. Instructors should provide samples of papers or other course requirements and indicate the relative priority among readings assigned. Finding time for feedback can be a problem, and the instructor may need new ways of managing time with students, including alternative methods to the lecture for the original presentation of information and concepts.

The skills for providing feedback are relatively easy to develop once instructors recognize the purposes. Instructors must listen to students, reduce the threat inherent in the evaluation, and make the suggestions impersonal and descriptive rather than value or grade oriented. The instructor is cautioned not to try to "analyze" individual students to determine the best feedback approach to use unless he or she has special training but to relate the performance observed to the model as spelled out in the course objectives.

A number of factors have combined to prevent college instructors from providing feedback. However, when it is provided at key points in the learning process, errors are minimized, instruction is efficient and effective, and instructors receive an enthusiastic student response.

6

❀ ❀ ❀ ❀ ❀ ❀ ❀ ❀ ❀ ❀

William J. Schiller
Susan M. Markle

Using the Personalized System of Instruction

❀ ❀ ❀ ❀ ❀ ❀ ❀ ❀ ❀ ❀

The Personalized System of Instruction (PSI), also known as the Keller plan in honor of its originator, Fred S. Keller, has rapidly become one of the most popular educational innovations of recent years. Since Keller (1968) first described this type of course, the method has inspired hundreds of research reports, a number of national and regional conferences, several handbooks, a PSI journal, and countless debates concerning the efficacy, utility, and desirability of PSI relative to other methods of instruction. These debates typically feature overwhelming evidence offered by PSI boosters

153

that PSI is the long-awaited educational panacea and repeated assurances by PSI detractors that this evidence is trivial at best and that, when PSI has been successful, it has been nothing more than a demonstration of a relatively long-running Hawthorne effect. The present chapter will contribute very little to the resolution of this debate. Although we favor the basic ideas, our purpose is not to proselytize for the method but rather to offer readers an overview of the PSI method and some how-to-do-it guidelines sufficient to enable them to conduct a fair test of PSI.

A Brief History and Overview of PSI

Keller's 1968 article entitled "Goodbye, Teacher . . . ," cited above, stands as the classic paper on the history and philosophy of PSI. In it Keller recounts the events leading to the development of what has come to be known as PSI in so clear and personal a fashion that we could not improve on it. Reading this paper is a must for anyone wishing to understand the roots of PSI.

The Personalized System of Instruction evolved over a number of years as a direct result of the discrepancy that Keller and his colleagues saw between conventional methods of instruction at the college level and the principles of behavioral psychology. They noted that the conventional lecture-text-midterm-and-final arrangement offered little opportunity for students to participate actively (respond) and to experience the feedback (reinforcement) that was the fundamental methodology in the behaviorists' studies of learning in the laboratory. Thus, when the opportunity to design an instructional system from the ground up presented itself in the form of the new University of Brasilia in 1962, they set about designing the system so that the principles of reinforcement theory would be used fully. The results of their initial effort were so encouraging that they developed similar courses within traditional academic institutions, beginning with Arizona State University in 1965. From the outset, Keller has viewed the PSI as a style of teaching that suited him and that he felt should be tried by others who share his feelings that conventional approaches do not take advantage of our knowledge of human behavior. Keller (1966, 1968) has carefully detailed the features of PSI that he feels distinguish it from conventional teaching procedures. These five features form the basis of any "pure" PSI course design:

1. The go-at-your-own-pace feature, which permits a student to move through the course at a speed commensurate with his ability and other demands upon his time.
2. The unit-perfection requirement for advance, which lets the student go ahead to new material only after demonstrating mastery of that which preceded.
3. The use of lectures and demonstrations as vehicles of motivation, rather than sources of critical information.
4. The related stress upon the written word in teacher-student communication.
5. The use of proctors, which permits repeated testing, immediate scoring, almost unavoidable tutoring, and a marked enhancement of personal-social aspect of the educational process (Keller, 1968, p. 83).

Those five features provide insight into PSI as a unified system, that can be compared with other instructional systems, both those of conventional design and others more innovative. The go-at-your-own-pace feature makes all students responsible for their own rate of progress through the course, both in completing assignments and in arranging for appropriate tests of achievement. The unit-perfection feature provides frequent checks on the students' progress and, where later units depend on abilities acquired in earlier units, provides for smoother progress through the total course. These two features are interdependent and in direct contrast to conventional instruction where students are subjected to a standard amount of instruction and all tested at the same time to see how much each has learned. Insistence on mastery (however defined—it need not be the 100 percent implied by term *perfection*) absolutely requires individualized progress through the materials or individualized remedial assistance for students who are unsuccessful under a standard treatment.

The third and fourth features of the PSI approach—the secondary role to which lectures are assigned and the dependence on the written word as the primary medium—follow logically from the

premise of student control over rate of instruction. Although lectures
to large groups may be a cheap medium for conveying information,
students are required to be in a place at a specific time, no matter
what level of mastery they have attained, and they do not have any
control over the pace of presentation. Written materials permit student control of both when and how fast information is processed as
well as control over the amount of repetition that each student
requires.

The last feature of PSI, the use of proctors or teaching aides,
is the major personalizing feature of the system, from which its name
was derived. The availability of proctors permits students to receive
immediate feedback on unit tests and individual prescriptions for
further work if their performance is below the mastery criterion. It
also puts each student into relatively frequent contact with someone in an instructional role within the course, thereby reducing the
impersonal ambience so often associated with large lecture classes.
This personal-social dimension was seen by Keller as immensely important in making the learning experience reinforcing, far beyond
the reinforcers that could be provided by less social forms of feedback, such as providing knowledge of results in various forms of
self-instructional materials. He asserted that the "pseudosocial" interaction with a teaching machine, to include computers, "would be
a poor substitute for a directly social interaction." (1968, p. 87).
The Keller system as a whole bears the stamp of Keller's own personality, deeply committed to fostering successful learning experiences and to human interaction as the primary role for the human
element in the instructional system.

The PSI system may fruitfully be compared to similar innovations sharing some of its features. The Mastery Learning system
developed by Benjamin Bloom from the model of school learning
proposed by Carroll (1963) includes the unit-perfection requirement but, in some cases, may involve all students working together
under a teacher's direction until performance on a mastery test
shows the need for remedial steps for some. In other words, individualization follows the test, with the students (typically elementary
ones in most cases) not free to decide when they are prepared for
the test. Some versions of Mastery Learning involve the purer form
of self-pacing. (See Bloom, 1968, 1974, and the papers edited by

Block, 1971, for further descriptions of the workings of this system in the schools.) Several other equivalent systems are in operation in elementary schools, under the titles Individually Prescribed Instruction (Glaser, 1968) and Individually Guided Education (Klausmeier, Morrow and Walter, 1968), with heavy support from the University of Pittsburgh and the University of Wisconsin, respectively, and government funding for extensive curriculum development.

At the university level, Postlethwait's Audio-Tutorial method (Postlethwait, Novak, and Murray 1969) provides another contrast. The audiotutorial system typically uses a multimedia approach often with study guides provided by audiotape rather than by written text. It uses a central study-laboratory where students can view films, inspect demonstration experiments, conduct simple experiments themselves, and work through other instructional materials at their own pace. Self-pacing and control over repetition are present; however, in early versions of the system, examinations were scheduled at common times and mastery was not enforced, with grades being given in the conventional manner. Later versions have instituted the mastery requirement and differ from PSI primarily in the heavy investment in media, which Keller (1968) did not rule out, but which he perceived as luxuries. All such self-paced systems create administrative problems in an educational environment that has typically been time bound, tied to units of measurement such as semesters or grade level in school, requiring units of measurement based on acquisition of skills and knowledge. Where a whole school unit adopts individualized progress plans, the administrative problems are less severe than is the case, typical of PSI and Audiotutorial so far, where one professor or one course team attempts to insert individualization into an otherwise time-bound conventional system. The problems of the lone innovator will be considered later on.

All systems that permit students free access to instruction, at the time if not the place of their own choosing, have a voracious appetite for instructional materials. It should be obvious that all presentations by the instructor have to be replaced by some more permanent form. Whether a lecture is committed to audiotape, to videotape, or to paper is not as important as the fact of its commitment to some medium to which each student can gain access when ready for exactly that piece of information. Conventional textbooks, most of us realize, were not designed for *self*-instruction, but rather as information-storing devices to be used by students under an instructor's direction and guidance. Whatever the instructor does in the normal classroom to facilitate use of a textbook, such as suggesting points to emphasize or asking questions in recitation sessions to check student comprehension or elaborating in lectures on known points of difficulty, must, in an individualized system, be put into writing or some other permanent form for use by students. Education has been called a labor-intensive system, and the truth of that assertion becomes clear to anyone who moves toward the more "capital-intensive" end of the continuum required by individual progress systems of any sort. Although the tutors in the PSI system may do some unavoidable tutoring, the main burden of instruction is carried by instructional materials.

In many ways, the points made by PSI advocates remind us of the early writings on programmed instruction, an earlier outgrowth of the behaviorist insistence on activity and feedback. Programmed texts, or programs presented via a teaching machine (see Skinner, 1968, for major papers by the originator), presented small amounts of information to students, asked them to respond in some way, and provided immediate feedback, with each student controlling the pace at which the material was handled. The most modern development, computer-assisted instruction (see Chapter Seven), represents the potential of a quantum leap into more sophisticated diagnosis and prescription than could be achieved by early versions of the teaching machine or any programmed textbook. Self-pacing is not the only dimension on which instruction can be individualized, but it is immensely important in enabling students to reach mastery, and it is common to both programmed instruction and to PSI. Keller himself pointed out that the size of step and size of response were the key differences between his approach and the programmed texts of that time. A frame or step in a programmed text might be limited to a couple of sentences of information, followed by an incomplete sentence or a question for the student to answer, representing a very small step toward mastery. Feedback typically consists of confirmation of the correct answer. As Keller expressed it, "The principal stages of advance are not 'frames' in a 'set', but are more like the conventional homework assignment or laboratory exercise" (1968, p. 84). The questioning following this sizable amount of activity can truly be called a test, and the feedback is personal interaction with a tutor who scores the student's responses and comments on them. Although modern programmed texts have broken away from the small step (Markle, 1969), the unit still tends to be smaller than the chapter or even the set of chapters that might contribute one module in a PSI course. PSI thus assumes a literate population of students, capable of handling large chunks of text with occasional questions and integrating activities at the end of the section. On occasion, PSI courses will employ programmed texts with their much heavier guidance of information processing, the heavy guidance being useful for very complex material or for less well-prepared students.

PSI instructional arrangements resemble more closely a relatively recent line of research in psychology called mathemagenics (Rothkopf, 1970), in which study questions, specific objectives, or both are provided to learners to increase the amount learned from large chunks of ordinary prose. The effectiveness of these questioning techniques in guiding the learning process is beyond question in psychological research reports (Anderson and Biddle, 1975), although many psychologists (and others, but psychologists should know better) continue to employ the passive lecture–text methodology in college-level teaching. As will be noted below, many instructors will begin by adopting "ordinary" prose—namely, textbooks and chapters from texts or other readings—as the starting point for developing the instructional capital they need to launch a PSI system. The instructor's main activity will be generating the objectives, questions, and other guides that enable students to use the existing written materials to achieve the goals of the course.

As a system that keeps students active, PSI has the same capacity that programmed instruction (PI) has always had for becoming an empirically based discipline. When students make errors, whether on PI's frequent small questions or on PSI's less frequent larger response requests, they provide data for instructors. These data may be used to guide decisions about students, but they may also be used to suggest fresh ideas about how to design the instructional materials. If more than a few students have trouble at some point, a conscientious instructor will question the instruction rather than the students. The use of data to determine where the instructional design is faulty is taken by some (Markle, 1970) to be *the* most critical aspect of developing good programs, although much of what is called programmed instruction has not been subjected to such trial and revision. Under the amusing title "The Rise and Fall of PSI in Physics at MIT," Friedman and others described the "chaotic" conditions resulting from a large-scale trial of the method in which several gross errors were made, "the first [of which] was to compose and use new study guides with the full 600 students without first trying them out on a small class" (1976, p. 207). First drafts are not always successful. PSI shares with PI the potential of self-improvement through careful use of the data students provide on how well the instruction is working.

The PSI system, then, is based on five interlocking features, some of which are absent in competing innovative systems and all of which are absent in the conventional system. Our how-to-do-it discussion will assume that the reader is interested in developing a true PSI course with all of these features intact. For those readers interested in a review of some of the recent research aimed at evaluating the relative contributions of each of these components to the total effectiveness of the method, the recent review by Robin (1976) is recommended.

What PSI Requires of Instructors and Students

Given the five key features, the PSI course emerges as basically a behaviorally oriented data-based approach to instruction. The features of a PSI course, when properly developed and implemented, produce a situation in which the students and the teaching staff are required to engage in activities that have been demonstrated to be functionally related to learning. In order to develop this view more fully, it is useful to examine some of the demands that the PSI makes on the instructor of such a course and on the student enrolled in such a course.

The first demand that PSI makes on the course instructor is to force careful consideration of the entire course content long before the start of class. Because the primary source of information to the student in the PSI is written materials that are intended to teach, the instructor cannot select a text on the basis of a quick estimation of its coverage of the area and hope to supplement its shortcomings with lecture material later. The instructor must select or prepare all of the course materials cautiously, since there will be little opportunity to add or change information presented in written form while the course is running (the instructor is too busy!). Similarly, the relatively short units of instruction that are used with the PSI mastery system necessitate sequencing the overall aims of the course in terms of a series of successive steps, through which the students will pass. This requires the instructor to break down overall goals of a course into the component goals and objectives to be achieved by each of the instructional units (see Chapter One). Due to PSI's behavioral orientation, it is common for instructors using this system to develop specific behavioral objectives and criteria for each of the units. Although distributing these objectives and criteria to students is not strictly required by PSI, it is in keeping with the overall success-oriented philosophy and can serve an important purpose in providing the student with information about the specific behavior that will be required at the evaluation of the unit.

We could think of the activities and procedures described above as nothing more than examples of the general concept of good teacher behavior in planning a course that could (should?) be employed regardless of course method of presentation. It is useful to note, however, that the PSI course establishes contingencies (or consequences) for the instructor that encourage such behavior to a much greater extent than do the contingencies of the conventional lecture course. McLeish (1976) has argued that the same careful analysis, detailed questioning of students, and feedback to the instructor on the effectiveness of the presentation could be built into the group-paced, face-to-face lecture, but, in our experience, it rarely is. A skilled lecturer can get away with a relatively extemporaneous presentation from hastily assembled notes, which the PSI commitment to written materials makes impossible.

The PSI approach requires the instructor to develop a series of units that comprise the course and requires development of multiple forms of examinations for each of these units in order to implement the mastery component. In effect, the instructor is designing a system that enables detailed records to be collected as students go through the course. Since all of the records of student progress through the units must be kept to facilitate tracking the students and determining final grades, it is relatively easy to use this information in assessing the effectiveness of the instructional materials, the objectives of the units, the effectiveness of the proctors, and so on. An example of how a simple tabular presentation of this information can provide a wealth of information about the course is presented in Table 1, developed by Howard F. Gallup for an introductory psychology course at Lafayette College. This summary provides information about the relative difficulty of each of the twenty units used for this twenty-week course, of which eight are presented. Units showing high incidence of failure on initial tests or high rates of repeated testing can then be further analyzed to determine the nature of the difficulty—for example, instructional materials that do not teach the behavior required by the tests, poor tests for the units, proctor difficulty with material or misinformation, and so forth. Note especially Units I and VII. It also provides information on how realistic the objectives for the course are and could provide some insights on alternate methods of presentation of the material or alternate sequencing of the instructional units. In short, the structure of the PSI course demands that the instructor collect the type of data that are necessary for successfully programming the course.

Perhaps the most difficult demand of the PSI system for most teachers to deal with is the role changes it forces. They must become course designers and course managers rather than performers. They must forego the immediate gratification of lecturing for the delayed gratification of improved student performance at the end of the course. In a conventional lecture course, there is immediate reinforcement from the group of students for careful preparation and whatever degree of polish is attained. The instructor faces a group of students—from a couple of dozen to hundreds—at least some of whom eagerly await each word, are seen to take copious notes, and are generally attentive to what is being said. Even when the lectures are less than exciting, students tend to appear in hopes of bettering their grades. On the other hand, any punishing effects of poor student comprehension are delayed until the hourly examinations. (We are assuming that the

Table 1. Summary of Student Performance Through the First Eight Units of a PSI Course.

Course Unit	Attempts at Passing Unit Test								Summary of Attempts by Unit			
	First		Second		Third		Fourth		Total Passing[a]	Total Failing	Total Tests	Mean Attempts To Pass[b]
	Pass	Fail	Pass	Fail	Pass	Fail	Pass	Fail				
I	109 (47%)	122	94 (41%)	28	26 (11%)	2	2 (1%)	0	231	152	383	1.66
II	163 (71%)	68	53 (23%)	15	12 (5%)	3	3 (1%)	0	231	86	317	1.37
III	194 (84%)	36	27 (12%)	9	8 (3%)	1	1 (1%)	0	230	46	276	1.20
IV	178 (77%)	52	43 (19%)	9	8 (3%)	1	1 (1%)	0	230	62	292	1.27
V	164 (72%)	65	53 (23%)	12	10 (4%)	2	2 (1%)	0	229	79	308	1.34
VI	193 (85%)	35	32 (14%)	3	3 (1%)	0	0	0	228	38	266	1.17
VII	108 (48%)	117	66 (29%)	51	32 (14%)	19	19 (8%)	0	225	117	342	1.52
VIII	205 (91%)	20	18 (8%)	2	2 (1%)	0	0	0	225	22	247	1.10

[a] Total passing equals total number of students in class. Changes in total passing reflects attrition in class.
[b] Mean attempts to pass equals total tests divided by total passing.
Source: Abridged from Howard J. Gallup (personal communication, 1976) and based on data collected in 1968 (mimeograph).

instructor in question accepts a degree of accountability for student achievement rather than blaming poor test results on the quality of the students or on their poor study skills.) The PSI course design reverses these contingencies. The subordinate role to which lectures are consigned has a predictable effect on student attendance. The instructor as performer is often faced with a considerably reduced audience, although the students who do attend are likely to be more interested and attentive, as well as better prepared for the presentation, than are students at the conventional lecture who often have put off the readings and other activities that would have made the presentation more meaningful.

As course designers, on the other hand, instructors are faced with delayed feedback, since a great deal of preparation has to be completed before any student appears. And not all of the feedback will be positive as students struggle to attain the objectives. A favorite way of handling a particular topic, which appeared to work on the lecture platform with its lack of feedback about student comprehension, will turn out to be inadequate. For concerned instructors, student failure will constitute a punishing contingency; their hard work did not get the intended results. The frequent testing and the mastery requirement force instructors to face these unpleasant facts.

It is certainly desirable to have a system that gives the instructor detailed feedback about the effectiveness of the course materials at frequent intervals and that gives the student equally detailed feedback about progress toward mastery (see Chapter Five). Such feedback systems can be built into group-paced live instruction and all mediated instruction, even if self-pacing is sacrificed in some of these designs. However, self-pacing and mastery requirements are not only the powerful variables that contribute to the effectiveness of well-engineered PSI courses but also the major reasons for the total redefinition of the instructor's role. Anyone considering adopting the PSI approach should be aware that the short-term effect will be a revision of the teacher's role from that of social performer to a more demanding (and in some senses more impersonal) one of course designer and course manager. Keller makes clear in his papers that he finds this role rewarding.

Just as the PSI makes certain demands upon the instructor, it also makes some demands upon the students that the conventional course does not make. Perhaps the most obvious of these demands is the requirement that the student prepare to be evaluated frequently throughout the course. The unit structure and mastery system forces the student to distribute study time more evenly over a greater period of time than does the traditional lecture class using midterm and final examinations. Distributing study time has long been considered an appropriate study habit, and so PSI is actually not demanding a new behavior that should be unique to such courses. As we all well know, however, infrequent midterm and final examination schedules are less likely to develop such regular study habits in students. It is easy to procrastinate until the examination is imminent. Therefore, even better students must make some adjustments in PSI courses. More directly, these ingrained study habits may lead some students to delay working on the course for some time. The PSI feature of going at your own pace allows students more freedom in setting their own instructional pace than does the conventional course, and delaying the start of work on a PSI course can cause these slow starts difficulty later on. Methods of dealing with this problem are mentioned later in the discussion of "doomsday contingencies."

A corollary of this demand is the general requirement that the PSI course makes on each student to assume more responsibility for learning-related activity in the course. The self-pacing feature allows students certain freedom in selecting the timing of instruction and testing. The reliance on written materials allows them more independence in learning than the conventional course but, at the same time, requires them to take a more active role in the learning process, since they must prepare and come to the course rather than sitting back and letting the instruction wash over them.

The use of proctors also requires each student to have more frequent contact with a member of the instructional team than is likely in a lecture format. The proctoring procedure typically requires some form of interview in conjunction with the testing procedure, and students are encouraged to come to the proctors and/or the instructor with any questions or problems that they have encountered with the instructional materials. Many students have not previously experienced this much contact with instructors, and some find it anxiety-provoking. The high degree of personal interaction, which many students believe they want, is in the context of evaluation of the student's performance, which is not necessarily what students have in mind when they complain of impersonality in large courses.

Since most courses do not use the small units of instruction, mastery of successive units, and repeated testing format of PSI courses, students taking PSI courses for the first time sometimes report feeling more pressure to perform in the PSI course, and many report feeling that the course was more work than a conventionally taught course. Because the PSI supports appropriate study behavior, most students in PSI format courses perform as well as or better than they do in traditional lecture format courses, and, for most, this improvement in performance helps to offset the impression that the course is more work. We know, however, of some better students (students with grade-point averages in the A range and doing the same level in the PSI course) who have withdrawn from PSI courses, stating that they felt they were required to work much harder for an A in the PSI course than they would in a conventionally taught course. These students are often enrolled for the maximum number of credit hours the college will allow and seem to have developed very effective student behavior for succeeding in traditional lecture courses in competition with their less-competent peers. This behavior is inappropriate in mastery-based PSI courses, and so they must adjust to the contingencies of the PSI course to succeed.

The question of amount of study time required for success in a PSI course has been examined in several research studies. Born and Davis (1974) and Born and others (1972) report analyses of data from a PSI course taught with all of the study materials—that is, texts, study guides, quizzes, and so forth—housed in a study center. Students were allowed to work with these materials only within the center, permitting careful logs of their actual study time. A matched group of students who were enrolled in a parallel conventional lecture course were told that the examinations for the course would cover only the material presented in the written materials available from the study center, that they must study these materials only in the center, and that the lectures for the course were optional but would be offered three times a week and would certainly supplement and explicate material presented in the study units. Comparison of the two groups performance on a common midterm and final examination showed significantly better performance by the PSI students. Comparison of the study times of the two groups also showed a significantly greater amount of time was spent at the study center by the PSI students. Born and Davis (1974) noted that this seems to suggest that the amount of time in contact with the course materials was greater for the PSI course. However, this would be true only if the time students in the lecture section spent in lectures was not considered. The addition of the twenty hours the average student spent in lecture to the total study time for the lecture group made the lecture and PSI groups very nearly equal in terms of total time spent on the course. Thus, the impression that PSI courses require more work may be the result of the student having to adjust to the active role that is required in the PSI rather than to any true increase in time required by the course format.

Despite the frequent report that students find PSI courses more demanding than conventional courses, every published study in which student course evaluations were used has shown that students enjoy PSI courses as much or more than conventionally taught courses. Kulik, Kulik, and Carmichael (1974) divided the research on student evaluations of PSI into three categories: (1) those using evaluation instruments that require the student to rate the overall course and some or all of its particular features on some scale of positive to negative, (2) those asking students to subjectively compare the PSI course they took with other conventionally taught courses they have taken, and (3) those who have compared evaluations of a PSI format course with evaluations of a conventional format course, usually carried out by researchers who have established both a PSI and a conventional course for purposes of making other comparisons between the two methods. Across these different approaches to obtaining student evaluation of PSI and across many different subject matters taught by the method, student evaluation of the approach remains at least equal to conventional courses. In fact, the evaluations have always favored the PSI course. Since it is never possible to rule out the contributing effects of the novelty of this approach in contemporary education, we shall take the most

conservative stance available and simply state that, to date, there is
absolutely no evidence that students find learning within the PSI
format less enjoyable than learning within the conventional formats,
despite the fact that they often view the PSI course as requiring
them to work harder and learn more.

Potential Benefits

Throughout the discussion of the demands of the PSI we
have attempted to point out also some of the potential benefits.
Before proceeding to the discussion of the actual mechanics of developing a PSI course, it is useful to summarize the benefits.

The structure of the PSI requires the instructor to evaluate
student progress at frequent intervals and over relatively small,
reasonably well-specified segments of instruction. In effect, the instructor must keep data on how well each student is able to learn
the materials presented in each section of the course. This allows the
instructor to evaluate course objectives, unit objectives, course
materials, demonstrations, evaluation instruments, proctors, and
the students in a much more detailed fashion than is allowed by
the conventional lecture format. Since this is the information that the
instructor requires to make reasonable decisions about redesigning,
supplementing, or otherwise changing the course, the process of
programming is greatly facilitated.

The fact that the PSI uses course materials presented in
relatively short "units" of instruction adds to the benefit of this
programming. The data that the instructor receives on any particular unit can help guide the selection of the materials for that
unit in the future. The unit structure allows the instructor to escape
some of the textbook tyranny and select materials that are appropriate for a particular unit independent of the source for materials
presented in other units. By following this procedure through several
iterations, it is possible to develop units that are very effective in
meeting the unit objectives. The entire structure of the PSI lends
itself to this type of research and development model of instruction.

A benefit that is an outgrowth of the gradual improvement
of the course is the reduction in instructor preparation time that is

required for successive offerings. Although the initial offering will require at least as much time as any well-prepared conventional course, and probably more, each successive offering typically requires less and less instructor effort until little is required beyond setting up the mechanics described below. We are assuming, of course, that the course content is not something that changes drastically in short periods of time (such as some cutting edge of a science or current issues in some field), which would argue against such intensive development. Perhaps the most important way in which this freed time can be used (educationally) is to allow the instructor to interact with the students in the course. Once the course materials are settled in to the point where they are reasonably effective at providing the student with the basic information, the instructor's time is freed to allow enrichment discussions with prepared students on topics that may be somewhat beyond the scope of the basic course. Thus, the PSI system allows a mechanism for dealing with the old problem of how to keep the advanced student interested without losing the less well-prepared or less-gifted student. The design of the course structures the materials to provide effective basic instruction for all students, and the reduced preparation time for the offering of the course allows the instructor to interact more frequently with the students on the types of enrichment topics that both instructor and advanced students find satisfying.

Finally, the PSI approach yields student performance and satisfaction at least equal to the performance and satisfaction levels produced by more conventional courses. Since we have stressed the notion that the PSI is essentially a data-based approach to instruction, we would not expect you to accept this claim without appropriate supporting data.

A great number of studies have directly examined the effects of PSI on student performance and satisfaction with the instructional method. Several reviews of this research by Kulik, Kulik, and Carmichael (1974), Kulik, Kulik, and Smith (1976), and Robin (1976) have been published, and it would be both unnecessary and beyond the scope of this paper to attempt to review this material here. As an overview of this research and as support for our statement about student performance and course satisfaction

Table 2. Summary of Comparisons of PSI and Lecture Groups.

Type of Comparison	Comparisons Favoring PSI		Comparisons Favoring Lecture	
	Significant Difference	Nonsignificant Difference	Significant Difference	Nonsignificant Difference
End of Course	34	4	0	1
Retention	9	0	0	0
Transfer	4	1	0	0
Overall Evaluation	7	1	1	0

Source: J. A. Kulik, C.-L. Kulik, and B. B. Smith, 1976.

in PSI courses, we offer the Table 2 taken from Kulik, Kulik, and Smith (1976) summarizing the results of sixty-two comparisons of the PSI approach and the conventional lecture approach with regard to end-of-course evaluation, retention past the end of the course, transfer to later course work, and overall comparisons involving these factors and others (such as student satisfaction with the method).

Although some of these studies employed procedures that restrict the conclusions that can be drawn from them (an unfortunately frequent fact in educational research in general, not restricted to PSI research), the studies do go beyond the single measure of outcome to include both retention and transfer. We agree with the statement that "in our judgment, this is the most impressive record achieved by a teaching method in higher education. It stands in stark contrast to the inconclusive results of earlier comparisons of college teaching methods" (Kulik, Kulik, and Smith, 1976, p. 29).

How to Develop a PSI Course

Since the PSI approach requires instructional materials that are capable of providing the student with the great majority of information to be learned, the importance of sufficient preparation time cannot be overstated. It is recommended that the instructor begin preparing the PSI course one full term (quarter, trimester, or semester) before it is to be offered, and certainly not less than four to six weeks ahead of time. Anyone not able to meet this requirement should consider using a more conventional format unless there are proven materials from a PSI course developed by someone else. Even in this case, however, the instructor will require considerable lead time to select and train proctors, set rooms and schedules, and create the necessary documents that will be specific to the course offering. The following discussion will assume that the instructor has this time available and will be developing the PSI course from the ground up.

The first step in the development of any instruction is deciding what is to be taught. Content coverage is, of course, a familiar aspect of this decision process. PSI is simply a method of instruction, and in none of its listed features can you find a specification of how the instructor should go about defining what is to be taught by the method. Indeed, many PSI courses are quite traditional in this aspect, covering exactly the same topics as a conventional course. The features do suggest some limitations on the definitions that the instructor can develop, however. The mastery feature requires that whatever the content of the course is the student should be able to demonstrate mastery of it. The written presentation feature requires that the content be presentable in an enduring format, and the repeated testing feature suggests that mastery should be defined in ways that lend themselves to alternate forms of tests. (It is possible to insist, for instance, on verbatim production of a set of thirty definitions of key terms, with the alternate forms of the test being any set of ten drawn at random from the set, but we would hope for more sophisticated objectives than that one. See Chapter Four.) The features of the method support an emphasis on defining the outcomes in terms of what students will know and be able to do as a result of having taken the course. The content of the instruction then becomes whatever is needed to allow students to perform in the desired manner.

It is frequently the case that instructors, even those with skill in developing course outlines of coverage, have trouble developing objectives that correspond closely to the types of activities that they expect *students* to demonstrate on sophisticated evaluation exercises. It is far easier to specify objectives for relatively simple forms of learning, such as remembering, than for complex forms such as problem solving and conceptual mastery. The result is often that objectives are written for a low level of learning, which the instructor (and often the student) find unsatisfying. A discussion of the various taxonomies of learning types and of the relation of such types of learning to the problems of sequencing information presentation and determining the kinds of student processing required is quite beyond the scope of this paper. Interested readers can find much discussion and further references on these topics in the classic paper by Bloom and others (1956) and more recent thinking in Gagné (1970) and Tiemann and Markle (1973). The rules for stating good objectives can be found in Mager (1975) or, in terms of the language used by Bloom, in Vargas (1972). See also Chapter

One. A review of these short programs is recommended to anyone lacking familiarity with forms of specific objectives.

Many instructors find that the use of a study guide complements the use of objectives and communicates to the students somewhat richer information about exactly what they are expected to be able to do than is possible with only the objectives. Such guides frequently include such information as pages to be read in a particular sequence, important terms to be remembered or related to each other, directions on topics to which the student should pay special attention, and sample questions are used to both make the student think about some point and to serve a facilitative ("mathemagenic") purpose in supporting the type of learning the instructor wishes the student to acquire.

In terms of systematic approaches to instruction, establishing the objectives for the instructional intervention is the rational first step. The actual procedure involved in accomplishing this end can vary between two limiting situations, which we will describe briefly.

The easiest method of establishing the content for instruction involves having the instructor review several available textbooks, selecting one that satisfactorily covers the area to be taught and accepting this book (and its structure) as the basic instructional material. The instructor then goes through the book deriving instructional objectives and developing study guides for each section. These are then used with the text itself to develop the evaluation instruments with a little basic information on how to accomplish these tasks; this approach can serve quite well for many courses of instruction that have mastery of a body of verbal information as their primary goal.

At the other end of the effort continuum is the full-scale development of a course by the instructor and other members of an instructional development team. In this situation, the instructor (along with other subject-matter experts for the area, such as other faculty teaching the course and/or professionals in the field) works with instructional development specialists (instructional psychologists, instructional design technicians, media specialists, and so forth) to develop the objectives of the course, analyze the content for appropriate teaching strategies, sequence the materials and objectives for maximum effectiveness, develop supporting media and procedures, and develop the entire course from scratch. Needless to say, the requirements of time, money, and other resources necessary for this latter course of action are greatly increased over the former and are probably out of the question for most instructors.

Both of these procedures, as well as all the procedures that fall between these two ends, can yield effective courses if properly done. The decision on exactly what level of effort to use is determined by the local circumstances the instructor faces. However, the procedure requiring the least effort does not capitalize on some of the features of PSI. Since PSI uses individual units of instruction and requires mastery of these units, there is no compelling reason to lock the student into a single source book for all of the information. We all realize that, with the exception of texts we have written ourselves, no textbook ever covers all of the topics we would like to present to our students in exactly the manner we would like to have them presented. Since PSI assumes separate units on separate topics anyway, why not put together the best possible set of units by using various sources? In many cases this can be accomplished without requiring the student to spend an exorbitant amount on texts by selecting smaller works on selected topics, by obtaining releases to duplicate chapters, or by obtaining reprints of various important papers. At the very least, the instructor should feel free to use the unit structure to allow resequencing of the material presented in any text, if the original sequencing does not preclude this procedure.

Although the PSI does not require the instructor to develop written objectives for each unit or extensive study guides, the development of these adjunct devices is strongly recommended and is in keeping with the increased responsibility that PSI places on the student in the learning process.

A further benefit of this increased documentation is its contribution to a rational analysis of how the system is fitting together. With specific objectives and study guides in hand, the instructor can check that it is indeed possible to learn the desired skills and knowledge from the assigned materials; the materials, in other words, should cover all points. It is well known that coverage and student mastery are not the same thing (the old maternal complaint "How many times do I have to tell you?" is relevant for instructors, too!) The rational analysis can be followed by the classic empirical techniques of programmed instruction (Markle, 1967); namely, one or more typical students can be asked to run through the units to see if they can do what has been specified. The information that an instructor can obtain from such a trial run usually provides a wealth of data on what is working and what is not effective and can, if time for revision is allowed, prevent the kind of disaster mentioned earlier that arises when a large class is subjected to untested instruction.

Once the instructor has developed the objectives and study guides and has settled on some materials for presenting this information to the students, the problem of preparing good tests for these units must be faced. For the mastery and repeated testing features to operate smoothly, past experience has shown that three forms of each unit test should be prepared. If students require more than three attempts at passing a unit of instruction, there is very probably something wrong with either the materials or the tests, and the instructor should immediately look over the types of errors that the students are making to determine where the problem lies. These kinds of problems should arise only in early versions of the course when only small numbers of students are involved.

The matter of developing three forms of a test for a unit should be given careful thought. There are several ways in which the various forms can be developed. One of the more popular methods is simply to select randomly one third of the unit objectives to be tested on each form of the unit exam. Although this method uses the features of random assignment to ensure that each form of each test will be representative of the material covered by the unit, it ignores some basic educational considerations. Most importantly, it assumes that all of the objectives of the unit are equally important. Although this might be true, it is unlikely to be the case for most courses or even for most units. More often, there will be some basic core of objectives that all of the students should master for a particular unit and other objectives that are worthwhile but not as important as the core ones. In these cases, the evaluation instruments should reflect this difference in importance by always evaluating student acquisition of the basic objectives and including some random sample of the other objectives. The only way you can ever determine if each student has acquired some objective is to evaluate performance on the objective until mastery is reached. To ignore this is to remove the primary benefit of the mastery feature of PSI. An excellent paper by Anderson (1972) covers some of the complexities of developing evaluation instruments aimed at assessing learning beyond the simple memorization of information (see also Chapter Four).

When the instructor has completed the tests described above, attention can be turned to developing the supplementary documents that will allow the course to run smoothly from the outset. Some of these may be educationally related, such as various practice exercises to supplement the unit materials, or enrichment materials for students who have interests in the subject matter beyond the basic scope of each unit. Others, however, are related to the basic operation of the course, and are intended to allow the student to fully use the benefits of the PSI approach. If most of the students have not had previous contact with a PSI course, a handout describing the features of the course is most useful. This should include a description of the exact sequence of events that the student is likely to experience, from meeting on the first day, through getting in touch with the proctors to take unit exams, to how the final grades will be determined. This handout should also spell out the policies and procedures, including when and how tests will be made available, the role of the lectures and/or demonstrations, the role of the proctors, the place where testing and feedback will be offered, and the lines of authority for the proctors, teaching assistants (if any), and the instructor, so that everyone is apprised of who is responsible for what, and what procedure to follow if any disagreements arise. Investing time in specifying these matters at the beginning will save countless frantic hours during the running of the course and, more importantly, allow the students to avoid confusions and misunderstandings that could hamper their progress. Many instructors prefer to use such a manual as the first unit, requiring each student to demonstrate mastery of the operation of the course before coming in contact with any of the substantive content. This procedure is strongly recommended, since it requires students to engage in all of the activities necessary for progress, gets them in touch with the proctors early, and forces them to begin working on course related matters from the first day of class.

The room in which the class is to be offered is much more important for a PSI course than for most conventional ones. Although PSI courses have been successfully conducted in rooms with fixed seating and conventional layout, these rooms are ill suited. In the PSI approach, regular lecture meetings of the entire class are rarely held; what is required is something approaching private areas where proctors can meet with students to give and evaluate examinations, discuss problems, and so on. In addition, it is usually desirable to have a study area where the students can sit and read or take their examinations in reasonable quiet while waiting to see a proctor. Also, since PSI courses often allow the proctors to schedule themselves at variable times that are convenient for their students, a regularly scheduled conventionally designed classroom would present some difficulties.

The easiest solution is a room that is not in general use through most of the day and that offers some areas of privacy or semiprivacy for the proctoring sessions. Many laboratory or small-group discussion rooms can serve nicely. With a little creativity, most instructors can find space that is amenable to the design features of the course or can modify available space (by moving furniture around) to make it more acceptable for the PSI design. The important point we are making is that this requires considerably more planning than does a conventional lecture course, and the would-be PSI instructor should begin scouting for an appropriate room early.

The average PSI course also requires considerably more paper than does conventional instruction. With objectives, study guides, multiple forms of exams, forms for student progress, data on student progress, and so on, many of these developed before the course begins, the instructor needs file cabinets or a lockable storage area to keep the forms in order. Establishing a logical filing system for the units and all of the materials that are coordinated with each unit will make the instructor's job and the proctors' jobs much easier once the course has begun. This storage and filing area must be accessible to appropriate instructional personnel but also reasonably secure to maintain the integrity of the tests and materials filed.

The selection of proctors for the course is often one of the last tasks to be tackled despite its importance to ultimate success.

The proctors will have the most frequent direct contact with the students, assuming many of the instructor's normal duties and responsibilities. Consequently, they are quite important to the students and to the course. There is no easy formula for determining who should be selected (or, more accurately, invited) to serve as a proctor, but we can provide some general guidelines drawn largely from experience with the system.

The most obvious qualification for a proctor is knowledge of the subject matter. Since proctors make decisions about the students' knowledge of course materials, they must be competent to do so. The instructor must be confident that the proctor knows the material sufficiently well to serve this function. Many PSI instructors select students who have completed the same course previously at the highest academic level. The decision to limit the pool of potential proctors to only A students, or only to A students who are also majors in the area, or any other restriction, is at the instructor's discretion subject to local constraints. The instructor's primary consideration is simply to select people in whom he or she has confidence, since they will be acting largely on the instructor's behalf throughout the course.

The second major selection criterion is that proctors be individuals who take their roles seriously and conduct themselves appropriately. This is definitely a fuzzy criterion, but one must be certain that the proctors will be individuals who are mature and responsible people. Because they will be largely responsible for guiding the students, they must be capable of such simple things as arranging their schedules to keep all appointments they make and maintaining a professional attitude toward their students.

Even the best selection criteria rarely yield proctors with all of the desirable traits or skills a proctor should have, so that specific training is called for. We highly recommend proctor training to maximize the benefits of the PSI features. Several authors of textbooks designed specifically for PSI courses have begun to include sections on how to instruct the proctors; for example, we can recommend the manual for instructors accompanying Keith Miller's *Principles of Everyday Behavior Analysis* (Miller, 1975) for an excellent description of a program for training PSI proctors and the many considerations involved in designing such a program.

If possible, the proctors should be trained before they begin seeing students, but at least the instructor should sequence the proctor training sessions to provide them with the basic skills of student interviewing as soon as possible. It is especially important that in further training sessions all of the proctors agree on the criteria for passing each test, although their test-grading reliability should be monitored throughout the course and adjustments in grades made where deviations occur. All of the proctors must understand exactly what authority has been delegated to them and what decisions the instructor reserves for him- or herself. The lines of authority, including any grievance procedures for dissatisfied students, must be clearly understood.

Although proctoring experience can be very rewarding and useful for an undergraduate student, real world pressures to complete degree requirements make it unrealistic to expect many students to elect to act as proctors simply for the experience. Thus, some form of payment for proctors should be established. The easiest form of payment, one that allows students to meet the demands for training mentioned above, is to offer academic credit. There are many mechanisms for such credit, from some form of independent study to a more formalized course specifically designed for proctors. This latter choice has been used successfully in a number of schools where the course for proctors is a course in education or human behavior management, complete with readings, regular meetings, and some form of evaluation. Thus, the proctoring experience is part of a laboratory course in human learning, with the proctors responsible for acquiring and demonstrating skills in guiding human learning. The proctoring course can also be developed as a practicum experience in teaching, offered as an elective for students majoring in the field.

When course credit cannot be offered, it may be possible to pay the proctors an hourly wage. Several schools have used some work-study monies or other resources to offer proctoring as a combination job and learning experience.

Financial and academic affairs of each institution will play a large role in determining what, if any, payment can be offered for the proctoring. Given the effort and responsibility that goes with the post, however, we would recommend some form of compensation, in order of preference: course credit, monetary payment, and volunteers. Even for volunteers, a major selling point is the opportunity to work closely with a faculty member in a teaching activity, which is very desirable for students intending to go on to graduate school. They get first-hand experience in academic endeavors and often get a friendly faculty member who can later write a letter of recommendation based on more than simple classroom contact.

Running the PSI Course

If the description of the preparations necessary for a PSI course has not dampened your enthusiasm, you will be happy to note that we have finally arrived at the point where the course is ready. You may have tried out some of the materials for the course on some students, but this is the real thing, the start of class. This section is considerably shorter than others, for a simple reason: the bulk of the work for a PSI course is done before the first student comes in the door on the first day of the class. Now that they are coming in, however, what happens next?

If you have developed a student manual containing the policies and procedures for the students to follow, you would present this to the students on the first day of class. Even if it will be the first unit of instruction, as we suggested earlier, it is a good idea to go over the material in a general way in a lecture-discussion format to reduce confusion. It may also be the last time that you see all of the students in one place at one time, unless you give a group final examination. Because PSI is new to many students, the necessary information on the roles of the student, the proctors, and the instructor need emphasis, as do the procedures for taking tests, retaking tests, and obtaining grades. This session also gives an opportunity to present whatever policy you decide upon for lectures and demonstrations, including your policy on attendance at these events and what, if any, proportion of the information presented in them is considered as testable material.

Although the pure PSI system relegates lectures to the role of motivational devices, many instructors compromise on the pure course by including a few mandatory lectures or demonstrations. As long as they are few, there is no real problem with this hybrid.

It is a good idea to indicate on the course outline when and where these will take place, to ensure that all students have a written record.

It is also useful to provide students with an idealized progress chart. Students tend to take some time adjusting to the self-pacing feature, putting off starting work until some time into the term, and hurrying to catch up or running the risk of not completing the course. This is especially likely when the students' other courses are not PSI ones and make more rigid demands on their time. Using the policies and procedures as the first unit helps to overcome this problem somewhat, but it does not totally eliminate it. A graphic presentation of what ought to be completed by what date in order to complete the course comfortably in the allotted time is therefore quite useful; students can be required to plot their progress on such a chart as feedback on how well they are progressing.

Even when students begin work promptly, the self-pacing feature can lead some to fall behind later as demands in other, non-self-paced courses become more acute. Deadlines for exams, papers, presentations, and other activities may lead the student to procrastinate. In an effort to discourage this behavior, many PSI courses include doomsday contingencies, time limits by which each unit must be completed in order to continue. Students who fail to complete a required unit by the appointed time must meet with the instructor before being allowed to go on and may be requested to drop the course because they are in danger of failing at their present rate of progress. Some instructors require that students meet these deadlines in order to avoid a failing grade, hence the name "doomsday." You may employ a true doomsday contingency and fail students who do not progress on some minimum schedule, or you may allow them one counseling session with the option to drop the course or catch up. Whichever you choose, such contingencies are useful devices that allow considerable latitude in student pacing without running the risk of having many students either fail to complete the course on time or be forced to withdraw late in the course. The key is to inform the students of the policy from the outset, so that they can allocate their time appropriately.

Students may be assigned to a particular proctor who has

hours convenient for the student, or any student may meet with the proctor who happens to be available. Regardless of which of these options is chosen, someone, either the instructor or a proctor, should be responsible for keeping track of each student throughout the course, reminding each laggard of the consequences of falling too far behind.

As with any human endeavor, there are always more things that can go wrong than we can anticipate beforehand, and you may have to make adjustments to the course while it is being offered. When the problem is large enough to involve some change in policy or procedure, the major difficulty will be communicating the changes to all of the students. Mandatory lectures or demonstrations may afford the opportunity to communicate the changes. If not, you must devise some way of getting the information to all students, if possible in written form and available at a number of times and places. The proctors can serve as one communication channel, explaining changes to the students with whom they have contact. Above all, keep careful records of the problems and your solutions so that they can be used in making the next offering of the course more trouble free.

Using the Data from the Course—Fine Tuning

We have repeatedly stressed that the PSI course is essentially a data-based instructional system that can be improved (dare we say perfected?) over repeated offerings. When you have completed an offering of the course, you will have considerable data on each student at each point in the course. These data isolate areas of instruction that were ineffective. Did most of the students require more than two chances to pass the exam for Unit X? What was covered in that unit? What questions on the examination gave them the most problems? Do their answers indicate any common misunderstandings or confusions? Can the proctors give you additional insights into what may have been the source of these problems? It is generally a good idea to arrange weekly meetings with the proctors during the running of the course to discuss just these types of problems; the data from these meetings can be valuable in preparing for the next offering of the course. Decisions on changes, additions, and deletions of course materials should all be made from the data you have collected for the last running. By careful examination of these data, you can make the course more effective and efficient each time it is offered.

As you improve your PSI course over several offerings, you will begin to encounter some questions of a more philosophic nature; we have reserved one of them for the end of this chapter. If you have made appropriate adjustments in the materials and strategies in successive offerings, you will find that you are able to communicate more of your objectives to more students in the same amount of time. Thus, the course is now more efficient, since it is teaching more effectively with the same amount of effort. What happens to the grading structure when this happens? If you elected to use some sort of criterion-referenced grading system, where a letter grade corresponds to successful achievement of some set of objectives, you will find that more and more students are earning higher grades. This is a cause of much concern on many campuses already, and you should expect that it may be a concern to some of your faculty.

One way out of this problem is to begin to require more and more objectives for each letter grade, so that the distribution of letter grades remains approximately the same. Of course, the course itself has now changed since students are now expected to learn more to earn the same grade (grade deflation?), but it will probably solve the problem for faculty who only look at the distribution of grades from a course as a way of selecting the best students. In any event, the problem of what to do about all these students who are learning so much from our courses is sufficiently novel that we are sure you will enjoy dealing with it if it arises. We also hope that the information presented in this chapter has increased the probabilities that you will experience it.

7

Alfred Bork

Computers in the Classroom

This chapter discusses use of the computer as a learning and teaching device within higher education. Computer programming as it is taught in many beginning computer science and physical science courses is of no concern, nor is the chapter concerned with teaching about computers. Rather, our interest is in the computer as an aid to students in learning almost any subject matter.

Computers are rarely used as learning aids in educational institutions around the world. Nevertheless, it is important to review current usage not only for the value of learning about existing practices but also because of what the future holds. Available evidence suggests that the computer will become a dominant device in teaching in higher education during the next twenty-five years.

The employment of computers for learning rather than just in programming had little influence on their initial development. Much of the early impetus for computing and many of the large-scale first attempts at building computers came from the sciences, particularly physics, where sizable research calculations are required. Research in the sciences, which involved numerical work, led to much of the early development; this work hinged on the fact that computers could do arithmetic very rapidly.

Discussions of computers around 1950 suggested that only a few would be needed in the entire country, since there were only a few specialized fields of research that would require them. Soon, however, research uses expanded, and many record-keeping and business processes were adapted to the computer; indeed these soon became the major market. Computers could perform numerical calculations very rapidly, make logical decisions, and manipulate a large class of symbolic information, including the symbolism of everyday language.

In most universities, computers were purchased for use in research and administrative activities; educational uses, such as direct student use other than learning to program, were not the driving force. Currently, we are seeing a crescendo of activity in the educational uses; sometimes these are competing for campus resources with research and administrative applications.

Computer development has been extremely rapid since the beginning, and it continues to evolve ever more rapidly. The first practical electronic computers employed vacuum tubes to create the internal logic decisions on which all computers, even today, depend. The second generation of computers came about 1958, when the first commercial use of transistors occurred. The transistor, replacing the vacuum tube, combined decreased size and cost with increased speed and reliability. Initially, transistors were discrete components —that is, individually manufactured items. The third generation in computing ability and power occurred about 1960 when we progressed beyond individual components to integrated circuitry, with many electronic components formed on a small area. Each of these three developments marked changes of many orders of magnitude. Computers became faster, cheaper, smaller, and easier to maintain.

We can safely say that technological development still has a long way to go before we finish this cycle of cheaper and faster computers. We are only beginning to see the first commercial use of large-scale integration (thousands of transistors and other components on a single chip) in available systems. New advances in the technology are occurring with increasing rapidity. Hence, dramatic continued decreases in prices of computers are almost certain; this is one of the factors that will hasten their acceptance in higher education.

It is difficult and, luckily, not necessary to say who first used computers as teaching devices. By 1960 several widely scattered groups were already known. Papers can be found in the literature of the early 1960s reporting activities of these pioneering groups. At that time the employment of computers in this manner was very uncommon. Even though today the computer is not a very common learning and teaching device in American colleges, its use has increased many, many fold since the initial period.

Computer Usage

In this section we review some major types of educational usage, describing these types in greater detail later. In considering various ways computers can be used in education, several major distinctions must be kept in mind.

First, two fundamental types of computer access are possible today. In the first type, characteristic of much older computer use in learning, the user—a student—presents a collection of punched cards (or perhaps punched paper tape) to the computing facility, with instructions to be carried out by the computer. Usually considerable time elapses between the presentation of this material to the operators of the computer and the return of the results. This type of interaction is called "batch computing." It contrasts with the second type, "interactive computing"; this is usually done through a student station or display, where the student enters material directly, commonly on a typewriterlike keyboard. There is almost instantaneous response from the computer, either in typed form or displayed on a screen similar to that in a television set.

The main difference in student access between batch and interactive computing is that of time. Minutes, hours, or days may elapse before a computer response is obtained for batch, whereas the time will be instantaneous or on the order of seconds for interactive computing. Educational use is largely dependent on the existence of interactive computing, although some limited activities in batch computing are possible. We can expect interaction to play an increasingly important role in the future. Interactive computer arrangements may involve several people using one computer, typically called "time-sharing," or they consist of each student employing a computer, a stand-alone or one-on-one system. This latter arrangement will become of greater importance (discussed more fully later).

In interactive computing, various types of student stations—locations for student-computer interaction—are possible. The common older stations were typewriterlike; recently displays—units that show material on a televisionlike screen—are becoming more common. Most of these systems employ cathode-ray tubes similar to those in home television sets, although other technologies are being investigated.

We should distinguish carefully between those types of display stations that can display only alphanumeric information—letters and numbers—on the screen and graphic displays—drawing lines or placing points—on the screen. Since pictorial material plays an extremely important role in all aspects of education, it is not surprising that there is a strong trend toward more and more such material in instructional use of computers. Most of the projects described in this chapter do employ graphics. Recall that the display stations, graphic or nongraphic, may connect to a (usually remote) computer or may themselves be complete computers.

Another critical distinction must be made between those situations in which the student is writing programs and those in which the student is employing programs that have been prepared by others, either the instructor in the course or teachers elsewhere. If students write programs, it is assumed they are writing such programs to aid in learning the subject, not to learn how to program. Indeed, the computer is often very useful for this purpose.

This type of usage corresponds closely to the student's later possible professional employment of the computer. The educational programs written by others, on the other hand, are more typical.

Finally, a distinction must be made between materials connected directly with student learning and materials connected with course management. We shall note examples of both kinds of usage in the following discussions.

Student Programming

When students use the computer to learn the content of a subject, through the medium of writing programs, they are employing the computer as an intellectual tool. For example, physics students might be studying a particular physical system, exploring the possible states of the system and the effects of various variables. Most realistic situations of this type are too complex for students to handle through hand calculations. The computer, though, extends the students' abilities and amplifies their intellects. The computer may be employed to augment traditional material, or it may make possible new and more interesting approaches that are characteristic of the subject area but not possible without the computer.

Although students typically must learn to program as part of this process, we must emphasize that the main goal of the activity is not simply computer programming but, rather, the use of this programming to aid in understanding the subject matter. The details of exactly how the computer will be employed will differ with the area involved. Auxiliary printed material is often necessary to support this activity.

If the student is to prepare computer programs within courses outside computer science, it is necessary that the learning of programming be considered carefully. As programming is not the main concern, it must be taught quickly and efficiently, employing only a small segment of the student's time. Interactive techniques have proved to be most effective. Working within the subject area rather than in a general programming context is an excellent setting in which to learn to program. The problems that students solve in the learning activity are problems taken from subject areas being learned; a relatively uniform student background allows preparation of more effective learning modules.

One approach I have found successful might be described as the "ten-finger" approach. The student sits at a student station and calls for the programming language that is to be learned. Then the student types in a set of statements given by the instructor, one by one; these statements are in printed or duplicated form. After each statement, the computer does something, and the student observes the computer behavior; the student might type "2 + 5," and the computer would reply "7." The printed material also poses questions about what is happening. Thus, students work through the various stages in learning the language, discovering its abilities. This way of learning might be compared to learning about a strange animal by stimulating it selectively and then observing its behavior in each case. In addition to promoting rapid learning, the ten-finger approach encourages students toward further experimentation in their use of the computer—trying out things to see what works.

Where the student will prepare programs, there may be a choice of the language or languages to be used in a course. Sometimes only one language may be accessible; in many small time-sharing systems, BASIC is the only one. In this case, naturally, the available language is the language students employ; most of the common languages can be involved in such activities.

But the instructor of the course or the students themselves may have a greater choice; several languages may be accessible. Or the instructor may play an active role in the choice of a new computer and so can influence the availability of computer languages. Then the teacher needs to consider the issue of what language is best for the application. The decision is clearly dependent on the academic discipline, with some general features always desirable. If possible, we want a computer language with good subroutining capabilities—that is, the ability of one computer program to execute a named segment of code so large problems can be thought of as collections of smaller ones. This is an important problem-solving mechanism. (BASIC is usually weak in this regard, providing only a very crude subroutining capability.) In some cases the existence of very powerful modes of computation, particularly those involving groups of numbers, is important. (APL is particularly strong computationally.) In some situations the instructor may be eager to emphasize the advantages of structured programming; then languages such as PASCAL will be very useful. In other cases the existence of convenient graphic capabilities within the language may be the most important determining factor.

Computer-Based Learning Programs

The other side of the coin are the programs prepared for students by others, usually instructors elsewhere or at the same campus. This type of usage is often called computer-aided instruction, or CAI; these and other common initials will not be employed in this chapter. Here, a wide variety of possibilities can be found; even the classification schemes for computer-based learning programs appearing in the literature show no common agreement. I favor a scheme that tends to emphasize the usage of the materials rather than emphasizing their nature as computer programs.

These computer programs designed specifically to aid learning tend to be inherently interactive and, in the best examples available today, typically employ graphics. Their use, particularly compared to the use of program running by students, is still relatively minor, but their potential for future use is far greater than the other (programming). Such programs have been developed for almost all academic areas.

The main advantage of this learning method over most others is that the student must interact with the material. The student is an active learner rather than a passive one. The interaction can proceed like a Socratic dialogue, with the student responding to questions designed to show the level of understanding involved. The computer can analyze each such response and so can react differently to each student. At its best, the experience can be like a personal interaction between student and teacher. Furthermore, the experience can be highly individualized to each student's needs and performance. The preparation of good material of this type is not a simple matter. The computer can also keep accurate records of student responses, and programs can be rewritten and improved.

The first category of computer-based learning material to be considered is drill and practice. In many areas instructors believe that students require detailed practice; the computer can offer an unlimited variety. Students are presented a series of examples and asked to solve them and to enter the answers. Many disciplines have tried such approaches; one could drill on French verbs or solve algebraic equations, for example. Records of student performance are maintained. Students are given aid, possibly directly from the computer, when difficulties occur in solving these examples; this may consist only in giving the right answer, or it may be in the form of extensive learning sequences that respond to the needs of each student.

The most common examples of drill and practice do not come from the university-level material but, rather, from elementary school areas; the materials developed by Patrick Suppes in reading and arithmetic are in widespread use in many parts of the country. Similar examples exist in many academic areas. Thus, if a student is learning vocabulary in a language such as French or is learning grammatical components of the language, it is commonly thought that sizable amounts of practice are desirable. In many areas debates exist as to the role of drill and practice, with some claiming that although it has played a major role in traditional learning activities, better modes of learning exist. But we need not resolve this controversy in the present chapter!

A second type of computer material is games as learning devices. Games, computer and otherwise, certainly have high motivational value, entrancing students in ways that many other academic materials do not. Computer-based games have been particularly successful in this direction. For example, science museums find that computer games are the most popular of all exhibits, both in numbers of people who interact with them and in holding attention. It is not easy, however, to develop games that have strong learning value in addition to their motivational value. Often game playing via the computer turns out to have little educational component. The clever instructor, concerned with how students learn, may be able to develop games that do have considerable teaching potential, particularly in aiding students to build intuitive notions of the subject area. A typical game, the lunar lander with the student "landing" a spacecraft on the moon, can, in some variants, be employed to give people an intuitive feeling of the Newtonian laws of motion (see Chapter Eleven).

Perhaps the most common material for computer-assisted learning is tutorial or dialogue. It is this material that competes most directly with the lecture or book, furnishing the student with the same basic type of learning assistance but with a moment-to-moment interaction missing in the other media. As already suggested, the computer has a tremendous advantage over the book or the lecture in being a truly interactive and responsive medium, encouraging active learning. That is, the student is not a passive recipient but is continually being asked to do something, to react, even if that "something" is a relatively small activity. Thus, the student may be asked to type a response to a question or to point to a location on a curve having a certain property. The student's understanding at each point can be probed and decisions made as to when to continue and when to offer additional work on a topic. Such material might be thought of as an interactive lecture and so is suitable in any area in which a lecture is suitable. Figures 1 and 2 illustrate a small fragment of such an interaction. These pictures are an incomplete representation of the student experience, as the time element is missing. Note, too, that perfect typing is *not* required.

The model for such tutorial dialogue usage is the conversation that might go on between a student and an instructor in the instructor's office, where the instructor is telling the student something and then posing questions for the student to answer, questions that assist in learning the material. In each case, office conversation and computer dialogue, the instructor is reacting immediately to the answers provided by the student. As with any human conversation, the student-computer conversation can move off in different directions depending on the replies that students are giving. Ideally, this material can be highly individualized to the needs and abilities of a particular student. The learning experience can be different for each student; in practice, existing materials often do not attain this full ideal, but materials are improving as we gain greater experience

You are probably familiar with the idea of measuring temperature in...

```
                  - a room -
                  - the outdoors -
                  - your own body -
                  - an oven -
```

What do you do to measure your own
body temperature?
?I'D USE A THERMOMETER!

That's correct!
We need a thermometer

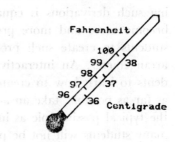

Figure 1

The reading on the thermometer is
initially below body temperature

Let us draw on past experience
with such measurements
Suppose you keep the thermometer
in your mouth for only a few seconds
and then take it out. Does it
read the correct body temperature?
?NO. IT WOULD NOT

97 deg.
F.

What would you do, then, to get a meaningful value?
?LEAVE IT IN SEVERAL MINUTES

Yes. That's it!

It's a common practice to wait at least two minutes,
and perhaps even try again to see if the reading has
ceased changing.

Type anything to continue...█

Figure 2

with the educational applications of the medium. Communication will not be 100 percent, but it is easily possible to respond appropriately in 90 percent of the cases.

A particular type of tutorial material important in science and mathematics is the interactive proof. Often in these courses instructors spend considerable time during classes deriving results for the students. The results are important, but the process of creating such derivations is equally important; we expect students to become more and more proficient in similar processes. Teaching students to create such proofs is often unsuccessful with present arrangements. An interactive proof dialogue attempts to aid students to learn how to create complex derivations by letting them, as far as possible, take an active role in the derivation rather than the typical passive role as in listening to a lecture. It may be that many students will not be prepared sufficiently at a given stage to assume this active role. In such a case the interactive proof dialogue will offer assistance; but it still will teach the important aspects of how one actually goes about creating such important proofs. In science courses such a dialogue may also fill in mathematical gaps in the student's background.

A related activity is that of providing assistance in problem solving; problem solving is a most important component in science and mathematics courses. Teaching students how to solve increasingly difficult problems is a major objective. We do not want the student to solve precisely the problems that have already been solved by the instructor but, rather, increasingly different variants of such problems. General problem-solving skills and strategies must be acquired. Traditional teaching methods often do not prove to be effective in assisting students with problem solving, but the interactive computer programs offer opportunities in this direction, opportunities being realized in some of the better materials now available. Figures 3 and 4 are from a problem assistance dialogue; the student did not mention the importance of drawing pictures, so the computer emphasized this.

Another type of activity is the controllable world, an attempt to provide a rich range of experiences to students, and therefore increase their *intuition* about the subject area. These computer-created experiences are not generally obtainable by the student or

```
Here is the problem
```

```
          A batter hits a ball over a 25 foot fence
                                  300 feet away.
          The ball is hit 5 feet above the ground
                          at an angle of 45 degrees.

          We want the speed at which the ball is hit.
          (The ball barely clears the fence.)
```

```
How would you get started with a problem like this??
??..I HAVE NO IDEA ■
```

Figure 3

```
You don't seem to have mentioned

the importance of a
```

PICTURE

```
at the beginning stages of problem solving
```

Figure 4

are obtainable only on a limited basis. Computer programs are often
called simulations, but simulations must consider carefully how the
student is to employ them before they become an effective controllable world. These are particularly valuable tools in studying those
areas of higher education in which the everyday experiences available to students are no longer relevant because of the advanced and
abstract nature of the subject matter or those areas in which much
practical experience is highly desirable. Although students can
discuss planets moving around suns, no one has "seen" this happen.

It is relatively simple to provide computer programs running on graphic displays where students can watch planets move around suns, with different initial conditions, with variants on the force law, and with several suns involved. Furthermore, students can see, in the literal sense, a wide variety of "abstract" spaces, plotting many different variables and thus observing the motion in ways that are impossible to observe without the computer (see Figure 5). Similar economic worlds can allow students to manipulate and control business situations that they cannot in their everyday experiences.

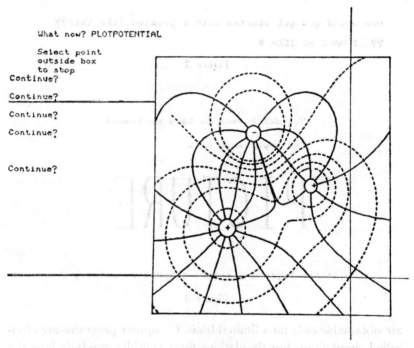

Figure 5

Thus far we have discussed the types of computer usage that are reasonably common today and represent what is possible in most teaching environments. There are several interesting possibilities for the future, existing now in experimental form, that should be mentioned. Many groups are working toward the possibility of allowing the individual user to have more control over the flow of the program, perhaps eventually taking over entirely. This approach can start with such simple things as allowing the skipping of sections, providing maps to aid the student to move around freely, and allowing for reviewing of sections.

A more complex mode is to try to respond to any student request. In such a program the student might be playing a more active role, querying the computer as well as responding to what the computer requests. Programs of this variety can store considerable information about the student, and can begin to achieve a level of "intelligence" in reacting to situations beyond those originally programmed by the author, at least in principle. Perhaps the most interesting existing program of this type is SOPHIE, developed by John Seeley Brown at Bolt, Beranek and Newman; it lets a student trouble shoot an electrical network by requesting various sorts of tests in the process. Programs of this kind are not currently practical for most educational environments but will be soon.

Computer Management of Instruction

A quite different aspect of the use of the computer in education is seen in a variety of management activities. Here the computer is not responsible directly for supplying learning material for the student but is responsible for a range of activities typically associated with classes that are described as course management. Such material can assist both the student and the teacher.

A class, particularly any sizable one, will require extensive record-keeping activities. Each activity contributing to the grade must be recorded, perhaps with auxiliary information such as when the activity was completed. Final grades must be prepared in most colleges, with various components for the grade added with appropriate weights; the students in the class must be ranked, perhaps with histograms prepared. This record keeping varies with the class; thus, in a self-paced (PSI) course, information about both passed and not-passed tests is important.

Students too should have access to information about their records, including their relative standing in the class, so they can check the records to determine whether they are accurate. Even in a self-paced course students like to compare their progress with that of others. A model system should give students pertinent information and allow for individual "letters" to students and to the instructor via an electronic mail system. The student can be given prescriptive guidance, guidance based on knowledge of the student's previous performance in the course and offering information about suitable learning modules for further progress.

Furthermore, instructors need a range of diagnostic tools to determine what is happening in the class. Thus, they should know which students are in what types of difficulties, which quizzes are giving trouble, which graders present problems. As with the other aspects, this information should reflect the latest data available for the class, data that changes constantly.

So far our discussion of computer-managed instruction has assumed mostly a conventional course. However, since the accumulation of the records is an important aspect of any such management activity, the use of computer-managed instruction is very much enhanced if the tests are given directly via computer, perhaps on-line with students taking the tests from individual student stations. Then the information about scores can be recorded at the time the test is taken; no additional secretarial or instructor assistance is needed.

Such tests also have the advantage of providing immediate feedback to the student; just as soon as the student has trouble with a question, assistance can be given to aid with precisely the difficulty noted. Thus, students know immediately what they have to study further; they encounter learning information at a moment when they are likely to be able to use it wisely—at the moment of taking the test. This immediate feedback is to be contrasted with tests in a traditional class where days or even weeks can pass before the student receives such information. Furthermore, such on-line tests can quiz the student in great detail about the subject, using a variety of techniques, in a way that can be more thorough than the typical written test. An example from on-line tests is given in Figure 6.

Although computer-managed instructional systems have not received as much general attention as some of the other aspects of the use of the computer in education, almost everyone who has been

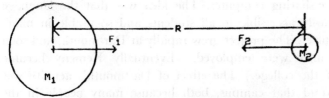

Let A_1 be the magnitude of the acceleration
the first body and A_2 be the magnitude
of the acceleration of the second body
Here are some statements with which you may agree
or disagree
    Answer YES if you agree or just
    press RETURN if you disagree

$\dfrac{A_1}{A_2} = \dfrac{1}{R^2}$...?

$\dfrac{A_2}{A_1} = \left(\dfrac{M_2}{M_1}\right)^2$...?

$A_1 = A_2$...?

$M_1 A_1 - M_2 A_2 = 0$...? YES ■

Figure 6

involved in a large class can appreciate the extremely valuable
assistance that this feature of the computer provides.

Important Projects

We shall now review selectively some major projects around
the world that are concerned with the production of computer-
based learning aids. The emphasis will be on a spread of different
kinds of uses and activities, characteristic of the entire area. Most
of the largest projects are represented in these descriptions.

Dartmouth College was one of the first institutions to establish a reputation for innovative uses of the computer in higher education. Dartmouth's activities started in the early days of educational
computing and were influenced by pioneering time-sharing projects
such as the JOSS system developed at the Rand Corporation.
John Kemeny and Thomas Kurtz became impressed with the possibilities of the computer as an aid to students; they developed a
simplified programming language, BASIC, and implemented it on

a small time-sharing computer. The idea was that the language would be easily accessible to all students and so usable in many different courses. The project grew rapidly at Dartmouth, and soon larger machines were employed. (Eventually Kemeny became president of the college.) The effect of Dartmouth's activity was felt far beyond that campus, both because many people in the region used it and also because of the national attention it received. Dartmouth's mode of operation is very much in the direction of "students as programmers," rather than in the development of instructor-generated, computer-based learning material. Displays are easily available to students. BASIC has expanded at Dartmouth and has been employed extensively elsewhere, although it still remains in many ways a relatively primitive language. Projects COEXIST and COMPUTE at Dartmouth, directed by Arthur Luehrmann, encouraged the development of learning modules using the computer; some of these modules, with both programs and associated printed material, are now becoming available.

The PLATO project at the University of Illinois has followed a very different tack from the Dartmouth activities. Developed by Donald Bitzer, PLATO evolved through a series of earlier stages to the present PLATO IV system. In the standard version the entire computer system is dedicated to instruction, with students using lessons prepared by faculty and other instructional designers. A systems approach has been followed; hardware and software combinations were designed for educational tasks. The initial intent was to achieve economy of scale by having large numbers of interactive student stations on the same large machine; typically five hundred displays are active. The initial displays developed for the PLATO system were based on the plasma panel, allowing graphics with selective erase capabilities and allowing projections of "slides" onto the panel.

The PLATO project also developed a powerful language, TUTOR, for assisting in the development of computer-based educational material. Because of the size of the project, schools elsewhere were encouraged to purchase displays; they can be found now in a wide variety of institutions. At the present time, the project is available commercially through Control Data Corporation (CDC) and is being marketed vigorously; it remains to be seen how many schools will acquire these systems. Since it is a very large time-sharing computer system, the initial investment needed to acquire a PLATO system is considerable. Although a wide range of learning material is available, the quality of the material varies. Until recently, the question of quality of lessons was left to each instructor. The best material, such as some of that in chemistry, is of very high quality. CDC and the University of Illinois have arranged for royalties for PLATO authors, which are based on actual usage of their materials. CDC has recently developed CRT-based terminals for PLATO.

Another large-scale project is TICCIT; the hardware was developed by the Mitre Corporation, and full course materials were prepared at Brigham Young University under the direction of Victor Bunderson. The system is smaller than PLATO, with 128 displays running from two minicomputers; but full-system costs are still considerable. The displays are modified Sony color television sets; this project was one of the first to see the advantages of color. The TICCIT material concentrates in beginning mathematics and beginning English, primarily for community colleges. The system, hardware and software, is based on a particular educational strategy, referred to as learner control, as previously mentioned. The student can move around freely within the material, using maps to guide these explorations. The system does not provide response to free-form student input in most parts of its teaching logic; all programs must conform to this logic, so authors are not free to follow their own inclinations. As with the other graphic systems described, the displays do not show development and motion. Because the television sets must be driven at television bandwidths, they must be relatively close to the central system.

Both the PLATO and TICCIT projects underwent a large-scale evaluation by Educational Testing Services, which was financed by the National Science Foundation (also the principal supporter of the two projects). Results of that evaluation are not yet available; delays in the material and other problems are said to have reduced the effectiveness of the evaluation efforts.

The Physics Computer Development Project at the University of California, Irvine, directed by Alfred Bork and codirected by Richard Ballard and Joseph Marasco, has also received its major support from the National Science Foundation. Unlike PLATO and TICCIT, it has worked with standard graphic displays and a general purpose, commercially available, timesharing system. Like PLATO and TICCIT, it has emphasized graphics. Materials have been concentrated in the beginning sciences area, particularly in physics.

In addition to development of underlying software to ease the task of creating student-computer dialogues, the Physics Computer Development Project has strived toward the creation of an effective authoring system. This will allow teachers with no previous computer experience whatsoever to make a full pedagogical specification of the material without learning any computer language. This approach encourages instructors to employ whatever teaching styles they have found effective in their previous experiences. Student programmers are responsible for the actual coding of the dialogues. The illustrations in this chapter are all taken from materials developed in the Physics Computer Development Project.

So far little in the way of marketing activities of computer-based teaching materials for the university level has taken place, although publishers and computer vendors have discussed the problem. The National Science Foundation has supported an organization to study the problems associated with transporting computer-based teaching material from one location to another; the problem is more complex than moving printed material. This organization, CONDUIT, has concentrated on programs that are relatively simple to transport to schools other than the developing school and has not yet attempted to move much of the more complex material described in this section. CONDUIT's strategy is first to have the material reviewed by several competent teachers, and then to study the material from the standpoint of technical transportability, the ease of moving the programs to many computer systems. The variety of different computers and different languages complicates such transportability.

The primary languages that have been employed in the CONDUIT materials are FORTRAN (in the form of the Bell Laboratory subset, PFORT) and BASIC. About fifty modules are currently available. CONDUIT has also prepared several extensive state-of-the-art reports, reviewing broadly the use of computers in different academic areas in higher education. They employ surveys, by academic discipline, of American colleges and universities as one of the bases for information. These reports furnish perhaps the best overall review available. CONDUIT's present headquarters are at the Computer Center at the University of Iowa; the director is James Johnson.

A system particularly oriented toward the individualizing of instruction has been developed by Allan C. Kelley. The TIP system is based on giving small tests to students, generally each week. These multiple-choice tests attempt to measure proficiency of the various objectives that the student is studying at that time. The results are entered on mark-sense cards, and these cards are evaluated by the computer. Each student receives a printout with individualized assignments based on the performance on the test. The teacher also receives reports on the overall performance of the class.

A number of interesting but smaller projects are going on in Great Britain, under the auspices of the National Development Programme in Computer-Assisted Learning. One of the projects, Computers in the Undergraduate Science Curriculum, involves three schools: Chelsea College, University College (both part of the University of London), and the University of Surrey. Simple simulations have been developed in a number of science areas, with emphasis on graphic equipment. The CALCHEM project, centered at Leeds University but involving many other British institutions of higher education, has concentrated on the development of computer-assisted learning modules in chemistry, with some emphasis on physical chemistry.

Once again, it should be stressed that this survey is far from complete; many active projects around the world must be ignored because of space limitations.

An Example of a Course Employing Computers

We have discussed the ways computers can be employed in education and described several developmental projects; still the reader may be left with an incomplete view of what an actual course might look like. Many such courses are in existence; some employ the computer in simple ways, whereas some make very extensive use of them. Because computer use to assist learning will increase greatly in the future, it seems reasonable to give an example of a class in which the computer played a major role.

The course I will discuss is Physics 3A at the University of California, Irvine, as offered in the fall of 1976. The course is the first quarter of a typical one-year beginning physics class. As with many beginning physics courses, the emphasis was on problem solving. The majority of the 300 students were premedical ones.

The class was taught in a self-paced, or PSI, format, with additional freedom allowing students to choose several "tracks" or paths through the course, based on several differing sets of course material. (See Chapter Six for further information about PSI courses.) Extensive learning dialogues on the computer were available to aid with the study of the subject matter—beginning mechanics. The computer dialogue material was only one mode for learning the course material; students were encouraged to employ whatever modes seemed best for individual purposes. As with other mastery-based courses, it was assumed that a variety of learning materials is important to accommodate students with different learning styles.

Course testing was also done on-line with tests that had extensive remedial help sequences. Several of the previous figures in this chapter are from such quizzes. Immediate assistance was given to a student having difficulty. In a class of about 300, over 10,000 tests were given at computer displays during the ten-week quarter. As with self-paced competency-based courses generally, the students repeated tests until they demonstrated that they had fully mastered the unit. Twenty-seven on-line tests were available, but not every student took each test. Typically, a given unit had several tests associated with it, and students could take the tests within the unit in any order. The course management system did not allow students to take the test unless they had successfully completed tests in previous units, as is common in PSI practice.

A full course-management system was developed and used for the course. On-line tests recorded information directly into the course data base, containing all the information about student performance. Students employed a program in which they could query their own progress in the course and could register complaints. The instructor was provided with information about: (1) where students were within the class structure, (2) students who were procrastinating, (3) students who were taking too many tests to pass a particular unit, and (4) overall performance for each of the tests. This information was available in graphic form, and it was dynamic in the sense that it changed during the quarter as the students moved through the course material. Figure 7 is designed to help the instructor determine which students need personal attention; each student is a point, with the horizontal axis representing weeks per unit for the student and the vertical axis tries per quiz.

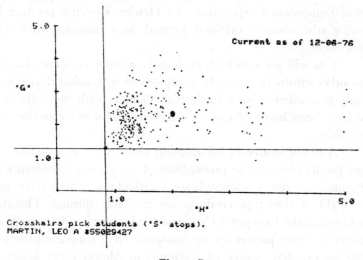

Figure 7

Complete descriptions of the Physics 3A course and the associated course management system are available from the Physics Department of the University of California, Irvine 92717, on request.

Getting Started

Instructors wishing to use the computer within classes in any of the forms suggested in this chapter should first attempt to find what has been prepared by others that might be usable. CONDUIT (Computer Center, University of Iowa) is a very good starting place for obtaining access to simple material. CONDUIT also publishes a useful journal, *Pipeline*.

Most computer vendors have user groups, and often these user groups will have an educational component. Sometimes program libraries will be available, often providing programs at no cost to the user. Furthermore, the user groups may be a way of putting the faculty member in touch with others with similar problems, at meetings of these groups in particular. If the user groups themselves do not prove to be adequate, perhaps direct appeals to the educational marketing managers of the computer companies will produce interesting materials. Some computer vendors also, particularly Digital Equipment Corporation and Hewlett-Packard, produce interesting educationally oriented journals in connection with their user groups.

You will want to find, perhaps from your computer facility, what other efforts in using the computer as a learning device have already proceeded at your institution. Contact with the individuals who have been involved can be extremely useful in suggesting new possibilities.

A major source of information about what is available and about possibilities are the proceedings of the annual Conference on Computers in the Undergraduate Curriculum. There have now been eight of these; proceedings are available through Theodore Sjoerdsma at the Computer Center of the University of Iowa. These conference group papers are by academic area; they comprise as a whole an excellent source of information. Almost every academic area is involved.

Another useful source of material about computer-based learning is the bulletin published by the Special Interest Group in Computer Uses in Education (SIGCUE), one of the special-interest groups of the Association of Computing Machinery. Information about membership in SIGCUE can be obtained from the Association of Computing Machinery, 1133 Avenue of the Americas, New York, New York, 10036. Journals in individual academic areas, particularly those oriented toward teaching, will typically carry articles about the computer and may even have program exchange mechanisms themselves.

Another way of orienting oneself to the possibilities is to visit active projects, those mentioned in this chapter and others, and actually run some of the available material. It is possible to do this in some cases directly from your own home campus. If you write to the individual projects, you may find that demonstrations are possible, without visiting the remote campus, via telephone lines connected to the computer. Unfortunately, this is not possible with all the systems discussed.

So far this discussion has assumed a campus in which usable computer resources are already available. If no resources are available, then the instructor must often, in combination with other faculty, be involved in making a case for them with the administration. Again, examples of use elsewhere, particularly in similar kinds of institutions, will be an important ingredient in convincing local authorities to acquire the needed equipment.

If you are anxious to develop materials as opposed to using existing ones, a whole new range of activities are necessary. First, it may be a waste of time to develop things that are already in existence, so the types of search mentioned above are still desirable. In some cases, however, it may be easier to develop them from scratch than to go through the laborious effort of moving them to a local computer system. Developmental activity does not have to assume that one person will do it all. Thus, an instructor may be particularly interested in the pedagogical problems of developing computer-based learning material, but may have very little interest in the programming. Often student programmers can take over the task, provided that the instructor gives the complete pedagogical specification of the teaching material.

An important component of development is to call on the experience of others. An experienced person can usually come to a college and offer a one- or two-day workshop, both reviewing the kinds of materials possible and stimulating faculty as a group to develop some small amount of teaching material. As an alternative, you can spend time with one of the active projects, assisting with whatever is currently being developed there at the time.

The Future of Computers in Education

As mentioned earlier, computers are still relatively little used in comparison with many of the teaching practices discussed in this book. But this situation is very likely to change considerably over the next decade and probably even more drastically after that. Eventually, computers will be one of the main devices for promoting learning at all levels of formal education.

The reasons for this prediction have already been advanced, but for emphasis they should be repeated. First, the computer is a very effective tool in individualizing learning—that is, in making learning a more active experience for students. It can react to individual differences and be responsive to a wide range of types of students, including the "new" ones who were not typically part of the university environment a few years ago. Second, computers are almost certain to continue to decrease drastically in cost as the technology advances and as we move toward mass production. By the year 2000 computers much more powerful than the large ones in use today will be available for only a few hundred dollars. These machines will have a far greater range of capability than those presently available.

Because of these two factors, we can confidently expect that the computer will be more available and that it will be widely used in learning. It may become the dominant device by which students may learn in all subject-matter areas. A study made by the Carnegie Commission on Higher Education, *The Fourth Revolution,* suggested that the period from 1990 to 2000 would be the period of very rapid introduction of computer-based learning modules. But this estimate, only a few years after it was initially made, now seems too conservative.

The more widespread use of computers depends on more than their effectiveness and their low cost. In many academic areas almost no effective computer teaching materials exist; in all areas the existing materials are fragmentary and only employed extensively in a few locations. Furthermore, little in the way of marketing incentives exist to encourage people to prepare such materials.

Few of the author aids that are available for other academic media are available for computers. An author who wishes to publish a book receives a variety of assistance from a publisher—reviews, editorial and artistic services, typesetting, printing, advertising, distribution, and royalties (including advances). Control Data Corporation is beginning to play such a role with PLATO materials, Educulture is starting to publish material for stand-alone systems, and other vendors are considering productions. But by and large the present writer of computer-based educational material has none of these resources and incentives. If computers are to be used widely in education, large-scale preparation and marketing of these materials will be an important aspect of encouraging teacher participation. Perhaps conventional publishers or computer vendors will play roles here; we may see new organizations developed especially for production and marketing of computer-based materials.

The process of development of computer-based units is presently a cottage industry; usually the individual is responsible for his or her own development. Furthermore, most authoring systems for computer-based learning assume that the faculty member will do all the work, including both the pedagogical and programming aspects. Authoring systems developed recently have shown that considerable efficiency can be gained by the use of specialists. In particular, the development of the program from a pedagogical point of view can be separated from programming; individuals can perform these tasks separately. We can expect a continual advance in production systems. The development of computer-based software in the future will be more efficient than it has been in the past.

Closely associated with the questions of how one is going to produce and market these materials is the question of the hardware on which they are to run. Presently transferability of elaborate materials is very limited. The best materials run in only a few locations and are accessible to only a very small percentage of students in colleges. We hope to influence the direction of evolution to make the new systems better for educational use.

In addition to the problems of transferability, current hardware presents some pedagogical limitations that can be overcome easily. Current inexpensive graphic displays usually do not have color available, often do not allow selective erase of only parts of the visual screen, and in no case allow full animation. Furthermore, few displays allow the designer to employ video sequences, slides, and audio messages where appropriate within the learning sequence, and all under control of the computer. All these are possible in systems that we can envision during the next few years; they are very desirable from a pedagogical viewpoint.

Another aspect of the hardware that must be considered is

whether interactive computing is likely to continue in the current time-sharing vein, responsible now for most of the instructional computing or with stand-alone systems with the computer activity almost all taking place at the student station. Some very large educational time-sharing systems have been proposed. I believe that stand-alone systems, integrating the computer and the display, are likely to be the major delivery systems, although time-sharing systems will still play an important role in the developing and testing process. The nature of large-scale integration, the computer technology just now being developed, is that design and development costs are more important than production costs; hence, the more units that can be produced the lower the cost per unit. This suggests that complete computers in the individual student stations are the most likely future mode.

Some aspects of computer-based education will still require communication, and so these student displays will occasionally connect to some other computer elsewhere. The educator must play a major role in encouraging the development of such systems. A very promising system has been produced recently under the encouragement of Kenneth Bowles at the University of California, San Diego. This system is available at a discount to educational institutions through an agreement with EDUCOM in Princeton, New Jersey. We can expect new and more powerful systems at reduced costs to be available continually over the next few years, and we can expect that existing new computer-based educational material will be increasingly available for such hardware.

As computers are used more widely in colleges and universities, the role of the teacher will be changed, too. The large lecture is one illustration of where the computer can compete and compete extremely well because of the possibilities of interaction. The use of lectures may decrease as more computer-based learning material is available. The recent evidence for the use of PSI suggests too that lectures are often not the most effective way for students to learn. Thus, the teacher may shift from large groups to more individual contact with students. Furthermore, the information that the teacher can receive from a course management system will encourage more contact with the students who most need this one-to-one assistance—

students having difficulty with learning the material that cannot be overcome by the other learning modes.

The computer may bring institutional changes, too. Some promising experiments with new institutional organizations of universities have occurred, quite independent of computer-based possibilities. The Open University in England, and such United States experiments as the University of Mid-America and Coastline College, are showing promising and often economical alternatives to conventional college education. This process will be accelerated by the enrollment difficulties all colleges and universities are expected to experience in the 1980s and by the increasing worry of the public concerning the support of education through taxes and, more generally, the cost of education. Widespread computer use will be appearing on the educational scene at a time of considerable turmoil and at a time when education will find itself under strong pressures.

The computer employed wisely can help institutions change or react favorably to these pressures. Computer displays with learning programs will soon be common in public libraries and soon after that probably in individual homes. Hence, the use of such capabilities will be less dependent on the student's presence at a particular location.

Therefore, education will change both within the university and without. This change may well be traumatic because the university is typically a conservative organization, resisting various impulses to change. Such change will be essential. It is hoped that the necessary leadership to guide it will be found during the decade of the 1980s.

8

❀ ❀ ❀ ❀ ❀ ❀ ❀ ❀ ❀ ❀

Thomas Clark

Creating
Contract Learning

❀ ❀ ❀ ❀ ❀ ❀ ❀ ❀ ❀ ❀

The recommendations of several major commission studies have resulted in heightened awareness of, and increased experimentation in, many colleges and universities with educational processes that operate to individualize the student's learning experience. The fundamental principle underlying contract learning is that individuals are different, they differ in a number of ways that are obvious but often ignored by educational practice. Individual differences that reflect how one attempts to learn include: chronological age, sex, race, socioeconomic class, ego stage development, learning objectives, motivation for learning, nature of past experience with formal education, the level of basic skill development, and preferred learning

212

style. All of these characteristics define learners and the needs and interests they possess as they seek to learn. Contract learning is a process that is responsive to these individual differences; it is by definition student-centered. The fact that contract learning is student-centered does not mean that students can "do their own thing," but it does represent a significant departure from many traditional "do-your-own-thing" practices for faculty members.

Principles and Processes

The contract process is one in which two individuals—a faculty member and a student—negotiate about teaching and learning. The process begins with a discussion of who the student is, what the student's goals and objectives are, why the student wants to study particular content and skill areas, how the learning will be accomplished, what resources will be employed, how the learning will be evaluated, and how much credit will be awarded. Similarly, the faculty member indicates what expertness he or she possesses, the alternative ways in which the learning can be accomplished, alternative resources that may be employed, and what level of student performance is expected. The process assumes that there are two active participants—not an active teacher and a passive student. This transaction between student and faculty member is the essential component of contracting.

The outcome of this process is a written agreement, usually called the learning contract. Although institutional practices vary somewhat, most learning contracts have four parts, these are descriptions of: (1) the student's long-range purposes, goals, or objectives, (2) the student's specific objectives for the period of time in which the particular contract is in effect, (3) the learning activities in which the student will engage, including a description of the content and/or skills to be mastered and the mode of study to be employed, a designation of what learning resources will be used, and the amount of credit the institution will award upon satisfactory completion of the learning activities, and (4) the methods and criteria or standards that will be used to evaluate the student's performance. Depending on institutional practice, the section describing the methods and criteria for evaluation may not include specific letter grades (the process of contracting for grades is described briefly later in the chapter).

The learning contract is a specific statement describing an intentional agreement about the structure of an individual student's learning and faculty member's teaching. It is important to note that as complete and precise as the written contract may be, it is at best only a representation of what the teaching–learning process will entail. A sample learning contract form (not necessarily a model) from Empire State College illustrates the four basic elements of most contracts. See page 215.

In brief, the learning contract is one of the most effective ways an institution can be responsive to the increasingly diverse students who are enrolling in postsecondary programs. It offers the opportunity for an institution to individualize the process of education to meet the needs of students in a variety of ways. When effectively carried out, it is characterized by sensitivity to individual differences, candor, intentionality, accountability, and closure; and it can be a valuable learning experience for the faculty member as well as for the student. As Timothy Lehmann (1975, p. 18) states:

> The contracting process itself has substantial educational benefits apart from the subject matter the contract addresses. The very act of negotiating a contract between a student and a mentor may be a valuable learning experience. By raising questions about a student's goals and life plans, the specific objectives for a particular learning contract, the kinds of learning activities and resources to be used and the ways in which the learning will be evaluated, the student-mentor dialogue stimulates the student to think seriously about his or her education. Such discussions tend to promote mature thought by a student about intellectual and self-development and about the relevance of a particular learning activity for that development. The contract format facilitates the student taking direct personal responsibility for learning and for gaining skills in self direction. By thinking carefully about the topics to be learned, by searching out learning activities and resources beyond the campus and by gaining evaluation experience in self-assessment,

Empire State College Learning Contract

STUDENT'S NAME (TYPE LAST NAME FIRST) Smith, John	SOCIAL SECURITY NUMBER		CONTRACT # 3	
ADDRESS	CONTRACT BEGINS ON 3/31/78	CONTRACT ENDS ON 11/2/78	FINAL CONTRACT?	
	MONTHS OF CREDIT: 2.75		FULL-TIME ☐	
TELEPHONE: HOME WORK	CHECK TYPE EXTERNAL RESOURCE USED		HALF-TIME ☒	
MENTOR'S NAME (TYPE LAST NAME FIRST)	ADJUNCT FACULTY ☐ INTERNSHIP ☐ OVERSEAS ☐	COURSE ELSEWHERE ☐ ISP ☐ RESIDENCY ☐	FIELD STUDY ☐ MODULES ☐ TV COURSE ☐	
LEARNING CENTER:	TUTOR ☐	OTHER ☐		

Give detailed description of: (a) STUDENT'S GENERAL PURPOSES, plans, or aspirations; (b) SPECIFIC PURPOSES of this Contract; (c) LEARNING ACTIVITIES to be undertaken and schedule by which they will be pursued and (d) methods and criteria for EVALUATION. Use the underlined as headings for the four sections of the Contract, and attach additional pages as necessary.

I. Student's General Purposes:

To earn a bachelor of science degree with a concentration in reliability and quality control.

II. Student's Specific Purposes:

In this contract, Mr. Smith seeks to:

1. Study the principles of reliability theory and sampling methods;

2. Carry out an in-depth study of an actual reliability/quality control problem where he works.

III. Learning Activities

1. Mr. Smith will enroll and complete CASM 761, Reliability at Rochester Institute of Technology.

2. Mr. Smith will prepare and teach a course in quality control sampling methods at the corporation where he is employed. He will provide his mentor with an outline and a brief written summary of the course.

3. Mr. Smith and his mentor will examine in detail a reliability/quality control problem(s) associated with Mr. Smith's work. In this study they will define the problems involved, critically examine the work already done, propose new approaches, and review the results. They will pay close attention to constraints such as cost, time, personnel, etc. Mr. Smith will prepare periodic written summaries of the status of the problem(s) and his evaluation of the progress of the work. He will hold extensive regular discussions of this problem with his mentor. At the conclusion of the project he will prepare a summary report describing the problem, conditions for a solution, approaches attempted, results and suggestions for how the process could have been improved.

IV. Methods and Criteria for Evaluation:

1. The instructor will evaluate the reliability course. A grade of C or better will be considered passing.

2. The mentor will evaluate the learnings Mr. Smith has gained through teaching quality control acceptance sampling. Specifically Mr. Smith is to show in his summary and outline that he can select topics in acceptance sampling relevant to his students' situation and background and present them in a clear, logical manner.

3. The reliability project will be evaluated by the mentor. Mr. Smith will be expected to develop his skills at problem analysis and definition, test design, and data gathering and analysis. He is to be able to identify and work within economic, technical and time constraints and to develop his own style of solving difficult engineering problems.

SIGNATURES	DATE
STUDENT	
MENTOR	
ASSOC. DEAN	

the student has prepared for a process of life-long learning that should carry beyond any given contract and the
achievement of a degree.

Elements for Individualization

Several components of the educational process can be individualized by the mechanism of the learning contract. The first component is the place where learning occurs; the use of field placements,
internships, mediated courses, and correspondence courses is
encouraged. These settings are frequently the focus of learning when
an institution has made those policy decisions that recognize and
accept the fact that learning can occur in a variety of settings other
than a campus classroom.

The second component is time. The pace at which the learning is pursued as well as the length of time that will be required for
completion of a single learning activity or series of learning activities
can be negotiated according to the individual's personal and professional commitments. A student can proceed at a full- or half-time
pace and study for one to six months. Although complete flexibility
is possible, many institutions offer the contract option within a traditional semester, trimester, or 4-1-4 academic calendar.

The third component of the individualized contract process
is that of the student's objectives. It is important to emphasize this
element because this is where the process begins. Clarification of the
student's objectives, goals, and purposes is an essential ingredient in
determining the other aspects of the learning contract. There are
often areas to be negotiated between the student's objectives and
those of the faculty member and/or the institution.

The fourth component that can be individualized is the content. Although some institutions use the learning contract to individualize a specific course, others use the method to provide the student
with an opportunity to approach the content in ways that make
most sense to that student and to his or her faculty instructor or
mentor. Contracts frequently describe learning activities in which
the content studied is organized in the context of one or more disciplines. Others organize learning activities that are interdisciplinary

in nature, thematic or problem oriented, and usually multidisciplinary; they may be professional and vocational and intentionally integrate practice with theory. The learning contract has demonstrated repeatedly its usefulness in accommodating these new content configurations that are negotiated by faculty member and student.

Learning activities and learning resources are the fifth and sixth components. The student's opportunity to pursue the study of a subject area in a variety of ways normally follows the recognition by faculty that effective mastery of a subject can occur in places and ways other than in the classroom. In the learning contract this awareness by faculty can be recognized quickly. Thus, a student may work toward understanding a topic through reading books and attending lectures, by using self-directed programmed materials, by using films, audio-tutorial, or television programs, or by using a field experience or internship in combination with appropriate readings. The greatly expanded number of available learning activities provides increased opportunity to match the needs of the learner with the nature of the learning in which he or she is engaged. The questions that faculty member and student must confront about these components are several:

1. How does the student learn best?
2. What learning activities are most appropriate for the subject or area to be studied?
3. What are the most appropriate learning resources for the agreed-upon learning activities?
4. Does the faculty member have the advising skills and knowledge necessary to assist the student in assessing his or her objectives, choosing learning activities, and finding available learning resources?

The seventh component of the individualized process is the evaluation of the student's work and the effectiveness of the faculty member. The learning contract causes the evaluation part of the learning process to be intentional and clear instead of mysterious and confusing. Most faculty who work with contract learning believe that evaluation is an integral and ongoing part of learning, in that it is "formative" as well as "summative"; evaluation is a

process in which both the faculty member and the student participate. A carefully constructed learning contract has a section that
details the essential parts of the process. These include the methods
or means that will be used in evaluating the student's work, the
criteria or standards that will be employed, and the evidence or
indicators that will demonstrate that the work has or has not been
completed and the level of proficiency that has been achieved. The
involvement of the student in the evaluation process as an active
rather than passive participant is often accomplished in two ways.
One way is for the faculty member to ask the student to present
orally or in writing an evaluation of the work completed. A second
way is for the student to write an evaluation of his or her own
work and an evaluation of the faculty member's work as well. Some
contracts are very specific in citing how much and at what level of
quality a student's work must be in order to receive a designated
grade.

The eighth and final component is *shared* authority and responsibility. A learning contract is the result of a negotiation or series
of negotiations between a faculty member and a student. The fact
that a series of learning activities is formulated on the basis of a
careful consideration of the student's objectives is a significant
change from the prescribed course that is centered on faculty interests or traditional patterns for presenting a particular content
area. The learning contract reflects the reality of shared authority
and has proven itself to be effective in assisting students to become
increasingly self-directed. The process in no way seeks to diminish
the authority of the faculty member as expert teacher–evaluator,
but it does seek to make operational the distinction between authority and authoritarianism. At the same time, it seeks to assist the student in taking primary responsibility for his or her learning.

These eight components of the individualized contract learning process constitute a useful guide for constructing and evaluating
a contract. A learning contract that addresses each of these components is probably complete and represents a completely individualized blueprint for learning. There are institutional variations because one or more of these components is not addressed or included;
for example, several institutions cannot make time a negotiable
aspect of an individual's contract because of strict adherence to the

semester as the academic calendar in which learning is to be accomplished. Others do not specify the methods, criteria or standards, or the evidence that is to be used in the evaluation process—merely indicating "Evaluation by Instructor." Still other institutions use the learning contract within the context of a class to individualize only the student's final project and the grade to be assigned. A learning contract can also be the vehicle for individualizing an entire class or seminar, to be discussed later in this chapter.

Faculty Roles

To negotiate a learning contract with an individual or group of individuals in an effective manner, the faculty member must: (1) ask evocative questions, (2) listen, (3) hear, (4) provide appropriate information regarding the institution, (5) discuss a number of alternative approaches to the content to be studied, (6) provide useful information about available learning resources, (7) assist the student in structuring an individualized set of learning activities, and (8) provide intentional and specific methods, criteria or standards, and examples of evidence or indicators that will be employed in the evaluation of the student's performance.

The outcome of the negotiation should be a written document which answers the following questions:

- *Who* is involved in the contract—the names of student(s), faculty tutor(s), field supervisor(s)?
- *Why* is the student engaged in a specific study, in other words what general and specific objectives are being pursued?
- *What* are the topics to be studied?
- *What* learning activities will be used?
- *What* learning resources will be employed?
- *What* methods, criteria or standards, evidence or indicators will be used in the evaluation?
- *When* is the contract in force, in other words, how much time is involved?
- *How* much credit is to be granted for successful completion of the contract?

The implementation of individualized contract learning by an increasing number of colleges and universities has prompted faculties to think carefully about these needed skills and about the development of new faculty roles, emphasizing those skills that the faculty member may not possess.

In the spring of 1975, faculty members and administrators from eight colleges and universities that use contract learning as the sole instructional model or as an option (State University College at Brockport [SUNY], Bunker Hill Community College, Community College of Vermont, Empire State College [SUNY], Metropolitan State University, University of Minnesota, New College at the University of Alabama, and Rockland Community College) convened in a workshop to discuss issues related to this and other nontraditional academic processes. Participants discussed the roles they performed in the implementation of contract learning; the following is a synopsis of their remarks.

The first role described was that of facilitator/counselor. These faculty members pointed out that it was difficult and inappropriate to lecture when working with students on a one-to-one or small-group basis. Others commented that it was almost impossible to avoid the counselor role when negotiating a learning contract because the individual's educational interests and needs are only one aspect of the individual's life and that these other responsibilities and demands enter into the discussion of learning activities. All agreed that although the role of facilitator/counselor is essential, few had had formal training for it.

The second role described was that of broker/negotiator. Faculty commented that the contract learning process caused them to become involved in negotiation. The contract process, except when a course is included as a learning activity, is rarely prescriptive. Since the learning activities contained in a contract represent a balance between student needs and interests and institutional requirements, each learning contract is a negotiated agreement unique to that individual. The role of negotiator is combined with the role of broker. This role emerges because a frequent outcome of a contract negotiation is the need for the faculty member to create or arrange a tutorial, internship, or field placement for the student.

The third role was that of instructor and/or tutor. This traditional faculty role is often performed specifically in cases in which the faculty member who negotiates the learning contract also serves as the primary source of instruction. This role was highlighted also because faculty often discovered that they worked in new ways particularly in cases when the student was studying content that was interdisciplinary, multidisciplinary, problem centered, or thematic in nature. This occurs because many learning contracts do not replicate content with which the faculty member may be working in courses that he or she is currently teaching. Many faculty indicated that involvement in contract learning caused them to work as both specialist and generalist in their field.

The fourth role was that of evaluator. Because the learning contract is usually very specific and intentional about how the learning activities are to be evaluated, this traditional faculty role was reported to be more difficult to perform than faculty had assumed prior to their involvement with the contract process. This difficulty is caused by the precision required when the methods, the criteria or standards, and the indicators or evidence to be used in the evaluation are specified. Other faculty commented that it was quite a change to have students actively involved in the evaluation of their work. This change occurs when the contract process called for summative as well as formative evaluation conferences between faculty member and student.

The fifth role was administrator. Faculty frequently reported that they served as the administrator of tutors and field experience supervisors when the student's contract contained learning activities that included the involvement of such individuals. The sixth role was that of the developer of learning resources. The activities involved in this role included the location of field placements in a variety of settings, such as business and industry, the location of internships in social and environmental agencies, and the development of contacts with libraries, museums, radio and television stations, newspapers, theater groups, and other resources in the community that may provide important learning opportunities for the student.

The seventh role was creator of instructional materials such as mediated and print based modules, and annotated bibliographies for interdisciplinary, problem-centered, and thematic studies. The emergence of this role occurred, the faculty said, because of the inappropriateness of some available materials in meeting the needs of some of their students. The eighth role was planner of individualized degree plans. This role emerges in many academic programs that use learning contracts because the student's entire degree program is individualized in the same way as is a single learning contract. This role is similar to that of facilitator/counselor in terms of the skills required to perform it but different in terms of the information about the institution with which the faculty member must be familiar in order to do an effective job. When working with adult students, this role may become more comprehensive since educational planning often involves career planning as well. The process is thus more complex than assisting the student in planning the learning activities for a single learning contract.

Except for the roles of instructor and evaluator, this set of roles was said to be new to the faculty involved in the academic programs that had implemented the contract learning process. Most of these faculty members indicated that the skills required to perform these roles were not developed in their traditional graduate degree programs and that development of them had been through the use of intuition and trial and error. These faculty members believed they needed ongoing work to improve these skills, particularly one involved in advising students, the evaluation of learning activities, the management of time and resources, and the administration of field-based tutors and intern supervisors. The consensus of this group was that the implementation of an academic program that individualizes the student's education through the use of contract learning should be accompanied by the initiation of a faculty development program that offers an opportunity for faculty to develop those skills necessary for effective program operation.

Contract Teaching

When a faculty member decides to individualize the educational experience for members of an entire class or seminar, a process similar in dynamics to that described earlier for the individual student can be used. This process, sometimes called contract teaching, has certain characteristics that should be noted. There is normally a common interest in the subject, topic, or problem under consideration among the enrolled students; however, each individual's level of interest is probably different, and there is typically a pluralistic set of needs or reasons for taking the course. Diversity is also characteristic of the individuals who make up the group—diversity of perspectives, values, and experience. This diversity is particularly apparent when the group is composed of nontraditional students. When carefully orchestrated, this diversity can enliven the process for each individual and add a richness to the group's experience—not possible in the one-to-one encounter.

When properly motivated, members of the group can offer psychological support to each other, engage in mutual criticism, and participate in the evaluation of each others' work (both formative and summative). Thus, the group can perform many functions that make the individual's educational experience more comprehensive than that provided in the one-to-one experience. The qualifier "properly motivated" is worth noting. If the group is not structured "properly motivated," few, if any of the aforementioned benefits of the group learning experience will occur. (In this context, the phrase "properly motivated" assumes appropriate subject matter preparation for the faculty member as well as careful attention to group process.) In fact, in the typical class little attention is paid to individual differences; all hear the same lectures, read the same books, take the same examinations, and so forth; perhaps the only thing that is individualized is the choice of topic for a final paper.

The individual student was considered earlier. The graph illustrates these group and individual sets of interactive characteristics:

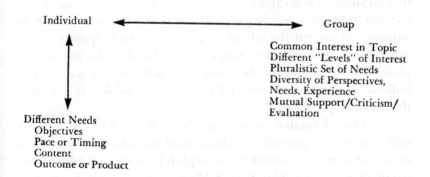

Individual ←————————————————→ Group

Common Interest in Topic
Different "Levels" of Interest
Pluralistic Set of Needs
Diversity of Perspectives,
Needs, Experience
Mutual Support/Criticism/
Evaluation

Different Needs
Objectives
Pace or Timing
Content
Outcome or Product

The process by which a faculty member can facilitate individualized learning in the context of a group has several variations,
but there are several common factors that characterize all of these.
The first two steps are identical to those for a single individual—a
needs analysis or inventory and the setting forth of an individual
contract. The plans need not be lengthy, but it is important to plan
carefully for all members of the group because of the intentionality
it brings to the overall design.

Step three involves the sharing of the individual plans; from
this, a decision about the extent of individualization can be made.
A faculty member with a group may decide that only some of the
learning activities will be individualized. Alternatively, the product
may be the segment that is individualized, or the faculty member
may decide that the individual objectives are unique enough to
require no more than a few group meetings for the presentation of
theoretical information and data necessary to provide a common
base for each member of the group. Step three can be accomplished
efficiently if steps one and two have been completed carefully. The
decisions made after the discussion of individual plans form the
plan for the group. This group plan will spell out the expectations
and responsibilities for each participant, including the faculty member. Thus, individual and shared activities become a blueprint for
the course.

If contract teaching is to be successful, the faculty member
will find that he or she has to play a series of roles. These include:
knowledge expert/subject matter authority, information resource,
facilitator, and evaluator.

The knowledge-expert/subject-matter-authority role is one
that all students will expect the faculty member to play. The faculty
member may elect to give an initial series of lectures, lectures in
sequence, or present the information in a more participatory discussion format. Whatever the plan, it is probable that this role will be
played. The existence of the group plan will provide some useful
indicators as to the amount and timing of the subject information
that must be presented.

The information resource role is necessitated by the fact that
individualization normally creates a need for information about a
variety of resources needed to accomplish learning activities. These
resources run the gamut from bibliographies, to specific author/

theorists, to social agencies outside the college or university setting. The role of facilitator is normally essential in implementing the individual needs analysis, the individual contract or plan, and the group plan. Satisfactory performance of this role requires group dynamics or group process skills. The role of facilitator is also necessary in implementing student participation in topical discussions. Group process skills will also help in facilitating effective discussion so that interaction or discussion will not be between student and faculty, but between student and student and student and faculty. The skills needed for facilitating group interaction include asking questions; listening to the answers given; linking points, questions, and issues expressed by students; using small groups so students talk to each other; and taking time to analyze what occurred during the group's work together.

The role of evaluator is critical if the process is to have the desired outcome. Attention must be paid to clarity in expressing anticipated outcomes as well as the methods, criteria, standards, and evidence to be used in the evaluation process. Evaluation at its best is both formative (in process) and summative (concluding). It is also beneficial if students are involved actively. In order for this to occur, the facilitator role must be employed. These five roles are all essential to contract teaching or individualizing learning within the context of the group.

Sample Model

A sample model may be useful in illustrating implementation of the contracting process. This model is based on the experience of a faculty member at another institution who has been experimenting for several years with a variety of techniques for individualizing education in the context of the group. Her assumption was that independent/individualized learning is compatible with group instruction, that by combining ingredients of both the group and individualized education, an enriched learning experience can occur. This model is based on a fifteen-week time block. The following outline describes the process:

Week 1: *Individual Needs Analysis and Presentation of Individual Plans.* This activity is characterized

by individual presentations regarding purposes, anticipated outcomes, learning activities, and evaluation strategies. Small groups are used to clarify, focus, and/or
expand the individual plans that individuals bring to the
first session. The discussion and small group interaction
are facilitated by the faculty member. Initial questions
about learning resources are answered at this point. A
variation is to do this part of the process before the beginning of the semester—for example, at preregistration.

Week 2: *Discussion and Development of Group
Plan.* The faculty member or a student task force from
the group presents several ideas that synthesize the common aspects of the individual plans and suggest a plan
for the group, which provides the opportunity for individual differences as well. Roles and responsibilities are
clarified also during this session, and agreement on the
group plan is achieved. More questions about resources
are answered, and the faculty member places students
in small task groups where there are specific shared
interests in content areas.

Weeks 3 to 6: *Information Core.* This particular
model calls for a four-week information core. The faculty member gives a series of four lectures, each of
which is followed by student discussion in small groups
and "reports" by each of the small groups to the whole
group. The faculty member is performing the knowledge-
expert/subject-matter-authority role as well as that of facilitator of the group discussion and report process.

Weeks 7 to 10: *Independent and Small Task
Force Work.* During this four-week period, students
work individually and in small common-interest task
forces in fulfillment of the activities described in each
individual's plan or contract. Since the model calls for
individual and small group projects as the major "product," this format was judged to be most appropriate.
The faculty member is available for consultation with
individual students and with the small task force groups.
The faculty member is performing primarily the roles of
knowledge expert/subject matter authority and information resource.

Weeks 11 to 14: *Forum.* This four-week period is a forum for presentation of papers and is sequenced to give those groups who need more time a later date on the schedule. A schedule variation that has been employed is to extend the independent and small task force work period to six weeks and have two forum sessions (or "double" sessions) each week (normally evenings) during weeks thirteen and fourteen. The forum provides the opportunity for each individual to be questioned by other students, to hear their criticisms, and to get a sense of their judgment regarding the work accomplished. During the forum sequence, the faculty member serves as knowledge expert/subject matter authority, facilitator, and evaluator.

Week 15: *Wrap-Up and Evaluation.* This week is spent in concluding the group study. Individual and small group meetings are scheduled—if deemed necessary—to discuss the work presented by the students, to engage in discussion of the evaluation of the student's work, and to complete the paperwork associated with the course. Students who may be deeply involved in a specific topic and need more time to pursue their work may elect at this point to negotiate for more credit or simply an extension of time, but the expectation will be that the individual plan or contract will be completed.

There are many models that could be designed to achieve the objective of individualizing the student's educational experience in the context of a group. Most models or variations require that the faculty member and the students perform a variety of roles and accept a variety of responsibilities. The present model is intended to stimulate discussion of the topic and to focus consideration of designs for educational experiences that foster individual and self-directed learning in the context of a shared group experience.

Variations on Evaluation

Evaluation of learning is a very difficult and complex process, and despite increasing attention to the measurement of individual behavior change, much work is still necessary (see

Chapter Four). Evaluation of learning in the context of a contract
is no exception. However, faculty members who have worked with
contract learning have made some suggestions that can push the
process beyond the level of intuitive judgment.

Because of the explicit nature of most well-written learning
contracts, the first suggestion regarding evaluation is to be as precise
and intentional as possible when describing how and by whom the
student's work or performance is to be evaluated. The section of the
contract devoted to evaluation is frequently divided into three sections (see Chickering, 1977a):

1. Methods. This part of the evaluation section should specify
   whether learning will be demonstrated in a paper, a written or
   oral examination, a performance, a display, a field observation
   with appropriate journal, or simulations. The vehicle that is to
   be used to demonstrate competence should be stated and described and understood by the student.
2. Criteria. This part should indicate what criteria or standards
   will be used in judging the work. The student should know the
   range of acceptable performance. It is helpful if the faculty
   mentor can discuss this range of acceptable performance and
   provide the student with examples of what is meant by, for example, passing work and excellent work.
3. Evidence or Indicators. This part should tell the student what
   evidence will be used to indicate that the criteria have been
   satisfied or the standards met.

When writing the evaluation section of an individual's
learning contract, it is useful to have a good idea of where the
student is beginning in terms of the learning being undertaken. This
will provide a better sense of what outcomes are realistic and how
they are to be measured. At best, writing explicit statements regarding the methods, criteria or standards, evidence or indicators
to be employed in evaluation is a difficult task. It is of particular
importance to involve the student in the process of negotiating the
methods, criteria, and evidence statements and to provide an opportunity for the student to be involved in self-evaluation. It is also
important to include both formative and summative evaluation
conferences. By so doing, work that is not progressing satisfactorily

can be corrected; thus, evaluation is an integral part of the learning process rather than simply a summary judgment of the student's performance. Specificity in the evaluation section of the contract also makes the preparation of the narrative evaluation a very efficient process.

Evaluation when contracting with a group has several variations among institutions. At some, for example, faculty provide grade option contracts to a class. The methods, criteria, and evidence to be used in evaluating work are stated; each student elects the specific level and quantity of work to be accomplished—which has a grade assignment—and contracts to do same. At the simplest level, this may mean performance on tests at specific levels. At more complex levels, a variety of contracts are prepared by a faculty member that provide students with alternative ways of fulfilling the objectives of the course. These contracts frequently contain sections that allow for even fuller individualization. Depending on the institutional practice, the rendering of the evaluation may be a grade or a comprehensive narrative evaluation.

Although the writing of narrative evaluations and the scheduling of evaluation conferences with students is a more time-consuming way of going about evaluation than assigning an alphabetical or numerical symbol, many faculty believe that these tie the evaluation function directly to the learning process. The narrative evaluation and the evaluation conference also work to demystify the process and thus provide students with an increased ability to engage in evaluating their own academic work.

Institutional Examples

Experimenting with the concept of individualizing the student's educational experience through the use of contract learning—on both a one-to-one and a group basis—often means simply a series of changes in an existing course or independent study or tutorial program. But some institutional changes may be needed as well, including one or more of the following:

• A change in institutional policy that makes individualized contract learning a option (this frequently occurs when an

institution initiates a program to serve nonresidential adult
students)
- A change in policy that makes the tutorial, independent study, or
  contract option available to an increased number of individuals—
  this occurs when a faculty removes restrictions that limit this option to students with a particular grade-point average or class
  (junior or senior) identification
- A policy change that initiates the contract process so that the
  independent study process has greater accountability and intentionality because of the existence of a written document and a
  process of negotiation
- A change in faculty teaching practices caused by the faculty
  member's frustration with "teaching to the middle"
- A change in the definition of faculty workload, so that a number
  of individual contracts constitute the equivalent of a course

A number of institutions have, or are currently engaged in,
significant use and experimentation with the individual and/or
group contract method of teaching. Several of these institutional
examples are worth noting (the institutions selected for comment
are illustrative of work going on at a number of other institutions
that are not cited here).

Empire State College (SUNY), an institution founded in
1971, uses the process of individualized learning contracts exclusively. The sample contract included earlier in this chapter is
similar in type to that negotiated with the more than 3,500 students
enrolled at the college's thirty-two geographic locations. The Empire
State College contract has four sections—General Purposes, Specific
Purposes, Learning Activities, Evaluation—and represents part of
the students' individually negotiated degree program. Students can
pursue their degrees either half or full time by completing a series of
learning contracts that can vary in time from one to six months.
They may use individually negotiated learning activities supervised
by a faculty mentor, courses at other institutions, SUNY independent study courses, educational television programming, field placements in job settings, industry, social service and other community
agencies.

The learning contract at Empire State College individualizes the place where the learning occurs, the time or pace, the student's objectives, the content, the learning activities, the learning resources, and the mode of evaluation to be used; it is a negotiated process. At the completion of the learning contract, the faculty mentor and student meet for an evaluation conference. The outcome of this conference and other meetings throughout the contract is the contract Digest and Evaluation, which is a narrative evaluation. The Digest and Evaluation contains a description in digest form of the Specific Objectives and Topics that were studied, the Methods and Criteria by which the work was evaluated, and a series of judgments by the mentor based on evidence presented in the student's work. Evaluations from field supervisors, assessments from tutors, grades from courses (when appropriate) may be included also in the faculty evaluation. The Digest and Evaluation becomes part of the student's transcript or permanent record at the college.

At Birmingham Southern College, an established residential college of arts and sciences, three types of contract learning or contractual study have been initiated recently. Each contract option provides the student with the opportunity to contract with the institution or an individual faculty member for incrementally smaller amounts of academic work—from an entire major to part of a course. The three options that have been developed are:

1. *The Individualized Major Contract.* Use of this option permits the student to negotiate with the institution through an advisory group an individualized major—a major that is not an option offered by any single department. The student carefully outlines the objectives for an individualized major, then identifies the learning experiences—classes, field studies, supervised work experience, or tutorials—in a variety of departments that make a consistent yet unique major for that individual. Examples of such individualized major contracts include: communication studies, women's development, medical illustrating. This result of the process is a specific contract that identifies the components of the student's major and is the student's individual academic blueprint.

2. *The Out-of-Class Learning Contract.* This contract provides the student with the opportunity to negotiate a field experience, an

internship, a reading course, a tutorial, an independent course when the regular course cannot be attended, or a work or travel related learning experience. This contract is individually negotiated with a faculty member and normally carries the credit equivalent of a single course. In this contract, objectives, learning activities, and the methods and criteria for evaluation are detailed.

3. *The In-Class Contract.* In this case, the student negotiates part of the work of an existing course with the faculty member teaching the class. A typical example is that of the student negotiating a project in lieu of a final examination.

In each variation, the process of contracting is similar and affords the student an opportunity to negotiate academic work based on individual interests and needs. (Neal Berte, the president of Birmingham Southern, has edited the definitive book on contracting 1975b, containing examples from other institutions and expert advice.)

At the Evergreen State College, Contracted Studies—both individual and group—is one of two kinds of programs (the other kind of program is Coordinated Studies). Based on a quarter system, Contracted Studies comprise learning activities that can be pursued as an individual or as a member of a small common-interest group; they are negotiated with a faculty sponsor. The sponsor may function as an advisor, instructor, or guide. If the area of work is outside the sponsor's specialty, a "subcontractor" on or off campus will be involved in the contract and report the evaluation of that specialized work to the sponsor. Sponsors usually work with no more than fifteen individual contracts at any given time. Evergreen is rather specific in suggesting that contracts (in their experience) work best for creative, highly motivated, advanced students. The current Evergreen catalogue (1975–1977, pp. 48–49) indicates that:

In preparing a contract, you and your sponsor work out:
• A short title for the project
• A statement of what you wish to learn through it and why
• A description of any previous experience you have had which relates to this project

- A summary of the activities which will take place—the materials and techniques you will study; the methods you will use; the facilities or locations you will be working in; the people who may be working with you
- The support to be provided by the sponsor (and other "subcontractors" on or off campus whose assistance is essential to the project)
- A description of the results which you wish to achieve
- A description of how you and your sponsor will evaluate the work
- A rough estimate of the duration of the contract, under the assumptions that four Evergreen units should represent one quarter of full-time effort but that contractual credit is awarded for the successful performance of the project, not for the amount of time spent on it

Group contracts bring together a group of fifteen to twenty individuals who share a common interest. Although emphasis is on shared work, this option does provide for individual concentration or individualized learning activities. These contracts carefully detail the objectives and learning activities that will be accomplished during the operation of the contract.

The Community College of Vermont uses the contract process as a strategy for individualizing the degree plan of those students who are seeking an associate degree in one of three programs of study: Human Services, Administrative Services, and General Studies. The student contracts with the institution to demonstrate a specific series of competencies in an individual way. Thus, although individuals can work to achieve a specific set of competencies, the contract provides the opportunity to accomplish this in an individual manner through a unique selection of field work and intern experiences, tutorials, classes and seminars, or independent study. The contract itself causes the individual to articulate Program Goals, Student Objectives, Learning Experiences, and the Evidence of Documentation, which will be used for judging whether competence has been attained. The contract is discussed and reviewed by a local review committee and is finally reviewed and amended or approved by the Community College of Vermont Review Board. This contract provides great flexibility for students who are pursuing degrees at this nonresidential statewide community college.

At New College of the University of Alabama, the contract learning process is a well-established pedagogical mode; it is the mechanism for organizing out-of-class learning and independent study. The New College learning contract involves a process of negotiation between faculty and student similar to that described in several of the previous institutional examples. There are five general headings for out-of-class learning and independent study: cross-cultural experiences, subcultural experiences, formal employment experiences, independent study, and internship experiences. The contract has several sections that cause the student to engage in individual planning: goals, objectives, methodology, and evaluation. The evaluation section contains six questions that must be answered: (1) Who will contribute to the evaluation—for example, faculty, field supervisors, tutors? (2) How long will the contract be in operation? (3) What method will be used to do the evaluation— for example, project, report, examination? (4) How much credit will be earned? (5) What tangible product or outcome is expected? (6) Who will render the final judgment regarding the quality of the work? This contract process has become a model that has been adapted by other colleges of arts and sciences where faculty have decided to experiment with individualized education.

Issues

There are many obvious similarities in the individualized contract learning process as it has been implemented at the above institutions. There are also a number of interesting differences.

The common motivation for implementing this process is a belief that individuals are different, have different needs and interests, and learn effectively in different ways. The contract learning process has been demonstrated to be an effective way of responding to these phenomena. The faculty involved with this process agree that effective advising is the core of this teaching method. Most agree that training in the development of advising skills, frequently through a faculty development program, is essential.

The contract process causes faculty to concentrate a great

deal of attention on the evaluation process. This is an area that needs ongoing development. Faculty working with the contract process also report a heightened interest in human development. Because the individualized contract process causes students to think continually about their own objectives, there is normally a closer integration of academic work and personal and professional development. Because of these issues and problems, I recommend that a concurrent program of faculty development accompany the implementation of any program that uses the individualized contract.

The advent of individualized contract learning also raises critical questions of faculty workload and the institution's reward system. There is a variety of institutional experience responses to these issues. It is not the purpose of this chapter to discuss these issues in detail. But there are positive institutional models in existence, and before an institution decides to implement even a pilot program using contract learning, these issues should be decided so that faculty involved in a new academic program do not discover that their energy in program development is appreciated but not rewarded.

Finally, it is important to note that the process of individualized education contains the rewards of a rich student–teacher relationship and may be a significant step in the development of self-directed learning—the key to lifelong learning.

9

❀ ❀ ❀ ❀ ❀ ❀ ❀ ❀ ❀ ❀

Gary A. Woditsch

Specifying and Achieving Competencies

The innocuous label "competency-based education" (CBE) encompasses a burgeoning curricular movement that will dominate educational thinking at least through the next decade and thoroughly shake, if not shift, educational foundations before it is done.

Already, the competency-based label is being attached to practically any curricular venture. All of the innovative instructional approaches treated in this book—from PSI through experiential learning—have been touted by someone as competency-based and not without reason. One seldom encounters a curriculum or pedagogy devoid of an intent to improve student abilities, and that intent sparks talk of competencies. But for this very reason, this chapter will slip blithely past at least 95 percent of contemporary curricular activity that would acknowledge the competency-based label and that is discussed in other chapters. While trying to convey some feeling for the overall movement—no matter how minimal its coherence—this chapter focuses on the less than 5 percent of competency-based education that attempts to grapple with what some of us have come to call "generic" skills or competencies.

Nature and Levels of CBE

It is genuinely difficult to limit the denotation of competency-based education because what makes a program or curricular venture competency-based is not worn on its sleeve. Some time ago, Harold Hodgkinson (1974, p. 2) observed that in competency-based programs "the curriculum which students study does not seem to be markedly different from those of other institutions, nor are the devices used to package or implement the curriculum very different. It seems clear to me that competency-based learning is first and foremost an innovation in the clarity of instructional goals and of the assessment of student learning." In firm support of Hodgkinson's view, one invariably encounters the following three characteristics among descriptions of the CBE approach.

1. Instructional goals are stated explicitly in terms of competencies learners are to acquire.
2. The instructional treatment is designed explicitly to bring about student acquisition of the specified competencies.
3. Assessment procedures are devised to gauge student achievement systematically, as well as the suitability of program goals and instructional treatments.

If these tenets serve to characterize the CBE approach (and no others seem to do it better), then CBE clearly has its roots in prehistory. There is little here that the very first curriculum development theorist would have found startling, though I must hasten to add that there is a good deal here that is quite radical in terms of dominant curricular practice. The key to CBE is simply the literal-minded intensity with which these three tenets are pursued.

A letdown? Perhaps. At least it explains why this chapter can bypass a great deal of CBE: You have already encountered much of it under other guises. Attend to what is said elsewhere in this volume about clarifying objectives, testing, feedback, personalization, flexibility, mastery learning, and computer assistance, and you will have marshalled and inspected the major paraphernalia of CBE. But what ties it all together? CBE is no cure-all instructional package, and it harbors no shake-and-bake solutions to perennial instructional problems. Has it really come so far simply by intoning the phrase, "behavioral objectives," in some ritual fashion?

In my search for a rallying point or a common totem for the clan, I keep returning to the view of CBE as a process, a way of embracing the instructional mission. Its uniqueness lies in the constant effort to shift what is *implicit* in the instructional act to a level of *explicitness* that makes it again focal and hence accessible to analysis, reassessment, and even reconstitution.

CBE attempts explicitness at various levels. First it strives to be explicit about the impact a given instructional unit is supposed to have on the abilities of the learner. At a second level, it tries to be explicit about the still more complex question of the impact a total program should have on the learner's ability to assume one or another societal role. Third, less frequently but with even greater temerity, it attempts to be explicit about the impact education should have on the total character and quality of an individual's existence.

These levels of CBE aspiration supply us with a crude, but useful, way of clustering major domains of CBE activity that are often confused. Although there is strong *process* kinship across domains, each attends to its own very distinctive instructional problem; and unless CBE proponents are quite clear about which domain they inhabit, they can easily make no sense at all of one another. There are course-related, role-related and life-related CBE domains.

Course-Related CBE

Much of CBE deliberately limits its concern to student abilities and performances as they relate to achieving the objectives of a given instructional unit. For example, an instructor wishes to increase the mathematical competencies students acquire as a result of involvement in a second-year calculus course. A good deal of mastery, PSI, modularized, self-paced, frequent assessment innovation fits in this domain. It forms the most palatable and popular sector of CBE for faculty in higher education, especially if they are not attached to professional or vocational programs. In part, this may flow from the fact that our first domain exerts next-to-no pressure for institution-wide change or mission review. Faculty who pursue some form of course-related CBE will be engaged in shaping course-confined changes in pedagogy and technique, aimed at improved instructional efficiency or effectiveness. Established program directions, not to mention the political and disciplinary structures of academia, need never be molested.

Role-Related CBE

Easily the greatest volume of CBE falls in this category. Here, CBE moves from the discrete course to the integrated program level and selects its competencies from those apparently required to excel in one or another socially prescribed role. Fully 90 percent of extant CBE programs have been devised to turn out teachers, but prototypes have emerged to serve social work, medical, legal, and other professions as well. Nor are the competency-specifying roles always work roles. Programs have been devised to develop the competent citizen, consumer, voter, and taxpayer. One will also find here the bulk of CBE assessment effort, which is as concerned with identifying and certifying possessed competencies as it is about developing curricula to foster them.

At the role-related CBE level, however, there is a significant erosion of academic autonomy. Instructional programs suddenly must respond to socially rather than academically established priorities. In good CBE professional programs, there are unprecedented amounts of information gathered about the context, characteristics, and constraints of effective role performance before a curriculum design finger is lifted. Faculty involved in the process will likely find themselves on interdisciplinary work teams engaged in diagnostic and program design activities. The process tends to make faculty articulate spokespersons for the role and leads their professional concerns to transdisciplinary orbits.

Life-Related CBE

Here, one finds the *rara aves* of CBE, in the form of two subtypes. One subtype consists of those efforts—sometimes within the scope of a single course, sometimes throughout an entire general education program—to develop highly generalizable abilities that are neither course nor role specific. The generic skills are pursued by this subtype, with heavy emphasis on the components of critical thought and precise communication.

The second subtype, which we will see is responsible for hatching much of the first, also boasts the most exotic plumage in CBE. Here are competency-based curricula that, in effect, orchestrate all the other domains we have discussed into total degree programs. Everything in the traditional two-year general or associates program or four-year baccalaureate program is subjected to the CBE process, with consequences that here and there are nothing short of breathtaking. No student of radical curricular change can afford to bypass the recent history of an Alverno College or Brigham Young University. As a model of the liberal arts college gone competency-based, Alverno is a classic in its own time, and Brigham Young is unparalleled in shifting the total curriculum of a large university to a competency-based assessment footing within a year (which, in terms of academic calendars, is literally overnight).

Given these three CBE domains, I will leave the first in deference to its treatment elsewhere in this volume. The second I will bypass because of its great scope and already ample bibliography (over five thousand published and fugitive titles at last count, some few of which are noted selectively later in the book). I will turn our attention to the third domain because, despite its comparatively diminutive stature, its story leads to a new (radically old?) and noteworthy model of instruction.

In 1973 a small group of institutions embarked on an attempt to develop competency-based liberal arts or general education programs, often with the stimulus of a grant from the Fund for the Improvement of Postsecondary Education (FIPSE). Places like

Alverno College, Milwaukee; Mars Hill College, Mars Hill, North Carolina; Sterling College, Sterling, Kansas; College IV of the Grand Valley State Colleges, Allendale, Michigan; Sangamon State University, Springfield, Illinois; Our Lady of the Lakes College, San Antonio, Texas; and Bowling Green State University, Bowling Green, Ohio, established lists of liberal and general competencies that, if one sketched a composite, would read something like this:

1. Command critical thinking and problem-solving skills; exhibit ability to use and acquire knowledge.
2. Demonstrate effective use of the written and spoken word.
3. Demonstrate awareness of values and commitments.
4. Demonstrate comprehension of humans' relationships to their physical and social cultures.
5. Demonstrate in-depth knowledge of one discipline or field.
6. Exhibit a comprehension of artistic and aesthetic dimensions of culture.
7. Exhibit proficiency in self-knowledge.

As shy of specifics as this list may appear, little more sufficed as the guideline for major curriculum revision at most of the above institutions. Usually the list bore the added sanction of being the consensual product of a deliberating faculty body. Some theoretical scaffolding would be found to sustain the program development effort—perhaps Bloom's taxonomy (1956) or possibly Phenix's "realms of meaning" (1964)—but not much time could be squandered on theory. Real courses had to be designed to flesh out idealized programs, assessment procedures devised, and the whole apparatus launched "by fall." Perhaps predictably, the serious questions were not phrased until the end of the second or the beginning of the third year. They were asked by front-line teaching faculty, and they would go something like the following: "I've been teaching critical thinking now for five quarters. And I'm beginning to wonder. What really *is* critical thought, what do we really know about it, and how is it best developed?" At just this point, where the rhetoric began to become real, there germinated a distinction between two types of CBE that has since grown to a distinction of moment. For want of better titles, I will call the dominant type of CBE "performance-based" (PB) and reserve "generic skills" (GS) CBE for the less-known alternative.

Performance-Based CBE

The PB approach is familiar, straightforward, and appeals to common sense. It merely requires that a desired set of behaviors, characteristics, or actions be identified. The educational objective is then the obvious one of bringing the student to the point of exhibiting those behaviors, characteristics, or actions. The source for objectives may be traditionally academic (as is the case for many master-learning- or PSI-oriented programs), vocational (where performance-based learning has for tens of centuries been *de rigueur*), any of a variety of social membership roles (parent, consumer, citizen, and so forth), a set of inter- or intrapersonal capabilities (leadership, followership, capacity for deferred gratification, and so forth), or what not.

Whatever behavioral objectives are selected, the *educational* problem is understood to be one of bringing the student, as efficiently as possible, to the point where he or she can exhibit those behaviors in a satisfactory manner. And how does one come to master new behaviors? Why, of course, by being exposed to them, by modeling them, and, once you get the hang of it, by practicing them.

Remember that we said CBE is tenacious about being explicit. A careful parsing of the simple road to mastery outlined above shows why many CBE programs are quick to acknowledge alternatives to classroom instruction. The classroom is simply not the best context for exposure to certain classes of desirable behavior. If the target behaviors are the sort that normally occur or are employed *outside* the classroom environment, perhaps a "real-life" context will better stimulate their acquisition. Apprenticeship truly is the covert ideal of the PB approach, an ideal that cannot quite be embraced because it lacks economy. Instead, the PB approach embraces a pedagogic strategy that holds that wherever possible, the conditions under which behaviors are *learned* should parallel the conditions under which those behaviors normally *occur*.

The PB approach exhibits a corollary tendency in assessment. Assessment techniques that elicit subject responses *most like* the target set of behaviors are preferred. Hence, the PB approach to CBE tends away from "paper and pencil" assessment and favors complex simulations of real-life situations that elicit the whole repertoire of desired behaviors from the student and permit experts to "judge" their adequacy. The criterion of competence is the degree of match between student performance and the prescribed target behaviors.

It should emerge from the above that, *in substance,* the PB approach, harbors a remarkably staid and unexceptional notion of the educational process. Competency-based education of the PB type gets into trouble with reigning educational practice not on grounds of fundamental incompatability but, rather, because CBE insists on being sober and relentless where the tradition has been somewhat casual, if not cavalier.

Generic Skills CBE

Oddly enough, GS-type CBE is the product of an even more compulsive explicitness. A small number of faculty who embraced the developmental objective of increasing student competence in problem solving and critical thought began to probe seriously the meaning of such terms as *cognitive skills, conceptual mastery,* and *problem solving.* They found that rather than resting on clear meaning (explicit referential content), such phrases depended on what Willard Quine (1966, p. 70) has called "an uncritical assumption of mutual understanding." As Quine observes in another context, such phrases are "promissory notes" that represent phenomena we understand poorly, but that we must nonetheless borrow against to sustain present discourse and that we hope some day to pay off in the specific currency of clear referential content.

These faculty sought to redeem at least partially the promissory notes. They augmented their own instructional experimentation with insights from the works of genetic epistemologists like Vygotsky and Piaget, anthropologists like Levi-Strauss and Casagrande, linguists like Whorf, Ullman, and Weinreich, and language theorists like Quine and Chomsky, all of whom contribute to a view of humans that suggests their most complex behaviors are the products of the mastery and recursive application of a relatively small set of core abilities. There appeared some hope that gains made in these molecular abilities might improve an individual's performance whatever his or her endeavor. For instance, an improved capacity to separate useful from trivial information would seem to advance all seven general competencies in the earlier composite list, from thinking critically to gaining proficiency in self-knowledge. So the GS approach does not search for desirable behaviors as much as for the common building blocks out of which an individual might construct legions of desirable behaviors.

Because it is concerned with the identification and development of highly transferable core abilities that advantage broad ranges of behavior, the GS approach does not especially favor alternatives to the classroom as an instructional vehicle, nor does it hunger to duplicate "real life" as a pedagogical strategy. Generic skills that comprise abilities like critical thinking may have broad real-life applicability and yet be cultivated best in highly synthetic and "unreal" ways. Certain of the most durable and transferable competencies yet identified—those in the cognitive and communicative domains—happen to be largely developable and accurately assessable by paper and pencil.

While attempting to forge some meaning for the generic skill catchwords that have long seasoned educational literature, some faculty slowly grew conscious of a set of assumptions that pervade current educational practice—including PB-type CBE—and conflict with their own emerging sense of the educational mission.

PB Versus GS: A Conflict of Basic Assumptions

That students come to us with basically predetermined abilities is the first, and perhaps most critical, of four dominant assumptions that PB does not challenge while GS does. The four are:

1. Fundamental development of human abilities occurs in early youth, well before formal postsecondary education. Any real hope of school influence on developing basic competencies lies with early childhood education.
2. An instance of performance implies competence.

3. Postsecondary curricula can assume and build upon basic conceptual and communication skills already attained, save in the
   case of uniquely "disadvantaged" students. When raised at the
   postsecondary level, development of basic competencies is a
   "remedial" issue.
4. The most promising strategy for change in postsecondary education involves retailoring curricula to address the expressed needs
   of society and the student.

   We shall gain some understanding of the GS approach from
its critique of the four assumptions.

   The tenet that basic abilities solidify early is one of the real
constants in educational planning. "Adapt the course material to the
student's ability," has to be among the ten commandments of curriculum development. If that ability were assumed to be flexible
rather than fixed, it might not seem so outrageous to attempt an
adaptation of student ability to the curriculum, and perhaps not all
the enormous federal funding that is directed to research on basic
abilities would be directed toward preteens. Counter to assumption
one, we know that certain very general higher order abilities can
barely emerge, let alone come to characterize our behavior, prior
to the midteens, and even then *need* not emerge. Quite contrary to
exhausting our capacity for growth early, we tend to be frugal in
developing higher abilities, and people can pass through adulthood
without generating critical and judgmental competencies well within
grasp. As with other biological organisms, there is a psychophysical
economy at work in human beings: We tend to function not at our
highest level of ability but, rather, at a level satisfactory to meet the
press of our circumstances and purposes. Since core abilities do not
irrevocably "set" at an early age, generic skills are a prime and
malleable target *throughout* the span of formal education, from
kindergarten to graduate school.

   Faith in assumption two ignores the ever-present human
capacity for mimicry. We quite commonly construct performances
without possessing the appropriate competence. The child "mimics"
the adult by constructing performances out of limited competencies
that look like products of higher order ones. That is how the bulk
of learning takes place. Particularly in formal education, where clues

regarding desirable performances are amply telegraphed, this capacity enables many to convey an impression of competence where little, if any, exists. A number of studies (Bauman, undated; Renner and Lawsen, 1973; McKinnon and Renner, 1971) suggest that evaluation of the kind that dominates education cannot distinguish the abilities underlying a given performance (see Chapter Four). We ascribe conceptual skill to certain student behaviors for no better reason than that we have already assumed the skills are there—somebody told us they were supposed to have emerged at age six or so.

The capacity to reproduce a set of desired behaviors is by itself not a sufficiently dependable sign that an individual is competent in that behavior. Give me time (as many PB-type CBE programs propose to do) and rote practice will enable me to deliver a passable piano concerto. Only when you hand me sheets of music I have not played before will you discover my musical ineptness.

Assumption three erodes as we uncover increasing numbers of students who might be classed as the "advantaged incompetent"—students with admirable secondary grades and standard scores who are incapable of developing, dismembering, or communicating an idea. The symptoms are not bound to ethnic or economic classes nor to the usual categories of "underachievers." It is simplistic to blame secondary education. At the college level, we see students now we did not see when self-selection, rather than social pressure, dominated college entrance. These students seem to show us that the demands life and schooling typically make of them are, in fact, not so strenuous as to trigger the development of abilities well within their grasp. The problem of getting people to develop competencies a step above those required to "get by" is much too pervasive to be considered remedial.

Assumption four, although attractively expedient, risks a strategy employed with other problems in the public sector, which is to segregate and treat the symptom. There is strong support for the view that education is a form of social welfare the job of which is to dispense a currency of skills that, in turn, are supposed to purchase useful and rewarding roles in society. If graduates cannot get jobs in glutted markets, aid them in career planning and teach job-specific skills for unglutted markets. If crime and social irresponsibility are rampant, teach values. The problem is that symptoms, by definition, are to be found under one's nose: causes are not. It is conceivable that public education could set itself an endless roster of explicit citizenry needs without ever improving an individual's capacity to serve his or her own needs. It may thereby totally miss society's basic want, which is for individuals whose range of self-directed action can support social existence.

While exploring their discomfit with these assumptions, proponents of the generic skill development concern in postsecondary education began to understand why talk of generic skills so often meets a cool or perfunctory reception, even from CBE proponents of the PB persuasion. The move from admitting to denying a place for generic skill concerns at the postsecondary level involves a fundamental shift of perspective. It is an epistemic shift, a change in the relationship we presume "knowing" establishes between us and our world. Consider . . .

If we assume that the business of the mind is to mirror what is real, the set of skills tagged as generic (we shall call them Set A) will be those that emphasize information acquisition and retention—the relatively passive "intake" skills. If, on the other hand, cognition is seen as responsible for *selectively shaping* the constructs we employ about our world, the skills seen as critical and generic become post-acquisitive, *constructural* skills. These are the active cognitive abilities (we shall call them Set B) by which we process information—decompose and recompose it—so as to better model experience given our purposes.

These two quite different epistemologies establish strong, implicit, and quite different predilections concerning what set of cognitive abilities is to be embraced as focal. Set A enjoys the sanction of the basically Aristotelian, common-sensical core of Western civilization. Set B enjoys the critically sound, but as yet culturally undigested, sanction of the leading scientific and philosophic minds of this century.

It is instructive to contrast the two skill sets. It happens that generic skill Set A comprises abilities that develop at a chronologically earlier age than those of Set *B*. The skills attendant to ostensive reception and retention are precisely those that acculturation requires of the child, and so they take shape quickly. If we count these as the primary cognitive abilities, it is no wonder that postsecondary educators eschew generic skills as an appropriate target. The *real* three R's of dominant educational practice—"Receiving, Retaining, and Reiterating"—are mastered quite early. Postsecondary education is not where they are developed; it is where they become team sports.

Quite a different case for Set *B* skills! It is not simply that these develop later (some of them may not even be *developable* prior to the midteens). It is that they need not develop at all. They are at once frighteningly optional and even more frighteningly essential. They are optional in the sense that an individual can wend his or her way convincingly through present-day society without them, whereas the absense of Set *A* skills is immediately and painfully evident and constitutes an overt handicap. The absence of higher-order skills, on the other hand, can go long undetected. In a world crammed with preprogrammed roles, there are even scientists who need not think critically. As long as they satisfy expectations, they can mime critical thought through routine behavior.

But Set *B* skills are essential from a societal point of view. Societies develop fatal dysfunctions, grow suicidal, and collapse without sufficient wielders of Set *B* skills. It should come as no surprise: If knowing is mirroring what is around you, the skills of the mimic are focal. The trouble with a mind whose attributes are those of the photocopying machine (copy, hence preserve, thus iterate) is its inability to assess the fitness of what it duplicates. Like the magic salt mill, it goes on and on till sweet waters turn bitter.

Once your epistemology allows you to prize set *B* skills, their claim on a central place in the postsecondary education mission grows gradually more insistent. These are not skills *preordained* to emerge in our behavioral repertoire. It appears that the higher and more complex the skill, the more explicitly we control whether it develops or atrophies. Consequently formal education, especially from secondary through postsecondary levels, will have very much to do with the relative presence or absence of Set *B* skill wielders. Also, since these are skills we control more explicitly, curricula would do better to address their development explicitly rather than implicitly, under the assumption that they are acquired like small change with other purchases.

The Generic Skills: What Are They?

People who collect definitive lists will be disappointed in their search for a roster of Set *B* skills, but then again such people should not be interested in education. There certainly is a sufficient list, far more precise than any that has thus far been used to guide large-scale curricular development. It is substantive enough to lead to its own systematic elaboration and modification, which means it has the quality of being "scientific." In order to arrive at the list, I take the path of mental measurement.

Some psychometricians, while engaged in the process of calibrating "intelligence," have concentrated on segregating the kinds of behavior that accompany problem-solving failure. Here is a typical list:

1. Subject exhibits random attention. Unable to sustain focus on the critical variables of the problem.
2. Subject scans compulsively and haphazardly. Does not probe a complex problem until all its components are identified.
3. Subject fails to test known relationships (prior knowledge) against potential relationships in the problem. Does not make analogies.
4. Subject guesses chronically. Does not assign priorities to regularities sensed in the problem but follows the first "lead" that occurs.
5. Subject fails to check solution. Does not review problem to see if the solution constructed (a) works and (b) is the best alternative.

At the CUE (Competency-Based Undergraduate Education) Center, Bowling Green State University, we found it exceedingly interesting to note that a student could exhibit any or all of these failure-prone behaviors and yet amass a thoroughly respectable grade-point average. In an environment as rich in behavioral cues as the college classroom, mimicry will apparently cover a multitude of incompetencies. Perhaps what is more interesting is that most new, "innovative" curricula tend precisely to compensate for these student failure-prone behaviors, obviating any need to develop the counterpart skill. Whether it be programmed text, PSI, or modularized learning, all are noted for (1) emphasizing the critical as opposed to trivial variables of a problem, (2) thoroughly decomposing the problem into its component elements, (3) drawing connections between new material and experience or knowledge the student might be presumed to have, (4) arraying evidence and deliberating the "best" approach, and (5) providing frequent feedback and solution checks.

In an astonishing number of cases, curriculum developers have lost the distinction between eliciting critical thought and doing the student's thinking. Too often an effort to reduce the instructor's assessment load results both in a reduction of required student effort and a *qualitative* shift in *type* of effort required (again, see Chapter Four). The distinction between stimulating and supplanting student effort is, in any case, an unfortunate one to lose, because the consequences snowball. A student who is not required to think has little to say or write and small cause to read.

Perhaps it will become more obvious that we are dealing with context-independent life skills if we transmute our failure-prone behaviors into their success-prone counterparts:

1. Selective attention: ability to control the class of stimuli that receive conscious focus.
2. Sustained analysis: a capacity to probe a complex situation until all its components are identified.
3. Analogizing: a capacity to test known relationships for similarity with those potential to a new situation.
4. Suspension of closure: assigning priorities to factors before shaping solution.
5. Autocensorship: testing a solution covertly, before affirmation.

It is difficult to imagine an area of purposive human activity that would not benefit by improved competence in these five molecular, hence transferable, hence generic, competencies. These and recursions and combinations of them represent a great portion of our Set *B* skills. If we prize individuals capable of self-illumination and self-guidance, they will wield these skills. Had we time and paper enuogh, we could show these to be skills prerequisite to conceptual thought, properly so-called, and also skills the exercise of which must precede any significant gain in the precise use of language (Woditsch, 1977).

Can Generic Skills Be Taught?

Generic skills can, and should, be taught both overtly and covertly. A leading exponent, not only of identifying generic abilities from this vantage but of developing them as well, is the psychometrician Arthur Whimbey, author of *Intelligence Can Be Taught* (1975). At CUE we had the benefit of Dr. Whimbey's assistance in developing college-level general education curricula that focus explicitly on articulating problem-solving abilities. Dr. Whimbey's course, which began as experimentation at Berkeley, matured at Dillard University and through work with the Washington State Board of Education, and received further polishing at Bowling Green State University, can be viewed as a model of the sorts of instructional emphases to be found among a growing cadre of faculty across the nation who are experimenting with the development of generic skills. The course drew upon 300 pages of problem-solving protocols, very much like those one would find in the item pool for an IQ battery. Math story problems and reading comprehension items of considerable complexity emerge from this collection to challenge the class, but not before such apparently simple, seemingly trivial, and invariably illuminating items as: "What day follows the day before yesterday if two days from now will be Sunday?"

Even the occasional graduate student exhibits lack of adeptness with the organized, sequential approach required to consistently solve problems of this kind. As members of the class vocalize their personal attack on the problem, it becomes clear that some will take a vague leap from Sunday after grasping only *some* of the relationships specified in the problem. Even among those who use the last part of the question to determine that today is Friday, some fail to see the two-component structure of the problem; they skip about unsystematically and then guess in frustration. Unproductive behaviors such as premature closure and guessing are caught in the light of day, and the class discusses and tries productive alternatives. Once grasped, these better strategies are employed, still with vocalization, to address increasingly varied and complex problems. Generally, Whimbey's course exhibits the following traits.

1. *The course compels students to verbalize their thinking as they solve problems, thereby alerting students to their own otherwise covert and unrecognized thinking patterns.* Whimbey pairs his students, who then alternate at making and criticizing vocal solutions to problems. More typically, courses focusing on the development of critical thinking competencies emphasize written verbalization and require the development and use, often by students as well as faculty, of a writing analysis ruberic (For example, see Haas, Browne, and Keeley, 1976). But whether the subject matter employed is highly literate controversy, IQ test items, or a series of problems in physics, emphasis is on making the *implicit* problem-solving behaviors of the student *explicit.*

2. *The course contrasts inadequate problem-solving strategies with good ones.* In Whimbey's approach, this is again done vocally. Students compare fruitless strategies with fruitful ones within their own ranks, occasionally contrasting their efforts with the "thinking aloud" protocols of outstanding problem solvers. Although there are written counterparts to this vocal approach, vocalization exhibits three significant advantages. Particularly where pairs are at work, the amount of passive classroom time per student is dramatically reduced. Second, because they experience the difference, students more readily transform the need to have right answers into a concern for improving their problem-solving ability. Third, bad problem-solving practices that normally would never be revealed are dragged into public view. This is particularly important because many bad practices have been deliberately inculcated by former schooling, such as "doing everything in your head," "avoiding scribbles and sketches," or "above all, be quick."

3. *Having helped the students identify the component problem-solving skills, the course demands their incessant practice.* The key to achieving easy transferance of these basic problem-

solving behaviors is to ensure their becoming habitual, and hence generic skills–oriented courses inevitably work students hard.

Perhaps the GS course displays CBE explicitness at its best. The whole point is to raise the processes through which problems are solved to a level of explicit consciousness, thereby making them amenable to student/instructor control. The approach is particularly useful in placing our five building-block skills under the student's explicit command.

However, developing a curricular component that success-fully addresses the formation of generic skills is the least of our prob-lems. Much more difficult is the task of providing *lebensraum* for such skills in the remaining curriculum. If not one change were made in the content of an undergraduate program but every estab-lished course were taught in such a way as to require student em-ployment of selective attention, sustained analysis, analogizing, suspension of closure and autocensorship, we would be closer than we have ever been to a curriculum for competent citizenry. As a result of studies CUE has initiated to probe the kinds of demands upon student skill levied by the typical college course (Keeley, Browne, and Haas, 1976), it can be said that wherever else our five skills may be in demand, their absence will not likely be detected in the classroom. Yet any content *can* be taught in such a way as to demand thought. An introductory Spanish course for developmental students, designed with Whimbey's assistance, has demonstrated an incredible degree of initial success because it applies a problem-solving paradigm to the business, say, of identifying correct pro-nomial endings (Whimbey and Barberena, 1977). Students come to exhibit good Spanish as a result of good thinking. If the basic skills we have identified are, in fact, to become characteristic of the student's posteducational behavior, his or her educational experi-ence must be heavily and consistently salted with demands for their exercise.

A New Instructional Role?

Faculty involved in GS-type CBE tend to be faculty who at one time or other taught a significant general education load. More-over, they received little intrinsic reward from the teaching and were sufficiently capable in their own disciplines to be cocky about addressing the bankruptcy of general education squarely. I have known a fair number of such faculty (there seem to be at least a few on each campus), and it seems they share a set of working assumptions that point to a new kind of classroom professional or at least a new embodiment of an old professional ideal.

The first working assumption is that the benefits usually ascribed to general education, if taken seriously, entail development of the most complex and least understood human abilities. They are difficult abilities to profile for the same reason they are to be prized highly—because they are generalizable, productively transferable to a broad range of life situations, and hence not as easily captured as the specialized skill in its confined and limited context.

Consequently, GS instructional experimentation is not "package" oriented. Involved faculty do not anticipate a terminal understanding of human ability, and hence they do not aim at a terminal critical thinking course design. Rather, they move toward better approximations in understanding and effectively developing basic abilities. Oddly enough, this makes them more careful about controlling the variables of instruction, since they know that better aim is a function of careful adjustment based on the results of prior aim. They are committed experimentalists who see instruction itself as an inherently problematic and hence experimental act.

Secondly, these are not faculty who are embarrassed by the classroom. They hold that the classroom harbors an archetypal, rather than artificial, human process—a seminal dynamic that underpins full human development, described from one pole as learning and the other as teaching. Nowhere is the process more accessible than in the classroom, and so GS faculty are convinced that careful inquiry there will eventually win profound and generalizable insight concerning the maturation of human abilities.

Finally, they are not faculty content to wait and be told by the "expert." The questions they raised about the relationship of instruction to the development of human abilities caused them to run out of experts very quickly. They have a sense of addressing a critical area that has been largely overlooked, and they feel quite capable of uncovering and contributing insight on their own.

"On their own" is perhaps the best descriptor for these instructor–experimenters. Their efforts typically receive no comprehension, let alone sympathetic support, from department, discipline, or institutional hierarchy. At best, they enjoy the rather tenuous collegium of a few like-minded instructor–experimenters on other campuses.

Perhaps because their professional demeanor conveys a sense of excitement about the instructional act, as though it were the unfathomable adventure it in fact is, I think of such faculty as the cream of the crop. This is not in all respects a happy image. An industry unable to find use for cream turns to homogenization.

A Future for the Generic Skills Approach?

Frankly, its chances are slim. The basic flaw of the GS approach is that it is on every count the more demanding path to change, and there is always a more easily grasped, more compatible alternative available. Evidence that the GS approach works, while the more palatable choices are ultimately trivial, will likely deter no one.

There is no need to explain the appeal of vocational and role-specific skill approaches to parents, teachers, or legislators. The appeal of that kind of performance-based instruction is as transparent as the skills themselves appear to be. Talk of generic skill, however, confuses and is presently fitting only in preambles to statements of educational mission or in decorative footnotes. If generic skills issues were to be taken seriously, large numbers of people would have to grow accustomed to (1) an unfashionable view of learners, (2) an unaccustomed view of teaching, and (3) an unsettling view of social and individual fulfillment. To epitomize these:

1. Our tendency to romanticize the learner as a kind of Rousseauian "Noble Savage"—naturally simple and forthright in dynamic, and thus in a sense "complete"—is signified in our willingness to speak of the student as a consumer rather than product of education. The generic skills approach almost requires a sense of

the student as inherently wiley and shrewd, with a kind of mild, unconscious, and hence unruly resistance to efforts that elicit and expand higher abilities. Where the former view demands that education be responsive to learner differences, the latter demands that education make differences in learners.

2. A great many faculty who consider themselves developers of skill are unaware that they are no more than attentive screeners of skill, like the coach who "taught" baseball by watching kids bat and singling out the ones who could. The production of instructors capable of influencing generic skill development would require major upheavals and reconstitutions of the dominant instructional role model. Disciplinary expertness, for example, would have to be reharnassed as a tool for, rather than a goal of, instruction, and instruction itself becomes increasingly experimental rather than increasingly programmed.

3. Next to its easy chair and its predinner martini, an older generation cherishes an image of its youth rising to privileged and secure futures. The violins of vocational and performance-based education do much to embellish that image. The generic skills approach, uneasy with social prognostics, fair or foul, that stretch beyond a few weeks, tries to root security and privilege in youth's ability to shape and reshape itself and its environment rather than its ability to adopt behaviors we ratify as advantageous today. Possibly no generation will ever find satisfaction in saying to its heir, "I'm not sure what is best for you, but here are some abilities you can use in pursuing what is better." That is, in fact, what the generic skills approach offers, and it requires quite a shift of contemporary bias to see that as *more* rather than *less* than one gains from role-specific education with its, "Here is what's best for you, and this is how you acquire it."

So the generic skills approach is unattractive and hence unlikely, whereas the vocational, role-specific skill approach is a shoo-in, probably because it makes explicit what has always been implicit in society's request for educational service. The ideal would be a limited victory for both approaches, with generic skill instruction underpinning more specialized preparation. But "generic skill" lacks sufficiently powerful protagonists to secure even minimal identity among *causes célèbres* in today's pantheon of educational issues. Despite know-how and a sense of need that excels any we have had before, generic skills will likely remain a rarely encountered target of the postsecondary instructional act.

10

❀ ❀ ❀ ❀ ❀ ❀ ❀ ❀ ❀ ❀

Charles F. Fisher

Being There
Vicariously
by Case Studies

A few years ago, as I entered the seminar room where I was about
to lead a case study discussion with a group of forty new academic
deans and vice-presidents, one of the participants began waving
his hand somewhat emphatically and, having caught the group's
attention, suddenly blurted out, "Chuck, before we get started,
you've gotta' admit to us, off the record, that this is *not* an *authentic*
case study—it just couldn't be true! No organization could have
so many problems or make so many mistakes, and certainly no in-

dividual could have been so naive as the dean at this institution. Come on now, isn't this really a case you have fabricated from several different accounts of college problems?"

Somewhat taken aback, even though I knew the authenticity of the case (having helped to develop and edit it), I nonetheless was caught in that temporarily awkward situation in which I was wrestling with an appropriate response that would not embarrass or intimidate the individual but, at the same time, would clarify the authoritative nature of the resource material and the validity of our group discussion. Before I was able to respond, one of the other participants came to my rescue.

"Let me take you off the hook," he said. "Just within the group here, as I read the case study, it became very evident to me that this was *my* institution and the dean in the case was *my* unfortunate predecessor!"

At that moment a very audible sigh of relief came simultaneously from three other participants. The first to speak, an academic vice-president, readily admitted that he had been virtually positive that this was *his* former institution and that, regretfully, *he* had been the naive dean who had made all of those incredible mistakes! He was wrong, of course, but our case study discussion was well under way—with gusto.

During the past decade I have had the opportunity to observe the case study method in action during ninety professional development programs involving altogether over 4,000 college and university administrators. While serving as a case discussion leader with over half of these participants, I have become particularly aware of the individual's personal involvement, the group dynamics, the participant "turn on," and the potential teaching/learning effectiveness of this instructional design.

The case study approach appears to provide a dimension of realism so often lacking in the structured learning milieu: an opportunity for greater participant identification and vicarious projection into real-world issues and circumstances, an opportunity to anaylze and solve problems in an informal, detached atmosphere in which peer wisdom is shared and in a manner conducive to sound, objective decision making.

I will be quick to suggest that the case study method is certainly not a panacea for all classroom instruction; nevertheless, the approach could well have much to offer for many programs and courses in the areas of professional and graduate school training, continuing and lifelong learning, and even in undergraduate courses that are concerned with human relations, organizational behavior, or, for that matter, any subject that addresses problem solving. It should be noted also that case studies do not necessarily deal with mistakes or deficient behavior; they simply present actual circumstances that involve realistic decision making on the part of the participants. The purpose of the method is to develop or enhance within the student a capacity to deal effectively with real-life problems in a complex and continually changing environment.

The case method of instruction, quite simply, is the use of cases to effect problem-centered learning. A case is a factual written record of a situation, condition, and/or experience. Bauer (1955) has defined several basic types: the *case problem*, which briefly presents the facts and the problem itself; the *case report*, which provides the basic elements with little supporting information and gives the decision(s) and results; the *case study* (or *history*), which is a longer, more complete account, not necessarily with a readily identifiable problem, but containing the results and sometimes the implications and analysis of actions; and the *research case*, which is the most comprehensive, including more on observable events, factors, and a complete diagnosis. Although this chapter focuses primarily on the case study, many of the observed characteristics, applications, and implications would apply as well to the other classifications.

In the sections that follow, I will attempt to describe further the case study method, its background and philosophy, some of its possible applications to the classroom, the design and development of case studies, teaching by the case method, and some evidence as to its effectiveness in the learning process.

Background and Philosophy

The earliest known use of cases was in the diagnostic training of social workers shortly after the Civil War. Later in the nineteenth century, the method was used by the Harvard Law School to present judicial decisions in a revolt against the less functional lecture method of legal education. In the early twentieth century, cases were employed by visiting teachers as aids to pupil guidance. It was in the early 1920s when the first intensive effort was made to apply the case method to any field of administration, with the initiative, not surprisingly, taken by the Harvard Business School. The case study approach to teaching has thus been referred to frequently as the "Harvard Case Method" of teaching human relations (Andrews, 1956). By 1940 the field of public administration began adopting this approach, and during the 1950s it was applied to the preparation of school administrators (Bauer, 1955).

During 1953–1955 the Harvard Business School, in cooperation with the National Association of Student Personnel Administrators (NASPA), developed a series of case discussion seminars for student personnel administrators. This experiment was apparently the first broad application of the case method to teaching college administration, and the success of the experience was a factor in the decision to establish the Institute for College and University Administrators (ICUA) in 1955. Several cases developed for the NASPA seminars were used in the early ICUA programs for presidents and academic deans; these formed the nucleus of the first cases in college administration, along with industrial management ones, which were made available through the Harvard Business Schools Intercollegiate Case Clearing House.

Not all categories of cases fall discretely into Bauer's four classifications, since the design is often determined by the intended use. Although legal cases are fairly specific, administrative and therapeutic (welfare) ones vary more in their purpose and style. Cases in business, public, or educational administration may fall into any one of the descriptive types. Those dealing with higher educational administration are usually case studies. The case used for the experiment briefly described later in this chapter was a *case study* by definition, one in which a major, exigent problem was not readily identifiable (perhaps not unlike the administrative process at times) but in which administrative decision making was very much in evidence and major educational issues were at stake.

A case study may be defined as the factual account of human experience centered in a problem or issue faced by a person, a group of persons, or an organization. It describes real situations in real settings that require or suggest the need for discretionary action. The case study method, then, is the process of using this written case to effect learning by involving the participant in at least three interdependent stages of activity: reading and contemplating the case by oneself; analyzing and discussing the case with others in a group session or sessions; and subsequent reflection upon the case, the discussion, and his or her own attitudes and behavior.

Every student brings a certain unique set of experiences, skills, and attitudes to the classroom setting. The purpose of the case method is to enhance these experiences, help the participants improve their skills, and provide them with the opportunity to examine their attitudes. While reading a case study in preparation for a discussion, the individual vicariously gains a new and different experience while formulating a tentative analysis of the case or problem. During the group analysis and discussion, then, each person contributes his or her own thoughts and reacts to those of others.

It is during this group discussion that the most significant aspect of the case method comes into effect. With an authentic case study as a common experience, a group of student colleagues as interested and vicariously involved partners, and a case leader as moderator, the ultimate in meaningful discussion can be accomplished. The participants can share and explore ideas, test their individual judgments, and play roles in realistic problem-solving exercises detached from the threat of actual consequences. Each contributes to, and learns from, the group's wisdom, benefits from group feedback, and gains greater insights into his or her own feelings and those of others. All sides of a question, issue, or problem can be explored quite thoroughly in an objective manner, approximating the ideal in real-world decision making while remaining once removed from real-world involvement.

The overall purpose of the case method, then, is to help participants develop human relations concepts, practical judgments, and decision-making acumen. Through active involvement, both cognitive and affective learning takes place. Participants gain a better comprehension of human roles and relationships and of how to apply theories and principles to concrete action and practices. They become more aware of behavioral concerns and of some of the analytical tools for more effective decision making. They sharpen their discernment and their ability to anticipate and analyze problems, to consider the feasibility and implications of alternative courses of action, and to avoid making premature decisions or over-cautious judgments.

Of course, the case method does not provide simple or necessarily correct solutions to human relations or administrative problems, nor does it indicate what is necessarily right or wrong. What it does do is provoke the critical-thinking processes, helping individuals realize that there are no "pat" solutions and that each problem is unique unto itself, requiring discretionary decisions appropriate to the specific set of circumstances. Nonetheless, through the method's reality testing, and particularly the simulated exploration of alternative decisions, the participants can acquire new concepts, useful generalizations, guiding principles, and valuable insights for sound, responsible decision making. In the course of this, some preconceived notions may be modified, whereas other attitudes may be reenforced, both of which are important learning outcomes. But perhaps the most important outcome of the case method is the fact that it helps participants learn how to learn, a quality indispensable to the lifelong education process.

What this suggests is that the case method provides a functional relationship between theory and process, between principles and practice, between the printed or spoken word and the actual process of doing. By relating to real-life problems, the case approach to learning is less confining and offers a greater potential for identification and exploration than do more traditional forms of classroom teaching. Although they provide more direct contact with reality, internships and practicums are lengthy in commitment and limited in opportunity. The case approach is perhaps the closest thing to actual apprenticeship that exists. It offers a happy compromise between precious time and extensive experience while bridging the gap between the classroom and the real world. It provides a concentrated, yet adaptable, learning opportunity in which the learners can vicariously acquire several years of real-world experience.

Application to the Classroom

My own involvement with the case study method has been primarily in the teaching of college and university administrators or, more accurately, in facilitating their own learning. For the most part, the students have been recently appointed presidents, vice-presidents, deans, and business officers—some brand new—though the typical participant has been in his or her post for almost a year. The majority have come from other positions in higher education, usually from the faculty or another administrative post. They have ranged in age from twenty-five to over sixty; the average age has been around forty-two.

The fact that these participants have been inservice professionals and obviously more mature and experienced than the typical classroom student no doubt has contributed to the popularity and success of the case method of instruction. In fact, as the study described later suggests, the case approach probably *is* somewhat more effective with older students; they are able to reflect upon a greater array of lifetime experiences, bring a broader analytical perspective, and relate their learning to their present job responsibilities and opportunities. But (this no doubt would apply in most all settings) older students tend to be more serious, dedicated, and aware of what they want to and/or need to acquire from a particular learning experience. They usually come, not only with more incentive, but with a greater accumulation of both practical and philosophical wisdom upon which to draw.

However, this is not to suggest that the case study method is applicable only to the older student. The younger learner, who tends to be more impressionable and probably more receptive to new ideas, can also discover a whole new way of learning by experiencing the method. (Indeed, he or she also may be able to bring some fresh insights into the seminar discussions!) Perhaps the ideal mix is attained (and I suspect that this too is true in most learning arrangements) when there is a range of ages and experiences present. Such a group composition would help optimize the opportunity for peer learning from different perspectives, which, after all, is what the method is primarily about. Nonetheless, with proper planning and application, with greater direction on the part of the teacher/case leader, even undergraduate courses involving mostly young adults could benefit from using the case study method, balanced with other, perhaps more conventional, approaches, as one refreshing alternative in college classrooms.

Although the case study approach probably could be adapted with a little imagination and some ingenuity to teaching courses in almost any academic area, the method really spans the traditional disciplines. It is most suitable for use in those areas of knowledge that deal with the dynamics of human, social, and organizational relations, behavior, and development. In other words, it would be more applicable to courses in the social sciences than the humanities, yet more suited to the humanities than to the physical sciences.

The case study typically presents the facts of a real problem or, in very elementary terms, circumstances that suggest a gap between what "is" and what "should be." With this simple notion, the creative reader may already be imagining the design of at least one case study that could be incorporated into his or her next year's course, be it in the basic disciplines or a graduate or professional training program. Although I trust the opportunities will become clearer in the remaining portions of this chapter, the following random examples may provide some glimpses into the unlimited range of possible problem areas:

- A high school teacher faced with a low-achievement student who has an IQ of 145
- A structural engineer who must devise a plan to salvage a rapidly weakening truss bridge
- A defense lawyer whose client has suddenly decided to plead guilty at the last minute
- An anthropologist who discovers that his archeological dig is strongly resented by the native inhabitants
- A college president whose board has just demanded a virtually impossible balanced budget for next year

- A news reporter whose editor refuses to print his scoop on corruption within the state political structure
- A history student with the challenge of reformulating the major battle strategies of the Korean Conflict
- A surgeon faced with the decision of a high-risk, but possibly life extending, major operation
- An elementary school teacher confronted by an irate father who claims that she is treating his son unfairly
- An urban mayor whose public is demanding his resignation if he does not improve the city's escalating crime problem
- A business executive who realizes that if he cannot increase his company's sales, it will be on the verge of bankruptcy
- A city planner who is charged with designing an adequate water source and supply for the next thirty years
- A university dean faced with the revolt of her faculty because of the "arbitrary administrative decisions on faculty retrenchment"
- An elected government official who is torn between appeasing his constituency and meeting the expectations of his political party
- A corporate manager confronted with unrealistic union demands for higher pay and extensive fringe benefits or a strike
- A biochemist who, with a life at stake, has twelve hours to come up with an antidote to a rare and deadly poison
- A district court judge who must decide on a case of reverse discrimination
- A personnel director who is faced with informing a long-time employee that his services will no longer be needed
- A social worker who has been assigned the case of an unwed "family" where the father just lost his job and the mother is expecting their third child
- A student personnel dean whose students are flagrantly violating the state and federal drug laws

It is readily apparent that these examples are drawn from many walks of life, are sometimes dramatic, often present exigent problems if not dilemmas, and sometimes deal with agonizing ethical questions. But so does real-life decision making! And this, too, is what the case study method is about.

The above examples tended to focus on the professions because they still seem to epitomize what we are concerned with primarily in higher education—providing pertinent learning experiences for those who will be assuming major societal and organizational responsibilities in the years ahead. Among others, some principal areas of study in which the case method would seem to provide an especially appropriate learning experience might include business administration, college and university administration, government, hotel management, human ecology, law, medicine, political science, public administration, secondary and elementary school administration, other social sciences, social work, and teacher training at all levels.

Possibilities for expanded use of the case study approach extend far beyond programs at the undergraduate, graduate, and professional school levels, however. The rapidly emerging areas of adult, continuing, further, extended, and lifelong education have assumed a whole new significance in the decade of the 1970s, and millions of additional Americans are realizing and taking advantage of the many opportunities each year (see Chapter Thirteen). These students *are* older, and whether they are participating in these programs to improve their job skills, for their professional development, for personal reasons, or simply for the sheer joy of it, exposure to the case study method could well enliven and enrich their varied learning experiences.

As a part of this trend, industry, government, medicine, and even higher education have been expanding the opportunities for the inservice training and professional development of their employees and constituencies. Numerous institutes, seminars, workshops, and other programs are being offered each year, an increasing number of which have been incorporating the case study method as one pedagogical technique. Just within higher education itself, there are currently well over 600 professional development programs for college and university administrators, sponsored by 100 different organizations, associations, and consortia, and several hundred individual institutions of higher learning (Galloway and Fisher, 1978). Many of these offerings, appropriately, are spinoffs from other earlier programs that perhaps had enlightened some of the administrator participants to the desirability of staff development and, at least a number of them I suspect, to the advantages of the case study approach to some very exciting learning. It would seem the classroom has no territorial limits.

Case Design and Development

Case studies may cover an unlimited range of topics, concerns, issues, problems, and opportunities that require judgmental decision making. An individual case may focus on one particular aspect or on many aspects of organizational operation and/or individual problem solving. It may involve a single individual or a whole cast of characters. It will present facts in such a way that the case is open for thought, objective discussion, and the evaluation of action. It will describe the setting, the issues and circumstances, the people involved, the events, and any other information pertinent to an analysis.

Among other things, a case study may be concerned with internal relations within or between departments, divisions, or groups, or between individuals; it may focus on external relations with the individual's or organization's various constituencies; or it may deal with a combination of any of these. It is even possible, of course, to have a case that does not directly involve other people but, rather, concentrates on the decision maker and his or her direct confrontation with a problem presented by the physical environment or circumstances. It is the task of the instructor or seminar program director to select or develop those cases most appropriate for a given class or group of conference participants on the basis of the course objectives, the most pressing concerns, and the most current pertinent issues.

No case study has a neat beginning or a neat ending, for each represents but a small chunk of reality out of the total dynamic process of human and organizational behavior. For this reason, it is never possible for a case study to provide *all* of the facts. But perhaps this is not that much unlike reality, for when actual decision making is called for, the decision maker seldom has, or is able to gather, *all* of the information one would like to have before the decision should be made. (Nor do those who make decisions usually use all the pertinent information they actually have available!)

Typically, the beginning of a case study presents a brief

overview of the problem or situation, thus involving the reader. The setting and other descriptive information follows. The facts are presented, either chronologically or else in a manner relating to salient aspects of the problem, so as to lead up to major decisions that must be made or to significant circumstances that require analysis and discretionary evaluation. Therefore, the ends are often left untied, with the outcome not known, the actions unjudged, and the motives not presumed. The participants are required to make their own analyses and judgements, assessing for themselves the consequences or implications of various decisions or actions.

Case studies are written in a completely objective style, using words that in no way reveal or imply the writer's own feelings. Personalities, antagonisms, pressures, and constraints, which are important for realism, are presented by relating incidents or including quotations that suggest the characteristic behavior and patterns of relationships of the major individuals involved. The case writer never passes judgment or even hints of personal bias, for this would defeat the intended effects of the case study method.

The most effective length for a case study normally is between 1,500 and 4,000 words, depending on what is necessary, to present in concise form a fairly complete picture of the actual situation. It should be sufficiently comprehensive to cover all the relevant facts but not so complex that it may be confusing or tedious. Topical headings at appropriate points in the text are helpful to the reader. Occasionally supporting documents that may be useful for reference are appended. Showing the reader the final action or outcome is often accomplished with a brief case supplement distributed toward the end of the session after the case has been thoroughly discussed, but with sufficient remaining time for group reaction. However, it should be noted that case outcomes, even if apparently appropriate and successful, are not necessarily *the* correct solutions; the participants must realize that *every* problem is unique unto itself.

A variation to the single case study is the sequential one in which parts of an unfolding set of events and facts are presented in episodes, each analyzed and discussed in turn, and each building on the earlier chapters of the case. In effect, this is a series of "mini cases" that usually deal with interrelated administrative problems contributing and leading to a larger organizational problem. The sequential case is not unlike the more typical case study except that a given set of facts is analyzed before additional facts are introduced.

Although the sequential case may offer a particularly effective variation in the case method approach to learning problem solving, it has the disadvantage of requiring more in-class time if each subsequent episode is read by the participants during the session rather than in advance. This necessitates longer sessions or else more sessions on the same case, which, within the always-present limitations of time, might deprive the participants of the opportunity to explore other case studies dealing with incidents perhaps just as important. Of course, there are occasions when greater in-depth analysis may be preferred to diversity or exposure.

Minicases themselves can provide bases for very useful group discussions. These are usually case problems, by Bauers' definition— brief two-to-three paragraph situational accounts requiring discretionary actions (not unlike the in-basket technique), as illustrated by the following examples from college administration:

> As the new academic vice-president of a large community college, you have decided to implement a merit salary program to reward equitably those faculty members who are doing the best job. Your deans, although sympathetic to your cause, cannot agree on how most fairly to assess faculty performance (for example, who should do the evaluating; how; should quantitative as well as qualitative factors be considered?), not to mention whether merit increases should be the only reward for outstanding service. At their request, you are meeting with them tomorrow to clarify your new policy and give them guidelines. How do you prepare?
>
> As the dean of students at a small, public, liberal arts college, one of your responsibilities includes the college's residency program. The director of residence has scheduled two female students, one black and one white, to room together. One of the students, for differences which she describes as "cultural," states (in rather adamant terms) that she would prefer to room with a member of her own race. Both the director and assistant director of residence refuse to move either of the students on the grounds that different people can, and

should, learn to live together harmoniously. In a meeting with you, the director and her assistant, both highly competent individuals, declare that they will remain rigid in their positions, even if threatened with termination of their employment at the college. What do you do?

You are vice-president for college services of a large urban college, and your registrar comes to you in a dilemma. He has just accidently discovered that the school's computerized transcript file has been tampered with, changing the grades of at least several students, including one of last June's graduates who is now in an Ivy League law school. He has a hunch that two or three of his employees are involved in this, including a student aide.

"How do we approach this messy situation?" he asks. "How do we determine the culpability and the extent of grade fixing? And what do we do about the offenders, particularly the graduate student?"

As you try to focus on all the ramifications of the problem, another agonizing thought comes to mind. Realizing that a serious transgression like this cannot be kept quiet, you wonder what effect it is going to have on the credibility of the records of the vast majority of your students who have earned honest grades. What courses of action should you consider? in what priority and how do you proceed?

The advantage of minicases is that, taken together, they introduce a much greater array of issues and concerns and the opportunity to cover more territory in less time but obviously with considerably less information. Minicases would normally be used as springboards to discussing those matters that the participants identify as being of greatest interest and relevance to them.

Anonymity is usually an important factor in case studies, and precautions are taken to protect the identities of both organizations and individuals. In most cases, the names of places, people, buildings, departments, and other identifiable characteristics are disguised to the extent possible without altering the basic qualities or essential facts of the case. This has the added advantage of precluding participant biases, discouraging the introduction of additional facts

from those who might happen to have known the organization or
the situation, and giving all participants an opportunity to discuss
the case on equal footing.

Case studies may be researched and written by virtually
anyone who has some knowledge of the circumstances and scene, an
appreciation of human and organizational behavior and the decision-making process, and some writing ability. Often the case
researcher or team of researchers will spend several days at the site
gathering and carefully recording pertinent facts from both primary
and secondary sources. Information may be compiled from available
reports, documents, letters, articles, or personal interviews. Sometimes the sensitivity and/or recency of the problem under study
may hamper the investigation, so timing must be planned carefully
and cooperation secured in advance. Case studies may be prepared
by the course instructor, colleagues in the field, alumni of the program, or, as part of the learning experience, even current students
or participants in the course. The first drafts usually have to be
edited, made more objective, perhaps better camouflaged, and modified somewhat to meet the specific course objectives, the needs of
the participants, and the conceptual framework of the case study
instructor.

Teaching by the Case Study Method

The case method of teaching might be likened most appropriately to the Socratic method of rational dialogue and questioning or, in the modern academic world, to the St. John's College
approach to learning. Through a program of seminars and discussions, St. John's students directly confront the great books that stand
among the original sources of our Western intellectual tradition.
This approcah to exploring, analyzing, debating, and understanding
some of the great minds of history is intended to develop the critical
intelligence of a liberally educated person. But it is not the content
and ideas alone that effect this result. It is also the method.

As with the St. John's seminar approach, the purpose of the
case method is to elicit genuine dialogue—candid, searching, and
purposeful discussion—from all participants. For this reason, it
makes special demands on the case discussion leader, who assumes

the role of seminar moderator and pilot rather than the more common role of classroom lecturer.

The case leader obviously must be knowledgeable about the subject matter and is usually an experienced teacher. He or she should also be a student of group dynamics and an astute observer of human reactions—qualifications that are essential to the role of stimulating meaningful, participant-centered discussions. The case leader's purpose actually is to serve as the professional guide to the group during its analysis and discussion of the case study, not as a teacher in the traditional sense, but more as the facilitating member of a learning resources team.

In accomplishing such student-centered learning, it is essential that all participants be able to see, identify, and interact with one another. For these reasons, the group size, classroom setup, and session duration are very important considerations. There should be a sufficient number of participants for maximum exchanges—probably at least a dozen—but not so many that discussion may be inhibited—perhaps forty at the most. Seminar-style or tiered conference-style seating, with large name tents for each participant, are most conducive to group dynamics. Sessions normally run from one to two hours, depending upon the length and complexity of the case (though sequential case studies obviously may run longer, incorporating appropriate breaks).

A suitable learning climate is another critical factor in the case method, and it is an important responsibility of the leader to establish and maintain an open, informal, and relaxed atmosphere throughout the discussion. If the group or any member of it is unfamiliar with the method, the leader should begin by explaining its philosophy, purpose, and format to maximize the value that the participant may derive from the experience. It should be pointed out, too, that the session will provide an unusual opportunity to test their own thinking by experimenting in the world of possibilities.

The case leader should also mention that a wide range of responses is normal and that there are times when some participants will become more involved than others. (In fact, reactions sometimes will vary to the point that one wonders if everyone has read the same material!) It should be stressed that there are no proper solutions to a case and therefore that everyone should feel free to express his or her own thoughts and to question, speak out, and help clarify anything that is said by others. Finally, the leader should emphasize that the participants are ultimately responsible for what they garner from the case study method; the more they involve themselves with it, the more they will benefit from it.

The objectives of the group analysis and discussion of a case are to: (1) identify and define clearly the major problem or problems and the subproblems, (2) examine the facts and evaluate the available evidence, (3) weigh the possible courses of action and the feasibility of responsible alternative actions, (4) establish priorities, deciding what should be done, when, in what order, and by whom, and (5) determine the most effective means of implementing the desired action. The discussants also analyze the causal factors to determine how the problem(s) may have been avoided and what might, or should, have been done differently.

There is no special point of departure for beginning a case discussion. Often the leader will start by asking such simple questions as "What is your general reaction to this case?" "Is there a problem here?" "If so, what is it?" This, in turn, may lead to posing such questions as "How did this problem begin?" "Is there anything distinctive about this problem?" "What would *you* have done under the circumstances?" The diversity of replies often suggests the need for the group to reexamine the data presented in the case, which, in turn, will lead to a clarification of the facts and the issues.

However, the case study method is typically a nondirective approach to teaching, with the leader providing only the amount of direction necessary to keep the discussion from drifting off onto tangents. The moderator does *not* direct opinion but, rather, attempts to give every participant the opportunity to speak and, at times, may even call upon those who have not contributed by asking them a nonintimidating question. Of course, more guidance is necessary with younger or inexperienced students than with those who are already seasoned in human behavior. Indeed, with more experienced participants, the nondirective approach is particularly beneficial since they are more apt to know what they want to derive from a given case and thus may concentrate their attention on those aspects and issues that are of special concern to them.

In this method of learning, it is the *feedback* that the participants receive from their peers that actually provides the most effective direction to the group discussion. The subtle, and sometimes not so subtle, cues of agreement from their own classmates or colleagues usually have much more potent impact on the learners than any overt attempt on the part of the leader to direct the group's thinking toward predetermined ends. Self-discovery is the key; the case and its leader are the facilitators.

During the discussion the leader, too, is continuously receiving feedback from the learners as he or she monitors and assesses the group discussion. This, in turn, may prompt the leader to provide at appropriate times subtle feedback of his or her own in the form of thought-directed questions that could help to promote group progress. Such questions may attempt to clarify opinions or points of agreement (or perhaps disagreement) that have been expressed and help relate them to the central concern of the discussion or to a major problem in the case. Other questions may allude to factors that have been overlooked, may help to distinguish facts from inferences, or may introduce controversial points to help stimulate the group discussion.

Sometimes the leader will enrich the discussion by sharing anecdotes from his or her own or others' experiences. However, the main purpose is always to evoke the participants' thoughts, insights, and theoretical concepts. To accomplish this, at times during and often at the completion of the session, the leader assists group members in summarizing their discussion and points of agreement, in relating their generalizations to current human behavior theory and principles, and in pointing out pertinent research studies and other applicable references that might be helpful.

Two teaching techniques quite often used with the case study method are buzz sessions and role playing. Buzz sessions are small discussion groups, usually of from three to six people each, designed to provide the participants with the opportunity to discuss the case, or aspects of it, on a more personal and informal basis. These sessions are especially useful in getting some of the more diffident or reticent members of the group to identify with the case method and become more involved in the discussion. Therefore, buzz sessions are quite helpful in increasing the self-confidence of younger or less experienced members. They may be scheduled at the very beginning of a case session or at a convenient point during the general group discussion.

In a sense, the case method is a form of simulation, since it involves participants vicariously, yet dynamically, in real-life circumstances. The ultimate in such involvement is attained, however, only when role playing is incorporated into the learning process. This may be introduced by design or extemporaneously with many case studies at various points during the discussion. If participants have been assigned specific roles to act out, they can better appreciate the dynamics and emotions of how they might react under certain circumstances, cope with various emotions, and influence the range of outcomes. Role playing is particularly beneficial for those who tend to empathize with only one side of an event. Assigning them a contrasting role increases their sensitivity to all sides of an issue and their appreciation of the difficulties sometimes involved in making sound decisions.

Impromptu role playing is possibly the most effective. Depending on circumstances, the leader may even wish to encourage participants in advance to feel free to assume roles whenever they would like during the group discussion. For example, a participant might decide to react to a position that someone expresses by suddenly assuming the role and speech of one of the adversaries in the case. Indeed, even the case leader might assume a devil's advocate role himself at appropriate points to help clarify positions and their implications. Once the role-playing notion is introduced, it becomes contagious.

Another value of role playing is illustrated by the results of an early study of mine in which I suggested that the roles some people assume in life and their conscious attitudes toward those roles could possibly be in conflict with the roles they would prefer to play subconsciously and the related attitudes with which they would feel more comfortable. In other words, some individuals may tend to assume a role and the decision-making behavior consistent with that role that they feel is expected of them rather than the role they might actually prefer. If there is any validity to this, then a role-playing experience might well free participants from such predispositions and permit them to more readily express subliminal feelings and attitudes as they experiment in the world of possible decision-making alternatives. (A fringe benefit, particularly with undergraduate students who have yet to decide upon a career, would be the opportunity to test their inclinations and role aptitudes.)

In conducting a case study, the leader inevitably will have an outline of the major aspects of the case that he or she has prepared in advance to help guide the group discussion as may be appropriate. Sometimes this serves merely as a check list because some groups, and especially the more experienced, are able to cover the salient points and issues with but a minimum of guidance or cuing from the leader. Since the leader is *also* a learner, he or she most probably will be *taking* notes on new ideas or concerns emanating from the group discussion, which can be used to modify and enhance the teaching outline for future case sessions.

To assist the group in an effective analysis of the case study, the discussion leader should be completely familiar with the decision-making process and have in mind an analytical scheme or problem-solving model to which the circumstances of the case may be applied. Although this is most readily used with cases in which a major, immediate, and clearly identifiable problem exists, it can be quite useful in discerning the relevant factors in any case study. It can help in keeping the discussion more focused and thus more productive by providing an overall picture of where it has been, is at any given point, and seems to be going. It also serves as a reminder of what major factors have not yet been considered.

This paradigm would allow for an analysis of the entire chain of causal events, contributing factors, pressing concerns, anticipated conditions, immediate and long-range goals, alternate means of attaining those goals, the desirability of each, conducive and impeding forces, and the implications or consequences of any decision(s). Any rendition of such an administrative problem-solving model would be inadequate at best. Nonetheless, I have attempted to diagram a conceptual framework for case study analysis that I have developed gradually and worked with over the past several years (see Figure 1). It has seemed to be a useful guide for case discussions and, in fact, for administrative problem solving in general.

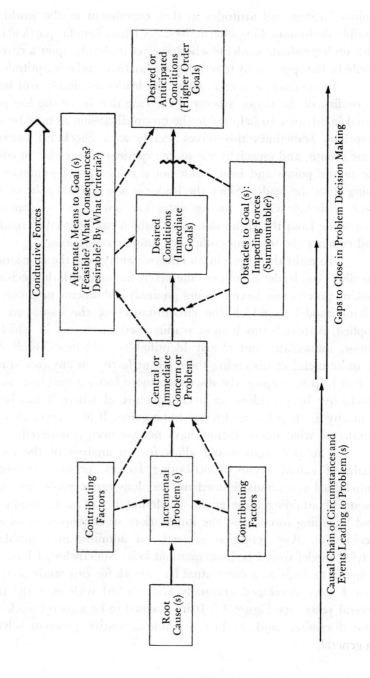

Figure 1. Problem-solving Model for Case Study Analyses.

In summary some brief guidelines that might be helpful for a case discussion leader/facilitator include:

Be familiar with:
* human and organizational behavior
* the self-discovery approach to student learning
* the dynamics and techniques of group discussions and the use of the seminar
* the decision-making and problem-solving processes
* the case study method itself
* the maturity of the participants
* the case study under discussion
* the subject areas it covers
* its basic principles and implications
* an appropriate analytical/diagnostic scheme

Attempt to:
* establish an informal, open, and relaxed learning atmosphere
* explain the procedures and anticipated outcomes of the case method
* encourage all participants to enter freely into the discussions
* emphasize that everyone's ideas and experiences are important to share
* draw out the reactions of all participants
* listen carefully to everything that is said
* facilitate the group discussion by providing appropriate guidance and feedback
* offer pertinent thought-directed questions at times
* help clarify points, comments, or ambiguities
* summarize the discussion, major points, and basic principles
* suggest further references for follow-up
* enjoy your role

Do not be:
* overly directive, evasive, intimidating, intimidated, uncomfortable, or unprepared

The several distinctive characteristics of the case study approach to classroom teaching might be summarized as follows: It deals with material that is current and/or relevant, and factual. It approximates reality in a way that arouses interest (not unlike a good short story) and enables the reader to be projected into the problem in an empathetic and active, rather than passive, way. It is designed to promote independent, constructive thinking, objective analysis, and intercommunication, and to inform, challenge, and motivate the participants. It is a purposeful, unified learning process that can help to effect more skillful problem-solving acumen and a greater awareness of the complex factors that enter into decision making and the formulation of organizational and operational policy. And finally, it can be an enjoyable way to learn—both for student *and* teacher!

Available evidence, which is mostly theoretical or impressionistic, would suggest the validity of these characteristics. Unfortunately, little has been done to test empirically the learning effectiveness of the case method. To my knowledge, the only existing study was one I conducted a few years ago in which I investigated the attitude changes of those who had experienced the case study method during one of the programs of the Institute for College and University Administrators.

Effectiveness of the Method

I was readily aware of the apparent effectiveness of the case study method as an integral facet of the institute's early inservice training programs for college and university administrators when, in 1971, I decided to conduct this study. Participants' evaluation forms and subsequent correspondence had frequently emphasized the helpfulness of this learning approach. Therefore, my purpose was to test it empirically during a session of the institute.

All evidence suggested that the case discussions were having a decided impact upon the participants' attitudes and their subsequent administrative behavior. However, the task of investigating the degree to which any behavioral change was attributable to the specific case study learning experiences was insurmountable, for it was impossible to determine the effects, if not the presence, of all of the intervening influences. Consequently, even behavioral change objectively observed by others would not conclusively indicate the effectiveness of a particular learning event in and of itself.

Nevertheless, assuming that behavior was in part a manifestation of attitude, then any change in behavior probably would reflect some change in attitude. Conversely, it was logical to assume that any change in attitude would influence any appropriate behavior that followed. Thus, the basic assumptions for the study were that: Attitudinal change is the sine qua non of behavioral change; attitudinal change could be attributed to an immediately concluded learning experience if there were proper experimental conditions; and comparing such change with a control group that had a different, but parallel, learning experience might suggest the relative effectiveness of the two teaching methods.

The thirty-six subjects, all academic deans and vice-presidents who were participating in the institute, were divided into two balanced subgroups matched in every feasible way by individual and institutional characteristics. One group experienced the case study method, and the control group, the more traditional but similarly designed position paper–seminar method. For the case group, I had developed a real, though disguised, case study about an institution, its president, and his plans and activities to expand the mission and programs of the college. The expansions were intended to meet changing societal needs and enhance educational opportunities more appropriately. For the control group, I used a cogent position paper authored anonymously by this same college president, purporting the same ideas, concepts, and beliefs and covering the same topics and issues. I served as discussion leader for both groups so that the teaching style and directiveness would be as identical as possible and thus would not be a differentiating factor.

All subjects were tested before and again immediately following their respective experimental sessions with an eighteen-item, seven-option opinion questionnaire that contained the major principles and positions common to both the case study and the position paper. Since the retest time lag was minimal, any attitudinal score changes could be considered real and, to the extent that they were significant, could therefore be attributed specifically to the respective learning experiences. With both groups, the process dealt primarily with the interaction of the cognitive and affective domains of knowledge—with concepts and judgments—rather than directly with the retention of specific factual information or with the strictly affective outcomes themselves.

Analysis of the subgroup, individual, and item score changes suggested that the case study method provided the more effective learning experience in terms of greater net, gross, and positive attitude change on the part of the participants. The questionnaire proved reliable beyond the .01 level, with attitudinal changes for the case study group showing significance beyond the .01 level (less than 1 percent probability of occurring by chance) using the t-test, and beyond the .05 level with the McNamar test. By contrast, the control group's attitude changes were insignificant—less than the .40 level in positive change, and not even reaching the .25 level overall.

Further analysis revealed that the case study group experienced greater internal consistency (less indecisiveness) in their questionnaire responses according to their fluctuation indices. This suggested that the greater focus, objectivity, and involvement of the case method may have facilitated the self-analysis of attitudes and the conviction of individual decisions. The implication, therefore, was that the case method was the more efficient approach to learning.

Additional findings indicated that the case method appeared to have greater relative impact on participants who were older (the age range was thirty to fifty-four) and/or who were more experienced in their respective current positions (they ranged from two months to three and one half years). And, interestingly, the final evaluations of the total institute week (which, other than for the experiment, was a common experience for all) disclosed not only a more favorable response from those in the case study group, but also a high positive correlation (significant beyond the .01 level) between their overall ratings and the positive direction and degree of their attitude change (in contrast to zero correlation in the control group).

I had selected the position paper-seminar method for the control group in this study because, among the more traditional techniques of teaching, the assigned reading and discussion approach seemed to offer the most similar design and the greatest potential (not unlike the St. John's Seminars) for approximating the group dynamics of the case study method. Since the case method was itself a type of reading-seminar exercise, comparing the learning outcomes of the two groups provided a fairly rigorous test of the relative effectiveness of the two approaches. Although in no way conclusive, the results certainly suggested that, in this investigation anyway, the case method of learning was more effective, more efficient, and more popular than the more common reading-seminar approach.

The question to be asked, of course, is "Why?" What was distinctive about the case method that may have led to the significant differences in the observed learning outcomes? Perhaps, as had been suggested by others, it was, in part, the aura of the living case study itself. Dealing with real people and real events, it may have promoted greater identification among the participants, enabled them to project more readily into the situation, and thus facilitated their active involvement; this led to more meaningful group discussion. Although one can only speculate as to the reasons for the seemingly greater learning impact with the case method group, the study, nonetheless, reinforced my own earlier observations of the apparent effectiveness of this approach to student learning.

Summary and Conclusions

A major report last fall from the National Research Council's Committee on Fundamental Research Relevant to Education (Scully, 1977, p. 5) admonished that: "Sustained inquiry is needed concerning lifelong educability and the character of higher-order abilities for tasks such as systematic problem solving and extended conceptual discourse that may develop after childhood." Somehow this admonition sounded to me as though a committee member or two might already have been familiar with the case study method. "Sustained inquiry, lifelong educability, systematic problem solving, conceptual discourse"—this certainly would be a cogent case for the case study approach to learning!

Indeed, if we hope to develop a true sense of understanding among our students—of whatever age and bent—and help to cultivate their critical thinking and decision-making processes, then perhaps the case study method does have something of particular value to offer in the course of these pursuits. By presenting students the opportunity to analyze problems as active participants in a vicarious real-life drama, very possibly those insights and discernable steps toward coordinating human effort will become more evident for them. Self-discovery, which is a significant outcome of any learning experience, is very central to the case study method; those who work out the abstract thoughts for themselves also tend to have a firmer and more enduring grasp of them. We must never lose sight of the fact that we are educating not only for today but also for those human endeavors and accomplishments of tomorrow.

Although reactions to human events are often predictable, they will at times be surprisingly diverse. In the introduction of this chapter, I related the accounts of several institute participants, each of whom thought that the case study under discussion was about them and/or their institution. And later, in the section on teaching by the case method, I observed that reactions within a case study group will sometimes vary to the point that one might wonder whether everyone had read the same written account. These very human responses suggest a paradoxical and yet quite significant advantage of the case study method and, indeed, provide an example of one of the essential components of any sound learning experience.

Whenever students are able to identify with the subject matter, the issues, the common learning materials, and the teaching method in such a way that they can individually and uniquely project themselves *into* the situation, even to the extent that their perceptions, reactions, and interpretations may differ initially, then they are becoming *involved and active* participants in the unfolding and dynamic group learning process. And this, after all, is the key so frequently advocated but too seldom turned. When the interest is there, so also is the motivation; just possibly a teaching/learning method that evokes such enthusiasm can help to at least nudge the door ajar.

In the preceding pages, I have discussed and admittedly

have been advocating the case study approach to student learning. I have explored briefly its background, philosophy, application, development, teaching method, and observed effectiveness. I have suggested that this method brings a vicarious, realistic enrichment along with a dynamic learning opportunity to all who participate. It provides a positive relationship between learning and appreciation, which, like a fascinating short story, offers a more interesting and enjoyable way to learn. (And, after all, learning should be fun!) Although evidence suggests that the case study method is probably more effective with older and more experienced students, it nonetheless has considerable and, for the most part, yet unexplored possibilities for application to the undergraduate classroom as well.

As I mentioned in the introduction, the case study approach to teaching and learning is by no means a panacea for teaching in postsecondary education. Not everything can, or should, be taught by this method, for certainly some subjects are much more suited to exposition and demonstration. In any event, the case method should not be the only teaching technique of any given course or program. If only for the sake of variety, it should be balanced with other proven approaches to student learning.

The case study method, nonetheless, does provide an opportunity for "being there . . . vicariously" and for gaining understanding from the experiences of others. Its teaching/learning potential has only begun to be realized, and the tremendous opportunities it can offer are limited only by the imagination. Those who do *not* learn from the experience of others are destined to relive their mistakes. Perhaps the case study method will have something to offer in our concerted attempt to restore that relevance to the classroom so essential for helping to develop today's student into tomorrow's leader.

11

Michael J. Rockler

Applying
Simulation/Gaming

The tension in the Cabinet Room increased. For the first time, President Granger appeared to be losing the outward calm which he had demonstrated throughout the crisis. Time was running out. President Granger reviewed the latest set of options received on the teletype. The first option was to launch a full-scale attack on the Soviet Union and hope that they would be caught off guard. The second option was to call the Soviet premier on the hot line and at the same time put all forces on full alert. The third option was to put all forces on stand-down status in the hope of convincing the Soviets that the bombers which had passed their failsafe points and which were on their way to the Soviet Union were there because of a mistake. The president could take no action and then the bombers would continue on their course toward the Soviet Union. If he did nothing, total war could result and perhaps total world destruction.

The President had already tried other alternatives. He attempted to reestablish radio contact with the bombers, but this had failed. The president, his national security advisors, and another group of advisors located in the Strategic Air Command (SAC) headquarters, worked to find a solution to the problem and avoid potential destruction. The Strategic Air Command group advised the president to launch a full scale attack and take the Soviets by surprise. The national security advisors argued for contacting the Soviet premier on the hot line and placing all forces on full alert. The president decided to listen to neither group and decided instead to contact the premier on the hot line while at the same time placing all forces on stand-down status in order to convince the premier of his sincerity. The Soviets distrusted this move. War seemed nearer. A new set of options appeared on the teletype. The President could decide to help the Soviets intercept the bombers by setting up a conference line between SAC and USSR which could help the Soviets find and destroy the bombers. The president could also continue to let the bombers fly, but he could indicate at the same time that he will ground all other US forces. After he received advice from SAC and from the national security advisors, the president decided to help the Soviets intercept the bombers. The Soviets used the information that was provided to them and destroyed the bombers, ending the danger. The President announced the results to the participants and they cheered. Mingled with the elation was a genuine sense of relief.

What I have been describing is an account of a group of students playing the computer simulation/game, Failsafe; this is an adaptation for the computer of the book by Burdick and Wheeler (1969). I have played Failsafe with many groups in many settings.

Sometimes a group follows a strategy that results in a peaceful solution to the crisis; sometimes the conclusion results in war. But whatever the outcome, certain things are always true. First, the players become totally involved with the crisis even though it is a simulation with nothing real at stake. It always becomes real to the participants, and the atmosphere is always charged with tension. Second, players learn about executive decision making, and as a result of the postgame discussion (debriefing), they have a better awareness of and empathy for the difficult task of executive decision making. Third, players learn about computers; they learn to use a teletype that has access to a computer program by telephone. The teletype provides players with a scenario, periodic time updates, and after each decision, a new set of options. Finally, students who play Failsafe have fun; this is useful for motivating them to learn.

Not all simulation/games use computers; many do not need expensive equipment and can be constructed by teachers with a minimum of difficulty. All good simulation/games facilitate involvement, learning, motivation and are fun. For these reasons I have come to be an advocate of their use; in this chapter I will attempt to explain, describe, and inform readers of the ways that they can be used in higher education. By way of further introduction to the process, definitions of a few terms may be useful to some.

Theories, models, and simulations are related phenomena. A *theory* is an hypothesis or generalization about relationships in the world that is descriptive, predictive, and has high credibility. A *model* is a subclass of a theory; it is a representation of a real-world phenomenon that is sometimes physical, sometimes an abstraction, and sometimes both. A central feature of models is that they are analogies, powerful tools that can be used to explain and to create. The value and importance of simulation/gaming comes in part from its relationship to modeling and to analogy. As model is a subclass of theory, so *simulation* is a subclass of model. The purpose of a simulation is to eliminate the potential danger and the cost that might be present if the activity took place in a real rather than a simulated setting. A simulation is a representation of a real-world event in a reduced and compressed form that is dynamic, safe, and efficient.

A *game* is a contest between two or more players that proceeds by a set of rules. The basic structure of a game (as opposed to a simulation) is that it is a zero sum event, which means that player A can win the game only if player B loses it. There are many variations of this from games in which everyone can win to those in which everyone loses but the basis of all of them is the zero sum relationship.

There is a hybrid form that combines the elements of a simulation (which can also be a research or evaluation device as well as a teaching tool) with the elements of a game (which can be pure entertainment) into a product which is called a *simulation/ game*. Those primarily for teaching purposes are called *educational* or *instructional simulation/games*. Rather than attempt to make unnecessary distinctions, and because this chapter examines daily practices in the classroom, I will follow the practice of calling all those techniques that are simulations, games, or hybrids and that are used for educational purposes *simulation/games*.

There is a branch of knowledge within the study of simulation and gaming called *games theory*, and although it has application to the problem of teaching, it is primarily concerned with mathematical gaming theory (which is beyond the scope of this chapter).

A simulation/game can be role play in which players assume specific roles (including those of themselves) to solve a problem or make a decision. It can also be a board game in which players attempt to reach a goal as a result of moving around a board (similar to the kind of activity that takes place in the commercial game, Monopoly). Many of those that are used for educational purposes are combinations of role playing and board activity.

Serious Games

My own children and I play a simple game (perhaps many reading this will recall playing it) in which each of us holds up either a fist (representing a rock), an open palm (representing paper), or a V sign (representing a scissors). The rules of the game are that the rock can break the scissors and win; the scissors can cut the paper and win; or the paper can cover the rock and win. When my children play this game with me, they are learning how to challenge and compete against an adult, and they are learning behaviors associated with winning and losing. They are obtaining this kind of socialization in a nonthreatening manner since nothing much is at stake if they lose, and it is fun to defeat Daddy on occasion. The point is to indicate that as in the title of Johan Huizanga's book, *Homo Ludens,* human beings are game-playing animals; the playing of games is serious business that can lead to improved opportunity for socialization. The appeal of simulation/ gaming as a teaching technique may be found in the proposition that a useful way to understand human social behavior and interaction is to understand it from the perspective that life is a game.

The role of games as socializing techniques has best been explained by O. K. Moore and A. R. Anderson (1960) in their description of the concept of "autotelic folk model." Moore and Anderson argue that people in society must learn to deal with problems caused by the natural environment. They must learn as well to deal with problems that involve human interaction and with those that are affective. They suggest that people learn to solve these problems in ways that are intrinsically motivating and hence autotelic. To learn how to participate in activity A (where failure may result in serious consequences) societies invent activity A′ (which is a simulation). Activity A′ lacks serious consequences but is similar enough to activity A to provide for genuine practice. Moore and Anderson call these activities *autotelic folk models.*

Moore and Anderson claim that there are four classes of these folk models. First, there are those of serious noninteractional problems; these are called puzzles. Societies create a variety of puzzles for people to solve, all of which involve little risk. These include crossword puzzles, those involving the manipulation of small pieces of plastic, and others. The whodunit, developed by Agatha Christie and many others, is also an example of a nonthreatening puzzle activity. Second, there are games of chance—for example, card games. Third, there are folk models of interaction. They are games of strategy; chess and tic tac toe are examples. Science fiction novels can also be viewed as strategy games in which the reader through the eyes of the protagonist must devise and test a strategy for dealing with a very difficult problem and thereby save the universe. Finally, Moore and Anderson describe folk models of the affective aspects of life; these are aesthetic objects treated autotelically. Examples of aesthetic folk models can be found in the variety of kits available that satisfy aesthtic needs—for example, paint by number, sculpture kits, and so forth.

Folk models have the effect of helping to socialize the young and of helping everyone to better understand the natural and social environment. These activities are serious games and accomplish the purpose of preparing people to interact in the natural and social world.

Simulation/games are useful teaching techniques because life may be analyzed from a games perspective. In games (and in life) players have goals that they attempt to achieve. In games (and in life) the action of players is regulated by a set of rules; violation of these rules may result in serious consequences. Eric Berne, developer of transactional analysis, wrote a best-selling book entitled, *Games People Play* (1964). Although Berne was interested in gaming behavior among severely neurotic people, his analysis was applicable to a much larger group, and the continuing popularity of the book supports the hypothesis that there is a connection between life and games.

Richard Duke (1976) also develops the argument that simulation/gaming is serious activity in *Gaming: The Future's Language*. Duke maintains that there are a variety of communication forms, some simple and some complex. Some complex forms are such that they enable us to communicate about the future in a way that enhances our ability to solve the future's problems. Flow charts, cartography, and simulation/gaming are examples of future languages. Simulation/games are future forms of communication because they are based on anology and can convey gestalt. They are able to create what Duke calls a "multilogue," which is a form of communication in which several persons interact simultaneously. This is an improvement over dialogue, which is a conversation between two persons, because it is more complex and therefore better able to deal with the problems of the future. The importance of future languages is that they allow us to examine alternative possible futures with enough lead time to be useful in the formulation of the solutions to problems. In Moore and Anderson's terms, future languages allow us to create many A' activities that are analogies and that are safe and nonthreatening as a way of testing for possible consequences of actions. In a present increasingly under siege from the future, the use of simulation/gaming as a defense is immensely important.

Simulation/gaming is an important technique to use in the classroom because (1) it aids the socialization process, (2) it can enable human beings to develop strategies for living, (3) it is a future's language that enables players to learn to deal with the future more successfully, and as will be indicated, (4) it aids in the development of certain attitudes.

Perhaps most importantly, simulation/gaming can demonstrate the idea of cause and effect more effectively than most other alternatives because it is able to convey gestalt. Understanding cause and effect is necessary in order to participate in social life and in order to understand the world. Yet as teachers we rarely provide students with opportunity to see the results of their own activities. In debriefing sessions students learn how their behavior led to the result that occurred. Many simulation/games allow for replay, and so in another round the student can try another strategy and obtain a different effect. Simulation/games collapse time, and this provides many opportunities for testing the relationship of cause and effect in a relatively short period.

Simulation/gaming is also an activity that provides cloture. The student is made aware of a problem; a simulation game is played. There is some kind of resolution to the problem, and there is a debriefing. This concludes the experience (although what was learned can be applied to another problem in the future). Compare this to the usual situation in which a student reads a chapter, hears a lecture, takes a test, and goes back to the beginning again. Because there is cloture, the process of understanding the cause-and-effect relationship is facilitated.

Simulation/gaming can change the role of the teacher or add to the role in a positive way. The model that many teachers follow is a didactic one in which the teacher serves as judge, selects the winners, and often punishes the losers by giving them low grades. In a classroom in which simulation/gaming is being used, the model is more likely to be an heuristic one in which the teacher is no longer the judge; winning and losing becomes a function of the activity allowing the teacher to take on the more pleasant role of being the facilitator of learning. The process can fail if an attempt is made to recast the experience into a more traditional didactic one. (The teacher, for example, observes a group planning strategy and in his or her wisdom suggests a more effective strategy for winning.)

Simulation/gaming reduces the gap between the successful and the less successful student; this is an advantage if the teacher wishes to help the less successful student become more successful. In a simulation/game there is usually an element of chance, and the less successful student may be lucky and win, even though in the contest that is an examination, he must always lose. Sometimes a successful experience may provide a student who has not been successful with a new sense of self-confidence, which may make a difference. (I do not wish to convey the impression that simulation/ gaming can work miracles. They can improve the performance of some students some of the time. In my value system, this is an important possibility.)

Certain critics maintain that because it is a simplified abstraction of reality, a simulation/game creates distortions of reality and therefore is not meaningful. It is true that distortions are created. *But this is true of any other presentation of reality that the student ever receives.* Every lecture ever given and every textbook description ever written is also a distortion (see Chapter Ten for vivid illustrations of distortions). The use of simulation/gaming can serve to supplement and extend the student's perception of reality more directly than any textbook or lecture.

Simulation/gaming is one technique of many; it is used most effectively in conjunction with other techniques when it is embedded in, and is an intrinsic part of, a course rather than if it is simply added on before or after as a means of introducing variety or using a new gimmick.

History

Simulation/gaming has an interesting history; it began as a part of the need to develop more effective military strategy. It was applied later as a technique for training management in business and industry, and then it came to be used as an educational tool.

J. R. Raser (1969) views it as being derived from decision theory, systems theory, and small group experimentation.

All people who study the history are convinced that the game of chess has its origins as a war game; I am generally in agreement with this although I have never seen any clear evidence that it is so. Nevertheless, the obvious relationship between the society simulated on a chess board and medieval society, as well as the aggressive nature of the rules, seems to be an example of the use of a simulation/game to attempt to create alternatives that can be pursued in medieval battle.

The development of war gaming began at the turn of the nineteenth century. It was first used by the Prussians, and by the end of the century it had spread to other countries including Great Britain. Perhaps the phenomenon reached its zenith in the Pentagon in the 1960s when computers were used to test alternative approaches to the war in Vietnam. The early war games were called *kriegsiel* and took two forms: rigid *kriegspiel,* in which the rules were carefully specified and followed, and free *kriegspiel,* a form that allowed for improvisation.

The next development was application in business and industry. In 1956 the American Management Association developed a simulation/game, Top Management Decisions, the purpose of which was to give potential executives the opportunity to try alternative strategies in order to obtain practice for making real decisions later. Eventually management simulation/games were used with computers for the purpose of refining them and making them more complex. Shortly after its development in business and industry, simulation/gaming was also applied to the problems of land use and urban planning.

It is interesting to note that the application to war, business, and planning are examples of the process described by Moore and Anderson (1960). They maintain that society develops socialization techniques so that persons may learn appropriate behavior in safe settings. Only an insane general would risk the lives of his troops unnecessarily simply to gain information about strategy; business executives would obviously prefer to train new managers as inexpensively as possible.

After development in war and business, simulation/gaming

was applied to formal education. It began as a device to train administrators (as a natural development from its use in training business executives). It was used in the early 1960s in the preservice education of teachers. This use was reinforced when it became an intrinsic part of many of the materials of the federally funded curriculum projects of the 1960s. The best example was in the High School Geography Project; this was perhaps the most successful of the curriculum projects, and it created many simulation/games for use in secondary classrooms. Once the use began in educational settings, it grew rapidly. The number of good classroom simulation/games now available is large; they are used at all levels.

In *Simulation and Society*, Raser (1969) argues that in addition to these historical developments, three other intellectual developments are also part of the theoretical basis for the development of simulation and gaming: decision theory, systems theory, and small group experimentation theory.

Decision theory is used in public administration as well as in political behavior. It is an attempt to understand the process of decision making, and it is used to give participants practice in making decisions. Raser argues that to do this, it would have been necessary to devise simulation/gaming if the process had not already developed in the manner described above.

The same argument, according to Raser, can be made with regard to the development of systems theory. To reduce complex systems to a size in which they could be studied and understood, it was necessary to create simulations of systems as a means of making them manageable. Hence, the process would have been created in order to devise small, manageable, and safe systems for the purpose of analyzing them.

Finally, the development of small group experimentation, according to Raser, is still another antecedent. Sociologists interested in social interaction concluded that simulations of social interaction in small groups was a way of studying the process in a controlled environment. This too necessitates the development of simulation/gaming.

Simulation/gaming developed from rich antecedents and for many purposes. I believe this rich background accounts for its growth and strength. Many educators viewed the development of

educational simulation/gaming as still another gimmick or fad
that periodically occurs in education. Nearly twenty years later the
technique has not passed from the scene, and it continues to grow
and develop.

The North American Simulation and Gaming Association
(NASAGA) is an interdisciplinary organization for all those on the
North American continent who are interested in simulation/gaming.
NASAGA meets annually for an examination of the state of the
art. Papers are given, new simulation/games are introduced, and
a great deal of intellectual stimulation takes place. NASAGA is one
of the few professional associations that is truly interdisciplinary.
It has its roots in the War Games Council, which many years ago
became an informal association called the National Gaming Council.
In Pittsburgh in 1974, the National Gaming Council formally
became the North American Simulation and Gaming Association,
an affiliate of the International Simulation and Gaming Association
(ISAGA). ISAGA also holds annual meetings around the world,
and thus simulation and gaming is a growing international
phenomenon.

Facilitating Learning

The process of learning is understood only to a limited degree, and claims about ways that simulation/gaming facilitates
learning are based on inferences of varying degrees of strength. Research has shown limited results, as I will indicate shortly. Nonetheless, based on my own experiences, the vast experiences of others,
and much inference, I am prepared to believe that the approach
facilitates many aspects of learning.

Many who share my beliefs claim that simulation/gaming
helps people learn how to learn. Moreover, it is an activity that
provides gestalt (it allows players to see problems in their totality
better than most other techniques). People can understand a process
better when they can see it as a whole and when it has cloture. At
the same time, students must be active participants rather than
passive recipients.

One unique aspect of the method is that it allows for individualization of instruction at the same time that it takes place in

a group. This is because a single simulation/game can be played simultaneously at different levels of abstraction by different players. For the slower learner, concrete experiences are provided; that is, the simulation/game occurs in the here and now. Average students may be involved because it is a concrete experience *and* because they are able to examine some aspects (perhaps cause-effect relationships) in more depth than would slow students. Meanwhile, advanced students may be examining sophisticated strategies and alternatives well beyond the range of slow and average learners. All three types of learners, however, are playing the same simulation/game at the same time. Because of the usually present element of chance, it does not follow that the superior student will always win.

Simulation/games allow students to experience content directly. Players participate in an event rather than experiencing it vicariously by reading about it. Through this participation, players have a concrete experience that may help them to understand an abstract event through an analogy. Students who have been characterized as the "new learners" (those who are new clients to higher education based on their poor performance on achievement tests) are often those for whom high levels of abstraction are difficult. Simulation/gaming may provide these students with activities that are motivating, involving, and concrete.

A widely accepted learning principle and one that has been documented is that learning is facilitated when the learner receives immediate knowledge of results or feedback (see Chapter Five). Unlike most traditional forms of instruction, a simulation/game provides prompt feedback. A decision to make one move or use one strategy usually leads to immediate results. Success or failure (demonstrated by winning or losing) is known at the end of the exercise. The debriefing that takes place immediately aids the player to learn from the experience. Compare this feedback with the processes of reading a text, hearing a lecture, writing a paper, taking a test, and then waiting days or even weeks for results.

The preceding presumed advantages are ones that simulation/gaming has over other teaching techniques that facilitate analytical and convergent thinking. I believe too that it is a far superior technique for facilitating creative behavior and divergent thinking.

In several books and articles E. P. Torrance (1970) has described techniques for facilitating creative behavior. Torrance maintains, for example, that it can be fostered (1) if the teacher's tendency to be a censor can be inhibited, (2) by deep student involvement, and (3) by placing an unproductive learner in contact with a productive one. Simulation/gaming is useful in meeting all of these conditions.

Torrance argues that creative behavior can be facilitated by the development of a tolerance for complexity and for a certain kind of disorder. (Simulation/games meet these criteria.) In addition, Torrance insists that creative behavior is fostered by incompleteness—that is, the sense that not everything is present in a setting all at the same time. All good simulation/games are based on this kind of incompleteness. Indeed, it is the usual task in any one of them to move from incompleteness to completeness. Still another way of encouraging creative behavior is through the use of sociodrama; many simulation/games are based on role playing. Torrance takes the position that creative behavior is facilitated by an accepting, respecting attitude; simulation/gaming can only be played if there is an accepting, respecting attitude. Creative behavior is improved when curiosity is encouraged and when one gives oneself over completely to a task. Curiosity is a motivating element in most simulation/games, and playing them usually results in total involvement.

It would be well to be able to conclude a section on the psychology of simulation/gaming by demonstrating the existence of a great body of research to support the inferences that have been made about the ways they facilitate learning. Unfortunately, the research evidence is not strong, clear, or consistent. Excellent reviews of this research have been published by Chapman, Davis, and Miller (1974), Lewis and others (1974), and Livingston and Stoll (1973). The reviews end with conclusions similar to the following: "The review of research to this point suggests the conclusion that games and simulations have little measurable impact on student cognitive learning when compared with other teaching techniques. Moreover, nearly all of the studies reviewed have research design limitations. This limitation involves population, test construction and validation, inadequate controls in the research design, and limited statistical analysis of data. It would be unwise to draw any firm conclusions about the impact of learning games on student learning from research to date" (Lewis and others, 1974, p. 68).

Although simulation/games have not been shown to be significantly more effective in terms of cognitive outcomes, they do seem to be effective in terms of attitudes. A. K. Gordon states: "One of the most promising hunches about educational games is that they can influence and alter the attitudes of participants. Specifically, this hunch applies to three areas. First, games can evidently be used to change attitudes about the particular issue a game treats. Second, and even more encouraging, experience with educational games can apparently improve the participants' attitudes toward learning and the school system in general. Third, games appear to influence the student's attitude about his own effectiveness in his own environment" (Gordon, 1970, p. 166).

Research since 1970 has tended to support these hunches about attitudes, and it is now generally agreed that simulation/ gaming has its greatest measurable effect in the area of attitudes.

Certain qualifications about the research are necessary. First, most studies have focused upon kindergarten through grade twelve settings. Whether similar results would occur in higher education settings is not known. Second, no research has been done on the relationship of simulation/gaming to the development of creative behavior. Since the technique does have positive effect on attitudes, perhaps it can be shown to have a positive effect on creative behavior as well. Third, the phenomenon is less than twenty years old, and it can be argued that the technique developed prior to the theory needed to support it. It is to be hoped that research will be continued and even accelerated in scope. Fourth, simulation/gaming is an art as much as a science. This complicates the research problems.

Since the purpose of this book is to inform readers about a variety of teaching approaches, instructors are encouraged to try simulation/games and discover whether they justify the claims. But there should be more than one attempt.

Using Simulation/Games in Daily Practice

Those who wish to add simulation/games to their daily practices must understand how to use them in the classroom, how to evaluate them, and how to design them. It is to these topics that I now turn.

The first step in using a simulation/game is to decide what objectives one wishes to achieve. Although this seems obvious, I am convinced that the selection of objectives is seldom the first step in instruction. This is unfortunate because without careful consideration of objectives, the possibility of effective instruction is diminished.

The second step is to determine whether or not a simulation/game is the most appropriate technique to accomplish these objectives. It is not easy to determine this until one has had some experience with the procedure. (Part of the decision, of course, will be determined by the availability of an appropriate simulation/game that can be used to achieve the objectives.) Some objectives may be better achieved by another technique, and sometimes it is not an appropriate decision for reasons relating to available time, the kind of activities that have come before and that will follow the simulation/game, the nature of the class, the nature of the course and its content, and even the cost.

The third step is to select a simulation/game (or perhaps to design one); this necessitates a knowledge of the available ones. (Some are annotated later in this chapter.) R. E. Horn (1977) has edited a massive guide; on a lesser scale, there is a guide edited by R. Stadsklev (1975) for simulation/games in social education. Catalogues available from publishers (Interact, Games Central, Education Manpower, Inc., to name a few) also provide annotations that are biased but helpful.

Having decided to use a simulation/game and having selected one, the instructor should now become familiar with it. This is the fourth step. The most effective way to do this is to play it with colleagues and friends. If this cannot be done, the instructor should, at least, read the rules and examine all the component parts carefully.

The fifth step is to introduce the simulation/game to the students. Most good ones provide instructions on how to do this, and if these instructions are followed, things will usually turn out satisfactorily. It is important not to provide information to players that might ruin the simulation/game, not to offer suggestions on strategy that appeal to the instructor, and not to so overwhelm the players with rules that they lose interest in playing.

The sixth step is to have the students play; the role of the instructor at this point is critical. The instructor ought not to play unless a particular stated role (such as moderator) is offered. The instructor should observe and serve as a resource person (who can sometimes pace the timing of events) with minimal involvement. The instructor can prepare for the debriefing while observing the process. The danger for beginning users is that they have difficulty changing from traditional roles and they may approach simulation/ gaming in a didactic fashion, lecturing on the rules, describing the outcome beforehand, lecturing on strategy, and urging players to one course of behavior and not another. These actions can destroy the possibility of success and interfere with the learning. Beginners often act in these ways because of the difficult transition for most people from that of traditional instructor to that of simulation/ gamer.

Another difficult aspect for beginners is the change in the nature of the classroom. An outsider may perceive noise, disorder, and perhaps chaos. (Once while I was having a simulation/game played in a university classroom, a colleague came in to complain, perhaps legitimately, about the noise.) The college instructor who is accustomed to the quiet turning of notebook pages and otherwise only the sound of his or her melodious voice needs to be prepared for and oriented to this change.

The seventh and final step is to conduct a debriefing session. The debriefing should refer to the objectives, which were the reason for using the technique in the first place. The instructor should avoid beginning a debriefing by evaluating the simulation/game itself (although this should be done eventually so as to give the instructor feedback about the effectiveness of the experience from the perspective of students). Debriefing should focus on the experience that took place, on an analysis of what happened, on conclusions that can be made from the events, on an examination of the feelings of the players, and on an attempt to discover if the conclusions can be generalized to other experiences. Most good simulation/games provide a debriefing guide that can be used as written or which can be adapted to the needs of the instructor.

Teachers must learn to evaluate the results of simulation/ games. There are three separate uses of such evaluation. First, it is

necessary to evaluate student achievement. Second, it is necessary
to evaluate from the perspective of those who have played to obtain
feedback on whether or not to use them again and, if so, which
ones. Third, it is necessary to learn to evaluate *before* they are used
as a means of deciding whether or not they should be used.

Some people argue that simulation/games are of limited
value because it is impossible to test students on what they learned
as a result of playing. The assumption that the only good activities
are those that can lead to examination questions is highly questionable; it is possible to write useful examination questions based on
experiences which take place during a simulation/game. The examination should be based on the objectives and on the debriefing
that, in turn, was based on the objectives.

The second part of evaluation is the question of whether or
not the simulation/game worked. Were students involved and did
their motivation increase? Were responses positive? There are many
good simulation/games available. An instructor who obtains some
experience with them can generally avoid ones that do not work
(although sometimes circumstances may lead to failure even with
the best). This kind of evaluation can be done after the debriefing,
partly by the instructor who analyzes the experience, and in conjunction with students who can share their feelings about the
simulation/game.

Finally, instructors must learn to evaluate simulation/games
before they are used to determine whether or not they should be
used. As one has experience, one develops the ability to do this. Several factors should be considered in deciding whether or not to use
a particular one. One that is too complex may be impossible to
understand and may need long, boring and confusing lists of rules.
A good simulation/game has a correspondence to reality that is
neither over simplified nor so complete a representation of reality
that it is no longer a simulation. Cost is another factor to consider.
Some are very expensive but are not any more effective than some
alternatives that might be available free. (See *Simulation/Gaming*,
which is a journal that often publishes simulation/games that can
be reproduced without permission.)

There are still other issues to consider. A simulation/game
may play well but have little value as a learning device. Many that

are commercial have this problem. Although they are fun to play, little is accomplished by their use, and they distort the real world so badly that they are capable of doing harm. Some educational products on the market use a simulation/game format but are devices for exercising rote memory; each carefully recited fact allows the player one more move on the game board.

The evaluation process can be summarized with the following questions: Does the simulation/game allow for accomplishment of objectives? Does it work? Do the students enjoy it? Can it be played in a reasonable amount of time at reasonable cost? Does the simulation/game correspond to reality in an appropriate way? Does it lend itself to meaningful debriefing? Does it leave players desiring to play another simulation/game on another day?

I would like to examine briefly the process of designing simulation/games. Design is one of the most difficult aspects of the process. There are hundreds of poorly designed simulation/games around. One should not attempt to design any until one has had considerable experience playing those designed by others. Some of the process of design is based on mimicry; thus, the first step in learning to design is to become familiar with what already exists. The next step *once again* is to determine the objectives one wishes to achieve. Then it is necessary to create a plan—what Richard Duke (1974) calls a "cognitive map"—in which the designer has a mental picture of how the simulation/game is arranged, how it proceeds, what kind of equipment is necessary, and how the parts fit together. Only then should the actual construction take place.

Designing a simulation/game involves the following as well. Whether it is to be a board game, a role play game, or some combination should be decided. A scenario must be created along with the parameters under which it will proceed. People who have experience with design always advise that in setting the parameters, it is necessary to focus on what to leave out as well as on what to include. Decisions must be made about how the simulation/game will operate with regard to the actions of the players. If they are to play roles, this should be decided and the roles created. The resources available to each player, basic moves required, and the decisions they must make should be determined. The way in which players interact with each other and with the setting needs to be specified.

A scoring system (if one is to be used) should be created, and a device for ending (lest it go on forever) should also be designed. Finally, a guide to debriefing is necessary.

An Interdisciplinary Technique

Well-designed simulation/games may be necessary more than ever in the future. Very early in this chapter I discussed the procedure as a future's language; gestalt can be conveyed, and as a result, alternative futures may be efficiently predicted. Moreover, here is a technique that is helpful in understanding the future because it is interdisciplinary.

As they are now perceived, the academic disciplines are arbitrary divisions of knowledge. They arose, with few exceptions, through a series of historical accidents. That they are arbitrary can be seen by the way in which they overlap (thus we have political sociology, social psychology, and biochemistry) and by the tendency for new interdisciplinary studies to arise to fill vacuums that exist among the disciplines (thus we have the cybernetics and demography). The problems that humankind faces on the planet are not ones that lend themselves to easy solution by the traditional disciplines. The energy problem, for example, will never be solved because of the efforts of any one discipline.

Three concepts that I believe are exemplars of future-oriented interdisciplinary ones are: decision making, model, and system. Decision making is a process of choosing among alternatives, and it is best accomplished where there is a large amount of information from a variety of sources. Model, which is described earlier in this chapter, is a representation of some aspect of the real world that is analogical. Models are widely used in a variety of contexts; the process of modeling is useful in problem solving. A system is an interrelationship of processes such that any aspect of the system affects any other aspect of the system. Systems analysis is an attempt to understand processes so as to be able to solve problems. Almost all simulation/games involve decision making; simulation/gaming is a subclass of modeling; a simulation/game can be perceived as a system.

Earlier I attempted to relate simulation/gaming to the pro-

cess of divergent thinking, which leads to creative behavior. This too
is an interdisciplinary process and one that can be related to the
future. As simulation/gaming facilitates creative behavior, it facilitates it in an interdisciplinary way. I believe that the development
of creative problem solving, based on divergent thinking (as an
addition to, not as a replacement for, convergent thinking) is a
necessary prerequisite to survival in the future.

Twelve Games

I would like to list and briefly annotate twelve simulation/
games that readers of this chapter might consider using. Any annotated list must be arbitrary. The ones I have selected for this
chapter are varied with regard to disciplines and are ones with which
I have had direct experience. They are simple enough for beginners
yet complex enough to have substance. And they are fun. Many of
them were developed for players who are younger than postsecondary students, but this should not deter anyone from using them
because they can be played at many levels of abstraction.

Beat Detroit (Antler Productions). This is a board game in
which players learn to deal with the problem of the automobile in
order to avoid going broke. Players are required to examine all of
the issues related to ownership (warranties, insurance, repair costs,
recalls, used versus new cars, and status) in a way that teaches improved strategies for automobile ownership. Beat Detroit can be
used with economics courses, consumer economics courses, and
those related to personal growth.

Culture Contact (ABT Associates). This is an exciting one
that examines the problems which occur when a group of sailors
are forced to land and to negotiate with a group of islanders. The
simulation/game can lead to either accommodation between the
two groups, or it can lead to destruction of one group by the other.
My experience has been that the players become so deeply involved
in the role playing that in the debriefing session it is easy to demonstrate the occurrence and intensity of conflict between cultures.
Culture Contact can be used in sociology and anthropology courses
as well as in ones that examine conflict.

Democracy (Western Publishing Company). This simulation/game, developed by James Coleman, is one of the better known and most successful. Players assume the role of legislators who try to pass bills into laws through a process of negotiation and lobbying. Democracy demonstrates the potential conflict that exists between a legislator's own point of view and the needs of his or her constituents. One feature of Democracy is that it consists of several versions which let the teacher introduce additional complexities of the legislative process as succeeding versions are played. This one can be used in political science courses as well as in those that examine decision making.

Energy X (Ideal School Supply Company). In this game, which is interdisciplinary, the energy crisis is examined thoroughly. This is essentially a role-playing game and is packaged with a multimedia kit that includes a slide tape presentation and other data, all of which are presented in an interesting and colorful way. Energy X is not difficult to play, but it is complex and somewhat lengthy; these characteristics seem appropriate for an activity that attempts to examine the problems of energy.

Failsafe (The Minnesota Education Computing Center). This one, designed by Bruce Tipple, is based on the book by Eugene Burdick; it is necessary to have access to a computer in which to store the program and to have a teletype available. Users will find Failsafe to be an exciting experience based on role playing. It examines executive decision making. Players attempt to arrive at a solution to the problem of runaway bombers that are aimed at the Soviet Union. In addition to the decision-making outcomes one achieves, Failsafe is a useful tool for acquainting students with procedures for using a teletype terminal in conjunction with a computer. This simulation/game could be used in courses in political science, ones that focus on decision making, and ones that teach computer science.

Future Decisions—The IQ Game (The Simulation and Gaming Association). This one involves role playing and attempts to orient the players to future studies. The scenario concerns the discovery of a drug that can raise IQ scores but is available only in limited quantities. Players must decide who gets the drug and become aware of the problems one might find in the future and the increasing difficulty of dealing with these problems. An interesting feature of Future Decisions is that it contains a systematic debriefing

procedure as part of the simulation/game itself. Sociology courses
and courses that examine future studies could use this one.

The Game of Farming (Macmillan Publishing Company).
This one, which is part of the High School Geography Project, is
based on actual events that affected Midwestern farmers during
three periods of American history. Players assume the roles of
farmers and try to anticipate climate and market conditions to make
a profit. The Game of Farming, which can be used in economics,
history and geography courses, demonstrates the multitude of difficulties involved in farming in the United States. It also develops
empathy for farmers, a quality often missing among those who
live in urban areas.

Inner-City Housing (Livingston and Stoll, 1973). Problems of inner-city housing are examined from the perspective of
both tenants and landlords. Players take first one role and then the
other. This feature allows them to gain insight into the problem
from the point of view of everyone concerned. Inner-City Housing
develops empathy for the landlords as well as tenants and in this
way achieves balance. It is useful in sociology, economics, and
geography as well as in courses that seek to develop sensitivity to
the poor.

Kommissar (Selchow and Rightler Company). This board
game is a commercial one rather than an educational one. It is a
parody of the Soviet system (a kind of Russian Monopoly game)
in which the goal of the players is to amass enough wealth so as to
be able to escape the Soviet Union. The game is fun to play. I have
found its educational value lies in the parody that is so broad it can
be used as a means of reality testing in conjunction with studies of
the Soviet Union. Kommissar could be played before and after a
study of Soviet government, for example, as a way of seeing to what
extent students have rid themselves of the many stereotypes that
people hold about the Soviet Union.

Nostalgia (Creative Communications and Research). This
one is difficult to describe and categorize, but it is fun to play.
Players draw cards that require them to play scenes based on events
which occurred in the 1920s and the 1930s. After they have followed
the instructions, the other players rate their performance, and the
higher the rating, the further the players may proceed on a game
board until one player reaches the end of the board and wins.

Nostalgia can be played in history, English, and drama courses; it could be used in many classes as a way of preparing students to role play.

Starpower (Western Behavior Science Institutes). Written by R. Garry Shirts, this is one of the best known and most successful of all games. Starpower builds a three-tiered society in which those at the bottom are placed permanently into a caste, whereas those at the top make rules and begin to discriminate against those below them. Starpower has great emotional impact. It teaches the effects of rigid social stratification more dramatically than any narrative description could ever hope to do. It can be used to teach sociology, human relations, and much else. The only disadvantage in using it is that it is so well known that its hidden agenda may not be so hidden anymore.

Values (Friendship Press). Here is a board game that forces players to examine their values. This simulation/game becomes more intense the longer it is played; it can be an emotionally mean-ingful experience. It is an excellent value-clarification exercise, and the object of winning is soon lost in the process of value examination that involves all the participants quickly. Courses that examine hu-man relations and development will find this one suitable.

This brief listing is but a small sample of the scope and variety of available simulation/games. Those readers who would like to use a game for the first time will find that any of the pre-ceding twelve will serve as a good introduction to the process.

An Example

By way of further introduction to the process, I would like to conclude this chapter by offering a simulation/game of my own de-sign. It is an interdisciplinary one that represents the decision-making process in higher education.

Interdepartmental Decision Making. Several objectives can be achieved by this simulation/game, including:

1. An understanding that decision making in a complex institution is affected by the values, perceptions, and experiences of the decision makers.

2. An understanding that in institutions of higher education, decision making involves many constituencies including departments, deans, and representatives of the public.
3. An understanding that department chairpersons tend to be more narrow in their views of institutions and attempt to protect their own constituencies. Deans are forced to arbitrate differences between department chairpersons, and they are in a better position to have a broader view of the institution.
4. An understanding that trustees are representatives of the public, and they tend to support the decisions made by institutions of higher education with little questioning.
5. An understanding that institutions of higher education have limited resources and there are usually unlimited demands on these resources.

Interdepartmental Decision Making contains the following *problem* statement:

Metropolitan College is a relatively small college located in a moderately sized midwestern city. Metropolitan has 3,000 students and only recently has become a four-year college after being started several years ago as a community college. Metropolitan consists of six departments: business, education, humanities, physical education, science, and social science. The college is administered by a president, who has primary responsibility for external relations, and a dean, who is responsible for the day-to-day operation. Metropolitan College is governed by a board of trustees who are elected by the voters of the city.

Through a series of errors and misjudgements, there is a surplus of funds available to Metropolitan College. This surplus has been discovered near the end of the current fiscal year. The surplus is not huge, but it is large enough so that it could help improve programs if it were used wisely. If the money is not used by the end of the fiscal year, which expires soon (so soon that there will not be time for another meeting), it will revert to the city's general fund.

Players assume the following *roles:*

Dr. Giles, Dean of Instruction. Dean Giles is fifty-one years old and has been with Metropolitan College since it was a community college. Dean Giles is very experienced and very patient. The dean would like to use the money and feels that it is imperative that a decision be made. At the same time the dean does not wish to anger the department chairpersons unnecessarily. For this reason, Dean Giles desires a compromise that will allow the sharing of the money with more than one department. If the money were to be shared by all the departments, however, there would not be enough to help anyone. Therefore, equal distribution is not an acceptable solution to the dean.

Dean Giles' career began as an English teacher in the city's public schools. Eventually the dean attended the state university, first part time and then full time. Following the receipt of a master's degree, Dean Giles obtained a position at what was then Metropolitan Community College. Eventually while working at the community college, Dr. Giles received a Ph.D. in English. The dean continues to have a strong interest in teacher education and has been a friend and supporter of the teacher education program at Metropolitan College.

Dr. Ledger, Chairperson of the Business Department. Dr. Ledger's department is a very popular one, and Dr. Ledger believes that the Department of Business is the most important one at Metropolitan College, given the current state of the economy. Most of the graduates of the department, and especially the secretarial science division graduates, have been able to find employment. Dr. Ledger is mild mannered, but this is deceptive. Dr. Ledger often wins these kind of battles despite the disarming manner. Dr. Ledger's needs are critical; the money would be used to replace several typewriters that are deteriorating.

Dr. Dewey, Chairperson of the Education Department. Teacher preparation is an important part of Metropolitan's mission, and Dr. Dewey is one of the most popular of all the faculty members at Metropolitan. Dr. Dewey has especially good rapport with Dean Giles. (In fact, Dean Giles and Dr. Dewey have been at the college for about the same amount of time, and they are personal friends socially as well as professionally.) Dr. Dewey is somewhat traditional with regard to the education program but has maintained splendid rapport with the area public schools. Dr. Dewey would use the money to provide honoraria for the teachers in the public schools who have been working with Metropolitan's student teachers. Dr. Dewey sees the ability to get this money as a test of the relationship with Dean Giles. For this reason, Dr. Dewey will fight hard for it.

Dr. Lark, Chairperson of the Humanities Department. The Humanities Department has been inadequately funded for many years, and Dr. Lark is disgusted. When Dr. Giles became dean, Dr. Lark thought that the dean's English background would result in better support for the humanities program, but this has not been the case and Dr. Lark is bitter and angry. The additional money would be used by Dr. Lark to provide better practice facilities for those in music classes. If Dr. Lark does not obtain the money, it may be necessary to eliminate the music program.

Dr. Strong, Chairperson of the Physical Education Department. This is Dr. Strong's first year as chairperson and as a member of the faculty at Metropolitan College. Dr. Strong is somewhat overawed by the other department chairpersons. However, Dr. Strong is not totally timid, and the needs of the Department of Physical Education are as critical as those of any other department, if not more so. The gymnasium in which most of the department's courses are conducted needs a new floor desperately. Not obtaining one may prove to be dangerous and physically hazardous. Dr. Strong's acceptance as chairperson among the other members of the department would be strengthened if the surplus were obtained.

Dr. Tube, Chairperson of the Science Department. Dr. Tube is relatively young and aggressive. Dr. Tube received a doctorate from a prestigious eastern university. It is Dr. Tube's wish to raise the level and quality of science at Metropolitan College. Dr. Tube feels that additional laboratory facilities are badly needed if the science program is to improve. Use of *all* the additional money will provide the department with a modest improvement in the laboratory facilities and Dr. Tube has come to the meeting to argue strongly for the science program.

Dr. Chart, Chairperson of the Social Science Department. Dr. Chart is an economist who has been at Metropolitan College since it became a four-year school. Dr. Chart was brought in to add prestige to the college. Dr. Chart has continued to develop a national reputation and has brought some prestige to Metropolitan

College. Unfortunately, Dr. Chart is also extremely arrogant and has little patience with others, particularly those whom Dr. Chart considers intellectual inferiors. If Dr. Chart obtains the money, it will be used for additional computer facilities for the social science department. Dr. Chart does not feel that the department can continue to grow in stature unless the additional computer resources are obtained.

Trustees of the College. The remaining members of the class assume the roles of the trustees of the college. In playing these roles, the students act as observers and react to what they hear as they would in real life.

Interdepartmental Decision Making is played in the following steps:

1. The instructor selects seven students and assigns them the designated roles. The instructor also describes the role of the trustees of the college, which will be assumed by the remaining members of the class.
2. The instructor serves as chairperson of the board of trustees and announces that the trustees have been invited to attend a special meeting of the dean and the department chairpersons.
3. The instructor then reads the problem statement and introduces the dean and the department chairpersons to the trustees. (The trustees should not read any of the role descriptions. Each player should read only his or her own role description.)
4. The dean opens the meeting and serves as facilitator and chairperson. The dean should try to obtain a consensus in the allotted time or less; the dean should avoid taking sides during the meeting.
5. If the department chairpersons reach no decision after approximately thirty minutes, the dean will have approximately ten minutes to make a decision, which is announced to the chairpersons and to the trustees.
6. The trustees of the college then discuss the decision briefly (either one made by the chairpersons, if they have agreed, or one made by the dean). The trustees can vote to support the decision or reverse or revise it. They should keep in mind that a

reversal or revision could cause the dean to resign and the trustees would not like this to happen.

This concludes the role-playing portion of the simulation/ game. The instructor should then conduct a debriefing session by asking the following questions (or others that the instructor would prefer):

1. To what extent do the results of this simulation/game reflect reality? Would the decision have been the same in a real college? (The students should realize that the most probable outcome is that the dean would have to make the decision since no consensus would come out of the meeting.)
2. To what extent do values, perceptions, and experiences affect decisions?
3. How is the behavior of the dean different from the behavior of a department chairperson? What accounts for this difference in behavior?
4. To what extent did the behavior of the trustees reflect reality? (Students should realize that in the real world, the trustees would probably support the dean.)
5. To what extent does the problem of the needs of the department reflect the problems of actual departments? (Students should recognize that this is the most realistic aspect of the simulation/ game. Limited resources and unlimited demands on them is a central feature of all economic systems and institutions.)

Readers who are familiar with simulation/games should find this one enjoyable and useful with students. Readers for whom the concept is new will find that this one is simple enough to serve as an introduction to the process.

12

❀ ❀ ❀ ❀ ❀ ❀ ❀ ❀ ❀ ❀

John S. Duley

Learning Through Field Experience

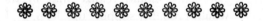

❀ ❀ ❀ ❀ ❀ ❀ ❀ ❀ ❀ ❀

Field experience is a comprehensive term that applies to many diverse course offerings and programs. Despite their diversity, all instances of field experience education have this in common: They are out-of-classroom learning activities sponsored by an institution or a faculty member in which the learner has the primary responsibility for the educational endeavor; usually the student has responsibility for a specific task or work assignment, which is the major vehicle by which the student learns. This broad definition is necessary because of the many uses of this type of education. There are at least seven broad educational goals that are frequently listed

314

singly or in various combinations in program descriptions. These goals are to help students:

1. Put theory into practice, develop the higher cognitive skills: learn how to apply, integrate, and/or evaluate knowledge and/or the methodology of a discipline or field
2. Acquire knowledge: engage in research, analyze the organizational structure of a firm or an agency
3. Acquire and develop specific skills: problem solving, interpersonal, group process, coping and/or psychomotor
4. Increase personal growth and development: increase self-understanding, self-confidence, self-reliance, and/or clarify values
5. Learn how to learn independently: develop the ability to use experiential learning theory or engage in cross-cultural learning
6. Explore careers: develop self-understanding and acquire and use career exploration skills
7. Become responsible citizens: develop a firsthand understanding of the political system, identify issues of concern, and develop the political and social action skills appropriate to citizenship

This type of education is used more extensively with undergraduates than many people realize. If Michigan State University is representative of institutions of higher education in the United States, the number of field experience programs is increasing. In a study at the university, forty-five undergraduate field experience courses were identified (Quinn, 1972). In 1974 there were sixty and in 1977, seventy-six such offerings (Nosow, 1975). The 1972 study described the diversity of field experiences as follows:

> One student visited and lived in abandoned World War II incarceration camps in California, interviewed former inmates, and compiled his findings into a book to be published. Another student lived, worked, and studied for two months in a California desert—a scientific research project. A young woman spent a term touring and acting with a West Coast theatre group. A young man lived with and observed the Amish as a means of getting background material for the project he

designed. Another young man established, edited, and published a newspaper for a religious organization. And another prepared both radio and television broadcasts for his field study. One student went abroad with a friend, where together they gathered data for a comparative study of the teaching techniques of British and American professors. Another student arranged interviews with a group of London businessmen for his self-designed study. One student did research for a senator, another interned in an attorney general's office, and still another spent time working and studying in the Democratic offices in the state capitol building. Experiences included jobs in a CAP firm, in an auditing department, with the Cooperative Service in Washington, in an office on campus, and with the foreign exchange students in another university. Some of the students described field education experiences in probation courts, in the police department, in reform schools, in juvenile homes, and in welfare agencies.

Service-oriented experiences abounded. Some of the students worked with small inner-city businesses as management consultants, planned and set up community recreation programs and centers, interned in day care centers, and worked with the physically handicapped, the emotionally disturbed, and the mentally retarded.

Other students were involved in cross-cultural experiences, encounter groups, leadership studies, family counseling, summer camps, and neighborhood surveys. One student studied some social problems of the inner city of Detroit; another, the social welfare system in Europe. One investigated the deterioration of housing in a specific area of a city; another worked at the socialization of former mental patients.

Some students participated in field experiences that took them away from campus for two to three hours a day at a time. Other field work lasted two or three weeks or an entire term. Students reported going to the Appalachian Mountains for geological study, to the deep South for a study of the park system, and to the East and South for forestry study (Quinn, 1972, pp. 32–33).

In their preprofessional and technically oriented professional programs, universities have traditionally encouraged activities outside of the classroom as a meaningful and necessary part of the educational experience. These out-of-classroom activities have been traditional adjuncts similar to term papers and library work. This has been true at agricultural colleges in such curricula as animal husbandry, crop and soil science, and fisheries and wildlife. Students have literally worked in the fields in these programs to supplement their classroom learning. Laboratory work has had the same role in engineering and the hard sciences. Student teaching and social work practicums are long established programs of a similar nature. These may have been the precursors of an attempt to increase the relevance of a college education for more undergraduates and the attempt to respond to the increased interest in the direct applicability of a college education to occupational and career development.

Developments in field experience education go beyond this, however. Educators are seeking ways to individualize learning opportunities and to customize education to fit the student's needs and readiness to learn. The growing awareness of the importance of the student in the learning process and of principles of learning and motivation have led educators to seek more opportunities in which the initiative for learning lies more with the student than it does in the relatively passive environment of the classroom. These concerns express themselves in increased opportunities for independent study, individual or group research projects as well as in field experience opportunities.

Participants and Their Roles

There are usually three principal participants in this educational process: the student, the sponsoring faculty member, and the work supervisor. The students' and faculty members' roles are significantly different from their classroom roles. The supervisor is a new actor not found in the classroom.

Field experience education is a valuable supplement to classroom learning because it provides different and educationally important role development opportunities to students that are not available in the classroom. The following list identifies and describes the additional roles in which a student engaged in field study may develop skill (Duley, 1974, p. 37).

Initiator	1. Identifies, seeks, finds, and secures the help and cooperation needed, often in an alien context
Problem Solver and Decision Maker	2. Functions in an open system, defining and solving the problems as they arise and making decisions in the course of carrying out the project that affect the student's life and the personal lives of others
Cultural Analyst and Strategist	3. Understands the cultural context well enough in which work is being done to function effectively in it
Interactor	4. Relates effectively with faculty supervisor, coworkers, clients, or customers, and is able to stay in touch with them and work through emotionally difficult relationships
Information Source and Network Developer	5. Develops personal information sources instead of relying on those provided by an instructor
Free Agent	6. Functions independently in a support system where rewards are given for workable solutions to particular and often unforeseen problems rather than for predetermined correct answers to set problems, and in an unstructured setting without the classroom support system assignment, syllabi, and tests
Value Clarifier	7. Makes value judgments in arriving at these workable (compromise) solutions or decisions that would not be expected in classroom work
Communicator	8. Is able to communicate effectively

| | | through the spoken and written word, through listening and reading nonverbal communication and to be emotionally involved in interpersonal interaction |
| Recipient | 9. | Is able to receive and utilize criticism constructively |

The quality of the performance of these roles is one pragmatic measure of education and maturity. When comparing the role descriptions of the chart with the usual classroom experience, a significant contrast emerges. For most students, the classroom is a familiar environment in which all the needed information is provided in lectures, the textbook, or through the reserve shelf in the library. The problems that are assigned in the course usually have predetermined correct answers, and neither they nor their solutions impinge directly on the student's life or the lives of others. In course work there is no need to develop interpersonal skills or to learn to work through emotionally difficult relationships. The payoff of the classroom-based course is in grades and credits earned for getting the predetermined work done well and on time. Classroom related learning places a high value on objectivity and emotional detachment as opposed to active, personal involvement.

Another major point of difference between classroom learning and field experience education is in who controls the learning activities and the dynamics of the learning process. This difference strongly influences the interaction of the student and the teacher. In the classroom the faculty member not only determines the learning objectives and the limits of what the course will cover, the instructor selects the knowledge content, how it will be presented, what will be done with it, what in it will be emphasized, and what the students will be held responsible for. The student has the responsibility to work with what is given. A student may have to use judgment in determining what, among all the material received, is most important to the professor. But that usually is the extent of self-direction expected. In the field experience setting the educational objectives and the limits of learning expected of the student are also controlled by the educator, although less directly and in a more flexible manner. But in this type of learning the student and the circumstances of the assignment exercise primary control over the learning process and determine the resources and the time and place of their use. In addition to differences in the control of the learning experience, the nature and the source of evaluation is different. The student is not solely dependent on the faculty for the evaluation of learning. Feedback is often direct, stemming from the evaluation inherent in the job and its performance or in the circumstances of the experience. The supervisor also shares in the evaluation process.

More self-direction is required of the student than in the classroom if the most is to be made of the learning opportunities provided in the placement. These opportunities will occur in unplanned ways as well as on the initiative of the student. On-the-spot determinations must be made as to how they will be used educationally, and a creative response must be given to negative as well as positive aspects of the experience.

The degree of freedom and responsibility and the affective demands in this type of learning are often unsettling to students. Their previous schooling experience has not provided opportunities for them to assume much initiative in directing their own learning. In addition, the fact that the student fulfills new roles, that the control of the learning processes are more in the hands of the student than in the classroom, and that the source of evaluation is more directly related to accomplishment in job performance and is multidimensional all contribute to a situation in which the dynamics of the relationship between the student and the faculty member change. A useful aid in the preparation of students for these new dimensions is *College Sponsored Experiential Learning—A CAEL Student Guide* (Nesbitt, 1977).

The faculty member's role is no less important, and it is significantly modified. This is so because the learning facilitated in these programs is not so much the mastery of subject matter content as it is the application and integration of knowledge and the acquisition of the skills necessary to an educated and mature person. Therefore, the faculty member's role shifts from one of the authoritative conveyor and interpreter of the knowledge and the methodological framework of an academic discipline to one of mentor. This means that the faculty member has to establish relationships with the students that provide insight into their special abilities, interests, and needs as a basis for suggesting placement possibilities, and use. Also involved is the ability to help students identify and describe their own learning objectives for their field experience. This requires ability to see the learning opportunities from the point of view of the students at their particular point of development.

This role requires a wide range of professional contacts and the development of a network of resources that can be used for the identification and development of placements. The development of a finely tuned sixth sense for matching students and placements is important. A creative imagination is needed for identifying new sources of placements where none exist or for identifying students with special abilities, interests, or needs. The documenting and reporting of learning is another aspect that requires additional skills. Not only do well-conceived assessable learning objectives have to be written, but reliable methods for reporting their accomplishment have to be identified or developed. Although there are some common practices, such as logs, journals, and performance analysis reports, creative imagination is needed to select or design methods that work well in each particular program.

In monitoring the learning acquired during the placement, the faculty sponsor has to keep in touch with students in a nonthreatening, nonjudgmental way to help them see and use the educational possibilities in their placement. The instructor must also develop working relationships of mutual trust with the work-site supervisors, informing them of the educational objectives of the program and of the student and supporting them in the accomplishment of the objectives. In short, this role requires the faculty, in addition to the use of regular academic skills, to develop and manage a learning environment that is not under direct control and is influenced primarily through informal personal contacts among a number of participants: students and supervisors.

What should the contribution of the work supervisor be to the educational process? Although that person's contribution may be limited, there are certain basic conditions that must be established in the placement if it is to be a good learning environment; these are the responsibility of the supervisor. The work responsibilities and conditions of placement, such as the amount of compensation, if any, the time to report to work, and the place of work, the resources and the equipment to be made available, must be clearly spelled out. A two-stage orientation of the students is needed. The first orientation should answer the questions: Where do I fit in? How do I get things done? What is expected of me here? The second stage of the orientation, after the students are well established in the placement, should help the students understand their roles in the agency and their relationship to the total mission and operation of the organization. This is part of the supervisor's ongoing responsibility for interpretation, helping the students see the relationship of what they are doing and the work of others and the agency as a whole. The supervisor is also responsible for the guidance and direction of the students in their work while on the site. The evaluation of the students' work, and, to the extent possible, the evaluation of the accomplishment of the students' learning objectives and those of the program are also the supervisor's responsibility. The supervisor will also serve as a model to the students for what it means to be a professional in that field. Often the interpersonal relations that develop between a supervisor and the students are highly significant in their growth and development.

In addition to the unique roles of students, faculty, and supervisor that require understanding, there is an eight-step process which the faculty member must carry out. This process includes: identification of institutional and student goals, development of learning objectives, arrangement of field placements, preparation of students for placement, placement of students, monitoring of student progress, assessment of student learning, and evaluation of program.

Goal Typology

Since the range of uses of field experience education is so wide, it is important at the outset to clearly specify educational goals and to ask the students to do the same. The following typology, first developed for the 1973 state-of-the-art conference of the Society for Field Experience Education and later refined for the Council for the Advancement of Experiential Learning (CAEL) faculty handbook, *College Sponsored Experiential Learning* (Duley and Gordon, 1977), identifies eleven types of programs and indicates the primary purposes served by each.

Cross-Cultural Experience. A student involves himself or herself in another culture or subculture of his or her own society in a deep and significant way, either as a temporary member of a family, a worker in that society, or as a volunteer in a social agency, with the intention, as a participant observer, of learning as much as possible about that culture and his or her own.

Work Experience (Cooperative Education). The National Commission for Cooperative Education has defined cooperative education as "that education plan which integrates classroom experience and practical work experience in industrial, business, government, or service-type work situations in the community. The work experiences constitute a regular and essential element in the educative process and some minimum amount of work experience and minimum standard of successful performance on the job are included in the requirements of the institution for a degree" [The National Commission for Cooperative Education, 1971].

Preprofessional Training. A student serves in assigned responsibilities under the supervision of a professional in the field of education, medicine, law, social work, nursing, or ministry, putting the theory learned into practice, gaining skills in the profession, and being evaluated by his or her supervisor.

Institutional Analysis. "A student has a temporary period of supervised work that provides opportunities to develop skills, to test abilities and career interests, and to systematically examine institutional cultures in light of the central theoretical notions in a chosen academic field of study" [Zauderer, 1973, p. 1].

Service-Learning Internship. "Service-learning has been defined as: the integration of the accomplishment of a task which meets human need with conscious educational growth. A service-learning internship is designed to provide students responsibility to meet a public need and a significant learning experience within a public or private institution for a specified period of time, usually 10 to 15 weeks" [Sigmon, 1972, p. 2].

Social/Political Action. A student secures a placement, under faculty sponsorship, which provides an opportunity to be directly engaged in working for social change either through community organizing, political activity, research/action projects, or work with organizations seeking to bring about changes in the social order. A learning contract is usually made with a faculty sponsor to be fulfilled by the student in this type of experience.

Personal Growth and Development. A student undertakes a program in an off-campus setting that is designed to further his or her personal growth and development, such as the wilderness survival programs of the Outward Bound Schools, an apprenticeship to an artist or a craftsperson, residence in a house of a religious order for the development of his or her spiritual life, or participation in an established group psychological or human relations program.

Field Research. A student undertakes an independent or group research project in the field under the supervision of a faculty member, applying the concepts and methods of an academic discipline such as geology, archeology, geography, or sociology.

Career Exploration. A student secures a supervised placement in business, government, industry, a service organization, or a profession in order to perform a useful service, to analyze the career possibilities of that placement, and to develop employment-related skills. The educational institution provides the means of structured reflection, analysis, and self-evaluation, the agency supervisor provides an evaluation of the student's work and career potential.

Academic Discipline/Career Integration. "A student is employed in a business, government, industry, service organization, or profession prior to entry into the educational institution. The faculty members and the educational institution provide the means of structured analysis and evaluation based on the academic discipline involved, integrating theory and practice and heightening the student's awareness and understanding of the world and his/her career in a conscious systematic fashion" [Currier, 1975, p. 5].

Career or Occupational Development. A student

is assisted in finding a series of two or more placements which are chosen, in consultation with an advisor, to provide the opportunity for advancement in skills and experience related to a specific career. This is particularly useful in technological programs when classroom and on-the-job learning are closely integrated.

In addition to assisting in the selection of broad general goals, the typology may also help resolve such issues as the relationship of the experience to the student's academic program—that is, in answering the question of whether it fulfills general education goals or reinforces the student's major. Other issues the typology may help resolve are the optimum time in the student's academic career for the placement to take place, the nature of the placement setting needed—business, industry, government agency, welfare or community organization or others—the time needed to fulfill the placement, full or part time, long or short span; and it will aid in the development of the much more specific learning objectives that will assure the attainment of the broad goals. Davis, Duley, and Alexander (1977, pp. 10–11) developed a checklist from this typology to assist program developers in selecting broad goal statements and for use by students in identifying their own goals and reaching agreement with faculty sponsors on acceptable common goals. The following checklist developed from the educational goals that are uniquely appropriate to field experience can be used also by staff and students for that same purpose.

Using the following code, fill in the blanks in the checklist below: (1) very important to me, (2) important to me, (3) not important to me.

The proposed field experience should give the student the opportunity to:

1. Learn how to apply, integrate, and evaluate knowledge   _____
2. Engage in research or organizational analysis   _____
3. Acquire the following skills:
   Problem solving   _____
   Interpersonal   _____
   Coping   _____

        Group process   _____
        Specific psychomotor   _____
4. Increase personal growth through improved:
        Value clarification   _____
        Self-understanding   _____
        Self-confidence   _____
        Self-reliance   _____
5. Learn how to learn independently through:
        The use of experiential learning theory   _____
        A cross-cultural experience   _____
6. Acquire and use career exploration skills   _____
7. Develop a firsthand understanding of the political
    system   _____
8. Develop the political and social action skills
    appropriate to citizenship   _____

Objectives

Having selected the broad educational goals for the program, the next step, the development of learning objectives, is the one that will be of greatest assistance in developing and managing a strong educational program. Knowing precisely what the program intends to accomplish is very important in executing the remainder of the six steps. Clearly stated learning objectives will help the instructor determine the content of the preparation or orientation sessions, the need for, and nature of, continuing interaction with the students in the field, or the need for a structured means of reporting and reflection in the monitoring phase of the program. Well-developed learning objectives also are valuable in the interpretation of the program to students, supervisors, other faculty, administrators and the general public. The most important contribution of these learning objectives will be their value in determining what the student has learned. The closer faculty can come to stating exactly what it is they expect students to be able to do or to know, the easier the assessment task will be (see Chapters One and Four). Well-stated learning objectives are also extremely useful in program evaluation, in decision making about both program improvement and continuation.

A learning objective involves four principal components. The first is a precise description of the end result desired, either knowledge to be attained or skill to be acquired. The key to the writing of that description is the verb. It has to be a verb that refers to some action which can be demonstrated or documented. Such verbs as *understand, grasp, appreciate, know,* and *determine,* which are quite appropriate in broad general goal statements, are not precise enough to identify acceptable performance for program planning or assessment purposes. Verbs such as *identify, list, draw, present, design, select, assemble, measure, distinguish between, solve,* or *apply* have been found to be more useful for this purpose.

In addition to a description of the end products desired, faculty also have to include three other elements in a learning objective. The first is a statement of the conditions under which the student will be expected to demonstrate the knowledge and/or skill. The second is a description of the minimum level of performance that will be accepted as evidence of the achievement of the objective. The third has to do with performance stability, how many times the behavior has to be demonstrated to be accepted as adequately learned. The following examples will indicate the various components of a well-stated learning objective. The four elements in each example are marked with the following code: *action verb,* **conditions** (minimal level of performance), and [performance stability].

1. **At the end of two weeks in the placement,** the student will be able to *diagram* the organizational components of the agency and **orally** *explain* the relationships of those components, (consistent with textbook use) of the terms authority, responsibility, departmentalization, and communication. (The diagram must include all positions) and both **the drawing and explaining must be done in one hour.**
2. **After three months in an intake office placement,** the student will be able *to distinguish between* a surrogate client's presented problem and real problems in a mock interview situation. **The test situation will involve five surrogate clients in simulations involving hidden agenda role-playing exercises in a mock office classroom setting with one-way mirrors.** The role-playing clients

will be skilled in providing clues to the "real problem" through acting in a previously agreed upon defensive manner. The student is *to use* interview and diagnostic procedures (elaborated in class and in written agency policy manuals). Evaluation of successful student performance will be (determined by a majority vote of three experienced social workers observing the student's performance) through the one-way mirrors. Students must arrive at (correct diagnoses) of "real problems" in ([three] of the five cases presented).

3. The intern will be able *to scribe* a flood plain map, including correction, layout, and lettering **using scriber, correction fluid, straight edge, curves, drafting table, and other standard drafting tools in a normal drafting room without referring to drafting manuals.** (The map shall be prepared according to the standards set by HUD for flood insurance studies and shall be correct according to these standards in [two] out of three cases). **The work will be completed within an eight-hour period.**

4. The behavioral technologist aide *will design and implement* [three] behavioral modification programs designed to increase the frequency of a behavior [in each of three different children] **while working on the 2–10 p.m. shift in the residential program at De Jeannette Center for Human Development during May term 1977. Each study must be repeated as a single-subject experimental study as reported in McGuigan, J. S.,** *Experimental Psychology,* with (six out of the seven parts being judged correct by the instructor).

5. **Given a hypothetical job opening, a person role playing an applicant for the job, and a predetermined number of evaluation instruments,** the student *will select* the appropriate instruments, *administer* those to the applicant, and *write* an evaluation of the applicant's potential for the job. (The choice of instruments and evaluation of the applicant's performance based on these must agree with the professor's. The performance in administering the instruments must meet the professor's approval. The student must pass [three] of four such exercises.)

In all of these examples the **conditions** describe the situation in which the student will be required to demonstrate the desired skill or knowledge. The conditions may include the aids or tools the student will be allowed to use, the restrictions that will be placed on the student, such as time limitations and the media of expression of the skill or knowledge such as written, verbal, in person, by videotape, or through a product. The performance standard ( ) is the minimal level of performance that will be accepted as evidence of the student having achieved the objective. These may have to do with acceptable levels of accuracy, the number of errors allowable, the speed with which it must be performed, compliance with criteria provided in a text or manual or in lectures. This minimal level of performance may relate to what other people do as a consequence of the performance. Performance stability [ ] simply indicates the number of times the skill or knowledge has to be demonstrated to be accepted as adequately learned. A study of the proceeding five examples will help clarify what these four components of a learning objective are.

A way to more fully understand what is involved in developing useful learning objectives is to analyze some existing ones. Secure some course description material from your institution and find within it a statement of one of the learning objectives of the program. See if you can use the four symbols to identify its various components. If you cannot, then modify it so that all four components are included. Try this on several of the learning objectives in a program to get a better understanding of what is involved. If there are no learning objectives, take one of the goals of the program and turn it into a learning objective that could be used in program planning or in assessing a student's learning (see Mager, 1975).

One of the difficulties in field experience education is in combining specificity of learning objectives with the kind of flexibility and openness to diverse options required by the widely differing placements available to students. All students in the same program are not provided with the same learning opportunities. Two students placed in the same agency at different times or even during the same period will not have the same opportunities for working on the attainment of a set of learning objectives. There is no way to control the work environment for learning purposes. Therefore, learning objectives that are too narrowly defined or too limited in choice are inappropriate. The way to provide for both specificity of learning objectives and the ability to use each placement to its fullest educational potential is to write objectives that describe major skills basic to most placement environments, such as interpersonal or problem-solving ones. A second way to cope with this condition of experiential learning is to provide a number of learning objectives from which the student, with the aid of the supervisor, can choose that are appropriate to the particular placement and of interest to the student.

Placements

The next step in the process is that of arranging for field placements. The process of arranging for the field placement should reflect the fact that the student role is significantly different in the field than it is in the classroom and that the uniqueness of field experience education is the opportunity it provides students to assume greater responsibility for their own learning. In practical terms this means placing as much responsibility as possible, consistent with the constraints of the program, on the students for the securing of placements. This process can begin even before the active search for placements. It can begin with decisions about which kind of field placements are best suited for their needs and interests. Nesbitt (1977, pp. 9–18) provides useful guidance to students on all parts of the process of placement selection. There are several important aspects of securing the placement for which students ought to assume responsibility. Having students develop résumés, correspond directly with firms or agencies and, where possible, make appointments by telephone and be interviewed in person by someone at the agencies are educationally valuable. It not only gets the students started in a manner consistent with the way they will have to function in the field, it provides faculty the opportunity to teach them how to develop résumés and participate effectively in interviews. Students develop self-confidence and self-reliance through securing their own placements as well as receive valuable training for seeking employment in the future. Shifting the emphasis from dependency on the teacher to greater self-reliance as a learner is also furthered when the student is required to develop personal learning objectives and, with the aid of the supervisor, to select from a comprehensive list the program learning objectives. Such a choice may mean delaying the final selection of each student's learning objectives until arrival at the agency and a conference with the supervisor is held. If the placement is in the same community as the school, this decision might be made by the student and supervisor in an interview before the placement begins.

The procedures suggested above do not mean that the educator is uninvolved with agencies and firms in arranging placements for students. The instructor will be continually lining up placement possibilities and making sure that previous ones are retained by developing close working relationships with supervisors and professionals in the field. The groundwork for securing these placements may have to be done by school staff, but the actual arrangement between the student and the agency or firm should be negotiated by the student in consultation with the faculty sponsor.

To make sure that the program goals and learning objectives are fulfilled and that the work needs of the agency are met, the following checklist may be useful in determining the acceptability of each placement.

Criteria for Accepting Placements

	Yes	No
1. Are the learning opportunities in the placement such that the student will have the chance to meet a significant number of the program learning objectives?	___	___
2. Is the placement compatible with the student's resources?		
a. Financial	___	___
b. Time	___	___
3. Can the student do the work expected in the placement?	___	___
4. Is supervision adequate?	___	___
5. Will the placement provide the student with sufficient opportunity to attain his personal learning objectives?	___	___

The chief concern in the preparation of students for placement is to prepare them to make the most effective use of the opportunity as a learning environment. This means, among other
things, that the student must clearly understand the learning objectives of the program and should have developed personal ones and
that the assessment process and the documentation methods are
understood. The student should also be required to demonstrate satisfactorily the recording and documenting procedures. If logs, journals, performance analysis reports, or reports of any kind are to be
required, a sufficient number should be submitted prior to departure to assure the faculty sponsor that the student can use the
procedures correctly.

There are certain general skills that people have to perform
effectively on work sites. These should be identified for the students,
and they should have the opportunity to become aware of and to
practice them. These include the observing and accurate recording
of observations, interpersonal interaction skills, such as awareness
of nonverbal cues and their importance, workable approaches to
informal information gathering, how to formulate and ask questions in a way that opens up communication, and value clarification
skills. In addition to these general skills, particular students will be
expected to have specific skills before they begin their assignments.
These may be research skills or language competency or skill in
such things as survey design, field testing, and implementation. The
nature of these specific skills will be determined by the placement
and the nature of the academic program. Students should have had
the necessary prerequisite courses or special training in these skills
before departing for their field experience.

In preparing the students, the faculty member must make
sure that all the arrangements have been completed and agreements
reached between the students and the agencies as to the students'
responsibilities and working conditions. The placing of the student
is an almost automatic consequence of the steps previously described.
It is a part of the process that requires very little of the faculty
member's time or energy. The faculty sponsor may wish to request
a report from the student during the first day of a placement to be
sure all students are on the job.

Once the student has begun the placement, another important aspect of the faculty member's work begins: that of monitoring the student's progress. The purpose of the faculty sponsor's work at this point is formative evaluation: to provide the student with feedback on progress in accomplishing learning objectives and encouragement and support through pointing out additional resources as they may be needed. Adjustments may have to be made in the learning objectives or the learning contract so that they conform more consistently to the learning opportunities available in the placement. The oversight of the student's work will also provide an opportunity to develop a personal relationship and a more significant role for the supervisor in the student's education. All these purposes are best accomplished by personal contacts through site visits, telephone calls, and individual conferences where possible. Monitoring also includes dealing with any problem that arises, including personality conflicts between supervisor and student, inadequate job performance by the student, excessive absenteeism or lateness, and any personal, financial, or cultural adjustment problems that the student may be having.

The nature of the placement has a major influence on the kind of monitoring of progress that is practical. Some of the determining factors are the geographic distance from the campus, whether or not there is a supervisor and whether it is full time or part time. Some options available for use when the students are within commuting distance of the campus are site visits, phone calls, concurrent weekly seminars, evening sessions, individual conferences, and close cooperative work with supervisors. When the students are some distance from the institution, some of the other means of keeping in touch with what is happening with the students are a midterm campus-based or regional weekend conference, periodic written reports from the students with feedback provided by the faculty sponsor and a midplacement formative evaluation by the supervisor to the faculty member, which is shared with the student.

All the responsibilities enumerated thus far, and the others yet to be described, obviously take much time to carry out even if the contact with the placement supervisor is done by letter or telephone. One of the continuing concerns of faculty involved in these programs is for the development of institutional policies that establish workload standards for faculty supervision of field experience education which are equivalent to the teaching load of faculty at the same institution. For example, the following policy has been developed and implemented at the University of Maine at Orono.

Supervision of three students is to be regarded as equivalent to one credit hour of classroom instruction; therefore, nine to ten students should be considered the equivalent of teaching a three-hour course when *all* the following functions are performed. When fewer functions are performed (as when placement sites are located and developed by the Cooperative Education/Field Experience Office) or when travel distances are minimal, a larger number of students would be normal. Please note that the standard is based on the number of students involved, not the amount of credits awarded, since the former is the major determinant of the work required.

The responsibilities of the course instructor are to:

1. Work with students to develop their field experience placements (general information giving, counseling, developing learning objectives for placement, matching students with specific placement). One should note here that the faculty member normally works with approximately one third more students than are actually placed.

2. Provide university supervision while on field placements. This includes at least three contacts during the semester with the student and placement supervisor, one of which is a visit to the placement site (except for out-of-state placements). The faculty member is also responsible for additional visits to a specific placement site when special problems arise.

3. Monitor and evaluate the student's performance in the field (that is, collecting student and employer reports, determining with the job supervisor whether learning objectives have been achieved, grading student reports or projects, giving the final grade).

4. Act as a liaison between the institution and the placement supervisor (to provide for feedback on program as a whole, employer attitudes, and so forth).

5. Some development of new placement sites (in cooperation with the Office of Cooperative Education/ Field Experience).

6. Work with the Office of Cooperative Educa-
tion/Field Experience on procedural or policy matters
when needed.

Instruction of a Cooperative Education/Field Experience course is a time-consuming and demanding
process. Unless a major problem arises, much of the
faculty supervisor's time is consumed in advance planning and coordination of student placements.

St. Mary's College of Maryland, a college in which the work
of developing placements, assisting students in securing them, and
building strong community ties is done by a separate staff, has
established the policy that the supervision of seventeen students in
field experience education is equivalent to teaching one course.
Each institution should establish its own faculty workload standards
that are consistent with its other practices.

Evaluation

For the educator and for the educational institution, the
most critical part of experiential education—in fact, of any kind
of education—is the evaluation of the learning. Faculty are responsible for ascertaining what the student has learned and how well it
has been learned as well as whether the student has learned what
was supposed to be learned in the particular course in which he or
she was enrolled. Assessment of learning is difficult under all circumstances but more difficult in this type of education because the
faculty member does not have the same kind of control over the
learning environment as in the classroom.

Another problem is that the learning objectives in field
experience education tend to be more complex than those of most
classroom-taught courses. They are from the highest levels of the
cognitive domain, such as application and integration, or involve
behaviors that require multidimensional skills, such as problem
solving or interpersonal skills. These types of learning do not lend
themselves to paper-and-pencil tests and sometimes can be judged
only subjectively by experts in that field. A good bit of work has
been done recently by professionals in business, industry, and government assessment centers where people are selected for promotion

to positions of higher responsibility on the basis of identifying the competencies needed to perform those functions and then designing assessment procedures by which means candidates for those positions are required to demonstrate the skills. Similar work has been progressing in education as well, not only in specific educational institutions but also through interinstitutional cooperation in the Council for the Advancement of Experiential Learning (CAEL—formerly the Cooperative Assessment of Experiential Learning Project).

The CAEL publication, *A Compendium of Assessment Techniques* (Knapp and Sharon, 1975) briefly describes, illustrates, identifies special problems, discusses technical considerations, evaluates the appropriateness of each, as well as provides a list of references for all of the techniques that have been developed for assessing experiential learning. The assessment procedures described include performance tests, such as work samples and unobtrusive observation, simulation, such as interviews, role playing, management games, leaderless group discussion, the case study method, and the in-basket test. Also described are essay examinations appropriate to experiential learning and objective written examinations, structured/ unstructured interviews, panel interviews, oral tests, oral reports or presentations, self-assessments, and ratings of product assessments.

The most recent and extensive research done on the assessment of experiential learning is reported in *The CAEL Validation Report* (Willingham and associates, 1976). It is based on a series of ten field studies involving more than a thousand faculty and students in twenty-four institutions throughout the United States. One of the conclusions of the research was that "it is reasonable to conclude that experiential learning can be assessed with acceptable rigor, though there are important qualifications to remember. . . . The field research indicated that faculty can agree reasonably well when appropriate conditions are met—and these are the important qualifications. It is necessary for institutions to develop clear policies and clear procedures for assessing experiential learning, and it is necessary for faculty to be experienced in such assessment. If any one of these conditions is not adequately met, results of this work suggest that the assessment process is likely to be poor, with resulting inequity to students" (Willingham, Valley, and Keeton, 1977, p. 59).

The five examples of learning objectives which are given

earlier in this chapter include assessment techniques within them. The first one uses a special type of written report, a diagram, and an oral presentation. The second one uses a simulation and expert judgment. The third uses a special written report in the form of a map. A performance test is used in the fourth, and a combination of simulation, written report, and performance test is used in the last example.

The essential elements in the selection of an appropriate assessment technique are well-written learning objectives and creativeness in identifying and modifying assessment procedures that are of reasonable cost to administer. The best assessment techniques will also be an ongoing part of the educational process and not an extraneous and irrelevant test administered at the end. A good assessment reinforces the learning or facilitates the development of further skill because it provides a realistic opportunity for the further use of the knowledge or the skill. The student views it as an appropriate assessment technique because it enhances learning.

The instructor will want to review continually the assessment techniques being used and evaluate their effectiveness in measuring the learning expected. Given the complexity of the task, it is doubtful that any perfect fit will be found between learning objectives, placement learning opportunities, and assessment techniques. Continual work will be needed in each program to improve the evaluation of student learning and to enhance the learning experience.

Since field experience education is much more individualized learning than a course with common syllabus, lectures, assignments, test and final examination, a letter or number grade on a transcript does not adequately describe the skill or knowledge acquired. Some faculty also feel it is difficult to assign a quantitative value to the learning that does it justice. A Pass-No Credit (P-N) grade is often given. When this or a letter or number grade is supplemented by a written evaluation of the student's performance that includes a description of the placement, an indication of the learning objectives, and a statement of the competence demonstrated by the student with incident specific examples from the experience, it can serve as very useful feedback to the student and as a basis for preparing letters of reference as they are requested for prospective employers or educational institutions.

Commenting on current trends in granting credit for learning that occurs outside of the academy, Valentine (1977, p. 3)
reflects on the whole problem of what credits actually mean in
American higher education: "Academic credits awarded in traditional ways stand as very crude measures of student achievement.
They serve mainly to certify that students receiving them were exposed to a certain kind of arrangement for learning, including a
teacher, a quarter- or semester-length course, a class and classroom,
and, at the end, a grade. Credits, in other words, tell more about
the opportunities afforded students to learn than they do about the
uses made of the opportunities." Commenting on the CAEL validation study (Willingham and associates, 1976) in the same article
(pp. 7–8), he acknowledges that faculty, when properly trained to
evaluate learning outcomes gained through experience, do so "with
degrees of agreement that probably would equal the agreement they
reach on ratings of conventional classroom products, such as essays
and term papers.

"Where faculty members tend to disagree is on the number
of credits that should be awarded for particular learning achievements. Whether this should be construed as a weakness in the assessment procedure or a weakness in the whole notion of credits is a
provocative question. My own view is that credits are such weak
and arbitrary measures of actual student competence, dominated
as they are by assumptions that length of time spent in class correlates with amount of learning, and that amounts learned in one
course equal amounts learned in other courses of the same length,
that judgments about how much credit to award are bound to be
highly debatable and hotly debated."

This point is one of the findings of the CAEL research and
illuminates it from a broader perspective. The central question confronting many faculty members and administrators is: On what
basis can judgments be made regarding the amount of credit to be
awarded for experiential learning? The amount of credit earned
should be firmly based on two things: content and level of learning.
If faculty have specified the competence in knowledge or skill that
they expect as a result of the learning experience and the level of
the knowledge or skill desired, a major step toward answering the
question has been taken, but one problem remains. How much

academic credit should be awarded for the knowledge and skill demonstrated? One basis for making that judgment is to compare the amount of documented evidence of learning and reports required in classroom courses. The purpose of such comparison is to find a basis for determining the equal amounts and levels of knowledge and skill acquisition in the more traditional models of instruction. The question of the amount of credit to be granted is less of a problem when the experiential learning is offered as a component part of a classroom-based course. Then its worth can be figured as a proportion of the total course credit. The crucial point is that "standards for crediting experiential learning should be the same as, or comparable to, standards for crediting other more traditional forms of learning. Neither should be more or less difficult to attain" (Willingham, 1977, p. 30).

Although it is discussed at the end of the chapter, program evaluation is something that should go on continually and during every step of program execution. It should not just be undertaken in moments of crisis when a decision has to be made about whether or not to terminate a program. The educator will want to do continuous program evaluation to create better techniques for selecting students and matching them with appropriate placements, for preparing them, monitoring their progress, and evaluating their learning. To be able to do this, a systematic means of collecting information on the various aspects of the program will have to be established and criteria and methods developed for using the data in evaluating the effectiveness of the program. This chapter may help in suggesting criteria. The program components on which data must be collected are: student application, selection and placement processes, the appropriateness of the learning objectives, the preparation of students, the monitoring of students' progress in the field, the educational opportunities provided in each placement and in different types of placements, the quality of the supervision and of the interpersonal relationships between the three principals— faculty, student, and supervisor—the quality of work done by the student for the agency or firm, the adequacy of the assessment procedures, and the cost in money and faculty resources and the recording and transcribing practices.

13

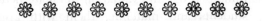

Milton R. Stern

Working with Older Students

Full-time studenthood is going the way of full-time motherhood. And frequently enough, the part-time mothers become the part-time students. In fact, the new majority in college classrooms already consists of older students, male and female, who are attending college part-time.

    Older students are not all that recent in their arrival in the classroom, of course. After World War II, we had literally and suddenly millions of older students, mostly male, in our universities. It was then that college teachers had to consider seriously—some did and some did not—the pedagogic implications represented by this distinctive group of new students. Simply put, the GIs were a different element in the classroom because they asked questions that younger students did not know enough to ask. They were more demanding; they were not passive; their questions came out of another experience than that of the conventional, four-year, full-time undergraduate.

Genuine alarm was expressed in the immediate postwar years about the quality of these then-new students, but the apparent danger of such democratization of admissions did not materialize. By and large, the invasion did not debase standards but rather enhanced them: The existing population of younger students was not conquered, but liberated, by their seniors. In any event, the GIs established the beachhead for older students as a permanent group. Now, more than a generation later, a mix of age groups has become familiar in many institutions, even in daytime classes. We have many more graduate students than thirty years ago, and we have increased numbers of adults returning to school after considerable interruption, to obtain degrees or for additional certification to continue their education as practicing professionals. As of 1972, a U.S. Department of Commerce study showed that only 10 percent of women between the ages of thirty and forty-four had college degrees. As they and increasing numbers of older people of both sexes become aware of opportunities now sanctioned, endorsed, and frequently paid for by society, the balance in the near future will shift steadily upward. It is reasonable to predict that before the century is out, the typical college student of today will be part of an atypical minority.

Beyond subject matter what should college professors know to teach these older students well? Is there a special pedagogy for them? Are there really "older" students, or, regardless of chronological age, may we think of *all* the men and women in our classrooms as students—no more different from each other than people ordinarily are? And in our teaching behavior and our teaching style, should we distinguish people of middle years or older, who are returning to school, from the customary college-age cohort? These are more than rhetorical questions. Many college teachers will acknowledge the fact of differences among students of varying ages as they confront two or three generations in the same classroom, but they may not recognize the full import of what such differences mean for purposes of instruction.

Some differences between the college-age generation and older generations may have been blurred in recent years by the student movement and its consequent effect of having college authorities and the courts accept the eighteen- to twenty-two-year-old cohorts as voting and drinking adults. Most large institutions these days treat their students as if they were responsible adults. If you are permitted by law to drink at the age of eighteen, then maturity is being redefined by the culture at large.

But in our thinking about teaching older students, if we look at those whose connections with formal education were severed at least five years ago or more and who have not been back to school since, the differences are major. (This eliminates those "stop-outs" who have left school for financial or other reasons but who have plans to complete a degree or certificate in the near future and consider their main role to be that of student.) The basic difference can be expressed in a colloquial way by asking students what they do. Ask them their occupation or profession. These older students' primary self-identification is something else than "student." They classify themselves in other social roles: worker, mother, housewife, manager. They have cut the umbilical cord with formal education and have made the transition to adult life. They identify themselves with their own social or working group or with their own family. They do not think of themselves as students or learners except to achieve other purposes.

They differ psychologically and culturally as well. They are not psychologically in tune even with their peers from their own age group with whom they may have attended elementary school, secondary school, or even college and who may have continued into graduate and postgraduate programs, let alone with today's college-age students. And they differ from chronologically younger people in their accumulated knowledge from work experience, family ties, and parental roles.

Such people, in short, not only *perceive* themselves to be different from the student whom most teachers in colleges and universities assume they are facing in the classroom; they are, *in fact,*

different. If we are to teach them well, we cannot afford to dis-
regard the realities of their lives.

Why Do Older Students Return to School?

The first reality in understanding them better is their motivation or purposes in returning to school. If you ask them—and I recommend that you do—many will most likely express themselves
quite positively about their priorities. There is frequently no single
reason, even if an explicit one is confidently offered, for the return
to the classroom. There may be, and typically is, a general unease
motivating older students about not knowing enough, a cultural
factor growing out of life and living in our time, a period so complex as frequently to be called "the learning society."* Yet it will
be useful to list a more precise classification under two major
headings.

Job-Related Reasons. The first broad category must be that
of employment. This is the most important reason, in its several
parts, why people go back to school, whether it be at lower school
levels or to community colleges and universities.

Many people want, or are required, to advance and update
their skills and knowledge to maintain their present positions. (Education, earlier or later, is thus a counterbalance to downward
mobility.) This motivates people at all economic levels, but the
skilled professionals in the largest numbers. It is now accepted in
the learning society, complex both in bureaucracy and technology,
that advanced professionals are constantly in a race with the new
knowledge that comes along after they have finished their formal
degree work or formal qualifying. It is not only that they feel a
professional and ethical necessity to do so, but they are increasingly
required to keep up. Relicensing laws in many states require that
people take programs in continuing education to maintain their
rights to practice in a given field. This is true throughout the
country and represents a growing trend; there are millions of stu-

*So named by an extension dean, the late Paul A. McGhee of New
York University, who defined the new era in a speech in 1959, "The Learning
Society," at the newly established Oakland University in Rochester, Michigan.

dents in continuing professional education programs who are not
volunteers for education but who are compelled to be there so that
they can continue to practice medicine, law, engineering, accounting, pharmacy—the list grows daily.

The issues constitute a complex political and social problem
intertwined with pedagogy. Continuing professional education will
be the gold rush of the 1980s, but colleges and universities will have
to hurry if they want to stake their claims. At the very least, those
faculty members involved because of their disciplines owe it to themselves and their institutions to become aware not only of the professional issues but of curricular implications. We are at the beginning
of a period in which there will have to be major rethinking of curricula for the first professional degrees. This will be necessary to do
in the light of what practitioners will have to learn later in their
careers. Not only what to learn, but *when,* is already of concern to
leaders in many professions.

In addition to the matter of adding on knowledge from the
base point of one's previous background, some students are being
required presently to earn degrees that were not asked of them in
the past—that is, certification required for maintenance of a present
job or position, where it was not so required in the first place. For
example, registered nurses are being required to return for bachelor
of science degrees despite many years of experience in the field. From
the point of view of employment, this is a necessity, not an option;
it is, in fact, compulsory adult education.

People who wish to increase their skills and knowledge to
advance to a higher position or a job have been familiar as students
in continuing education programs both in and out of universities
for scores of years. Indeed, this particular group still is a stereotype
of the whole group and also of our upwardly mobile society. It is a
sentimental reduction by the press and media to concentrate on that
goal as the easy way to characterize millions of older people in universities today. "Grandma Gets Her Degree" is still a standard
June headline. It is true that these are the men and women who
have been identified as the students in adult education, of night
school, from the beginning. But, although they remain important,
they are by no means the only group that must remain in this listing
of those motivated to return to the classroom.

Traditionally, with regard to the job-related goals, we have the group of poor people and unemployed. They now have many more opportunities than before to attend colleges and receive stipends. This has been a development of the last two decades; it is presently at a level that can no longer be regarded as disguised welfare. A moral problem in admissions remains: Is provision of access and funding enough? A problem of appropriate curriculum and of psychology of instruction exists for college teachers. These students have more "threshold consciousness" than most other older students.

Finally—and an expression of a somewhat newer symptom of a leisure-oriented society—there are the growing numbers of men and women who want to change careers. Sometimes this is a necessity: People laid off from jobs, retired service personnel, or civil servants who retire early feel in an inflated economy that it is necessary to undertake a second career to survive. Just as frequently, many such people, and others, feel a psychological necessity as well. It is symptomatic of the crises of adults in their middle years, whether these pressures occur once or more times in one's life, that many of them see a now-or-never chance to train for a better or more satisfying career. We are in a confusing time, when one's life style seems to be something one has to invent for one's self rather than get given from the culture or by economic circumstances. Such freedom brings anxiety. "We never had it so good?" . . . perhaps, but probably it is not, and was not ever.

Personal Factors. Job maintenance, improvement, or change are not the only reasons that people go back to school. Personal reasons, a phrase that may be a catchall for everything else than jobs, runs a close second in importance. Moreover, it is difficult to separate people's motivations. For example, mid-career changes are not only caused by economic need, as has been noted, but also because people become restless and *want* a change. The increased lifespan has created a situation in which for the first time there is statistical significance in people surviving in larger numbers and having to be thought of as an important continuing element in society (and they think of themselves that way too!). Indeed, programs for learning in retirement, in effect, for enforced leisure, are becoming increasingly common in the country. People over sixty-five do not make much of an impact in degree programs, but in the typically noncredit programs of continuing education in universities, many of which give reduced rates or charge no fees to retired persons, they have become increasingly important. As for the community colleges, their public source of funding makes the two-year schools dote on those over sixty-five. People do not retire from voting, particularly if they have a need or grievance. From the teachers' viewpoint, although retired men and women are not statistically important in the college classroom, they nevertheless require attention.

What happens in the learning society begins to fulfill More's (1965, p. 76) predictions in *Utopia:*

> In Utopia they have a six-hour working day—
> three hours in the morning, then lunch—then a two-hour
> break—then three more hours in the afternoon, followed
> by supper. They go to bed at 8 P.M. and sleep for eight
> hours. All the rest of the twenty-four they're free to do
> what they like—not to waste their time in idleness or
> self-indulgence but to make these free periods on further
> education, for there are public lectures first thing every
> morning. Attendance is quite voluntary, except for those
> picked out for academic training, but men and women
> of all classes go crowding in to hear them—I mean, dif-
> ferent people go to different lectures, just as the spirit
> moves them. . . . They never force people to work un-
> necessarily, for the main purpose of their whole economy
> is to give each person as much time free from physical
> drudgery as the needs of the community will allow, so
> that he can cultivate his mind—which they regard as
> the secret of a happy life. . . . Admittedly, no one's al-
> lowed to become a full-time student, except for the very
> few in each town who appear as children to possess un-
> usual gifts, outstanding intelligence, and special aptitude
> for academic research. But every child receives a pri-
> mary education, and most men and women go on edu-
> cating themselves all their lives.

Are we already in the brave new world? As we know, the doctrine of secondary causation will confuse the effect, but there is reason for cheer and, of course, sober planning.

We are beginning to expand what is meant by the wise use of leisure because now we are beginning to have leisure to be wise. There is increased respect for learning today. It is not hyperbole to speak of the love of learning as more than an attribute of immolated academics but as a quality shared by many in the group of older students. When people have time, they use it in unexpected ways. And it is one of the joys of teaching older students that their responses are frequently drawn from contemplation, reflective of the life examined outside the classroom. Although it is claimed that philosophy, humanities, and the arts are most often the areas in which older students find satisfaction, the speculative and ruminative aspects are present when men and women take courses in management, and most certainly in applied human relations.

Recreation, sport, and dozens of avocational interests—spelunking, raising Arabian horses, antiques—name it, and you discover interested people and almost always a point of collegiate reference. It is a tribute to the catholicity of intellectual concern in the American university that our academic frame of reference is generally close to the reality frame of so many older students. If an extension course is offered in hang gliding, there is not only a classical reference to Icarus but to aerodynamics. Scuba diving involves functional uses for underwater engineering and reference to the natural sciences, to say nothing of the aesthetics of the sometime dangerous "ecstacy of the deep."

The professoriate has been late in the field in recognizing that *learning* has become part of the life style of millions. People *learn* to play golf and *learn* to paint, and some become quite good at both. A major part of the pleasure principle, of satisfaction to be derived from the experience, is that they will have learned to do each well.

Under the summary heading of personal reasons is the matter of improvement of one's relationship with others, whether it be at work or to one's married or unmarried mate. During the thirty years I have worked in continuing education in universities, increasing numbers of people have taken an immense variety of programs of study because they felt the need to know other people better and to know themselves better.

In the late 1940s and early 1950s, such programs were essentially translations of standard psychology courses, but by the

1960s practical applications and programs drawn from the human
relations frontier were the rule. Transactional analysis, biofeedback,
rolfing, gestalt encounter groups—just name a new approach in
human relations and it has been offered in an extramural class
whose predominant audience consisted of older students. Although
this interest will be an important part of future programs for them,
I would hazard the guess, based on recent observation, that the
1980s will see a cyclical return to consideration of what others
are feeling and thinking as against feeling one's own pulse, which
has been the recent trend. Classroom and related experiential learning will pick up again in a social framework rather than encouraging the individual to concentrate on his or her self-centered emotional responses to the circumambient world.

Another dimension of personal motivation is the obverse
side of the coin of purposes related to jobs. Modern technology has
made many jobs redundant, although people still work at them.
Indeed, it may be possible to allege that somewhere between twenty
and forty million jobs in the United States are featherbedded. In
any event, millions of people are educated in the first place for jobs
that then become unnecessary or necessary only to keep them off the
streets. They find themselves unhappy because they lack the psychological rewards of work, while at the same time leisure is not yet
fully sanctioned. In this situation self-expression through the arts
has become a significant aspect of continuing education programs,
most important in universities because universities represent a
source of high cultural sanction.

As an instance, the last four or five years has seen the revival
of programs in writing in many urban extension programs as a
healthy practical way of self-expression. In the 1930s and 1940s,
people took writing courses—novels, poetry, short stories—and then
moved into radio and television. This faded in the late 1950s and
throughout the 1960s. In part, psychologically based courses in self-
expression filled the gap, but now writing courses are again on the
rise. It is not only that writing has become once more a romantic
profession or that television as an experience has become less
satisfying (it always was). One might almost guess the cheerful
hypothesis that a new floor of literacy is being built under literature
and culture and that a new sensibility demands novel expression.

The universities are the chief providers. In effect, people go where the action is, namely the growing edge of the university, where such continuing education programs are done outside the walls—that is, outside the captive culture of undergraduate or graduate departments.

One cannot leave the field of personal motivations without discussing the new high-energy approach of women. Many women return to school out of basic dissatisfaction with their lives, and these days they return with considerable cultural support. Some consciously or unconsciously take up study as the beginning of a way out of an unsatisfying marriage—that is, as a prelude to divorce, a time during which they acquire skills that will enable them to become economically self-sufficient. There is, also, the "now-it's-my-turn" syndrome—the mother, who having supported children and perhaps a spouse through school, now wants her chance at a college degree. Then there's the "empty-nest-now-that-the-children-have-grown-I-have-nothing-to-do" feeling. Mothers, then, return to school to renew their interests in a world outside the home.

Frequently enough, women's motivation is economic. The pressures of our time demand that both marriage partners have jobs to pay the mortgage or put the children through college. Then the wife returns to school to update or learn new skills to be employable. An acknowledged motive for some women is that the husband has moved to an executive position, and her education or lack of it prevents her from enjoying the social group into which she has been thrust. In reverse, it is much less common that the male partner acknowledges a parallel situation.

The changing mores of our time for both men and women puts the matter of motivation to return to school in a decisively personal category: The motives are idiosyncratic and to some extent cannot be classified save in the largest of terms. People are responsive to the whole range of opportunity made available through the continuing education programs of universities. To those of us concerned with the vitality of our culture, the pervasive individuality and variety of human motivation to learn is encouraging. When we teach adults, we teach in a school for optimists.

The reasons mature students return to school make it plain that as a group they are distinctly different from younger students.

Whatever the specifics, the older group usually has a clearer idea of what it wants from school and appears to be more energetic in its motivations. By and large, they earn higher grades, when these are applicable, than do traditional college-age students. For example, studies of World War II veterans returning to college under the GI bill showed that as a group they did better than students of the eighteen to twenty-two age segment. Perhaps older men and women are easier to teach simply because they have more motivation to learn; certainly they are more interesting to instructors. Their own range of experience provides challenge in teaching. In general, they have an intrinsic self-motivation, and they tend not to be as resistant or hostile to the teacher as an authority figure as are pubescent students who may be struggling with their first identity crisis. Mature students, most of the time, tend to be more tolerant of the university or college as an institution because they have had more experience with the way in which the world works—the social framework is familiar to them. This is not to say they are less than harsh in their criticism of inadequate instruction. Indeed, the basic and abiding characteristic of older students is that they are not a captive audience, and, although they tend not to riot (the decade of the 1960s included few examples of older students in this category), they vote with their feet by walking away from programs that are inadequate to their needs. Because so much of the study upon which older students engage is noncredit in character and has no reference to the carrot of a degree, the institutions which are just discovering that the older students are their new audience will find it very difficult to assign inadequate instructors to teach them for very long. This latter point is important because it goes against the conventional wisdom. For years, campus departments have tended to assign junior instructors and older, inferior members of the professoriate to the evening classes in which most older students enrolled. That just will not do today.

Transition Problems

I do not intend to give a picture of older students as full of confidence and moving assertively in all situations. When they return to school, they frequently tend to do so hesitantly. For them school may well be an experience about which they have forgotten during the interval of adult living. For some the recovery of what it is like to study and to take tests, to go to class in a student rhythm, is rewarding and pleasant. For others, it may come as a distinct shock. There are no adequate statistics on survival rates among older students except in very specialized circumstances. Attrition rates among them can be attested to in limited situations only. The unreliable index of the drop-out rate in community colleges, which is very high indeed, does not really tell us much about their survival rate in comparison to younger students.

Suffice it to say, males or females returning to school must expect changes in life styles coupled with sacrifices of money and/or time. Part-time students who return for an evening program are full-time adults, and whether pursuing degrees or not, they are using evenings for a specific purpose that takes them away from significant others. To be sure, the decisions have been conscious and deliberate and, from our point of view, are virtuous, but they are taking time away from family, social activities, hobbies, other work. Furthermore, in addition to attending classes, the employed adult has the extremely difficult task of finding time to study and a place to study. (The carrel in the library is almost unheard of.) He or she does not have the luxury either of the ritualistic preliminaries to study—turning the radio on, turning the radio off, getting a glass of milk and a cookie, calling a friend, and so forth—that younger adults have. Older students have to give up other activities. The reduction of available time from the multitude of adult joys and chores are particularly difficult for women ("Men work from sun to sun; women's work is never done"). The mother-housewife-student has to give up time with her children or husband. She may find frequently that her husband is more demanding and that the children are as well. They will, willfully or not, create crises the night before an examination or when assignments are due.

Think of the exact reversal of the situation as it applies to the younger classmate whose family has not only sacrificed to send him or her to college but who, even if living at home, has an absolutely reduced schedule of obligations and demands. Unless the corporate employer pays, the mature student returning to school full-time or part-time must adapt to a lower standard of living and must adopt a rigid schedule over a long period. In addition to family and social restrictions, the adult returning to school may well have problems of psychological adjustment. Many people think of themselves as rusty and out of practice in study, and many, if not most, tend to be somewhat fearful about returning to the competitive school experience with younger students. More frequently than not, they tend to underestimate their own skills and abilities. This is particularly true of women who, when returning to college, underestimate their writing abilities.

This initial adjustment is more difficult when older students are integrated with the younger ones. Most often, the formal vocabulary and concepts of a discipline are unfamiliar; the academic patois is strange. It may take some time to become comfortable with the language and ritual of this, to them, new experience. They get over their initial feeling that their younger classmates have an advantage, and, when they discover that they can play the discussion game well, they come into their own. It is a truism that the mature students come to realize as a result of their experiences of life that they have a deeper understanding of the material. Once they learn the new language, they become a far more compelling and contributing group of students than their younger classmates.

Characteristics of Older Students

There is just as wide a range in abilities, learning styles, and personality among older students as among the younger. They are somewhat less likely, if they have been successful in their chosen occupation or profession or in life, to accept the tradition of psychological distance between professor and student. They do not respond to the conventional image in which the student is expected to be appropriately awed and deferential and the professor appropriately aloof and paternal. They are less likely to regard higher grades as the only goal, and they are much more likely to challenge faculty and ask questions that younger students would not think of, or, at least, would not think of asking. Their expectations of school tend to vary according to their previous individual experiences in the classroom. If the previous experience was negative, they are more likely than not still to harbor a low self-concept.

Older students just do not think of their teachers as parents or parent surrogates, friendly or unfriendly. They are more likely to have a sense of equality with the teacher or, in the discipline in which they are studying, to assign the teacher the role of *primer inter pares*. They will regard the teacher as having clear authority in the limited area in which he or she works but will tend to discount his or her opinion in other areas. They will include the instructor as a peer at the same time they find it difficult to relate to younger students.

As we have discussed the several differences in motivation among age groups along with transitional problems and basic characteristics of older students, college teachers will readily see implications for their role in or out of the classroom. The qualities that make for good teaching will be the same for mature students as for the younger. Knowledgeable instructors, who will state clear objectives, give sound assignments, and present well-organized lectures with opportunities for discussion and interaction, will have no difficulty in teaching older students. If they choose to develop new formats, they will find responses on a common-sense basis. If willing to have ideas challenged without getting defensive, they will find the new majority more exciting at the same time they are more demanding. It is of the utmost importance that the instructor recognize that older students, typically part-time, are full-time adults, with other demands on their time. That may affect the tempo of instruction. The fact that these students have had experience significantly different from classroom experience should help instructors get to the point faster with the older students, who use such experience naturally in their learning.

Older students are more likely to be critical of instructors than are younger undergraduates who tend to give instructors high ratings. Teaching a class of older students tends to contradict self-congratulation as a teaching style. Anyone who has it in mind to *teach* has embarked upon an enterprise that can only be deemed successful if the students are satisfied. Most mature students are responsive to serious instruction. They are students, not members of an audience seeking superficial histrionics. They do not expect to be entertained, and the excitement of learning for them is not in laughter or even the tragic catharsis described by Aristotle. Older students are deeply aware that education has its own quality and purpose, an increase of capability to deal with life. When they come back to the classroom, most adults know what they want. It is up to us as teachers to know them.

14

❀ ❀ ❀ ❀ ❀ ❀ ❀ ❀ ❀ ❀

Audrey D. Landers

Evaluating Teachers

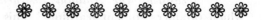

American universities spend more money on salaries for teachers than on anything else. As a result and as part of the impact of the current era of accountability, litigation, and tight budgets, they are being asked by trustees, legislators, and the general public for clear-cut information about the quality of their instruction. A glimpse of things to come may be the recent decision of Idaho's State Board of Education that henceforth student evaluations must play a part in faculty tenure and promotion decisions. At the same time, decreasing faculty mobility is bringing with it increasing numbers of faculty being considered for tenure and promotion, and for their own benefit and protection, these professors themselves want evidence of their teaching effectiveness that is of higher caliber than that produced in the gossip mill or intuited in the ubiquitous smoke-filled room.

355

Thus, "to be evaluated or not to be evaluated" will not be the question much longer. A new question—"how to be evaluated"—is taking its place. Hopefully, this new question will be answered with the selection of appropriate, valid, and reliable measures of teaching effectiveness. Currently, according to a recent survey of the ways by which institutions evaluate teaching for faculty personnel decisions, the most widely used method involves gathering the opinions of an instructor's faculty colleagues, but fully 95 percent of the institutions surveyed avoid classroom visits with which to form these opinions, either because of expense, subjectivity, or faculty resistance (Seldin, 1976). The gap between what is preached and what is practiced is *enormous*. Consider what is preached and practiced about several approaches to evaluation.

Approaches to Evaluation

Measuring the Amount Learned. "Good teaching is that which produces student learning." This statement summarizes the view of a fairly large constituency, which holds that student learning or student achievement is the only valid measure of good teaching (Kerlinger, 1971). This position has an undeniable directness about it, which is appealing, and since it is a popular one, it deserves careful scrutiny. But it is neither as simple nor as straightforward as it seems. First, there is no general agreement on what students should learn. Is learning simply the acquisition of facts or detailed information? Is it important that students learn to think critically and/or independently? Does learning involve appreciation of the subject matter? If so, how does one measure that? Does learning mean a reexamination of or possible change in values? Is learning a growth experience? How are these things measured? Furthermore, is learning of any of these types always recognized at the time it occurs, or is it possible for the realization that learning has taken place to occur some time in the future? Also, a somewhat troublesome aspect of the learning-equals-effective-teaching argument is that it allows for the possibility an unenthusiastic, disorganized, generally disliked instructor may possibly come out "smelling like a rose." The more troublesome problem is one in which the trite is true: Another instructor may do an excellent job of leading students to the well of knowledge, but this does not guarantee that the students will drink from it. They must present some degree of thirst and a minimum mechanism required for swallowing.

In addition, critics of this approach argue that some parts of teaching simply cannot be evaluated by student learning alone. These may involve procedures, such as testing and grading techniques, or content, such as the suitability of reading assignments (are they current, at the appropriate level of difficulty, and academically sound?). Generally these aspects of the conduct of a course bear some relation to student learning, but simple measures of student learning offer few clues about those aspects needing improvement. Thus, other measures than merely the amount students learn are required as well for the most useful evaluations; and colleagues, department heads, deans, outside experts, and students themselves have all been suggested as potential evaluators of these aspects.*

Classroom Visitations. The limitations of direct measures of learning have led to the use of outside observers of an instructor's classroom performance to provide further evidence of teaching effectiveness. As implied above, however, raising the idea of classroom visitation often goes over about as well as a lead balloon. Indeed, inviting faculty participation in a classroom visitation program seems to serve as a stimulant for much hard work and creativity directed toward convincing the proponents of visitation to change their minds. Several questions arise: Who will be visited? Who will do the visiting? How often will visitation occur? What will be the form and content of the report of the visit? And how will the report be used?

A highly readable introduction to the issues and emotions that can be provoked by the idea of visitation appears in Eastman's article, "How Visitation Came to Carnegie Mellon University" (1970). And Borich and Madden (1977) offer a concise view of several instruments that can structure classroom observation. Some

---

*Advocates of direct measures of learning may question how much can be learned about teaching effectiveness from other procedures. Yet it is not unusual to hear of faculty members producing course syllabi *for the first time* when they are requested by a department head or dean; in such cases, simply requesting materials would seem to hold promise for the improvement of teaching.

sort of coding or measurement along the lines they illustrate seems
essential if observer reliability and validity are to be checked and,
perhaps most important, if usable feedback is to be given to the
teacher.

Advocates of visitation should be prepared for several
criticisms. First, it is often argued that the key to a successful performance when one is being observed is nerves of steel, not teaching
skill. A second, related criticism is that the very act of observation
of a phenomenon often changes the phenomenon itself (see Chapter
Four). In terms of classroom visitation, this means that the presence
of a visitor may change the teaching behavior of the instructor and
even the general mood of the class. Finally, the instructor may be
influenced by a self-imposed need to respond to certain demand
characteristics: In other words, to teach "unnaturally," in a way
designed to please the particular observer. These criticisms are not
intended as ammunition to fight proposals that visiting classes be
employed as an evaluation technique; they are presented more for
those overly zealous advocates who may believe that "anything
students can do, we can do better; we can do anything better than
they." Realistically speaking, advocates of visitation should even
be prepared for complete defeat. Losing the battle, though, for
visitation might mean winning the war. In one case on record
(Miller, 1974), it was when agreement was reached on dropping a
colleague evaluation form and using, instead, a form completed by
the department head that general resistance to an overall evaluation program just about vanished.

Informal Interaction. The classroom is not the only place
where students learn. Likewise, the classroom is not the only setting
in which faculty have the opportunity to teach. Indeed, they often
interact with students in several other roles, ranging from academic
adviser or personal counselor to beer buddy or tennis partner. The
importance of out-of-class interaction has received increasing recognition, as illustrated in these remarks from an address by Chancel-
lor Weidner of the University of Wisconsin–Green Bay to its faculty:
"We must give up the comfortable old idea that professors meet
their classes and post office hours (two or three hours a week) and
then hide the rest of the week. . . . Of course, you must have
formal office hours, but we are at the time now when we should

be available the clock around. If a month goes past and you have not had any students in your home, then there's something wrong with your approach to students; and if a week goes past and you have not had coffee with some students, if you have not got lost in some of our new people pockets, then there is something wrong. . . . If any of us are uncomfortable with students outside the classroom, then we ought to find another job, because the time is gone when higher education is a thing that takes place in the classroom" (Fischer, 1971, p. 27).

Buttressing these remarks are findings that faculty members who interact most with students receive the greatest number of nominations from both students and colleagues as teachers who are outstanding and who have had the most impact upon students' lives (Wilson and others, 1975). Therefore, this out-of-class interaction should be taken seriously, measured systematically, and weighted more heavily than is usually the case in determining faculty evaluations and rewards.

Advising. The relationship of the teaching faculty to advising is one that varies widely between and within institutions and between and within individual departments of a single institution. Despite an obvious teaching component inherent in the advising process, it is not at all uncommon to encounter college teachers who view advising students as an activity falling outside their teaching province, rather than one that is a natural extension of their teaching role. Yet, forces are converging to force attention on the importance of quality advising. There are student complaints about "unadvisers," who are uninformed, uninterested, and even unavailable. There is a growing awareness among academic administrators and enlightened faculty about the relationship between good, personal advising and retention of students, an issue of increasing concern in a period of steady-state and declining enrollments. More than ever, we seem to be witnessing conferences and seminars on the improvement of advising, ad hoc committees to investigate the local state of the art, and brochures and pamphlets designed for both advisee and adviser. (One of the most clever adviser aids—admirable for its insightfulness as well as its design and substance—is Drake University's "Everything You Always Wanted to Know About Academic Advising but Were too Experienced to Ask.") And advising, when successfully woven into the fabric of professorial garb, is an activity deserving of attention in the evaluation of instruction. Instruments exist to assess its effectiveness in some detail (Miller, 1972). At the very least, it is easy enough to determine whether or not advisers are knowledgeable and accessible.

Critical Incidents. Critical events, or rumors of them, have probably had more influence on decisions concerning the evaluation of teaching than one might imagine. A disgruntled student or student group reporting to a department head or dean that a teacher gave an impossible exam, assigned an unreasonable workload, or graded a set of term papers unfairly produces an unknown result. Conceivably, such complaints may not surface at the time they are made but may appear later in promotion and tenure discussions. Unfortunately, at that date the teacher is often absent and no defense is available.

Nonetheless, critical incidents have a place in the evaluation of teaching—if they are handled with care. Such care requires that they be kept in written form, with a written reply from the teacher. Furthermore, in that elusive best of all possible worlds, the critical-incidents record would include positive, as well as negative events, such as participation in faculty development programs related to the improvement of teaching, nominations for outstanding teaching awards, invitations to "favorite faculty dinners," and so forth.

Self Evaluations. The notion of self-evaluation expresses itself in two forms: (1) teachers providing information about their teaching, in particular or (2) teachers providing information about their personality, values, and so forth. This latter approach, though not widely discussed as a means of teachers' supplying information about themselves that is related to teaching, deserves more than a passing glance—especially as one realizes that there are certain personality characteristics associated with good teaching which repeatedly emerge from student ratings of instruction, and that many forms for self-reporting values and ratings of classroom teaching are available.

One might question whether teachers would ever be critical of their own teaching if given an opportunity to comment on it. For whatever reason, be it sheer lack of interest or a belief that self-degradation is an unnatural act, not much effort has been devoted toward finding an answer to that question. A 1977 survey found that academicians do not think they are teaching well, and such a finding, be it true or false, does demonstrate that self-reports may, indeed, yield something other than simply self-praise. Maybe we should seek them more often (Ladd and Lipset, 1977).

A 1973 study addressed a critical, related question: How do ratings teachers give themselves compare to student ratings of them? The principal finding was that students and faculty evaluate teaching differently (Centra, 1973). A 1974 investigation complicated the picture by adding ratings of department heads but it also concluded that although modest agreement exists between students and department heads on some specific aspects of teaching, the three groups show little agreement about what constitutes effective instruction (Sagen, 1974).

Thus, if there is a "bottom line" in the issue of self-evaluation, it must be that self-evaluation can be viewed as one additional source of information for the evaluation of instruction. Also, just the very experience of engaging in such introspection—even if only because it is demanded by a superior—might raise teaching consciousness. That would be a desirable end in itself.

Student Evaluations

Student ratings of instruction receive the largest amount of attention by writers and researchers concerned with teaching evaluation, and the popularity of student ratings as a way to evaluate faculty as well as the frequency with which such ratings are used in decisions concerning faculty status is increasing. Discussion of the issues and the instruments involved in using students' ratings thus comprises the lion's share of the rest of this chapter.

That most attention in the literature has been paid to student evaluations may reflect no more than the possibility that student evaluation lends itself to scrutiny more easily and with less threat than do other evaluation methods. Alternatively, one might argue that the methods most scrutinized are least accepted, in that a high degree of scrutiny reflects a high degree of suspicion. And admittedly, students cannot tell us everything we want to know about effective teaching; hence the other methods discussed above deserve continued attention. Moreover, student evaluations do not escape the problems that nonstudent evaluations face. Basic questions of validity, reliability, and interaction with other variables—discussed below—must be confronted. But we should not be afraid to ask students for their assistance in evaluation. And Hughes, addressing the 1975 International Conference on Improving University Teaching, summed up much current thinking in his statement that "systematic student evaluation was the only method which received wide endorsement from the literature, from university deans, and from conferees" (1975, p. 6).

Are Student Evaluations Valid? Sooner or later (probably sooner), every proponent of student evaluation of teaching faces the question of validity. Sometimes the question comes in straightforward fashion: "Are student ratings valid?" Other times the question is raised obliquely and appears in such forms as: What do students really know about good teaching? Isn't student *learning* the best measure of effective teaching? Do student ratings agree with ratings made by peer-colleagues of "experts" in instruction? In any event, understanding the notion of validity is crucial to one who attempts to extract method from what may appear to be the mad proliferation of literature dealing with the issues and instruments in student evaluation of college instruction. In simple, general terms, validity refers to how well something does what it is supposed to do. Complications arise, however, when disagreement exists about what the thing is supposed to do. Educators are well known (indeed, revered) for their ability to disagree and disagree eloquently and voluminously. Such has been the case with the issue of validity of student ratings of teaching.

One extremely articulate and persuasive faction argues that student ratings are intrinsically valid; that students are the consumers of instruction, and consumer satisfaction is important (McKeachie, 1969b). Clearly, it is hard to argue with the position that no one but students can provide us with information about how well an instructor "presents ideas in a manner understandable to the student," "stimulates student thinking," or "establishes rapport with students easily." In short, advocates of this view believe that students are the recipients of lots of instruction. They view one instructor many times during a term or semester. They experience many instructors during the course of their college or university career. Therefore, they ought to know.

Nonetheless, that students are accurate judges of good teaching has been questioned. This questioning has produced a group of studies that seek to find out how well student ratings of instruction agree with ratings made by such other groups as measurement specialists, teaching assistants, peer-colleagues, or otherwise defined experts in teaching. Such studies generally obtain expert opinion by asking the experts to either watch videotapes, listen to audiotapes, or actually visit the instructor's class. Then these judgments are compared with the students' ratings.

Correlation coefficients, measuring the extent to which the ratings of students and experts agree, seem to indicate that there is a fair amount of agreement between the two groups.* Although the extent of agreement does vary, the variability seems to be related to how well the particular quality of the teacher who is being judged is defined. For example, agreement on how well an instructor "accepts student feelings and ideas" is a lot harder to come by than is agreement on whether or not the instructor "speaks clearly." Later, attention will be directed toward an examination of variables affecting student ratings of instruction. At this time, however, it seems only reasonable to point out that ratings of experts are also influenced by factors extraneous to the instructional process (such as instructor rank or research productivity) and therefore cannot be regarded automatically as "the real truth."

It is not surprising, then, that a vast amount of research has been conducted in attempts to provide information about the relationship between student evaluations of teaching and various measures of student achievement or learning. Unfortunately though, the results of such research have been both inconclusive and in-

---

*A correlation coefficient is a statistic that measures the strength and direction of the relationship between two variables. It can take values from -1.00 to $+1.00$, inclusive. Negative values—those between 0 and -1.00—indicate negative, or inverse, relationships, in which increases in one variable are associated with decreases in the other. Positive values—those between 0 and $+1.00$—indicate positive, or direct, relationships, in which the variables move together in the same direction. The closer the correlation coefficient is to either -1.00 or $+1.00$, the stronger is the relationship. Thus, a correlation coefficient of -1.00 represents a perfect negative relationship; $+1.00$, a perfect positive one; and 0.00, no relationship at all.

consistent. The correlations between student learning and student ratings range from high negative to high positive. With studies varying as widely in their methodology as these do, the confusion might have been expected. If pressed to generalize about the relationship between student learning and student ratings, the best one could say at this point is that the relationship seems to be moderate and positive. Nonetheless, it is difficult, and probably unwise, to blind oneself to carefully executed studies that use several student-rating instruments and fail to find significant relationships between any instrument and student achievement (Greenwood and others, 1976).

Are Student Ratings Reliable? Reliability is often confused with validity. Reliability, in nonjargon language, refers only to consistency or, to put it another way, stability. A rubber measuring tape is not reliable. However, if a steel measuring tape was used to measure instructors' head sizes, and those measurements were taken to indicate effectiveness of instructor teaching, those measurements would, indeed, be reliable. They could be replicated; anyone could replicate them fairly errorlessly. But, obviously, head size of the instructor is not a valid measure of instructor effectiveness. Although the measure is consistent, it does not do what it is supposed to do.

Reliability can be measured in a number of ways, and predictably, the reliability of instruments that are used by students to evaluate instruction has been measured in a number of ways. For example, the internal consistency of an instrument may be determined by comparing responses on odd-numbered items with those on even-numbered items (called odd-even reliability) or by comparing responses on the first half of the instrument with responses on the second half (called split-half reliability). High, positive correlations between the two groups of items indicate a high degree of reliability. Stability over time may be determined by administering an instrument more than once to the same students during the course of a semester. High correlations between the two sets of responses indicate a high degree of reliability (called test-retest reliability). Reliability also may be determined by examining the consistency of ratings given by all the students in a class. Alternatively, one might compare ratings given to a single instructor teaching two sections of the same course. To make a long story short, student evaluations have proved highly reliable. Generally, the correlations used to indicate reliability have been in the .80s and .90s. Remember, however, that reliability is generally viewed as a necessary, but not sufficient, condition for the validity of an instrument.

Are Student Ratings Affected by Things Other than Simply Teacher Effectiveness? Virtually all discussions of student evaluation of teaching contain questions about factors that may influence or bias student ratings. Some of the most common questions are: Don't student ratings really just reflect how well the student does in the course? Aren't students just rating the personality of the teacher? How are student ratings affected by class size? A vast research literature that attempts to provide answers to these and similar questions has evolved. What follows is a highly selective effort to highlight that literature.

No less than seventy-five characteristics of students have been studied in terms of their relationship to student ratings of teaching (de Wolfe, 1974). In short, if it is a characteristic of a student, someone somewhere has asked the question: Is this characteristic related to student evaluation of teaching? Familiar things have been investigated, such as student age, sex, race, major, class level, socio-economic status, marital status, and grade-point average (overall as well as in the particular course). Students have been grouped by less formal characteristics too, such as those who prepared for class versus those who did not, those who have participated in class discussions versus those who have not, and those who held preconceptions of enjoyment which would be received from the course versus those who did not. Investigators have even examined the relationship between students' attitudes toward the value of student ratings and the student ratings themselves. What follows represents major conclusions from research that answers the questions most often asked. Nonetheless, if one may be so bold as to declare that the status of the inquiry has advanced to the point where some general rules exist, be assured that there are, indeed, exceptions to every one of them; more empirically stated, researchers have called into question and at times failed to replicate even the most often-cited findings.

Taken alone (as opposed to in interaction with other variables), student sex seems unrelated to student ratings. Though some research suggests that a student's major may determine what kind of teaching behavior is viewed as ideal, student major does not seem to affect student evaluation of instruction. Similarly, neither student age nor student rank in college is strongly related to student ratings. Furthermore, when statistically significant relationships have been found between student ratings and such demographic variables as those mentioned, the magnitude of the relationships is generally so small that it raises the age-old question: Is this finding that is of statistical significance really of practical significance?

The relationship between student ratings and student grades seems to have received more attention than it deserves. Faculty seem to be reacting to the feeling that if giving high grades means receiving high student evaluations, then the easy professor will come out more favorably than the one who maintains high standards of academic rigor. However, it might be argued that students who do well in a course may truly believe that their performance was, indeed, related to high-quality instruction, and they evaluate their instruction accordingly. That appears to be such a logical argument that one might wonder whether there should not, in fact, be a relationship between student grades and student ratings. Placing the logic aside, and moving to the data, the huge amount of research on this issue indicates that if a relationship exists, it is a weak one. The highest correlations reported between student grades and student ratings are in the vicinity of .40, indicating that only 16 percent or less of the variability in student ratings can be accounted for by the relationship that student ratings bear to student grades.*

On the basis of a much smaller body of research, a grade-related variable that seems to be more strongly related to student ratings than are grades alone has emerged. That variable is "expected grade." Discrepancies between grades students receive and

*Squaring the value of the correlation coefficient produces a statistic called the coefficient of determination. The coefficient of determination measures the proportion of variation in one variable that can be accounted for by the relationship which that variable bears to a second one. Note in the example above that although student grades can account for 16 percent of the variability in student ratings, 84 percent of the variability in student ratings has nothing to do with grades—that is, comes from some other source(s).

grades they expect to receive seem to suggest to students that the instructor may be unfair or whimsical in her or his grading practices, and their evaluations seem likely to reflect this view. So, C, D, or F students cannot be automatically assumed to produce low instructor ratings. If, however, these same students expected As or Bs and received their Cs, Ds, or Fs, then it seems that conditions are ripe for low student evaluations, and they may be warranted, since under such conditions something is obviously amiss in the student-teacher communication process.

If one had to single out a student-related variable which is more highly related to student ratings than any other, that variable would have to be the general attitude of the student toward teaching or toward courses. Once again, research investigating this relationship has not produced correlations in excess of .40, and many correlations have been much lower. Here, too, far more of the variability in student ratings is left unexplained than is explained by the relationship the ratings bear to the student's general attitude toward instruction.

Only about half as many teacher characteristics as student characteristics have been investigated in terms of their possible relationship to student ratings of instruction (de Wolfe, 1974). Faculty sex, age, rank, tenure status, salary, experience, and research productivity have all been studied as potential correlates of student ratings. Instructor appearance, verbal self-disclosure, actual body accessibility, and even attitude toward student ratings of instruction have also received researchers' attention. If it is a recognizable characteristic of a teacher, someone has asked the question: How does this characteristic affect student ratings of teaching? A sample of the results of this research follows.

Interestingly, most teacher personality traits do not seem to be related to student ratings of teaching. This is especially the case when teachers describe their own traits. When students or peers describe an instructor, however, these correlations increase a bit. Out of a great number of personality traits which have been investigated, those that have been reported to be somewhat related to teaching skills are enthusiasm, vigor, self-confidence, emotional stability, and original thinking.

One might suspect that more experienced teachers would

receive higher student ratings than less experienced ones. If professional rank is taken as an index of experience, such does not seem to be the case. Correlations between rank and ratings have been not only weak but mixed—positive as well as negative. The only reasonable conclusion seems to be that if a relationship exists at all between teacher experience and student ratings of instruction, it is, at best, not a very strong one.

The relationship between student ratings and an instructor's intellectual ability and knowledge of the subject matter also has been studied. Possibly because college-level instructors all generally possess a good deal of expertise in their speciality areas, these studies have not produced much. The lack of a relationship here seems to be a good sign; it may indicate that academia does not contain stupid instructors, with little knowledge of their subject matter, who fall at the low end on measures of knowledge and ability.

The question "Do student ratings bear a relationship to a faculty member's research productivity?" is a particularly emotional one. An often-expressed student sentiment is that faculty members are only interested in doing their research, and teaching is just something they have to do to keep their jobs. Faculty, on the other hand, report that active research involvement is necessary to keep abreast of new developments in the field and to maintain enthusiasm for learning and teaching. The data fail to provide support for either constituency. Apparently, one can be an excellent teacher from the perspective of students and do no research, and a prolific researcher may not be an excellent teacher. At most, the relationship between ratings and research is positive and small, accounting for too little of the variability in ratings to make much of a fuss over.

Though not exactly what one would call "teacher characteristics," some activities of instructors do seem effective. From the students' viewpoint, good teachers know when students understand, increase students' appreciation of the subject, satisfactorily answer impromptu questions, achieve the objectives of the course, and explain complicated topics by using examples.

Teachers rarely exercise complete control over the conditions under which they teach, but do factors such as class size, course level, the time at which a course meets, or whether a course is required or elective influence student ratings?

Studies of the relationship between class size and student ratings yield equivocal results. A tendency for smaller classes to receive higher ratings than larger classes has been reported several times, but a failure to find a relationship between size and ratings is not uncommon either. It may not make good sense to become particularly embroiled in this issue, since student ratings, when used appropriately, involve interpretation based upon appropriate groups. The level of a course may bear some relationship to the ratings its instructor receives: There is some tendency for higher-level ones to receive higher ratings. The time of the day a class meets may bear some relationship to the ratings its instructor receives: Some tendency has been reported for morning classes to receive higher ratings than evening classes. And teachers of elective courses may have a slight advantage over teachers of required courses with regard to student ratings of instruction; but, the difference seems to be quite small. Nonetheless, if, in some context, the dichotomy between required and elective courses seems important, it may be handled easily and appropriately by using it in the selection of comparison data.

Unlike teaching conditions, the conditions under which student evaluation forms are administered can be controlled. Therefore, there is no excuse for student evaluations to be administered in ignorance of, or insensitivity to, the relationship between conditions of administration and ratings. Students produce higher ratings when they believe that the ratings will be used for decision-making purposes, such as tenure and promotion, than when they believe the ratings will be used for the instructor's benefit only. With so many uncontrollable elements in the system, the message with regard to instructions seems clear: Instructions make a difference; the stated purpose of the evaluations as well as the conditions under which they are collected must be viewed with great care.

Unfortunately for researchers, factors affecting teaching and teaching evaluations do not occur one at a time, in isolation from one another; rather, they occur in interaction with each other. For example, a lower-level course may be taught by a charismatic instructor to a mass of students, some of whom are taking the course because it is required, others of whom are taking it for elective credit. Perhaps because the research endeavor becomes more and more difficult as one gets closer and closer to approximating reality, relatively little research has been done on the interaction of the factors that may affect student evaluations of teaching. A few trends have emerged, however.

In a fashion that tempts one to think in terms of a congruence model, student personality and teacher personality interact in their effect upon student ratings. Similarity seems to produce more satisfied students—that is, higher ratings—than dissimilarity. Class size and class level interact. Large, lower-level courses generally yield lower ratings than small, upper-level ones. Several studies support the presence of an interaction between teacher style and student ability. Here again, a sort of congruence model is suggested. Teachers who direct their classes to bright students receive higher ratings from the brighter students. Conversely, teachers who direct their classes toward poorer students tend to receive higher ratings from these students than from the brighter ones. In short, in the dynamic classroom, with different teacher types affecting different student types differentially, the conscientious interpreter of student ratings seems committed to hoping for a random distribution of these factors.

Do Student Evaluations Improve Teaching? One purpose of student evaluations is to provide the instructor with constructive feedback regarding teaching (as opposed to providing administration with data to support decision making). "Do instructors use this feedback to improve their teaching?" becomes a relevant question. For a question so critical, surprisingly little effort has been devoted toward finding the answer, but what few data exist are encouraging.

Student evaluations tend to be most influential when they indicate a discrepancy between the way teachers perceive themselves and the way students perceive them. For example, teachers who expect good ratings but do not receive them are the best candidates for improvement, whereas those who expect mediocre or poor ratings and get them are not as likely to improve. In sum, discrepancies, rather than realities, seem to be what is necessary for quick change. But interestingly, data also indicate that when confronted repeatedly with negative feedback, even instructors for whom this feedback does not necessarily indicate a discrepancy do make some modest improvements in their teaching. Ironically, students tend to believe that student evaluations of teaching will lead to improved teaching.

Perhaps there is a missing link in this process. The message that "something is wrong" cannot, alone, be reasonably expected to lead to improvement of instruction. That message may be a bit like a diagnosis without a prescription. Knowing what is the matter is not enough: One must know what to do about it and be able to do it. It is because of this sort of understanding and sensitivity that offices of evaluation services (or similarly functioning outfits) often operate in direct association with, or make referrals to, specialists who can counsel, advise, or otherwise help out the instructor who seeks such services. The need for support services to supplement evaluation services is widely endorsed in the literature. It just makes good sense.

Student Rating Instruments

Many instruments used by well-meaning individual faculty members or departments to get student opinions are unfortunately constructed in armchair fashion. In other words, someone just sits down and thinks about questions inviting answers that ought to relate to the quality of teaching. The word *unfortunately* is used here for two reasons: First, the procedure involves much reinventing of the wheel; and second, several well-researched instruments are generally available, and the group of them probably does contain "something for everybody." Some are available at little or no user cost, depending on how much scoring and interpretation of the instruments the user institution wishes to take on.

Homemade Instruments. Despite the great amount of effort that has already gone into construction and validation of standardized instruments, individual faculty members, departments, and entire colleges often feel a need to construct their own. To be sure, this I'd-rather-do-it-myself phenomenon with regard to instrument development has not come about because test construction is so much

fun. Rather, it owes its popularity to the fact that ownership enhances acceptability.

The ownership issue may be expressed in a variety of ways,
some of which can sound fairly hostile: "I don't want my ratings
compared to ratings of teachers all over the country. Alabama psychology students aren't like psychology students in Baltimore,
Detroit, or Los Angeles!" or "I don't care about some of the things
this questionnaire asks, and there are some things I do care about
that it doesn't ask!" or "I should be compared to my colleagues
here, not my colleagues at Harvard!"

Yet, doing one's own thing can be dangerous, especially
when the stakes are high. Perhaps if those in search of an instrument could be acquainted with the many already available, the
selection of a favorite from among the existing potpourri might
personalize the selection process to a point that promotes a feeling of
ownership. And despite the fact that more often than not the ob-
jections to comparisons with normative data are voiced by individuals who come out on the short end of such comparisons, norms
are an asset, not a liability; and their existence certainly does not
force their use. Whether one is compared with national norms,
regional norms, campus norms, departmental norms, or no norms
at all is a decision open to negotiation, as is the decision about the
interpretation and use of such comparisons.

Standardized Instruments. Construction of standardized instruments generally begins with a large, sometimes even huge, pool
of items thought to be related to good instruction. These items may
come from a variety of sources: available literature, faculty, students, administrators, alumni, or any other source that stands a
chance of making a helpful contribution. Next comes a content
analysis; obvious duplications are eliminated. The result is a smaller
group of items, written in a format suitable for a rating form. (The
word *smaller* is used advisedly here, since at this stage of test construction, one is still likely to be dealing with anywhere from one
to three hundred items or statements.) It is at this point that the
instrument is generally considered ready for its first field test. Based
on the responses of a large number of students to this preliminary
instrument, the instrument undergoes further modification and
shortening. Items that fail to differentiate between good and bad

instruction and items that evoke largely neutral responses are eliminated at this stage. The result, hopefully, is an instrument of reasonable length, with the ability to distinguish good teaching from bad.

Most well-researched instruments have been factor analyzed. Simply stated, factor analysis is a statistical technique that analyzes a large number of responses and provides information about which ones tend to cluster together (because they are responded to in a similar fashion) and form a subscale or factor. Generally, the longer the instrument, the more subscales it contains. In simplest form, a two-subscale instrument would most likely contain one subscale about the course itself and a second subscale about the instructor. More subscales than two generally reflect components of the course and components of the instructor.

Depending on the sophistication of the resources available (for example, hands, test-scoring service, or first-rate computer), a variety of statistical information may be obtained from student rating forms beyond the raw scores or "marginals." Basically, though, the information consists of the number of students who responded to each test question, a distribution of responses to each question (in absolute terms as well as in percentages), and the average response to the question. This information is generally printed out by subscales, with a "collapsed" subscale average. In addition, if appropriate normative data are available and of interest, instructors may receive information regarding how their ratings compare to those of instructors of courses of similar size, class level, or meeting time. The appealing aspect of subscales is that they help indicate areas of strength or weakness which are often difficult to discern from unfactored instruments.

Choosing and Using an Instrument. Ideally, faculty members would be eager to receive information about their teaching. At present, we seem far from that condition, with evaluation often forced or not too subtly encouraged, rather than embarked on with enthusiasm. Gathering "student reactions" rather than "student evaluation" may help some. People seem to like "reactions" better than "evaluation." The different names of the rating instruments may be something to consider.

Allowing individuals to choose an instrument from the many available seems both to encourage involvement in the evaluation process and to reduce the anxiety and defensiveness that often accompany it. Several instruments have supplementary items or provision for inclusion of additional items constructed by the user. It is even possible to individualize not the instrument but its scoring, according to the importance the instructor attaches to each of several possible course objectives. Flexibility of this kind also allows for the choice of a common core of items of general interest to all members of a department or college and other, different items of specific interest to certain individuals.

The interpretation and use of the data that evaluation instruments yield are as important (maybe, more important) to the reception the whole evaluation process receives as is anything else, including the selection of an instrument. Notice, for example, that when means and medians are used in interpretation and/or decision making, some faculty have to fall below those points. In other words, everyone cannot be "above average," even in a group full of winners. The use of absolute rather than relative standards would handle the issue raised here. The more basic point remains, however; in an age of computer-oriented number worshippers, it is wise to remember the old adage that "figures don't lie, but liars do figure," and to make every effort to ensure that evaluation data receive the benefit of an honest and articulate interpreter.

Conclusions

Many states, for better or for worse, have moved toward formula funding of higher education. It would not be surprising and not a bad idea, to move toward a type of formula evaluation of teaching. Indeed, this has already been suggested (Ballard, Rearden, and Nelson, 1976). Although somewhat intimidating at first blush, such a scheme allows for the various sources of information about a faculty member to be used in clear-cut fashion. Colleague evaluations, advising competence, out-of-class activity, student ratings—all can be weighted and then combined to yield a better picture of a faculty member's teaching than any one of these indices alone can yield.

Evaluation of teaching is an issue of moment. Its time has come, and it is probably here to stay. One can only hope that the responsibility for teaching evaluation will be in the hands of informed, sensitive, progressive individuals.

In a recent address to the National Association of Student Personnel Administrators, former Health, Education, and Welfare Secretary David Mathews (1977) said, "there is no good vision of education that can begin anywhere else than with a good vision of what society ought to be." Let us hope we are not so conservative that the notion that professors communicate (and, indeed, should communicate) their values as well as their knowledge strikes us as too radical to be taken seriously. For that notion, with its implications for an expanded role of the college teacher and its concomitant implications for an expanded kind of evaluation of college teaching, contains an energizing hope that can ensure our future.

Ohmer Milton

Rapprochement
for Learning

As author-editor, I now exercise certain liberties, including offering editorial opinions about the topics of the preceding chapters and alerting readers to other useful materials about them.

I mentioned earlier that in my judgment the weakest area of classroom instruction is that of specifying course objectives. This is why Robert M. Barry's chapter on these objectives is Chapter One. He quite properly avoids the unwarranted simplicity of much that is written about college course objectives—a simplicity especially true of many treatises about "behavioral" objectives. All too often this concept has been carried to ridiculous extremes and has earned a resulting contempt. Behavioral objectives can help make

376

many of our traditional concepts about teaching and learning operational. Thus, beyond applying Barry's lessons, readers concerned about clarifying their own objectives for their courses should study a sound and humorously written little paperback by Robert Mager (1975) on *Preparing Instructional Objectives*. They will clarify their own thinking about such concepts as "appreciate" and "understand" and, as a result, will know better when a student appreciates and understands.

I agree with John Satterfield that lectures should be improved rather than discarded, but I must emphasize even more forcefully than he does that the first route to better lectures is fewer of them. Hutchison (1966, p. 437) asserted, "Even the omnicompetent and the inexhaustible are usually giving too many lectures per week. . . . It is not uncommon for clergymen to feel that one twenty-minute sermon deserves two days' preparation. Academic lecturers, working with less divine and no secretarial assistance, probably should not inflict fifty minutes of scholarly material . . . without equivalent preparation." Lacking the requisite time and energy, most lecturers should substitute other teaching methods for some lectures to concentrate their lecturing ability on the rest.

In view of the widespread use of discussion as an alternative to lecturing, it is puzzling that so little appears in the literature about how to lead discussions. One recommended reading beyond that cited by Patricia W. Barnes-McConnell in Chapter Three is Chapter Six on discussions in Eble's *The Craft of Teaching: A Guide to Mastering the Professor's Art* (1976).

In my chapter on classroom testing, I did not discuss grading at any length because I really do not know the way out of that morass. I think the fundamental problem with grades is that they just plainly *cannot* fulfill one of their primary functions: personnel selection. But since the nation *believes* they are good selection devices, they continue to be used for that purpose. As George Bernard Shaw lamented, "There is no harder scientific fact in the world than the fact that belief can be produced in practically unlimited quantity and intensity, without observation or reasoning, and even in defiance of both by the simple desire to believe founded on a strong interest in believing." For the most recently marshaled evidence about the invalidity of grades as indicators of occupational success, see Nelson's

monograph for the Civil Service Commission (1975). If you examine the survey by Collins and Nickel (1975) you will be amazed
at the tremendous variations among grading policies and practices.
Regarding testing, in addition to the books referred to in Chapter
Four (Gronlund, 1977 and Ebel, 1972), I recommend the one
edited by Lindquist (1966).

Beyond C. R. Carlson's thorough discussion of feedback in
Chapter Five, the only word I can add concerns the importance of
positive feedback. Simply put, positive feedback works better than
negative feedback. Historically, schooling has been associated with
negative feedback; it is as though unpleasantness, anguish, and pain
are obligatory for significant learning to occur. For example, a
colleague once told me that he encouraged his students to learn to
spell technical terms by *subtracting* points from their test scores and
term paper grades for misspelling. He was startled when I proposed
he *add* points for correct spelling—a notion that had never occurred to him.

My only advice about PSI beyond William J. Schiller's and
Susan M. Markle's excellent presentation in Chapter Six concerns its
self-pacing nature. With scholarly cautiousness, the authors state:
"Even when students begin work promptly, the self-pacing feature
can lead some to fall behind as demands in other, non-self-paced
courses become more acute." I have to emphasize the severity of
this problem for the PSI novice. Unfortunately, many students are
just not accustomed to going it alone; they lack self-discipline to
pace themselves. They procrastinate, especially in their first PSI
course, because no one prods or cajoles them. As a result, incom-
pletes are rampant, withdrawals numerous. Currently, more advocates of PSI seem more concerned about overcoming this problem
than any other—including that of handling registrars and faculty
committees who believe everyone should grade on the curve. Departmental and institutional funding on the basis of credit hours
earned requires that PSI students complete their courses—otherwise
no funds. The fact that so many students have not learned to
manage their time even in college demonstrates the veracity of
Robert Frost's observation, "We put helpless old people in hospitals.
. . . We put helpless young people in college."

The technical aspects of computers are changing so rapidly

that published materials become outdated quickly, and thus, for Chapter Seven, Alfred Bork and I agree that customary references to existing literature would be inappropriate. But for ideas about the computer's great adaptability to teaching and learning challenges, see the several annual *Proceedings* of the Conference on Computers in the Undergraduate Curriculum.

When learning via contract (Chapter Eight), students frequently engage in independent study. This is encouraging because so few students in the past have had the opportunity (and responsibility) of studying independently (Dressel and Thompson, 1973). Further examples about contract learning are contained in the volumes edited by Berte (1975a, 1975b).

Additional works that explore competency-based education (Chapter Nine) include Knott (1975), O'Connell and Moomaw (1975), Peterson (1976), and Trivett (1975). But for information about competency-based liberal or general education programs, the several institutions listed by Gary Woditsch as developing them are the best resources. These institutions are in a position to illustrate competency-based grading—a very different approach to evaluation than conventional grading.

The case method (Chapter Ten) may be thought of as a modified or simulated version of experiential learning. Beyond Charles F. Fisher's chapter, further enlightenment about it can be found in McNair and Hersum (1954), Bruner (1968), Hunt (1951), and Bock (1962). Readers interested in simulation and gaming (Chapter Eleven) may wish to consult Greenblatt and Duke (1975), Inbar and Stoll (1972), and McClean and Raymond (1975). And for further information about field experience learning (Chaptel Twelve), readers may wish to consult the comprehensive paper by Chickering (1977b), the volume on *Experiential Learning* edited by Keeton (1976) and, for examples of specific programs in such fields as agriculture, business administration, chemistry, engineering, and mathematics, issues of the *Journal of Cooperative Education*.

Common to all those students discussed by Milton R. Stern in Chapter Thirteen who return to campus after a long absence from schooling is anxiety (sometimes severe) about their ability to perform adequately. Their anxiety is aggravated by the widely shared myth of a decline in mental ability with age. In trying to dispel this myth, Comfort (1976, p. 45) summarized extensive research with this statement: "The human brain does not shrink, wilt, perish, or deteriorate with age. It normally continues to function well through as many as nine decades." (See pages 9–33 and 118–122 in Comfort and pages 18–33 in *Time* [1977] for further evidence reassuring to these older students—and to us in welcoming them back to class and using their wisdom and talents to help the eighteen to twenty-one-year olds to learn.)

Formal faculty evaluation (Chapter Fourteen) is a relatively new phenomenon, and student questionnaires currently constitute the preferred route to it, probably because of their seeming simplicity in both preparation and use. But, as Audrey D. Landers points out in her chapter, unless faculties become enlightened properly about this type of measurement many will be harmed. Once they are aware of the severe limitations of hundredths of points differences in student ratings for important decisions about their own futures, however, faculties may be more concerned than in the past about the injustices inflicted on students via hundredths of grade-point-average points. Unfortunately, much of the published literature will not help them because it is written by specialists for specialists, but the book by Doyle (1975) is an excellent follow-up on student ratings of instruction.

Finally, two reminders may be in order here. First, the focus of the preceding chapters on different approaches to teaching should not be interpreted as suggesting that instructors should choose only one approach from among this repertoire. On the contrary, we advocate the reverse. Rather than proselytizing for any single approach, my colleagues and I urge a rapprochement among them and experimentation with all of them. Why should the professor assured at lecturing believe it necessary to shift entirely to discussion or case study or contracts? No one should assume this is our intent. Instead, we suggest consideration of all these approaches as supplements, variations, and occasional options more than as replacements. Experimentation may well lead some instructors to an eventual substitute—for example, to full-fledged PSI. But experimentation with variety is our message more than the adoption of one alternative.

Second, as Landers notes in the previous chapter, classroom instruction is only one of our responsibilities as professors for helping students learn. Counseling, advising, and out-of-class contact are no less important, and our emphasis in this volume on classroom instruction should not be interpreted as neglect of these other avenues for teaching. In a comprehensive investigation of faculty influences on students, which included eight institutions and hundreds of students and faculty members, Wilson and others (1975, p. 167) concluded: "Repeatedly, one of the overriding differences found between faculty and students who engage in effective teaching and learning and those who do not was the *amount of interaction*— both inside and outside the classroom—that students and teachers have with one another." Until approximately thirty years ago, such contacts were taken for granted; their importance may be foreign to many of those entering college teaching now. But, as they enter teaching, the graduates of even the most impersonal and bureaucratized university probably recall their appreciation of at least one former instructor or professor who held a wider conception of teaching than that of lecturer or group leader, one who even involved a glimmer of personal friendship. The Wilson volume contains much information for such newcomers, and it deserves the attention of all readers of this volume. Indeed, those professors and prospective college teachers who are concerned enough about their effectiveness to be reading this volume may not need to be reminded of the importance of out-of-class contacts with their students; they already know enough about teaching not to believe that it stops at the classroom door. But they can use Wilson along with our reminder here to make sure that administrators, trustees, and legislators also remember this fact and take it into account in faculty personnel policies, instructional standards, and general institutional planning. American colleges and universities are more than classrooms, and American faculty members deserve reward for more than classroom instruction.

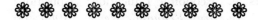

References

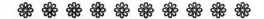

ABT, C. C. *Serious Games*. New York: Viking Press, 1970.

ALEXANDER, L. T., and ABRAMSON, J. H. *Using a Discussion to Teach. Teaching Lab Workshop: Small Group Discussion.* East Lansing: Michigan State University Press, 1975.

ALEXANDER, L. T., and DAVIS, R. H. *Writing Useful Instructional Objectives*. East Lansing: Michigan State University Press, 1977.

ANDERSON, R. C. "How to Construct Achievement Tests to Assess Comprehension." *Review of Educational Research,* 1972, *42,* 145–170.

ANDERSON, R. C., and BIDDLE, W. B. "On Asking People Questions About What They Are Reading." In G. Bower (Ed.), *Psychology of Learning and Motivation.* Vol. 9 New York: Academic Press, 1975.

383

ANDREWS, K. R. (Ed.). *The Case Method of Teaching Human Relations and Administration.* Cambridge, Mass.: Harvard University Press, 1956.

ARISTOTLE. *The Poetics of Aristotle.* (P. H. Epps, Trans.) Chapel Hill: University of North Carolina Press, 1942.

BACH, G. L., and SAUNDERS, P. "Economic Education: Aspirations and Achievements." *American Economic Review,* 1965, *55,* 329–356.

BACH, G. L., and SAUNDERS, P. "Lasting Effects of Economics Courses at Different Types of Institutions." *American Economic Review,* 1966, *56,* 505–511.

BALCH, J. "The Influence of the Evaluating Instrument on Students' Learning." *American Educational Research Journal,* 1964, *1,* 169–182.

BALLARD, M., REARDEN, J., and NELSON, L. "Student and Peer Ratings of Faculty." *Teaching of Psychology,* 1976, *3,* 88–89.

BAUER, R. C. *Cases in College Administration.* New York: Teachers College Press, Columbia University, 1955.

BAUMAN, R. P. "Teaching for Cognitive Development: A Status Report." Mimeographed paper. Birmingham: University of Alabama, undated.

BERGEN, T. J., JR. "Teachers for the 21st Century." *University College Quarterly,* 1976, *220,* 26–28.

BERNE, E. *Games People Play: The Psychology of Human Relationships.* New York: Grove Press, 1964.

BERGQUIST, W. H., and PHILLIPS, S. R. *A Handbook for Faculty Development.* Washington, D.C.: Council for the Advancement of Small Colleges, in association with the Colleges Center of the Finger Lakes, 1975.

BERTE, N. R. (Ed.). *New Directions for Higher Education: Individualizing Education by Learning Contracts,* no. 10. San Francisco: Jossey-Bass, 1975a.

BERTE, N. R. (Ed.). *Individualizing Education Through Contract Learning.* University: University of Alabama Press, 1975b.

BLACK, M. *Critical Thinking: An Introduction to Logic and Scientific Method.* Englewood Cliffs, N.J.: Prentice-Hall, 1946.

BLAKE, H. "Case of Institutional Renewal: Oaks College, University of California, Santa Cruz." Paper presented at summer conference, Project on Institutional Renewal Through the Improvement of Teaching, Sewanee, Tenn., July 1977.

BLOCK, J. H. (Ed.). *Mastery Learning: Theory and Practice.* New York: Holt, Rinehart and Winston, 1971.

BLOOM, B. S. "Changing Conception of Examining at the University of Chicago." In P. L. Dressel (Ed.), *Evaluation in General Education.* Dubuque, Iowa: C. Brown, 1954.

BLOOM, B. S. "Learning for Mastery." *Evaluation Comment,* 1968, *1* (2).

BLOOM, B. S. "Time and Learning." *American Psychologist,* 1974, *29,* 682–688.

BLOOM, B. S. *Human Characteristics and School Learning.* New York: McGraw-Hill, 1976.

BLOOM, B. S., HASTINGS, J. T., and MADAUS, G. F. *Handbook on Formative and Summative Evaluation of Student Learning.* New York: McGraw-Hill, 1971.

BLOOM, B. S., and OTHERS (Eds.). *Taxonomy of Educational Objectives.* Handbook I: *Cognitive Domain.* New York: McKay, 1956.

BOCK, E. A. (Ed.). *Essays on the Case Method in Public Administration.* New York: Inter-University Case Program, 1962.

BOK, D. "On the Purposes of Undergraduate Education." *Daedalus,* 1974, *103,* 159–172.

BORICH, G. D., and MADDEN, S. K. *Evaluating Classroom Instruction: A Source Book of Instruments.* Reading, Mass.: Addison-Wesley, 1977.

BORN, D. G., and OTHERS. "College Student Behavior in a Personalized Instruction Course and in a Lecture Course." In G. Semb (Ed.), *Behavior Analysis and Education.* Lawrence: Department of Human Development, University of Kansas, 1972.

BORN, D. G., and DAVIS, M. L. "Amount and Distribution of Study in a Personalized Instruction Course and in a Lecture Course." *Journal of Applied Behavior Analysis,* 1974, *7,* 365–375.

BOYER, E. L. "Changing Time Requirements." In D. W. Vermilye (Ed.), *Learner-Centered Reform: Current Issues in Higher Education 1975.* San Francisco: Jossey-Bass, 1975.

BROWN, D. G., and HANGER, W. S. "Pragmatics of Faculty Self-Development." *Educational Record,* 1975, *56,* 201–206.

BRUNER, J. S. *Toward a Theory of Instruction.* Cambridge, Mass.: Harvard University Press, 1968.

BULLMER, K. *The Art of Empathy.* New York: Human Sciences Press, 1975.

BURDICK, E., and WHEELER, H. *Fail-Safe.* New York: Dell, 1969.

CAEMMERER, R. "Creativity and Visual Thinking." Paper presented at Indiana–Michigan Regional Conference of the Danforth Associate Program, Angola, Ind., 1977.

CARPENTER, F. "Basic Psychology for Teachers." *Contemporary Psychology,* 1975, *20* (7), 569–570.

CARROLL, J. B. "A Model of School Learning." *Teacher's College Record,* 1963, *64,* 723–733.

CASTANEDA, C. *The Teachings of Don Juan: A Yaqui Way of Knowledge.* (1st paperback ed.) New York: Simon & Schuster, 1974.

CENTRA, J. A. "Self-Ratings of College Teachers: A Comparison with Student Ratings." *Journal of Educational Measurement,* 1973, *10,* 287–295.

CHAPMAN, K., DAVIS, J. E., and MILLER, A. *Simulation/Games in Social Studies: What Do We Know?* Boulder, Colo.: Social Sciences Education Consortium, 1974.

CHICKERING, A. W. "Evaluation in the Context of Contract Learning." *Journal of Personalized Instruction,* 1977a, *2,* 96–100.

CHICKERING, A. W. *Experience and Learning.* New Rochelle, N.Y.: Change Publications, 1977b.

COHEN, A. M. *Objectives for College Courses.* Beverly Hills, Calif.: Glencoe Press, 1970.

COLLINS, J. R., and NICKEL, K. N. "Grading Policies in Higher Education: The Kansas Study/The National Survey." *Wichita State University Bulletin,* University Studies 103, 1975, *51,* 5–57.

COMFORT, A. *A Good Age.* New York: Crown, 1976.

CROUSE, R., and JACOBSON, C. "Testing in Mathematics—What Are We Really Measuring?" *Mathematics Teacher,* 1975, *68,* 564–570.

CROW, M. L. *Teaching on Television.* Arlington: Faculty Development Resource Center, University of Texas, 1977.

CURRIER, G. "El Centro College Grant Proposal." Grant proposal submitted to the National Institute of Social Sciences, New York, January 1975.

CURWIN, R. L., and FUHRMANN, B. S. *Discovering Your Teaching Self.* Englewood Cliffs, N.J.: Prentice-Hall, 1975.

DAVIS, R. H., ABEDOR, A. J., and WITT, P. W. F. *Commitment to Excellence: A Case Study of Educational Innovation.* East Lansing: Board of Trustees, Michigan State University, 1976.

DAVIS, R. H., DULEY, J., and ALEXANDER, L. *Field Experience.* East Lansing: Michigan State University, 1977.

DE WOLFE, V. A. *Student Ratings of Instruction in Postsecondary Institutions.* Vol. 1. Seattle, Wash.: Educational Assessment Center, 1974.

DOBBIN, J. E. Personal communication, 1976.

DORSEL, T. N. "Effect of Mastery and Test Item Distribution on College Classroom Performance." Paper presented at the annual meeting of the American Psychological Association, San Francisco, August 1977.

DOUGLASS, H. R., and TALMADGE, M. "How University Students Prepare for New Types of Examinations." *School and Society,* 1934, *39,* 318–320.

DOYLE, K. O., JR. *Student Evaluation of Instruction.* Lexington, Mass.: Heath, 1975.

DRESSEL, P. L., and THOMPSON, M. M. *Independent Study: A New Interpretation of Concepts, Practices, and Problems.* San Francisco: Jossey-Bass, 1973.

DUKE, R. *Gaming: The Future's Language.* New York: Halsted Press, 1974.

DULEY, J. (Ed.). *New Directions for Higher Education: Implementing Field Experience Education,* no. 6. San Francisco: Jossey-Bass, 1974.

DULEY, J., and GORDON, S. *College Sponsored Experiential Learning—A CAEL Handbook.* Columbia, Md.: Council for the Advancement of Experiential Learning, 1977.

EASTMAN, A. "How Visitation Came to Carnegie Mellon University." In K. E. Eble (Ed.), *The Recognition and Evaluation of Teaching.* Salt Lake City, Utah: Project to Improve College Teaching, 1970.

EBEL, R. *Essentials of Educational Measurement.* Englewood Cliffs, N.J.: Prentice-Hall, 1972.

EBLE, K. E. *The Craft of Teaching: A Guide to Mastering the Professor's Art.* San Francisco: Jossey-Bass, 1976.

ELIOT, T. S. "Chorus from 'The Rock.' " In T. S. Eliot (Ed.), *The Complete Poems and Plays.* New York: Harcourt Brace Jovanovich, 1958.

Evergreen State College Bulletin. 1975–1977, pp. 48–49.

FISCHER, J. "Survival U is Alive and Burgeoning in Green Bay, Wisconsin." *Harpers,* 1971, *242,* 20–27.

FISHER, C. F. "The Use and Effectiveness of the Case Study Method in the Inservice Training of College and University Administrators." Unpublished doctoral dissertation, Columbia University, 1973.

FOWLER, H. W. *A Dictionary of Modern English Usage.* (2d ed.) New York: Oxford University Press, 1965.

FOX, R. S., LIPPITT, R., and SCHINDLER-RAINMAN, E. *Towards a Humane Society: Images of Potentiality.* Fairfax, Va.: NTL-Learning Resources Corporation, 1973.

FRIEDMAN, C. P., and OTHERS. "The Rise and Fall of PSI in Physics at MIT." *American Journal of Physics,* 1976, *44,* 204–211.

GAFF, J. G. "New Approaches to Improve Teaching." In D. W. Vermilye (Ed.), *Learner-Centered Reform: Current Issues in Higher Education 1975.* San Francisco: Jossey-Bass, 1975.

GAGNÉ, R. M. *The Conditions of Learning.* (2nd ed.) New York: Holt, Rinehart and Winston, 1970.

GALLOWAY, S. W., and FISHER, C. F. *A Guide to Professional Development Opportunities for College and University Administrators.* Washington, D.C.: American Council on Education, 1978.

GAYNOR, J., and MILLHAM, J. "Student Performance and Evaluation Under Variant Teaching and Testing Methods in a Large College Course." *Journal of Educational Psychology,* 1976, *68,* 312–317.

GHISELIN, B. (Ed.). *The Creative Process: A Symposium.* Berkeley and Los Angeles: University of California Press, 1952.

GLASER, R. "Adapting the Elementary School Curriculum to Individual Performance." In *Proceedings of the 1967 Invitational Conference on Testing Problems.* Princeton, N.J.: Educational Testing Service, 1968.

GORDON, A. K. *Games for Growth.* Palo Alto, Calif.: Science Research Associates, 1970.

GREENBLATT, C. S., and DUKE, R. E. (Eds.). *Gaming-Simulations: Rationale, Design, and Applications.* New York: Halsted Press, 1975.

GREENWOOD, G. E., and OTHERS. "A Study of the Validity of Four Types of Student Ratings of College Teaching Assessed on a Criterion of Student Achievement Gains." *Research in Higher Education,* 1976, *5,* 171–178.

GRONLUND, N. E. *Constructing Achievement Tests,* (2d ed.) Englewood Cliffs, N.J.: Prentice-Hall, 1977.

Group for Human Development in Higher Education. *Faculty Development in a Time of Retrenchment.* New Rochelle, N.Y.: Change Publications, 1974.

HAAS, P. F., BROWNE, M. N., and KEELEY, S. M. "A Clarified Rubric for Assessing Critical Thinking." Mimeographed paper. Bowling Green, Ohio: CUE Center, Bowling Green State University, 1976.

HARRIS, T. A. *I'm O. K., You're O.K.* New York: Harper & Row, 1969.

HODGKINSON, H. L. "Issues in Competency-Based Learning." Keynote address to the National Conference on Competency-Based Learning, Cincinnati, Ohio, February 15, 1974.

HOFSTADTER, R. *Anti-Intellectualism in American Life.* New York: Vintage Books, 1966.

HOOD, E. F. *Educating Black Students: Some Basic Issues.* Detroit, Mich.: Detroit Educational Consultants, 1973.

HORN, R. E. *The Guide to Simulation/Games for Education and Training.* Cranford, N.J.: Didactic Systems, 1977.

HUGHES, A. M. "Systematic Student Evaluation of Faculty Teaching Effectiveness: A Proposal for UMUC." *The Faculty Forum,* University of Maryland, November 1975, p. 6.

HUNT, P. "The Case Method of Instruction." *The Harvard Educational Review,* 1951, *1,* 175–192.

HUTCHISON, W. R. "Yes, John, There Are Teachers on the Faculty." *The American Scholar,* 1966, *35,* 430–441.

INBAR, M., and STOLL, C. S. *Simulation and Gaming in Social Sciences.* New York: Free Press, 1972.

JOHNSON, D. W. *Reaching Out—Interpersonal Effectiveness and Self-Actualization.* Englewood Cliffs, N.J.: Prentice-Hall, 1972.

JOHNSON, K. R., and SULZER-AZAROFF, B. "PSI for First Time Users: Pleasures and Pitfalls." *Educational Technology,* 1975, *15,* 8–17.

KAISER, L. R. "Increasing Professional Effectiveness." Paper presented at seminar on high level wellness, Estes Park Institute, Pacific Grove, Calif., March 1977.

KAUFMANN, W. *The Future of the Humanities.* New York: Reader's Digest Press, 1977.

KEELEY, S. M., BROWNE, M. N., and HAAS, P. F. "Cognitive Activity in the Classroom: A Comparison of Three Kinds of Raters Using the Cognitive Activities Rating Scales (CARS)." Mimeographed paper. Bowling Green, Ohio: CUE Center, Bowling Green State University, 1976.

KEETON, M. T. *Experiential Learning: Rationale, Characteristics, and Assessment.* San Francisco: Jossey-Bass, 1976.

KELLER, F. S. "A Personal Course in Psychology." In R. Ulrich, T. Stachnik, and J. Mabry (Eds.), *Control of Human Behavior.* Glenview, Ill.: Scott, Foresman, 1966.

KELLER, F. S. "Goodbye, Teacher . . ." *Journal of Applied Behavior Analysis,* 1968, *1,* 79–89.

KERLINGER, F. N. "Student Evaluation of University Professors." *School and Society,* 1971, *99,* 353–356.

KLAUSMEIER, H. J., MORROW, R., and WALTER, J. E. *Individually Guided Education in the Multiunit Elementary School: Guidelines for Implementation.* Madison: Wisconsin Research and Development Center for Cognitive Learning, 1968.

KNAPP, J., and SHARON, A. *A Compendium of Assessment Techniques.* Princeton, N.J.: Educational Testing Service, 1975.

KNOTT, B. "What Is a Competency-Based Curriculum in the Liberal Arts?" *Journal of Higher Education,* 1975, *46,* 25–39.

KULIK, J. A., KULIK, C.-L., and CARMICHAEL, K. "The Keller Plan in Science Teaching." *Science,* 1974, *83,* 379–383.

KULIK, J. A., KULIK, C.-L., and SMITH, B. B. "Research on the Personalized System of Instruction." *Journal of Programed Learning and Educational Technology,* 1976, *13,* 23–30.

LADD, E. C., JR., and LIPSET, S. M. "The Faculty Mood: Pessimism Is Predominant." *The Chronicle of Higher Education,* October 3, 1977, *15* (1), 14.

LEHMANN, T. "Educational Outcomes from Contract Learning at Empire State College." Unpublished paper. Saratoga Springs, N.Y.: Empire State College, 1975.

Laurence Levine v. *George Washington University,* Civil No. 8230-76 (Sup. Ct. of the District of Columbia, September 7, 1976).

LEWIS, D. R., and OTHERS. *Educational Games and Simulations in Economics.* New York: Joint Council on Economic Education, 1974.

LINDQUIST, E. F. (Ed.). *Educational Measurement.* Washington, D.C.: American Council on Education, 1966.

LIVINGSTON, S. A., and STOLL, C. S. *Simulation Games.* New York: Free Press, 1973.

MCCLEAN, H. W., and RAYMOND, M. J. *Design Your Own Game.* Lebanon, Ohio: Simulation and Gaming Assoc., 1975.

MCGUIRE, C. H. "An Evaluation Model for Professional Education-Medical Education." In *Proceedings of the 1967 Invitational Conference on Testing Problems.* Princeton, N.J.: Educational Testing Service, 1968.

MCINNIS, M. "Academic Dismissal—The Developing Role of Due Process." Paper presented at the annual meeting of the Association for Study of Higher Education, Chicago, March 1977.

MCKEACHIE, W. J. *Teaching Tips: A Guidebook for the Beginning College Teacher.* Lexington, Mass.: Heath, 1969a.

MCKEACHIE, W. J. "Student Ratings of Faculty." *AAUP Bulletin,* 1969b, *55,* 439–444.

MCKEACHIE, W. J. "Research on College Teaching." *Educational Perspectives,* 1972, *11,* 3–10.

MCKEACHIE, W. J. "Psychology in America's Bicentennial Year." *American Psychologist,* 1976, *31,* 819–833.

MCKINNON, J. W., and RENNER, J. W. "Are Colleges Concerned with Intellectual Development?" *American Journal of Physics,* 1971, *39,* 1047–1052.

MCLEISH, J. "The Lecture Method." In N. L. Gage (Ed.), *The Psychology of Teaching Methods.* The 75th Yearbook of the National Society for the Study of Education. Chicago: University of Chicago Press, 1976.

MCNAIR, M. P., and HERSUM, A. C. *The Case Method at the Harvard Business School.* New York: McGraw-Hill, 1954.

MCNAMES, N. "Summary of Responses to 'Testing Practices' Questionnaire." Unpublished paper. Kansas City: Kansas City Regional Council for Higher Education, May 1977.

MAEROFF, G. I. "Writing Tests for Colleges Is Urged." *New York Times,* January 25, 1976, p. 1f.

MAGER, R. F. *Preparing Instructional Objectives.* (2nd ed.) Belmont, Calif.: Fearon Publishers, 1975.

MAIER, N. R. F. *Principles of Human Relations.* New York: Wiley, 1952.

MAIER, N. R. F. *Problem-Solving Discussions and Conferences.* New York: McGraw-Hill, 1963.

MARGOLIS, D. R. "A Fair Return? Back to College at Middle Age." *Change,* 1974, *6,* 34–37.

MARKLE, S. M. "Empirical Testing of Programs." In P. C. Lange (Ed.), *Programed Instruction.* The 66th Yearbook of the National Society for the Study of Education. Chicago: University of Chicago Press, 1967.

MARKLE, S. M. *Good Frames and Bad.* (2nd ed.) New York: Wiley, 1969.

MARKLE, S. M. "Programing and Programed Instruction." In S. G. Tickton (Ed.), *To Improve Learning: An Evaluation of Instructional Technology.* New York: Bowker, 1970.

MATHEWS, D. "What Do You Profess, Professor?" *NASPA Journal,* 1977, *16,* 34–38.

MEYER, G. "An Experimental Study of the Old and New Types of

Examination." *Journal of Educational Psychology*, 1935, *26*, 30–40.

MILLER, L. K. *Principles of Everyday Behavior Analysis*. Monterey, Calif.: Brooks/Cole, 1975.

MILLER, R. I. *Evaluating Faculty Performance*. San Francisco: Jossey-Bass, 1972.

MILLER, R. I. *Developing Programs for Faculty Evaluation: A Sourcebook for Higher Education*. San Francisco: Jossey-Bass, 1974.

MILTON, O., and EDGERLY, J. W. *The Testing and Grading of Students*. New Rochelle, N.Y.: Change Publications, 1976.

MONTAGU, A. *Culture and Human Development*. Englewood Cliffs, N.J.: Prentice-Hall, 1974.

MOORE, O. K., and ANDERSON, A. R. "Autotelic Folk Models." *Sociological Quarterly*, 1960, *1*, 206–216.

MORE, T. *Utopia*. (P. Turner, Trans.). Middlesex, England: Penguin Books, 1965. (Originally published 1516).

National Commission for Cooperative Education. *Colleges, Universities and Community Colleges Offering Cooperative Education Programs*. New York: National Commission for Cooperative Education, 1971.

NELSON, A. M. "Undergraduate Academic Achievement in College as an Indicator of Occupational Success." Professional Series PS-75-5. Washington, D.C.: U.S. Civil Service Commission, Bureau of Policies and Standards, Department of Commerce, 1975.

NESBITT, H. *College Sponsored Experiential Learning—A CAEL Student Guide*. Columbia, Md.: Council for the Advancement of Experiential Learning, 1977.

NOONAN, J. "Evaluation and Inquiry in the Arts School." Unpublished paper, Virginia Commonwealth University, 1977.

NOSOW, S. "Students' Perception of Field Experience Education." *Journal of College Student Personnel*, 1975, *16* (6), 508–513.

"Now, the Revolt of the Old." *Time*, 1977, *110*, 18–28.

O'CONNELL, W. R., JR., and MOOMAW, W. E. *A CBC Primer*. Atlanta, Ga.: Southern Regional Education Board, 1975.

OLMSTEAD, J. *Small-Group Instruction: Theory and Practice*.

Alexandria, Va.: Human Resources Research Organization, 1974.

PETERSON, V. T. (Ed.). *Renewing Higher Education: The Competency-Based Approach.* Toledo, Ohio: Center for the Study of Higher Education, University of Toledo, 1976.

PHENIX, P. H. *Realms of Meaning: A Philosophy of the Curriculum for General Education.* New York: McGraw-Hill, 1964.

PIFER, A. *The Higher Education of Blacks in the United States.* New York: Carnegie Corporation of New York, 1973.

PIPHO, C. *Update V: Minimal Competency Testing.* Denver, Colo.: Education Commission of the States, 1977.

POLLAK, O. *Human Behavior and the Helping Professions.* New York: Halsted Press, 1976.

POSTLETHWAIT, S. N., NOVAK, J., and MURRAY, H. T., JR. *The Audio-Tutorial Approach to Learning.* (2nd ed.) Minneapolis. Burgess, 1969.

QUINE, W. *The Ways of Paradox: And Other Essays.* New York: Random House, 1966.

QUINN, M. E. "An Investigation of Undergraduate Field Study Experiences at Michigan State University." Unpublished doctoral dissertation, Michigan State University, 1972.

QUINN, M. E., and SELLARS, L. "Role of the Student." In J. Duley (Ed.), *New Directions for Higher Education: Implementing Field Experience Education,* no. 6. San Francisco: Jossey-Bass, 1974.

RASER, J. R. *Simulation and Society.* Boston: Allyn & Bacon, 1969.

RENNER, J. W., and LAWSEN, A. E. "Piagetian Theory and Instruction in Physics." *The Physics Teacher,* March 1973, *11,* 165–169.

RIGDON, B. "The Teacher–Student Relationship." Paper presented at Indiana–Michigan Regional Conference of the Danforth Associate Program, Angola, Ind., 1977.

ROBIN, A. L. "Behavioral Instruction in the College Classroom." *Review of Educational Research.* Baltimore: University of Maryland, 1976.

ROGERS, C. R. *Freedom to Learn. Studies of the Person.* Columbus, Ohio: Merrill, 1969.

ROTHKOPF, E. Z. "The Concept of Mathemagenic Activities." *Review of Educational Research,* 1970, *40,* 325–336.

SAGEN, H. B. "Student, Faculty, and Department Chairmen Ratings: Who Agrees with Whom?" *Research in Higher Education,* 1974, *2,* 265–272.

SCULLY, M. G. "How Do College Students and Other Adults Learn?" *Chronicle of Higher Education,* September 26, 1977, p. 5.

SELDIN, P. *How Colleges Evaluate Professors.* Croton-on-Hudson, N.Y.: Blythe-Pennington, 1976.

SHERMAN, J. G. (Ed.). *Personalized System of Instruction: 41 Germinal Papers.* Menlo Park, Calif.: W. A. Benjamin, 1974.

SIEVERT, W. A. "A California Campus Where Adults Can Return to College 'On Their Own Terms'." *Chronicle of Higher Education,* December 12, 1977, pp. 5–6.

SIGMON, R. L. *A Notebook on Service Learning.* Raleigh: North Carolina Internship Office, 1972.

SKINNER, B. F. *The Technology of Teaching.* New York: Appleton-Century-Crofts, 1968.

SNYDER, B. R. *The Hidden Curriculum.* New York: Knopf, 1970.

Southern Regional Education Board. *Priorities for Post-Secondary Education in the South: A Position Statement.* Atlanta: Southern Regional Education Board, 1976.

SPENCER, R. E., and STALLINGS, W. *The Improvement of College-Level Student Achievement Through Changes in Classroom Examination Procedures.* USOE Project No. 6-1174, Contract No. OEC-3-7-061174-0271. Urbana: University of Illinois, 1970.

STADSKLEV, R. (Ed.). *Handbook of Simulation and Gaming in Social Education.* Part 2. University, Ala.: Institute of Higher Education Research and Services, 1975.

STICE, J. E. "A First Step Toward Improving Teaching." *Engineering Education,* 1976, *66,* 394–398.

STRUNK, W., JR., and WHITE, E. B. *The Elements of Style.* New York: Macmillan, 1962.

Tennessee Higher Education Commission. *The Competent College*

Student. Nashville: Tennessee Higher Education Commission, 1977.

THOMAS, L., and AUGSTEIN, S. *An Experimental Approach to Learning from Written Material.* Uxbridge, England: Center for the Study of Human Learning, Brunel University, 1970.

TIDBALL, M. E. "Perspective on Academic Women and Affirmative Action." *Educational Record,* 1973, *54,* 130–135.

TIEMANN, P. W., and MARKLE, S. M. "Remodeling a Model: An Elaborated Hierarchy of Types of Learning." *Educational Psychologist,* 1973, *10,* 147–158.

TORRANCE, E. P. *Encouraging Creativity in the Classroom.* Dubuque, Iowa: W. C. Brown, 1970.

TORRANCE, E. P., and MYERS, R. E. *Creative Learning and Teaching.* New York: Dodd, Mead, 1970.

TRIVETT, D. A. *Competency Programs in Higher Education.* ERIC/Higher Education Research Report No. 7. Washington, D.C.: American Association for Higher Education, 1975.

VALENTINE, J. A. "Learning: Questions of Standards and Credits." *New York University Education Quarterly,* 1977, *8,* 2–8.

VARGAS, J. S. *Writing Worthwhile Behavioral Objectives.* New York: Harper & Row, 1972.

WALES, C. E. "Data: How You Teach Does Make A Difference." Unpublished paper, West Virginia University, 1977.

WALES, C. E., and STAGER, R. A. *Guided Design, Part I.* Morgantown: West Virginia University Press, 1976.

WERT, J. E. "Twin Examination Assumptions." *Journal of Higher Education,* 1937, *8,* 136–140.

WHIMBEY, A., and BARBERENA, C. J. *A Cognitive Skills Approach to the Disciplines: Intelligence Beyond Arthur Jensen.* Bowling Green, Ohio: CUE Project Technical Paper Series, no. 2, Bowling Green State University, 1977.

WHIMBEY, A., and WHIMBEY, L. S. *Intelligence Can Be Taught.* New York: Dutton, 1975.

WHITEHEAD, A. N. *The Aims of Education.* New York: New American Library, 1949.

WILLINGHAM, W. W., and ASSOCIATES. *The CAEL Validation Report.* Princeton, N.J.: Educational Testing Service, 1976.

WILLINGHAM, W. W. *Principles of Good Practice in Assessing Experiential Learning.* Princeton, N.J.: Educational Testing Service, 1977.

WILLINGHAM, W., VALLEY, J., and KEETON, M. *Assessing Experiential Learning—A Summary Report of the CAEL Project.* Columbia, Md.: Council for the Advancement of Experiential Learning, 1977.

WILSON, R. C., and OTHERS. *College Professors and Their Impact on Students.* New York: Wiley, 1975.

WODITSCH, G. A. *Developing Generic Skills: A Model for Competency-Based General Education.* Bowling Green, Ohio: CUE Project Occasional Paper Series, no. 3, Bowling Green State University, 1977.

WRIGHT, D. "Tests for Psychology Vocabulary Should Not Be Vocabulary Tests." *Teaching of Psychology,* 1976, *3,* 187.

ZAUDERER, D. *Urban Internships in Higher Education.* ERIC/ Higher Education Research Report No. 9. Washington, D.C.: American Association for Higher Education, 1973.

Index

❀ ❀ ❀ ❀ ❀ ❀ ❀ ❀ ❀ ❀